THE LANGUAGE OF BUSINESS

An introduction to business finance

(Fourth edition)

Andrew Mills

British Library Cataloguing-in-Publication Data

A catalogue record for this book is available from the British Library.

Published by:

Kaplan Publishing UK

Unit 2 The Business Centre

Molly Millar's Lane

Wokingham

Berkshire

RG41 2QZ

ISBN: 978-1-78740-573-8

Fourth edition © Andrew Mills, 2019

Printed and bound in Great Britain.

The text in this material and any others made available by any Kaplan Group company does not amount to advice on a particular matter and should not be taken as such. No reliance should be placed on the content as the basis for any investment or other decision or in connection with any advice given to third parties. Please consult your appropriate professional adviser as necessary. Kaplan Publishing Limited and all other Kaplan group companies expressly disclaim all liability to any person in respect of any losses or other claims, whether direct, indirect, incidental, consequential or otherwise arising in relation to the use of such materials.

All rights reserved. No part of this examination may be reproduced or transmitted in any form or by any means, electronic or mechanical, including photocopying, recording, or by any information storage and retrieval system, without prior permission from Kaplan Publishing.

CONTENTS

		Study Text Chapter	End of Chapter Exercises
Chapter 1	The Statement of Financial Position	1	36
Chapter 2	The Statement of Profit or Loss	45	71
Chapter 3	Long term finance for the business – debt versus equity	89	121
Chapter 4	Pricing and Profitability	133	153
Chapter 5	Introduction to Costing and Marginal Costing	165	200
Chapter 6	Absorption Costing	211	239
Chapter 7	Budgeting	251	275
Chapter 8	Standard Costing and Variance Analysis	283	315
Chapter 9	Capital Investment Appraisal	331	364
Chapter 10	Cash flow	379	406
Chapter 11	Working capital management	417	444
Chapter 12	Performance appraisal	459	486

INTRODUCTION

Ask a typical Business student *"what is the fundamental aim of any business"* and they will confidently (and quite correctly) reply that it is to make a profit. However, then ask the same student exactly *what* profit is, or how it differs from cash, or how to maximise it …. and their answers will always become more hesitant !

You probably did not embark on your chosen degree course with an insatiable appetite to learn the finer points of accounting and finance, and were probably attracted to your course by the prospect of more alluring subjects such as *'Marketing'* or *'Business Strategy'*. After all…. if you had really wanted to study accounting and finance then surely you would have applied for an Accounting and Finance course in the first place wouldn't you?

The over-riding aim of this book is to introduce you to what Warren Buffett described as **"the language of business"** in a way that is interesting and accessible, but moreover in a way that is relevant to your future aspirations.

You might see a future career for yourself working in sales or marketing, or you might even see yourself a future entrepreneur trying to bring your own business ideas to the market.

The point is that regardless of what part of business you end up working in there is one truth of which you may be certain …You *will* need a 'working knowledge' of accounting and finance!

- Human Resource Managers need to be able to compile and interpret budgets
- Marketing Mangers need to understand break even points
- Operations Managers need to understand labour efficiency
- Sales Managers have to understand the effect of price discounting on profitability

So don't see the study of accounting and finance as a diversion from your 'real' studies. See it as (arguably) the ultimate core module you are taking as you prepare yourself for a career in business.

After all, if the fundamental aim of any business is to make a profit, then it might be a good idea for you to really understand the ultimate underlying reason for your future employment!

Andrew Mills, 2019

HOW TO USE THIS BOOK & ICONS

This Study Text has been carefully designed to make your learning experience as easy as possible and to give you the best chance of success in your assessment. It includes a number of features to help you in the study process.

It has been written in a practical and interactive style using clear definitions of key concepts and terms, lots of examples to put your knowledge into context and both end of chapter questions and an extra section of additional practice questions to reinforce your learning.

Calculation

Definition

Example

Key Point

Overview

Test Your Understanding

Tutorial Note

FORMULAE AND DISCOUNT FACTORS

General

Accounting Equation: Assets – Liabilities = Equity

Gross Profit (£) = Sales Revenue (£) – Cost of Sales (£)

Cost of Sales (£) = Opening Inventory (£) + Purchases (£) – Closing Inventory (£)

Annual Depreciation Charge = (Initial Cost – Residual Value) / Anticipated Life

Pricing

Gross Profit (%) = Gross Profit (£) / Selling Price (£) x 100%

Mark Up (%) = Gross Profit (£) / Cost Price (£) x 100%

Price Elasticity of Demand (PED) = Percentage Change in Demand / Percentage Change in Price

VAT Inclusive Selling Price = VAT Exclusive Selling Price x 1.2   *(assuming 20% VAT applies)*

VAT Exclusive Selling Price = VAT Inclusive Selling Price / 1.2   *(assuming 20% VAT applies)*

VAT element = VAT inclusive Price / 6 *(assuming 20% VAT applies)*

Investment Appraisal

Accounting Rate of Return (ARR) = Average Profit / Average Investment x 100%

Internal Rate of Return (IRR) = $A + \dfrac{NPV(A)}{NPV(A) - NPV(B)} \times (B-A)$

Performance Ratios

Gross Profit (%) = Gross Profit (£) / Sales Revenue (£)   x 100%

Operating Profit (%) = Operating Profit (£) / Sales Revenue (£)   x 100%

Return on Capital Employed (ROCE) = Operating Profit (PBIT) / Total Capital Employed   x 100%

Return on Equity (ROE) = Profit after Tax / Equity   x 100%

Efficiency Ratios

Inventory Turnover (days) = Inventory / Cost of Sales   x 365

Trade Receivables (days) = Trade Receivables / [Credit] Sales   x 365

Trade Payables (days) = Trade Payables / Cost of Sales   x 365

Operating Cycle (days) = Inventory Turnover(days) + Trade Receivables(days) – Trade Payables(days)

Working Capital Management

Working Capital = Current Assets – Current Liabilities

Current Ratio = Current Assets / Current Liabilities

Quick (acid test) Ratio = (Current Assets – Inventory) / Current Liabilities

The Language of Business

Investor Ratios

Dividend per Share = Dividend for Year / No. of shares in issue

Dividend Cover = Profit after Tax / Total Dividends

Earnings per Share = Profit after tax / Number of shares in issue.

Price/Earnings (PE) ratio = Market price per share / Earnings per share

Lending Ratios

Gearing = Debt Finance / Total Capital Employed x 100%

Interest Cover = Operating Profit / Interest costs

Variance Analysis

Sales Profit Volume Variance = Flexed Budget Profit – Original Budget Profit

Sales Price Variance = Actual Sales Revenue – Flexed Budget Sales Revenue

Direct Labour Total Variance = (Std. Hours x Std. Rate) – (Actual Hours x Actual Rate)

Direct Materials Total Variance = (Std. Quantity x Std. Cost) – (Actual Quantity x Actual Cost)

Total Overhead Variance = Budgeted Overheads – Actual Overheads

Net Profit Variance = Actual Net Profit – Flexed Budget Net Profit

Direct Labour Rate Variance = (Actual Hours x Std. Rate) – (Actual Hours x Actual Rate)

Direct Labour Efficiency Variance = (Std. Hours x Std. Rate) – (Actual Hours x Std. Rate)

Direct Materials Price Variance = (Actual Quantity x Std. Price) – (Actual Quantity x Actual Price)

Direct Materials Quantity Variance = (Std. Quantity x Std. Price) – (Actual Quantity x Std. Price)

year on year variance % = the variance £ ÷ original figure x 100

DISCOUNT FACTORS

Years (n)	1%	2%	3%	4%	5%	6%	7%	8%	9%	10%
1	0.990	0.980	0.971	0.962	0.952	0.943	0.935	0.926	0.917	0.909
2	0.980	0.961	0.943	0.925	0.907	0.890	0.873	0.857	0.842	0.826
3	0.971	0.942	0.915	0.889	0.864	0.840	0.816	0.794	0.772	0.751
4	0.961	0.924	0.888	0.855	0.823	0.792	0.763	0.735	0.708	0.683
5	0.951	0.906	0.863	0.822	0.784	0.747	0.713	0.681	0.650	0.621
6	0.942	0.888	0.837	0.790	0.746	0.705	0.666	0.630	0.596	0.564
7	0.933	0.871	0.813	0.760	0.711	0.665	0.623	0.583	0.547	0.513
8	0.923	0.853	0.789	0.731	0.677	0.627	0.582	0.540	0.502	0.467
9	0.914	0.837	0.766	0.703	0.645	0.592	0.544	0.500	0.460	0.424
10	0.905	0.820	0.744	0.676	0.614	0.558	0.508	0.463	0.422	0.386
11	0.896	0.804	0.722	0.650	0.585	0.527	0.475	0.429	0.388	0.350
12	0.887	0.788	0.701	0.625	0.557	0.497	0.444	0.397	0.356	0.319
13	0.879	0.773	0.681	0.601	0.530	0.469	0.415	0.368	0.326	0.290
14	0.870	0.758	0.661	0.577	0.505	0.442	0.388	0.340	0.299	0.263
15	0.861	0.743	0.642	0.555	0.481	0.417	0.362	0.315	0.275	0.239
16	0.853	0.728	0.623	0.534	0.458	0.394	0.339	0.292	0.252	0.218
17	0.844	0.714	0.605	0.513	0.436	0.371	0.317	0.270	0.231	0.198
18	0.836	0.700	0.587	0.494	0.416	0.350	0.296	0.250	0.212	0.180
19	0.828	0.686	0.570	0.475	0.396	0.331	0.277	0.232	0.194	0.164
20	0.820	0.673	0.554	0.456	0.377	0.312	0.258	0.215	0.178	0.149

Years (n)	11%	12%	13%	14%	15%	16%	17%	18%	19%	20%
1	0.901	0.893	0.885	0.877	0.870	0.862	0.855	0.847	0.840	0.833
2	0.812	0.797	0.783	0.769	0.756	0.743	0.731	0.718	0.706	0.694
3	0.731	0.712	0.693	0.675	0.658	0.641	0.624	0.609	0.593	0.579
4	0.659	0.636	0.613	0.592	0.572	0.552	0.534	0.516	0.499	0.482
5	0.593	0.567	0.543	0.519	0.497	0.476	0.456	0.437	0.419	0.402
6	0.535	0.507	0.480	0.456	0.432	0.410	0.390	0.370	0.352	0.335
7	0.482	0.452	0.425	0.400	0.376	0.354	0.333	0.314	0.296	0.279
8	0.434	0.404	0.376	0.351	0.327	0.305	0.285	0.266	0.249	0.233
9	0.391	0.361	0.333	0.308	0.284	0.263	0.243	0.225	0.209	0.194
10	0.352	0.322	0.295	0.270	0.247	0.227	0.208	0.191	0.176	0.162
11	0.317	0.287	0.261	0.237	0.215	0.195	0.178	0.162	0.148	0.135
12	0.286	0.257	0.231	0.208	0.187	0.168	0.152	0.137	0.124	0.112
13	0.258	0.229	0.204	0.182	0.163	0.145	0.130	0.116	0.104	0.093
14	0.232	0.205	0.181	0.160	0.141	0.125	0.111	0.099	0.088	0.078
15	0.209	0.183	0.160	0.140	0.123	0.108	0.095	0.084	0.074	0.065
16	0.188	0.163	0.141	0.123	0.107	0.093	0.081	0.071	0.062	0.054
17	0.167	0.146	0.125	0.108	0.093	0.080	0.069	0.060	0.052	0.045
18	0.153	0.130	0.111	0.095	0.081	0.069	0.059	0.051	0.044	0.038
19	0.138	0.116	0.098	0.083	0.070	0.060	0.051	0.043	0.037	0.031
20	0.124	0.104	0.087	0.073	0.061	0.051	0.043	0.037	0.031	0.026

JARGON BUSTER

Absorption Costing	The costing of goods and services including a fair share of any fixed production overheads
ACCA	Association of Chartered Certified Accountants
Accounting Equation	Equity = Assets – Liabilities
Accounting Period	See Financial Period
Accounting Rate of Return	A capital investment appraisal method which reports the (accounting) return on (accounting) investment
Accounting Reference Date	A company's chosen date on which to draw up its annual accounts
Accrual	An expense which has been incurred but not yet charged for
Accrual Accounting	Reporting performance in accordance with the accruals concept
Accruals Basis	Use of accruals concept
Accruals Concept	Accounting concept which states that profit is measured by recording sales when earned, and expenses when incurred
Acid Test Ratio	See quick ratio
Activity Based Costing (ABC)	Costing method that assigns overheads into activities and hence into cost objects
Adverse Variance	A difference between actual and budgeted performance which will result in lower profitability
Aggressive Funding Policy	The funding of working capital with increased reliance on short term finance
Allocation	Directly assigning an entire cost to just the department that relates to that cost
Alternative Investment Market (AIM)	A sub-market of the London Stock Exchange for the trading of the shares and loan stock of newer and emerging public companies
Amortisation	Alternative term for Depreciation, specifically used for intangible non-current assets
Annual General Meeting (AGM)	The annual meeting of company shareholders where the directors present the year's results and offer themselves up for re-election as directors
Annual Report	Comprehensive report on the financial year just finished prepared by the company's directors and filed at Companies House for public viewing

Apportionment	Sharing a cost across two or more departments which use that cost
Articles of Association	A company document submitted to Companies House stating the rules by which the company will be run with regard to shareholders
Assets	Items owned by the business
Audit	The scrutinising of a company's accounts by an independent auditor to provide users of those statements reassurance of their accuracy
Audit Exemption	Relaxation for smaller companies of the general company requirement to have an annual audit
AVCO	Average Cost - A system of inventory valuation that constantly updates a weighted average cost for items of inventory
Avoidable Costs	Costs which can be avoided or reduced by adopting a certain course of action
B2B	Business to Business.
B2C	Business to Consumer
Balance Sheet	UK term for the Statement of Financial Position
Balanced Scorecard	A method of whole business appraisal which aims to set out the key priorities for a business from four different perspectives
Bear Market	A market where investors are selling and hence share prices are falling
Break Even Point	The sales volume at which profit contribution = fixed costs i.e. no net profit or loss
Budget	A financial plan expressed in financial and/or other quantitative terms which extends forward for a period into the future
Bull Market	A market where investors are buying and hence share prices are rising
Bundle Pricing	Selling several products together as part of an attractively priced sales package
Capex	Capital Expenditure
Capital Assets	See Non-Current Assets
Capital Expenditure	Expenditure which has lasting value and is therefore gradually charged to the P&L over the life of the capital assets
Capital Rationing	Lack of available funding to undertake all proposed capital investments, necessitating a selection process

The Language of Business

Cash Accounting	Not using the accruals concept and instead simply recording cash inflows and cash outflows
Cash Basis	Use of cash accounting principles
Cash Purchases	Purchases made from suppliers in immediate exchange for cash
Cash Sales	Sales made to customers in immediate exchange for cash
Committed Costs	Expenditure where a legal obligation now exists and regardless of any decision to be taken will still therefore be incurred
Companies Act	The primary UK legislation governing the operation of companies
Companies House	UK registrar of companies responsible for their registration and administration
Company	A legal entity created from which to operate a business which has a separate legal identity from that of its owners
Competitive Pricing	Basing selling prices on what the competition is selling similar goods or services for
Confirmation Statement	Annual return submitted to Companies House providing basic details of a company
Conservative Funding Policy	The funding of working capital mainly from long term finance
Contribution	The profit that is left over when all the variable costs have been deducted
Corporation Tax	Profit based UK tax paid by UK resident companies or companies trading in the UK
Corporation Tax Return	Tax return submitted to HMRC by companies detailing their profits and the corporation tax due
Cost Centre	The collection of costs into specific departments (used in Traditional Absorption Costing and Responsibility Accounting). Also used to describe a sub-division of an organisation which holds responsibility for control of expenditure budget
Cost Driver Rate	A calculated rate that describes how much of a particular activities overheads should be absorbed by the products subject to that activity
Cost Object	A product or service whose cost is being determined
Cost of Capital	The % discount factor a business applies to future cashflows to compensate it for receiving them later rather than sooner
Cost of Sales	The cost of the goods or services sold during a financial period

Cost Plus Pricing	Setting selling prices by first calculating the base cost of a product or service and then adding the required profit margin.
Cost Pools	The collection of costs into specific activities (used in Activity Based Costing)
Costs	See Expenses
Credit Purchases	Purchases made from suppliers with an agreed period of grace before the corresponding payment is due
Credit Sales	Sales made to customers with an agreed period of grace before the corresponding payment is due
Creditors	See Payables
Current Assets	Assets which are expected to be used within 12 months.
Current Liabilities	Liabilities which are expected to be settled within 12 months.
Current Ratio	A measure of a business's liquidity (= Current Assets / Current Liabilities)
Debt Finance	Long term finance for a business derived from borrowing (e.g. bank loans or issuing corporate bonds)
Debtors	See Receivables
Depreciation	The spreading out of capital expenditure over the financial periods during which economic benefit is derived
Direct Costs	A cost which can be directly and exclusively linked to a particular cost object
Direct Labour Efficiency Variance	The difference in profit purely attributable to the number of labour hours used compared to that in the flexed budget
Direct Labour Rate Variance	The difference in profit purely attributable to paying a higher or lower labour rate from that in the flexed budget
Direct Labour Total Variance	The difference in profit purely attributable to the amount spent on direct labour from that in the flexed budget
Direct Materials Price Variance	The difference in profit purely attributable to paying a higher or lower unit cost for direct materials from that in the flexed budget
Direct Materials Quantity Variance	The difference in profit purely attributable to the quantity of direct materials used compared to that in the flexed budget
Direct Materials Total Variance	The difference in profit purely attributable to the amount spent on direct materials from that in the flexed budget

The Language of Business

Direct Materials Usage Variance	See Direct Materials Quantity Variance
Director	An officer of a company who holds legal responsibility for the running of the company
Discount Factor	The mathematical factor applied to future cashflows to ascertain their Present Value. Depends on both Cost of Capital and the time delay in receiving funds
Discounted Cashflow	See Present Value
Dividend Cover	A measure of how affordable the level of dividends are for the company
Earnings	See Profit
Earnings per Share (EPS)	The Profit after Tax (PAT) attributable to each individual share
EBITDA	Earnings before Interest Taxation Depreciation & Amortisation. Rough measure of cash generation from operating activities
Equity	The value of the net assets in the business that belongs to the shareholders
Equity Finance	Long term finance for a business derived from shareholders (e.g. share capital and retained profit)
Expenses	The outflow of wealth from a business in relation to its ordinary operations
Favourable Variance	A difference between actual and budgeted performance which will result in greater profitability
FIFO	First In First Out - A system of inventory valuation which assumes that the oldest inventory is always sold first
Financial Accounting	The branch of the accountancy profession which focuses on the production of financial information for external users e.g. shareholders
Financial Period	A period of time (e.g. week, month, year) for which a set of financial statements are prepared
Financial Reporting Standards (FRS)	The UK based standards which govern the production, format and content of financial accounts
Fixed Assets	See Non-Current Assets
Fixed Cost	A cost whose total value remains constant regardless of the level of activity
Flexed Budget	A budget revised to the actual level of activity encountered

Full Costing	See Absorption Costing
Gearing	What percentage of a business's long-term finance derives from debt (aka Leverage)
Goal Congruence	Aiming to align the objectives of different parties (e.g. company directors and shareholders)
Gross Margin	See Gross Profit
Gross Profit	Sales Revenue less the corresponding Cost of Sales. Can be expressed as both £ and %
Hard Capital Rationing	Externally imposed restriction on available funds for capital investments (e.g. by bank)
Herd Instinct	The tendency of share investors to follow the common trend of either buying or selling
Hi-Lo Method	A method of analysis used to calculate the variable and fixed components of a semi-variable cost
HMRC	Her Majesty's Revenue & Customs. The UK tax authority.
Horizontal Analysis	The analysis of a financial statements by comparison between corresponding figures from different time periods
ICAEW	Institute of Chartered Accountants in England & Wales
ICAS	Institute of Chartered Accountants in Scotland
Imposed Budgets	Budget setting process which does not consult with those who will be subsequently responsible for its achievement
Income	The inflow of wealth into a business from its ordinary operations i.e. sales of goods and services
Income Statement	See Statement of Profit or Loss
Income Tax	UK tax paid by individuals on their income from employment, self-employment, pension income, savings interest, share dividends and property rental income
Incorporated Business	A business which is being run from within a company or other corporate body
Incremental Budgeting	The setting of a budget by applying incremental changes to past performance
Indirect Cost	A cost which cannot be directly and exclusively linked to a particular cost object
Input Tax	The VAT which a business suffers on its purchases of taxable supplies from VAT registered suppliers

The Language of Business

Interest Cover	The number of times the interest costs of a business could have been paid out of operating profit, and hence how affordable the level of interest payments are for the company
Internal Rate of Return (IRR)	A capital investment appraisal method which calculates the discount factor at which the Net Present Value of the project would be zero
International Financial Reporting Standards (IFRS)	International standards which govern the production, format and content of financial accounts
Inventory	Raw materials, work in progress and finished goods held by a business for subsequent resale
Inventory Days	A measure of the level of inventory held i.e. How many days would it take to sell the inventory held?
Investment Centre	A sub-division of an organisation which holds responsibility for the achievement of budgeted investment returns
Irrelevant Cost	A cost which will not be affected by a certain decision
Joint & Several Liability	The liability of a partner not only for his partnership actions and debts, but also those of his/her partners
Just in Time (JIT)	A philosophy that aims to reduce or even eradicate the holding of inventory by receiving raw materials 'just in time' for manufacture
Key Performance Indicator (KPI)	A quantitative method of measuring business performance by reference to a few key metrics
Leverage	See Gearing
Liabilities	Items owed by the business
LIFO	Last In First Out - A now obsolete method of inventory valuation which assumed that the newest inventory is always sold first
Limited Liability	The protection enjoyed by the shareholders of companies from the debts and claims made on the company (also enjoyed by the members of an LLP)
Limited Liability Partnerships (LLP)	An incorporated partnership sharing features of both companies and conventional partnerships
Limiting Factor	Any production resource (e.g. materials or labour) whose scarcity will limit production
Liquidity	The ability of a business to pay its debts as they fall due by virtue of being able to access cash
London Stock Exchange (LSE)	The world's oldest stock exchange for the trading of the shares and loan stock of the largest public companies
Management Accounting	The branch of the accountancy profession which focuses on the production of financial information for internal users e.g. directors and managers

Margin	See Gross Profit
Margin of Safety	Expresses by how much the budgeted (or actual) sales volume exceeds the break-even sales volume
Marginal Cost	The cost of producing one more of a particular item (which consists of just the variable costs of that item)
Mark Up	A method of calculating (or quoting) the profit margin on a product or service by relating it to the corresponding cost price
Market Capitalisation	The valuation of a company by reference to its current market share price
Memorandum of Association	A company document submitted to Companies House stating that the company will be formed and what its general aims are
Net Present Value (NPV)	A capital investment appraisal method which takes into account all cash flows from a project, discounted to their equivalent present value
Net Profit	A generic term covering profitability after deduction of overheads from Gross profit
Net Profit Variance	The total difference in profit from that in the flexed budget due to all factors
NIC	National Insurance Contributions. Contributions paid on earnings (i.e. from employment & self-employment) to fund various state benefits
Non-Current Assets	Assets which are expected to still be held by the business in 12 months' time
Non-Current Liabilities	Liabilities which are not expected to be settled within 12 months
Operating Cycle	The average length of time that elapses between actually paying for inventory and receiving the cash for its eventual sale
Operating Profit	Profit before Interest & Tax (PBIT). The key measure of operating performance
Opportunity Benefits	The loss of potential cost as a result of a certain decision
Opportunity Costs	The loss of potential revenue as a result of a certain decision
Optional Pricing	Encouraging customers to purchase optional extras with main purchase
Output Tax	The VAT which a VAT registered business must add to its sales of taxable supplies
Over Absorption	Lower than expected overheads or higher than expected activity, leading to excessive absorption of production overheads into cost objects

Overhead Absorption Rate (OAR)	A calculated rate that describes how much of a particular departments overheads should be absorbed by the products passing through that department
Overhead Variance	The difference in profit purely attributable to the amount spent on overheads from that in the flexed budget
P&L	See Statement of Profit or Loss
PAR values	Target stockholding of each item of inventory used to formulate replenishment orders
Participative Budgeting	Budget setting process which consults with those who will be subsequently responsible for its achievement
Partnership	Two or more individuals jointly operating in business and not trading via a company
Partnership Act	The primary UK legislation governing the operation of partnerships
Payables	Amounts owed by a business to its suppliers for goods and services purchased from them on credit terms
Payables Days	A measure of the level of payables i.e. How many days' worth of credit purchase payments are outstanding
Payback (Period)	A capital investment appraisal method which reports the time required for the cash inflows from a project to repay the initial cash outflow
Penetration Pricing	Initial setting of a low selling price to gain a foothold in an established market
Period Cost	Production overheads not assigned to the cost of a product, but instead charged directly to the P&L
Premium Pricing	Selling at an artificially high price to convey the impression of a premium product
Prepayment	An expense which has been charged for but not yet incurred
Present Value	The equivalent present value of a future cashflow found by applying the appropriate discount factor
Price Earnings Ratio (PE Ratio)	Ratio expressing the market price of a share compared to the Earnings per Share for that share
Price Elasticity of Demand (PED)	A measure of the responsiveness of demand after a change in selling price. PED = % Change in Demand / % Change in Price
Price Skimming	Initial setting of a high selling price in the belief that keen/loyal customers will pay a high price to access a new product
Principal	The initial sum borrowed in the form of a bank loan

Private Limited Company (Ltd)	Company designated by the letters 'Ltd' who are limited to trading shares on a private basis i.e. not via a stock exchange
Product Cost	Production overheads which will be assigned to the cost of a product and hence ultimately form part of the Cost of Sales
Production Departments	Any department that works directly on the products being manufactured
Profit	The difference between income earned and expenses incurred
Profit & Loss Account	See Statement of Profit or Loss
Profit after Tax (PAT)	The final profit figure attributable to the shareholders of the company
Profit before Tax (PBT)	Operating Profit less Finance Costs. Used to calculate corporation tax liability
Profit before Interest and Tax (PBIT)	Operating Profit. The key measure of operating performance
Profit Centre	A sub-division of an organisation which holds responsibility for achievement of profit budget
Profit Contribution	See Contribution
Psychological Pricing	To convey the impression of a lower price e.g. £1.99 instead of £2.00
Public Limited Company (PLC)	Company which is able to trade shares publically i.e. via a stock exchange.
Quick Ratio	A more robust measure of a business's liquidity which ignores inventory (= [current assets less inventory] / current liabilities)
Receivables	Amounts owed to a business by customers who have purchased goods and services on credit terms
Receivables Days	A measure of the level of receivables i.e. How many days' worth of credit sale receipts are outstanding?
Registered Office	The address to which official correspondence concerning a company is sent. Companies often use their accountant's address as their registered office
Relevant Cost	A cost which will be affected by a certain decision
Responsibility Accounting	A system used by large organisations whereby responsibility for achievement of financial targets is delegated to key managers
Retained Profit	Company profit which has not been distributed to shareholders as dividends but instead retained as onward investment within the company

The Language of Business

Return on Capital Employed (ROCE)	A measure of the profit return from the total capital employed in a business
Return on Equity (ROE)	A measure of the profit return of a company purely from the shareholders perspective
Revenue Centre	A sub-division of an organisation which holds responsibility for achievement of the sales revenue budget
Revenue Expenditure	Expenditure which has no lasting value and is therefore immediately charged to the P&L in its entirety
Sales	See Income
Sales Price Variance	The difference in profit purely attributable to the change in average selling price from that in the flexed budget
Sales Profit Volume Variance	The difference in profit purely attributable to the change in activity level from that originally budgeted
Sales Revenue	See Income
Sales Volume	The number of units of a particular product or service sold
Scarce Resource	See Limiting Factor
Secured Loan	A loan which provides safeguards to the lender in case of default by the borrower e.g. signing over certain company assets in the case of default
Semi-Variable Cost	A cost whose total value increases with activity (which is not nil at Zero activity) because it includes both variable and fixed components
Service Departments	Any department that does not work directly on the products being manufactured, but which indirectly supports production
Share Capital	The amount originally paid by shareholders to purchase newly issued shares in the company
Share Options	The right (but not obligation) given to an individual (e.g. company director) allowing them to purchase company shares in the future at a stated price
Shareholders	The legal owners of a company who have invested in a share of the company
SIC Code	Standard Industrial Classification of economic activity. System used by Companies House to categorise the business sector of UK companies
Soft Capital Rationing	Self-imposed restriction on available funds for capital investments (e.g. in capex budget)
Sole Trader	A self-employed individual operating in business on their own account i.e. not in partnership with others and not trading via a company

Standard Costing	A costing technique utilised when the various costs of production are subject to operational variations
Statement of Capital	A company's declaration to Companies House of its share structure and ownership
Statement of Cashflows	Financial statement which records the various cash inflows and cash outflows of a financial period
Statement of Changes in Equity	Financial statement that describes the change between the opening and closing values of equity over a period of time
Statement of Financial Position (SOFP)	Key financial statement which reports the position of a business at a point in time by reporting its assets, liabilities and equity
Statement of Profit or Loss	Financial statement that describes the profitability of a business over a period of time
Static Budget	A budget which once set is not amended to take into account actual levels of activity
Step Cost	A cost which appears fixed for a certain range of activity, before jumping to an increased amount for a higher level of activity
Stock	See Inventory
Subscribing	The original purchase of newly issued share in a company (as opposed to the second-hand purchase of existing shares)
Sunk Costs	Expenditure which has already been spent and regardless of any decision to be taken cannot be 'unspent'
Taxable Supplies	Goods and Services which fall within the VAT regime
Term	The length of a time for which a bank loan is arranged
Time Value of Money	The concept that cash received in the future is worth less than cash received now due to inflation, foregone investment opportunities and risk
Total Capital Employed	The total long-term capital in a business (both debt finance & equity finance)
Total Costing	See Absorption Costing
Traditional Absorption Costing	Costing method that assigns overheads into production departments and hence into cost objects
Turnover	See Income
Unavoidable Costs	Costs which cannot be avoided or reduced despite adopting a certain course of action

Under Absorption	Higher than expected overheads or lower than expected activity, leading to insufficient absorption of production overheads into cost objects
Unincorporated Business	A business which is not being run from within a company or other corporate body i.e. a sole trader or partnership
Unlimited Liability	The lack of protection for sole traders and partnerships whereby they are personally responsible for the debts and claims on their business
Value Added Tax (VAT)	The UK sales tax applied to the sale of many goods and services (ultimately borne by the end consumer)
Variable Cost	A cost whose total value increases with activity (but which is nil at zero activity)
Variance Analysis	A technique to analyse the various differences in profitability due to variations from a product's standard costs
Vertical Analysis	The analysis of a financial statement by comparison between different figures from within the same time period
Work in Progress (WIP)	Partially manufactured goods which form part of a business's inventory
Working Capital	The required funding to allow the day to day operation of a business (= Current Assets less Current Liabilities)
Working Capital Ratio	See current ratio
Zero Based Budgeting	The setting of a budget without reference to past performance

Chapter 1
The Statement of Financial Position

INTRODUCTION

In this first chapter we will start by looking at the main different forms of **business entity** and then move on to consider different types of **financial information** and what makes such information useful.

We then look at our first financial statement '**The Statement of Financial Position**' which introduces the concepts of assets, liabilities and equity.

OVERVIEW AND OBJECTIVES

By the end of this chapter you should able to:

- Describe different types of business entity

- Assess different forms of financial information

- Understand the concepts behind The Statement of Financial Position

    …..and answer questions relating to these areas.

1 The Statement of Financial Position

1.1 Different types of business entity

There are three basic different ways in which a business can be formed and operated

1) **Sole Trader:** Where an individual trades (i.e. runs his/her business) on his/her own account with no legal distinction between the identity of the individual and that of the business.

2) **Partnership:** Where two or more people trade on their own [joint] account, again with no legal distinction between the identity of the business and that of the partners.

3) **Company:** Where a new legal entity (the company) is specifically created from which the business is run. The company has its own legal identity which is completely separate from that of the owners of the company (the shareholders).

Each of these will now be considered in turn, as well as some variations to the three basic types of entity listed above.

1.2 Sole traders

This is the simplest form of business entity where an individual simply operates on his/her own account. This is typically how many small businesses originally start to trade, and in fact many continue as sole traders on a permanent basis (presumably because they cannot see a good reason to change). Whilst it is true that operating as a sole trader is often typical of trades such as those of shopkeepers, plumbers and the like, they can also include professionals such as barristers.

A sole trader can employ any number of people and enter into contracts and there is no *theoretical* limit to the size of business that could operate with sole trader status. However, for various practical reasons it is often the case that as a 'fledgling' sole trader business starts to grow, the trader then often decide to 'incorporate' as a company.

Starting to trade as a sole trader is very straightforward with few legal requirements. The key requirement is to inform the tax authorities (HMRC) that the individual has started to trade, as in due course he/she will need to pay income tax and national insurance contributions (NIC) based on his/her profits.

The time limit for informing HMRC that a new self-employed business has commenced is the 5th October in the *second* tax year of trading. Tax years always run from 6th April in one year to the 5th April in the next year e.g. Tax Year 2018/19 runs from 6th April 2018 to 5th April 2019. So a new sole trader business that commenced anytime during tax year 2018/19 would have to notify HMRC by 5th October 2019.

> ⚠️ **KEY POINT**
>
> The key feature of trading as a sole trader is that there is **no legal distinction** between the business and the individual.
>
> This is the case even if the sole trader adopts a 'trading name' e.g. a builder called Robert Matthews trading as *'Bob the Builder'*.
>
> From a legal perspective the individual (Robert Matthews) and the business ('Bob the Builder') are **one and the same legal person**.
>
> This lack of legal separation means that if a legal claim is made against the business, then it is in effect being made against the individual.

> **EXAMPLE**
>
> Imagine that our sole trader builder is negligent in some way and causes a serious injury to a customer whilst working at their house.
>
> The customer may then be able to sue the builder in court for damages. The level of damages the court awards to the customer will not necessarily be limited to the value of the assets of the business (van, tools etc.), but can include the value of the builder's personal possessions as well ... including (if they own it) the house his family live in!
>
> In other words the sole trader has unlimited liability and this is one of the major disadvantages of operating as a sole trader.

All businesses (sole traders, partnerships & companies) should ensure that they are adequately insured against any potential claims that may be made against them by employees, customers and members of the public, but this is especially true for sole traders and partnerships who would otherwise face unlimited liability. Insurance companies operating in the small business sector typically offer 'All Risk' insurance policies which provide comprehensive cover for business risks.

1.3 Partnerships

We have just seen that a sole trader is simply an individual trading on his/her own account (i.e. *not* having created a separate legal entity such as a company from which to carry on his/her trade). Taking this idea one step further, a partnership is simply *two or more* people trading on their own account (i.e. again *not* having created a separate legal entity such as a company from which to trade).

The law covering partnerships has been in place since 1890 and is still going strong! **The Partnership Act 1890** defines partnership as *'the relationship which subsists between persons carrying on a business in common with a view of profit.'* In practice this means that a partnership *automatically* exists as soon as two or more people work together in business with the aim of making a profit. They do not need to formally decide to be in a partnership ... it is automatically the case!

The Partnership Act 1890 then further defines certain default rights of the partners, such as the right for all partners to have access to the partnership's accounts (which is probably non-contentious) and the right for all partners to share equally in the profits of the partnership (which may *not* be what the partners intended if some partners are more involved in the business than others!).

In order to override some of the default conditions of the Partnership Act 1890, it is wise for partners to agree exactly how they wish *their* partnership to operate by drawing up and signing a partnership agreement. This would typically include clauses governing such matters as

- Contribution of time & money to the partnership
- Decision making & authority levels
- Conflict resolution
- Admission & retirement of partners
- The sharing of profits.

1 The Statement of Financial Position

> **TUTORIAL NOTE**
>
> This last point is especially important. A good partnership often contains a complimentary mix of skills and involves different partners making different levels of contribution to the partnership.....whether that be in the form of cash invested, time spent, or knowledge/expertise brought in.
>
> It is therefore often the case that the partners will agree to *not* share any profits equally, but instead to adjust each partner's 'profit share' based on their individual contribution. Obviously, to avoid future conflict these arrangements should be formalised in a partnership agreement.

Both sole traders and partnerships share the same major disadvantage of having 'unlimited liability' for the individuals concerned. In the case of a partnership the business is legally indistinguishable from the partners, and in fact each partner has a *'joint and several'* liability. This means that anyone with a claim against the partnership business may pursue (in court) either *all* of the partners, or *any* single partner. This means that each partner cannot only be held legally responsible for his/her actions, but also those of their partners.

The partnership as a whole does not pay tax. Instead each individual partner is responsible for paying income tax and national insurance contributions (NIC) based on his/her own share of the profits (according to the same basic tax principles as for sole traders). Partners are solely responsible for their own tax affairs … the principle of *'joint and several liability'* does not extend to the personal taxation of individual partners. The time limit for notifying HMRC that a new partnership has commenced trading is the 5th October in the *second* tax year of trading (i.e. the same as for sole traders).

Partnerships (just like sole traders) can employ any number of staff and enter into contracts with suppliers or customers. A partnership is relatively simple to set up and administer and although drawing up a partnership agreement is not legally required, it is nonetheless highly recommended to ensure a future harmonious partnership.

1.4 Companies

A fundamentally different way to trade is via a limited company which has an entirely separate legal identity to that of the owners of the business. New companies must be set up and registered at Companies House, who are responsible for administering more than 3 million companies in the UK.

Setting up a new small company is nowadays quite a simple process and can be quickly processed online at: www.gov.uk/government/organisations/companies-house.

The key information which needs to be declared when forming a new company includes:

- **The name of the company** - Which must not only be unique, but also different enough from other company names to avoid confusion. Some companies actually continue to trade using a 'trading name'(aka 'business name') instead of trading under their company name. The trading name should be registered as a trademark to protect it from being copied.

- **What business sector the company will operate in** – By quoting the 'SIC code' *(=Standard Industrial Classification of economic activities)* e.g. The SIC Code 56101 would designate that the business is a licenced restaurant.

- **The registered address of the business** – Which will be made publically available and where official correspondence will be sent to. This must be a physical UK address (i.e. not a PO Box) and companies often use their accountant's address for this purpose.

- **The names of the Director(s)** – A company must have at least one director (aged over 16 and who is not disqualified from being a director). The names and addresses of the directors will (normally) be made publically available.

- **The 'Statement of Capital'** - i.e. How many shares of each 'class' (type) will be issued and at what value, and the names of the initial shareholders (known as 'subscribers') and the rights attached to each class of share. It is often the case that there is only one class of share called 'ordinary shares' and fledgling businesses often start with a very low value of share capital (which could even be a single £1 share!).

- An **'Accounting Reference Date'** - Which defines when the company's financial year-end will be and therefore the accounting period for which the financial accounts will be prepared.

There are two key documents which a company is required to submit to Companies House:

i. **The Memorandum of Association** – Which is simply a document from the initial shareholders ('subscribers') stating that the company will be formed and what the general aims of the company will be. There is a standard template available on the Companies House website which can be used to simplify this requirement.

ii. **The Articles of Association** – which act as the rulebook for how the company will be run with respect to any matter that involves the shareholders. There is a standard 'model' set of Articles of Association available on the Companies House website which can be adopted, which will suit most needs. Alternatively a new company can draw up its own Articles (probably with the help of a solicitor) to exactly correspond to any unique requirements it may have.

Companies come in all shapes and sizes with varying amounts of complexity, but the very simplest companies can be created online in under 30 minutes for a total set up fee of £12 payable to Companies House.

The newly created company will be assigned a company registration number which must be shown on the company letterheads, order forms and websites etc. together with the address of the registered office and whether the company is registered in England & Wales, or Scotland, or Northern Ireland. It is also necessary to signify that the business is actually a limited company and this can be easily achieved by simply including the company's full name including 'Ltd' or 'Limited' or 'PLC' (covered later).

A company can employ any number of people ranging from a single employee (who might also be the sole owner of the company) to employing tens of thousands of employees. Since the company is a 'legal person' in its own right it can also enter into contracts. The point is that in the event of a legal dispute it is *the company itself* which would be pursued **not** the individual within the company who signed the contract on the company's behalf, nor any of the shareholders. In fact the company designation *'limited'* refers to the fact that the shareholders' liability is limited to just the share capital they have invested.

1 The Statement of Financial Position

> **KEY POINT**
>
> The **protection** that this **limited liability** offers individuals is a strong incentive to run a business from within the relative safety of a company. The other tempting feature of companies is that they offer more **flexibility for tax planning** compared to the taxation of the self-employed (both sole traders and partnerships).
>
> Additionally, some customers and suppliers regard sole trader businesses as lacking **credibility** and would rather trade with a limited company. The irony of this is that in the event of a dispute this often worsens the position for the customers and/or suppliers as they can only claim against the assets of the company and not those of the owners (shareholders) of the company.
>
> For all of the above reasons there is a growing trend away from unincorporated businesses (e.g. sole traders and partnerships) and towards incorporated businesses (e.g. companies).

Percentage of Companies compared to Sole Traders and Partnerships, 2011-2016 (Office for National Statistics)

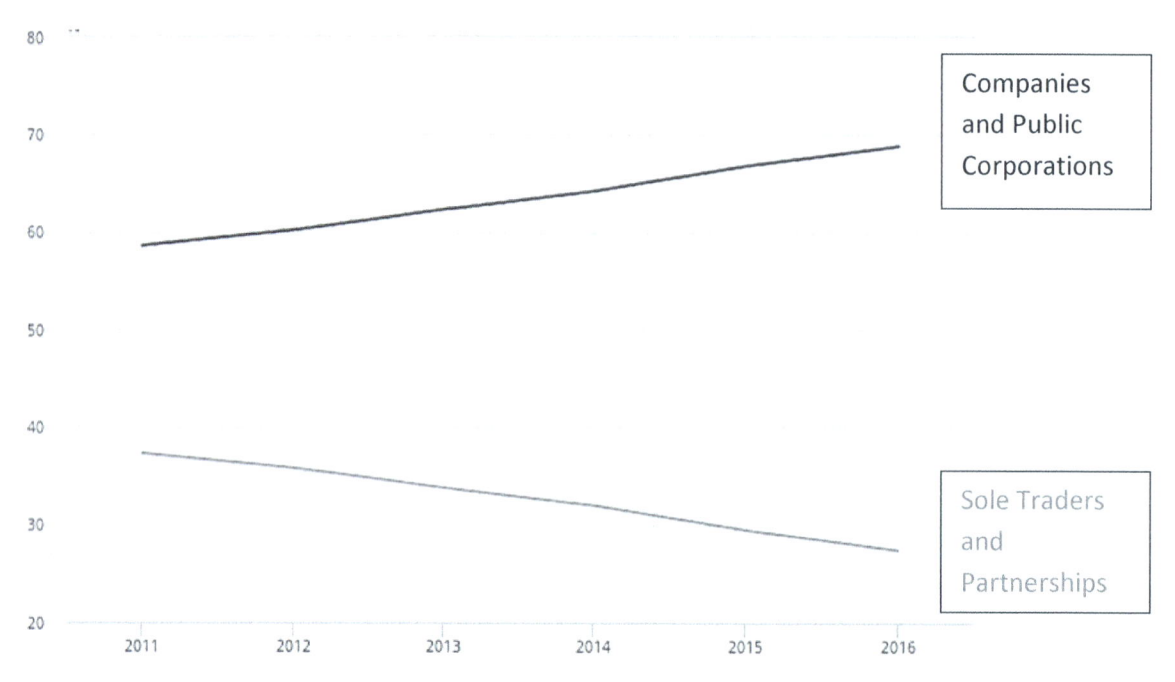

There is however a price to pay for gaining limited liability. All companies are required to submit two separate documents to Companies House on an annual basis:

i. A 'confirmation statement' (previously known as the Annual Return) which confirms basic details about the company such as the industry sector worked in (SIC code), the share capital issued and details of who owns those shares. If any details have changed from the previous year they must be updated.

ii. A set of financial accounts (aka Annual Report) and explanatory notes, together with a Director's statement.

Much of the above information is then made publically available by publishing it on the Companies House website. In contrast the ownership details and financial accounts of sole traders and partnerships are *not* required to be made publically available.

Addtionally, companies must submit a corporation tax return to HMRC (which is *not* made publically available).

1.5 The different parties involved in a company

From a legal perspective there are **three main parties** involved in a company:

i. **The company itself** – which is an entity in its own right with a separate legal identity from both that of the shareholders and the directors. The company itself will be liable to pay corporation tax on the profits it makes.

ii. **The director(s) of the company** – who are legally responsible for the running of the company. The directors are usually employed by the company and will be liable to pay income tax and national insurance contributions on the salary they receive.

iii. **The shareholder(s) of the company** – who actually own the company. The shareholders will hope to receive a share of the company's profit each year which is paid as a 'dividend' and the shareholders will potentially pay income tax (but not NIC) on the dividend income they receive.

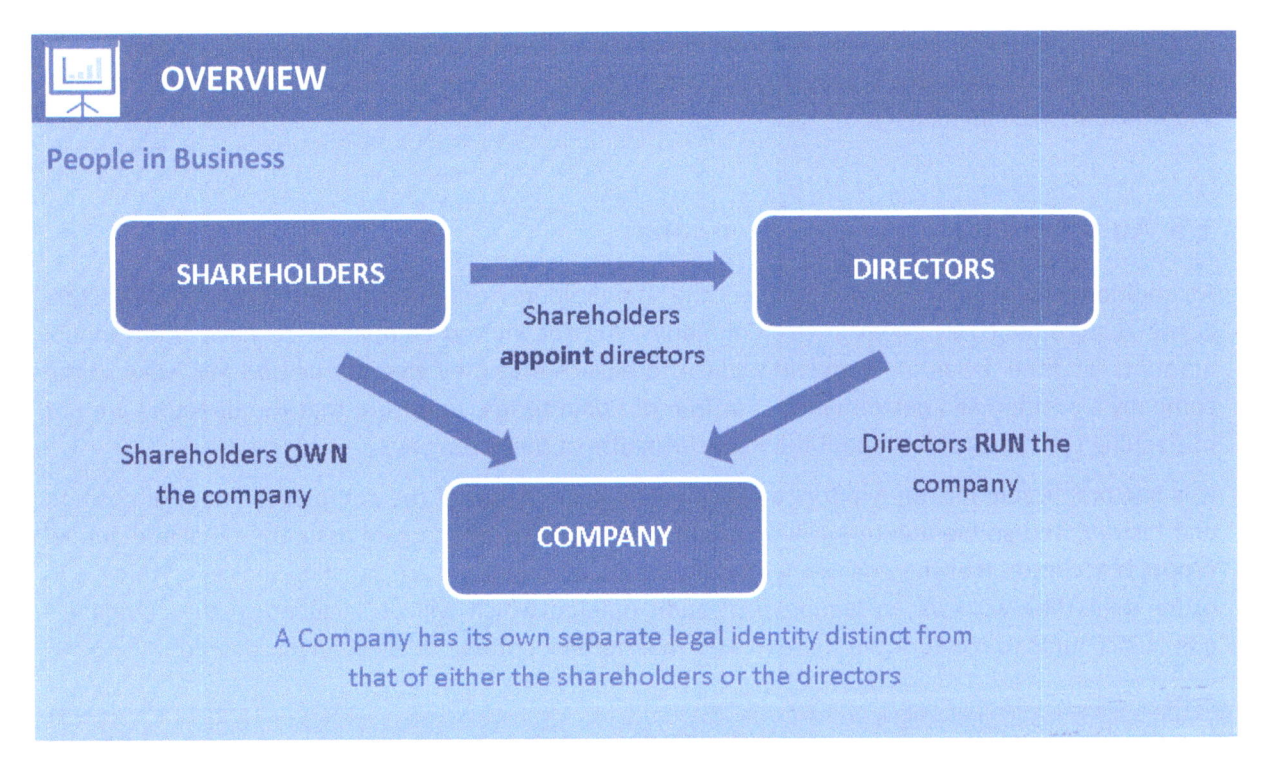

> **OVERVIEW**
>
> **People in Business**
>
> SHAREHOLDERS → DIRECTORS
>
> Shareholders **appoint** directors
>
> Shareholders OWN the company
>
> Directors RUN the company
>
> COMPANY
>
> A Company has its own separate legal identity distinct from that of either the shareholders or the directors

There are many small one-person companies which are both 100% owned and solely run by the same person. In these cases the shareholder and the director are in fact one and the same person.

At the other end of the scale there are many large companies where the shareholders who own the company are individuals (or indeed financial institutions such as pension funds) who have absolutely nothing to do with the running of the company. In these cases the directors are running the company on behalf of the shareholders and this is an example of an agency relationship where the 'principals' (the shareholders) have authorised their 'agents' (the directors) to run their company on their behalf. The problem with this sort of agency relationship is ensuring that the directors are in fact acting in the best interest of the shareholders ..... and not in their own best interest!

The standard technique used to ensure the necessary *'goal congruence'* between the aims of the directors and those of the shareholders is to ensure that the directors are in fact *also* shareholders themselves, as well as being company employees. The directors would then be unlikely to initiate any action which is not beneficial to the shareholders, as this would hurt their own interests.

1 The Statement of Financial Position

Ensuring that the directors are shareholders themselves can be achieved in various ways:

i. By inviting them to buy shares in the company (possibly at a discounted price)

ii. By simply 'gifting' a number of shares to the directors.

iii. By awarding 'share options' to the directors which allow them to purchase a number of shares sometime in the *future* (when hopefully they are worth more) but for a lower price based on their *current* market value at the time the option is granted. The directors are immediately incentivised to do everything in their power to encourage the share price to increase so that they (and all the other shareholders!) will enjoy higher ultimate gains on their shares.

The other final sanction which the shareholders (the 'principals') have over the directors (the 'agents') is that they can vote them out of office. Most companies hold an Annual General Meeting (AGM) each year and one of the standard agenda items concerns the election (or re-election) of directors.

If enough shareholders are dissatisfied with how *their* company is being run, they can ultimately vote the directors out of office…. which is another good incentive for the directors to act in the shareholder's best interests!

1.6 Audit requirements for a company

An additional factor which helps to protect the shareholders from potentially unscrupulous directors is the requirement laid down in the Companies Act for limited companies to have their annual accounts 'audited' by an independent auditor to ensure that they give a *'true and fair'* view of the company's position and performance … or in more bold terms, to ensure that the directors are not misleading the shareholders about the financial health of *their* company.

It is not practicable for the auditor to check every single detail of the companies financial position and history, and so the auditors will use sample-testing in order to gain assurance that the annual report is accurate. If at the end of their audit process the auditors are satisfied that everything is in order then they will give an *'unqualified'* audit opinion which will be included in the company's annual accounts to reassure the shareholders that nothing untoward has been discovered.

> **EXAMPLE**
>
> **An Unqualified Audit Opinion :** *"In our opinion the company's financial statements give a true and fair view of the state of the company's affairs as at 31st December 2018 and of its profit [loss] for the year then ended".*
>
> **Conversley**, if the auditors are *not* satisfied that all is well, then they will issue a *'qualified'* audit opinion, which will alert both exisiting (and potential future) shareholders that there are serious issues.

> **EXAMPLE**
>
> Audits can only carried out by **qualified auditors** who will normally be members of one of the following professional bodies:
>
> - Association of Authorised Public Accountants (AAPA)
> - Association of Chartered Certified Accountants (ACCA)
> - Institute of Chartered Accountants in England and Wales (ICAEW)
> - Institute of Chartered Accountants of Scotland (ICAS)

One potential flaw in the audit process is that it is the directors who choose which accountancy firm to use to conduct the audit, which immediately raises the potential for the 'independent' audit to not be completely independent! However, to counter-balance this, the shareholders are asked to confirm the director's choice of auditor by way of a vote at each Annual General Meeting and can therfore override the director's choice.

Successive govenments have been keen to avoid over-burdening small businesses with excessive regulation and small private limited companies are able to take advantage of an 'audit exemption' to avoid the need for an audit at all if they have at least two of the following:

- an annual turnover of no more than £10.2 million
- assets worth no more than £5.1 million
- 50 or fewer employees on average.

However if the shareholders require an audit, or if this is a requirement laid down in the articles of association, then even small private limited companies must also then comply.

By contrast, public limited companies always require an audit regardless of size.

1.7 Tax planning for 'owner managed' companies

The smallest companies are often owned by a single individual who also works for the business. In other words they are an employee of the company they own! Additionally they will also probably be the sole director of the company.

This (quite common occurrence) means that the individual in question has no less than three separate legal connections to the company:

i. As a director they have legal responsibility for the running of the company and exercise day to day control over the operations of the company.

ii. They are the sole shareholder of the company and are therefore entitled to receive whatever share of the company's profits the director proposes, *but luckily for them they also happen to be that director!*

iii. They are an employee of the company (which is a separate issue to being a director) and will receive a salary as set by the director……. *which again is themselves!*

1 The Statement of Financial Position

> **EXAMPLE**
>
> To get a basic understanding of why the above arrangement can be so tax efficient let us consider what the situation would be if the individual had not incorporated their business and instead had run it on a sole trader basis.
>
> As a sole trader they would typically pay 40% income tax (on any income in the 'higher rate' tax band) plus NIC on *all* the profits their business makes *regardless* of whether the individual intended to 'extract' that profit for their personal use, or simply leave it invested in the business to help it grow.
>
> By contrast a company will only initially pay 19% corporation tax on its profits, and the business owner then has various options of how to extract the cash they personally require whilst suffering no further tax liability on profits left invested in the company.
>
> Since the individual has complete control of the company they can decide how best (i.e. most tax efficiently) to extract profits for their own use.
>
> The options for the individual include:
>
> i. Paying themselves a salary which will be potentially subject to income tax and NIC.
> ii. Awarding dividends to themselves which result in lower rates of income tax and no NIC
> iii. Awarding themselves various employment benefits such as child care vouchers or paying money into their pension scheme which are potentially exempt from income tax
>
> Additionally, many small business owners *personally* own their business premises and rent them to their business. The rental income the owners receive from their company is liable to income tax but not NICs.
>
> These smaller owner-managed companies are often initially launched at least partly because of the greater flexibility in tax planning that a company offers, compared to that of self-employed people (both sole traders and partnerships).

1.8 Private and public limited companies

There are in fact two distinct types of company that can be created:

- Private limited companies (Ltd)
- Public limited companies (PLC).

> **OVERVIEW**
>
> **Private Limited Companies (Ltd):**
>
> - Designated by including 'Limited' or 'Ltd' in their name
> - Can be formed with as little as £1 of share capital
> - Relatively easy to set up
> - Less ongoing administration required
> - Less financial disclosure required
> - Can only sell shares on a private basis i.e. not via a stock exchange

> **OVERVIEW**
>
> **Public limited companies (PLC):**
>
> - Designated by including 'PLC' in their name
> - Must have minimum of £50,000 share capital
> - More complex to set up
> - More ongoing administration required
> - More financial disclosure required
> - Can sell shares publically if it is listed on a stock exchange

Only the shares of Public Limited Companies may be publically traded on a stock exchange such as:

- The **London Stock Exchange** (LSE), originally founded in 1571, which is the world's oldest stock exchange. It is reserved for the very largest public companies, is highly regulated and places even more disclosure requirements on the listed companies.

- The **Alternative Investment Market** (AIM) which is a sub-market of the LSE intended for newer and smaller emerging companies. It was founded in 1995 and is far less regulated and therefore less costly to gain an AIM listing than a full LSE listing. Being listed on AIM is often a stepping stone to a full LSE listing.

The fact that a company has PLC status does not mean that it is actually listed on a stock exchange but that it potentially *could be,* if desired, and if all the additional requirements of the individual stock exchange were met.

1.9 Limited liability partnerships (LLP)

A special kind of partnership exists that is a hybrid between a conventional partnership and a company. Although Limited Liability Partnerships appear similar to conventional partnerships in many respects, they are in fact corporate bodies. Hence they have a distinct separate legal identity from that of their owners (the partners of the LLP or 'members' as they are usually called).

One of the drawbacks of a conventional partnership is that each partner has 'joint and severally' liability for claims facing *any* of the partners. This would be difficult enough for a small 'firm' (as partnerships are often called) where all the partners work in the same premises. However, certain professions (most notably solicitors and accountants), which have always traditionally traded as partnerships, have in recent years grown enormously and often become international. For example, KPMG (accountancy partnership) now operates in over 150 countries, which presents quite a leap of faith for a new prospective partner in accepting joint liability for *any* of their partners' actions!

In response to this, the Limited Liability Partnership Act 2000 *(quite new by partnership standards!)* introduced the concept of a Limited Liability Partnership, which, although a limited liability corporate body (like a company), was in every other respect akin to the conventional form of partnership used for many years by firms of professionals. Thus all of the operational, profit share and taxation arrangements continued unaltered, apart from there now being a cap on an individual member's liability equal to the original capital investment he/she had made into the LLP. This is similar in concept to the liability of company shareholders being limited to their original investment in share capital.

Since an LLP is in fact a corporate body it must be registered at Companies House and comply with many of the annual filing requirements of companies. However, unlike a company, the LLP does not

1 The Statement of Financial Position

itself pay tax. Instead the individual 'members' (as the partners of an LLP are known) are taxed in the same way as the partners of a conventional partnership. That is, their personal share of the LLP profit is assessed as self-employment income on each 'member' separately.

> **OVERVIEW**
>
> **Limited liability partnerships (LLP):**
>
> LLPs offer large professional firms a way of maintaining many aspects of their partnership tradition, whilst offering the individual members the same sort of limited liability as the shareholders of a limited company.
>
> Again, the price to be paid for the 'corporate body' status is that an LLP is required to file annual returns and accounts at Companies House which will be put on the public record.

1.10 Summary – different types of business entity

	Sole Trader	Conventional Partnership	Limited Liability Partnership (LLP)	Private Limited Company (Ltd)	Public Limited Company (PLC)
Legal Form	Individual	Individuals working together	Corporate Body	Corporate Body	Corporate Body
Owned by	Sole Trader	Partners	Members (= Partners)	Shareholders	Shareholders
Transfer of Shares	N/A	N/A	N/A	On private basis	Via Stock Exchange
Minimum Share Capital	N/A	N/A	N/A	£1	£50,000
Day to Day Control	Sole Trader	Partners	Members	Directors	Directors
Liability	Unlimited	Unlimited	Limited	Limited	Limited
Taxation	Sole Trader liable to Income Tax & NIC on profits	Partners liable to Income Tax & NIC on their share of profits	Members liable to Income Tax & NIC on their share of profits	Company liable to Corporation Tax on profits. ************ Share-holders liable to Income Tax on Dividends received	Company liable to Corporation Tax on profits. ************ Share-holders liable to Income Tax on Dividends received

Main types of business entity

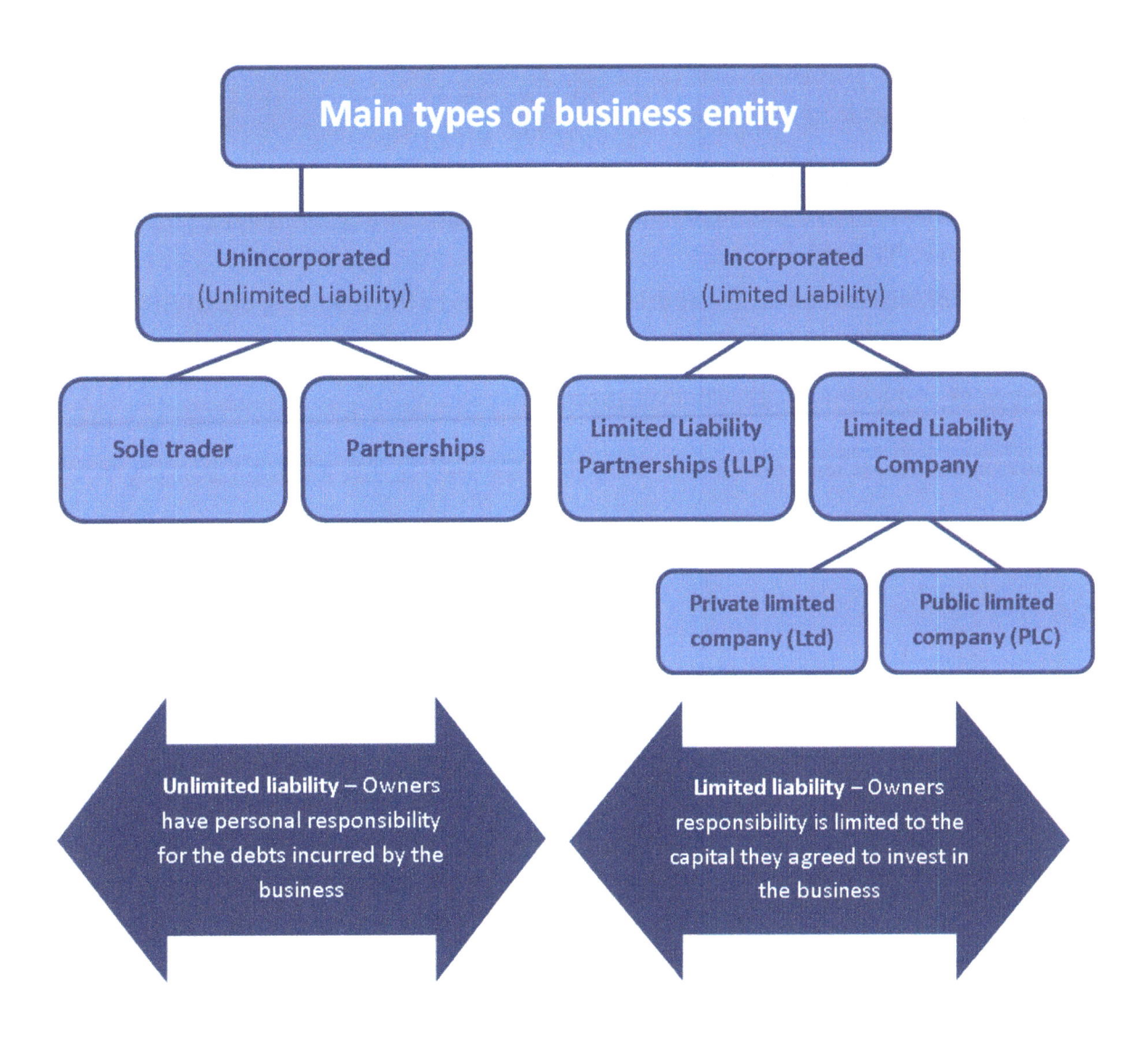

- **Unincorporated (Unlimited Liability)**
  - Sole trader
  - Partnerships
- **Incorporated (Limited Liability)**
  - Limited Liability Partnerships (LLP)
  - Limited Liability Company
    - Private limited company (Ltd)
    - Public limited company (PLC)

Unlimited liability – Owners have personal responsibility for the debts incurred by the business

Limited liability – Owners responsibility is limited to the capital they agreed to invest in the business

1 The Statement of Financial Position

TEST YOUR UNDERSTANDING 1

A business can be operated in a number of different forms or 'entities' such as: Sole Trader (ST), Partnership (P), Private Limited Company (Ltd), Public Limited Company (Plc), Limited Liability Partnership (LLP)

Which form of business entity (or entities) corresponds to the following descriptions (there may be more than one in each case):

Single owner and business legally indistinguishable _____

Business is a separate legal entity from owner(s) _____

Must file accounts at Companies House _____

May keep finances confidential _____

Can be set up with £1 share capital _____

Requires £50,000+ share capital _____

Results in single owner having unlimited liability _____

Results in owners having 'joint & several' liability _____

Gives limited liability to owners _____

Shares may be traded on London Stock Exchange _____

Shares may only be traded privately _____

Owners directly pay income tax on profits _____

Business pays corporation tax on profits _____

Can employ staff _____

Small fledgling businesses _____

Growing businesses wanting limited liability _____

Firm of Solicitors wanting to limit liability _____

The answers to 'Test Your Understanding' questions can be found at the end of each chapter

1.11 Users of financial information

We will now turn our attention to financial information - what makes it useful, who uses it and the main two branches of accountancy, known as management accountancy and financial accountancy.

In order to understand the wide range of people who use financial information, it is convenient to consider each of the various stakeholders of a company in turn (though most of the following will also apply to sole traders and partnerships etc.).

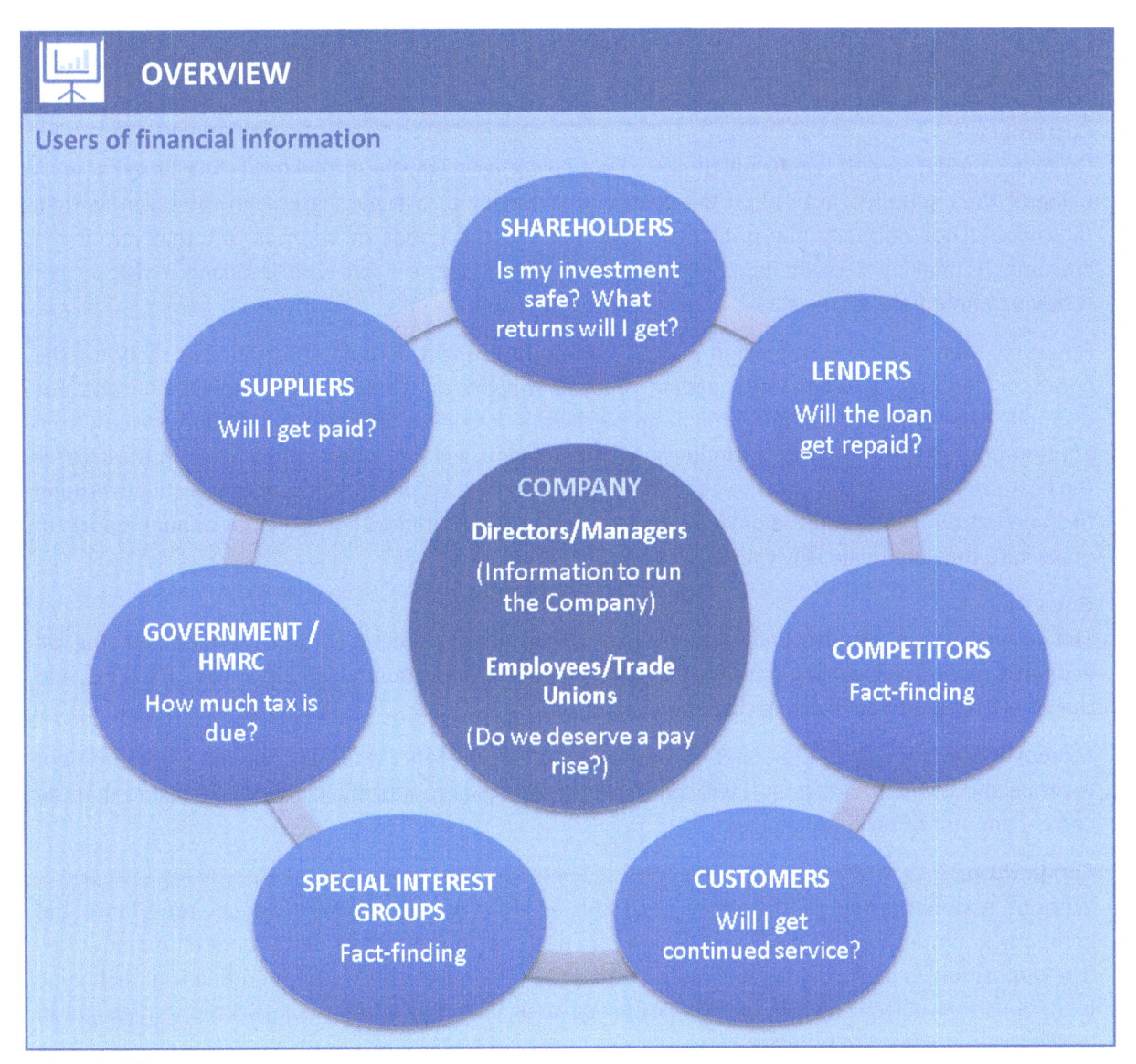

OVERVIEW

Users of financial information

- **SHAREHOLDERS** — Is my investment safe? What returns will I get?
- **LENDERS** — Will the loan get repaid?
- **COMPETITORS** — Fact-finding
- **CUSTOMERS** — Will I get continued service?
- **SPECIAL INTEREST GROUPS** — Fact-finding
- **GOVERNMENT / HMRC** — How much tax is due?
- **SUPPLIERS** — Will I get paid?
- **COMPANY** — Directors/Managers (Information to run the Company); Employees/Trade Unions (Do we deserve a pay rise?)

Shareholders

The shareholders actually own the company but may well have nothing to do with the day to day running of the business. They therefore need to know that their company is being run properly (by their 'agents' – the directors) and to understand how well it is performing and how safe their investment is.

The shareholders need this information to decide whether to invest or further invest in the company, or alternatively whether to withdraw their investment i.e. a 'buy or sell' decision.

Lenders

Before banks and other lenders will consider lending money to a company they will want to know that the business has the ability to pay both the interest on the loan and repay the original capital sum borrowed.

1 The Statement of Financial Position

The lender will therefore wish to assess the future prospects of the business and in particular its ability to generate the cash with which to make these payments.

Suppliers
Most business to business (B2B) transactions are made on a credit basis i.e. the supplier will provide goods or services now and allow a certain number of days credit before expecting payment. This obviously involves the supplier trusting the business to actually pay the bill when due.

The supplier (or quite possibly a credit rating agency) will look at the financial statements of the business to judge its ability to pay the debt when due, and to also ascertain the typical length of time the business actually takes to pay its suppliers.

Customers
On first consideration it is difficult to see why a *customer* might be interested in the financial well-being of their supplier. After all, if the customer is making a cash purchase from the business then they would not normally pay until they had received the goods or services. Alternatively if the customer is making a credit purchase, then it is the business itself who is taking a risk by not receiving immediate payment.

However, there are occasions when a significant deposit might be paid in advance of receiving the goods or services, or when the ongoing product support or warranty are highly significant. For example, one business (customer) might be purchasing a multi-million pound computer system from another business (the supplier) including a 10 year support and enhancement package. In these cases the customer business will want to assure themselves that their potential supplier will still be around for the next ten years, and the obvious starting point is to scrutinise their previous annual reports to make sure they are financially viable.

Government
The government is keen to know how British industry is performing to better understand the UK economy on both a local and national level e.g. growth in the economy, employment prospects, and the potential need for stimuli packages etc.

Moreover, the corporation tax paid by companies on their profits is a major source of government revenue and HMRC (the taxman!) will scrutinise the annual accounts of a company to ensure that the correct amount of tax has been paid.

Competitors
Without a doubt some of the most assiduous readers of a company's annual report are the company's competitors, who will scrutinise every detail in an attempt to better understand how well 'the opposition' is performing and what direction they are moving in. A common financial technique is to 'bench-mark' your own business's performance against that of your competitors to highlight in which areas you need to improve.

Special Interest Groups
Certain companies attract the attention of special interest groups either because of the sector they operate in (e.g. oil companies, animal testing etc.) or because of a local issue (proposed expansion of an airport etc.). In either case they are likely to face close scrutiny from pressure or protest groups who will want to glean as much information about the subject of their cause as possible, including its financial performance.

Employees / Trade Unions
One of the most interesting (and sometimes eye-popping!) parts of a company's annual report is the section where the board directors are forced to disclose their salary, bonuses and share options etc. (and by deduction how much these have increased by from the previous year).

This can then set the expectations of the rest of the workforce for what sort of annual salary increase they might be entitled to!

Directors / Managers

The directors and managers of a company are absolutely dependent on receiving 'useful' (see next section) financial information to allow them to perform their three main activities:

  i. Planning
  ii. Control
  iii. Decision Making

TEST YOUR UNDERSTANDING 2

There are many different users of financial information each wanting to use the information for a range of different purposes.

Give an example of one possible reason **why** the following groups might use financial information:

Shareholders _____

Lenders _____

Customers _____

Suppliers _____

Employees / Trade Unions _____

HMRC _____

Directors / Managers _____

Competitors _____

Special Interest Groups _____

1 The Statement of Financial Position

1.12 Characteristics of useful information

In the absence of the appropriate information, managers and directors will be little more than guessing what to do. They can only make informed decisions if they are supplied with the appropriate information.

We will now consider what actually makes information useful, but to begin let's first distinguish between 'data' and 'information'. These two terms are sometimes used interchangeably but have very different meanings!

'Data' means basic unprocessed 'raw data' which by itself is of little use. In contrast, 'information' means data which has been processed in some way to give it meaning, which will then make it useful in making informed decisions.

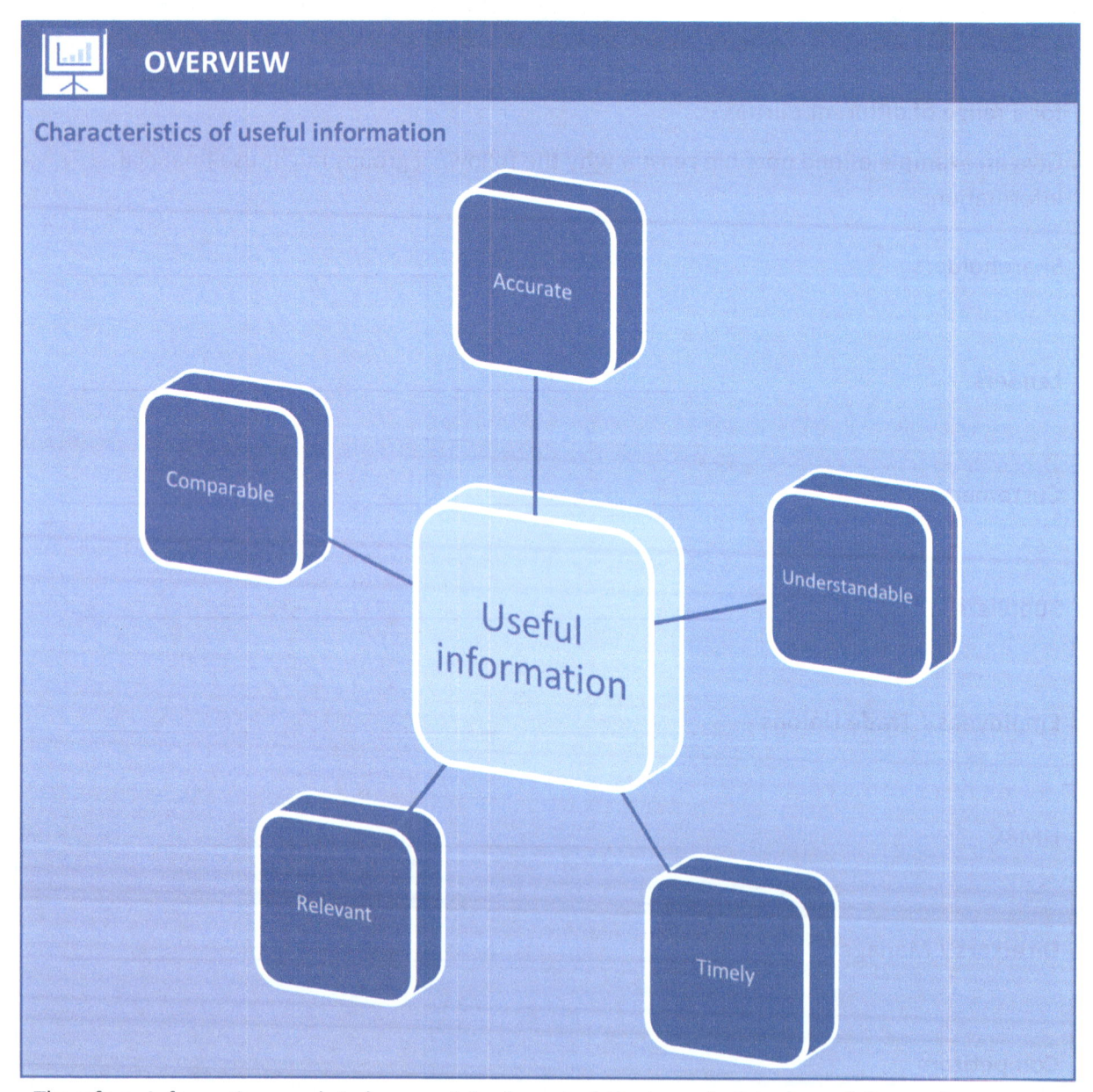

OVERVIEW

Characteristics of useful information

Useful information: Accurate, Comparable, Understandable, Relevant, Timely

Therefore, information needs to have certain characteristics to make it truly useful, namely:

Accurate
Obviously if information is not accurate then it will be potentially misleading and can lead to wrong decisions being taken. However, in the real world 'accuracy' is a relative term, and a more

meaningful statement might be that information needs to be *sufficiently* accurate for a given purpose.

Relevant

Supplying irrelevant information not only fails to assist the decision making process, it actually hinders it. A *'less is more'* approach should always be adopted when decision making. Only relevant information should be considered to avoid the potential confusion and stagnation of the process which can be caused when a whole raft of irrelevant information is also introduced.

Timely

Ideally information should be available almost immediately so that decisions are not based on out of date information. However, this presents a potential conflict in that the sooner information is made available the less accurate it is likely to be. In order to ensure that information is fully accurate we may need to wait for it to all become available and to be properly checked and verified. Unfortunately the time needed to accomplish this then means that the information ceases to be timely.

A judgement needs to be made as to the appropriate balance of speed versus accuracy!

Understandable

This characteristic cannot be over-stated. If information is not presented in a way that is immediately understandable *(to the end-user ... not to the author!)* then it is of little use. There is a real art in presenting information in a logical, easy to follow manner, complete with the necessary headings, units and formatting emphasis, to result in the information 'jumping off' the page or screen to the end-user. Conversely, if it is presented as an incoherent unintelligible mess, then it has no value whatsoever.

Comparable

We shall see that merely presenting figures in isolation is of limited value. In order to turn the 'data' of an isolated figure into 'information' we typically need to compare it to another figure. For example, stating that the sales revenue for July was £120,000 means very little because we do not know whether this level of sales is good, bad or indifferent! In contrast, if we added the fact that the previous July's sales revenue (i.e. the same month a year earlier) was £100,000 then we can immediately see that the July sales have increased markedly year on year, which is clearly good news.

The three most common ways of comparing information are:

i. Year on Year (as just described)

ii. Against a target 'budget' figure (i.e. what we had planned to achieve)

iii. Against a competitor 'benchmark' figure (where available)

The other 'comparability' issue when we are comparing two figures is to ensure that both of them have been produced on the same basis. For example, there is no point comparing this July's sales revenue (including VAT) with last July's sales revenue (excluding VAT). The two figures have been produced using different assumptions and are simply not comparable!

1 The Statement of Financial Position

1.13 Financial Accounting versus Management Accounting

There is not one single type of accountant for much the same reason that there is not one single type of doctor or solicitor. Different areas of work require different accountancy specialisms and these can be as diverse as working with companies in financial difficulty (as an 'Insolvency Practitioner'), or being an expert witness in legal proceedings (working as a 'Forensic Accountant'). However the two most common broad categories of accountancy are Financial Accountancy and Management Accountancy.

> **DEFINITIONS**
>
> **Financial Accountancy** is where the primary objective is to provide a 'true and fair' view of a business's activities to *external users*.
>
> **Management Accountancy** is where the primary objective is to inform *internal users* of the business to assist in planning, control and decision making.

Financial Accounting

We have already briefly considered the agency relationship that exists between

- The directors of a company (who are responsible for its day to day operation) … and
- The shareholders (who actually own the company but may play no part in its day to day operations).

In order for this relationship to work there needs to be a robust mechanism to inform the shareholders on all relevant aspects of the company's financial performance. It is for this reason that the Companies Act requires that annual accounts are made available to the company's shareholders and filed at Companies House, who make them publically available via their website.

A company's accounts must be filed at Companies House no later than:

- 9 months after the end of the company's financial year end for private companies
- 6 months after the end of the company's financial year end for public companies

These annual accounts typically include:

- Statement of Profit or Loss - to show the performance over the previous year
- Statement of Financial Position – to show the year-end closing position
- Notes to the accounts – to explain the accounting methods used
- A directors' report including a business review or strategic report
- An auditors' report *(hopefully!)* confirming that the accounts are a 'true and fair' view

The process of recording the numerous transactions of the business and presenting them in a set of accounts for external users such as shareholders (who 'own' the company, but do not work within it) is the field of Financial Accounting.

As we shall see, accounting is not always a black and white topic and often involves making estimates and various judgements which in turn can make a company look more or less profitable, and indeed worth a greater or lesser amount. This is not particularly useful to the shareholders who want a robust and objective assessment of their company's performance and position, which has not been biased or embellished by directors who are trying to paint a slightly different picture of reality!

This very real problem is the reason why financial accounts (i.e. those for external users) must be prepared in accordance with strict financial reporting standards which specify which accounting treatments may or may not be adopted, in an effort to reduce the potential for 'creative accounting'. The use of the same accounting standards by different companies also ensures 'comparability' when the financial results for two companies are compared. In the UK these standards are known as 'Financial Reporting Standards' (FRS).

Additionally, as our world becomes increasingly global it is becoming more important to ensure comparability of financial information between companies located in different countries and for this reason there is now a move towards the use of international accounting standards known as 'International Financial Reporting Standards' (IFRS) or their older equivalents 'International Accounting Standards' (IAS).

The good news is that there has been a 'convergence' of accounting treatments so that a UK FRS and its corresponding international IFRS might actually prescribe similar accounting treatments. Currently over 100 countries have adopted International Financial Reporting Standards (including the European Union and most G20 countries) meaning that most large companies now use these as a common set of reporting standards to ensure meaningful comparisons between different companies in different countries on a like-for-like basis.

Management Accounting

By comparison to financial accounting, management accounting initially seems to be quite simple and straightforward….however that belies a far greater level of detail!

If financial accounting is intended for the external users of a business, then management accounting is intended for the internal users i.e. management accounting is used by the managers! Because management accounts are only intended for internal users they do not need to be strictly regulated in the same manner as financial accounts. If the managers of a company wish to adopt a certain format for their management accounts that is absolutely fine … so long as the corresponding financial accounts produced for the outside world do comply with the appropriate financial reporting standards.

The term 'management accounts' is a blanket term coined to cover any and every form of internal report used by the managers of a company (though the bank manager will also ask for monthly management accounts if the bank is providing an overdraft facility).

Management accounts will cover a massive array of information including:

- Sales reports by product, branch or sales person … or whatever else is required
- Profit and Loss information
- Budgets covering planned sales revenue, expenditure, profit and cash flow
- Production schedules and resource targets
- Inventory information detailing fast / slow moving items of stock and reordering requirements
- Comparisons of performance against budget, previous year or competitor benchmark

…. and whatever other information is required by the managers of a business to assist them with planning, control and decision making (the three principal management activities).

Different management accounting reports will be produced at different frequencies (daily, weekly, monthly, quarterly, annually) unlike financial accounting which is predominantly an annual exercise.

1   The Statement of Financial Position

Additionally, unlike financial accounting which only ever reports historical information, management accounting will report both historical performance and forecast future performance (to assist in forward planning).

Whereas financial accounts are published months after the year-end (and possibly after an audit) which ensures their accuracy, management accounts are produced as soon as possible (before their contents becomes 'ancient history') which means that they will inevitably include a higher degree of estimation and will therefore not always be 100% accurate.

OVERVIEW

Comparison of Financial and Management Accounting

	Financial Accounting	Management Accounting
Users	**External Users** Primarily intended for shareholders, but also used by customers, suppliers, lenders, HMRC etc.	**Internal Users** Directors and Managers … though other parties may insist on receiving certain information e.g. bank
Type of Information	**Annual Report** Plus other information as required e.g. interim financial statements or profit warnings	**As Required** To ensure the proper running of the business.
Historic / Future	**Historic Reporting** Factual reporting of actual results	**Historic & Future** Widespread use of budget forecasts for planning and co-ordination
Accuracy	**Highly Accurate** Based on actual (audited) results	**Contains Estimates** To enable information to be supplied to managers faster.
Timely	**Slow to Produce** Not required until 6-9 months after financial year end	**Quick to Produce** Up to date information required as quickly as possible
Level of Detail	**Broad Overview Only** e.g. sales revenue for year might be quoted in a single figure	**Very Detailed** e.g. sales revenue detailed by week / product / branch / customer etc.
Purpose	**General Purpose** Aims to give shareholders etc. an overview of the company's performance and position	**Numerous Specific Purposes** To provide each manager with the information needed.
Frequency	**Annually** Plus additional reports as dictated by a particular stock market etc.	**Daily, Weekly, Monthly etc.** As required by the needs of the business

TEST YOUR UNDERSTANDING 3

Accounting can be broadly categorised as being either *"Financial Accounting"* or *"Management Accounting"*.

In general terms would each of the following be more usually associated with Financial Accounting ('FA') or Management Accounting ('MA')?

Weekly Sales Reporting _____

Available for public scrutiny _____

Very detailed _____

Only consisting of historic information _____

Consisting of historic + future projections _____

Possibly reviewed by external Auditor _____

Possibly scrutinised by potential suppliers _____

Less accurate _____

Very out of date when first made available _____

Presentation & content highly regulated _____

Typically annually _____

Quick to produce _____

Intended for internal use _____

Filed at Companies House _____

Not regulated _____

1 The Statement of Financial Position

1.14 The Statement of Financial Position

By the end of the book we will have covered the four most important financial statements, namely:

i. The Statement of Financial Position
ii. The Statement of Profit or Loss
iii. The Statement of Cash flows
iv. The Statement of Changes in Equity

To conclude this chapter we shall look at the first of these: **The Statement of Financial Position (SOFP)**, also known as the **'Balance sheet'**.

> **DEFINITION**
>
> **The Statement of Financial Position** reports on a **business's position** at a point in time, by detailing the:
> - 'Assets'
> - 'Liabilities'
> - and hence the 'Equity' of a business…
>
> …..at that point in time.

Let's begin by examining each of these new terms in turn.

Assets

> **DEFINITION**
>
> **Formal definition:** *"An asset is a resource controlled by the entity as a result of past events and from which future economic benefits are expected to flow to the entity."*
>
> **Or put more simply …..** What the business **owns**.

Assets can be either:

Current Assets — Which are expected to be realised within 12 months i.e. used up and no longer existing within the business.

e.g. Cash, Inventory (stock held for manufacture or resale), Receivables (unpaid debts from credit customers)

In each of these cases we would expect the asset to have been used within the next 12 months e.g. the cash will have constantly changed as money goes in and out of the bank. Hopefully the inventory will be sold as soon as possible and the credit customers will have paid their outstanding amounts.

or …

Non-Current Assets — Not expected to be 'realised ' within 12 months i.e. not used up and therefore will still exist within the business.

e.g. Land & Buildings or Plant & Machinery ('tangible' non-current assets) or Goodwill or Trademarks ('intangible' non-current assets).

The Language of Business

In each of these cases we would expect the asset in question to still exist within the business. The Land & Buildings, Plant & Machinery and Goodwill & Trademarks will [ordinarily] still be present in the coming years. Non-current assets are also known as 'Fixed Assets' for this very reason.

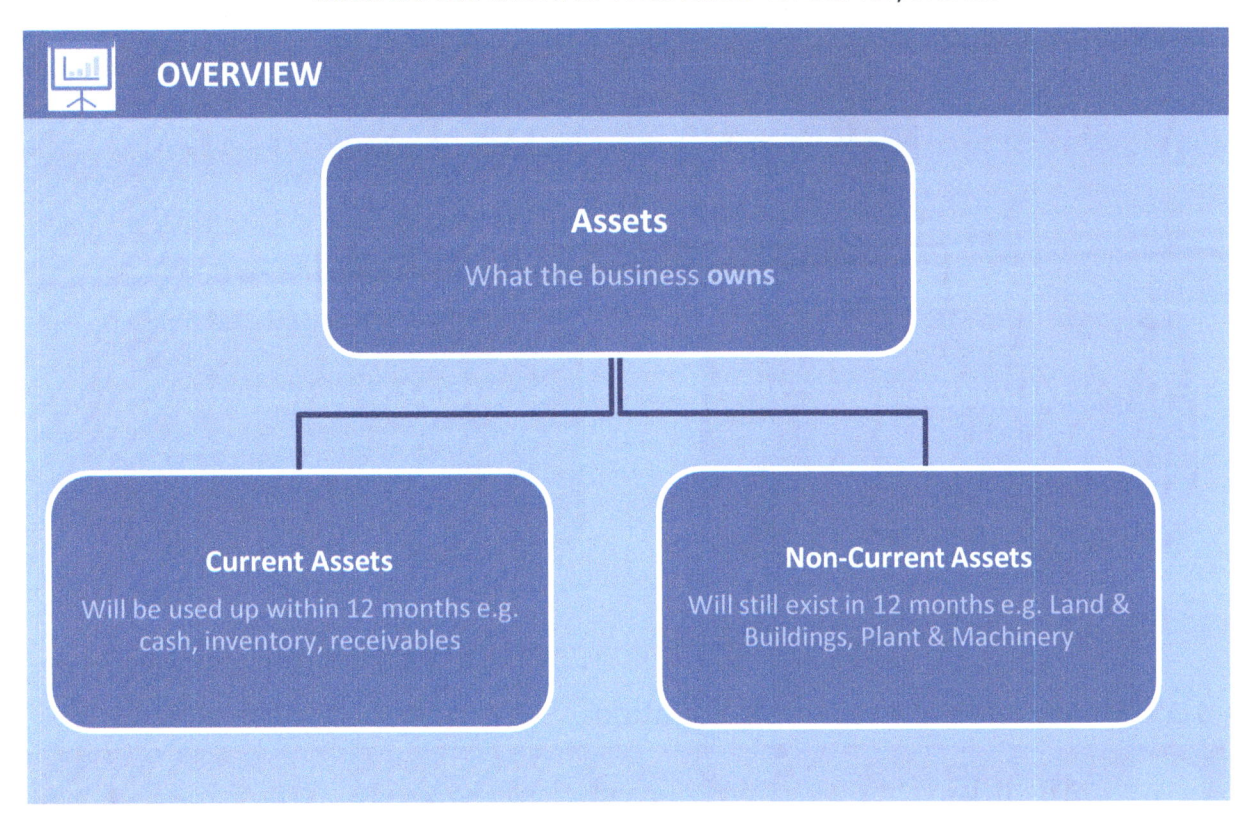

OVERVIEW

Assets
What the business **owns**

- **Current Assets** — Will be used up within 12 months e.g. cash, inventory, receivables
- **Non-Current Assets** — Will still exist in 12 months e.g. Land & Buildings, Plant & Machinery

Liabilities

DEFINITION

Formal definition: *"A present obligation of the entity arising from past events, the settlement of which is expected to result in an outflow from the entity of resources embodying economic benefits."*

Or put more simply ..... What the business **owes.**

Liabilities can be either ...

Current Liabilities Expected to be settled within 12 months

E.g. Bank overdraft, Tax owed to HMRC, Payables (unpaid debts owed to credit suppliers).

In each of these cases we would expect the liability in question to have been settled. The suppliers will have been paid. HMRC will have received the tax owing. Overdrafts are technically repayable on demand and so at any point the bank could ask for immediate repayment.

or ...

Non-Current Liabilities Not expected to be 'settled 'within 12 months

E.g. long-term bank loan (due for repayment > 12 months).

In this case we would expect the bank loan to still be outstanding in 12 months' time because it is not due for repayment during this period.

1 The Statement of Financial Position

> **OVERVIEW**
>
> **Liabilities**
> What the business **owes**
>
> **Current Liabilities**
> Will be settled within 12 months e.g. overdraft, tax bill, payables
>
> **Non-Current Liabilities**
> Will not be settled within 12 months e.g. long-term bank loan

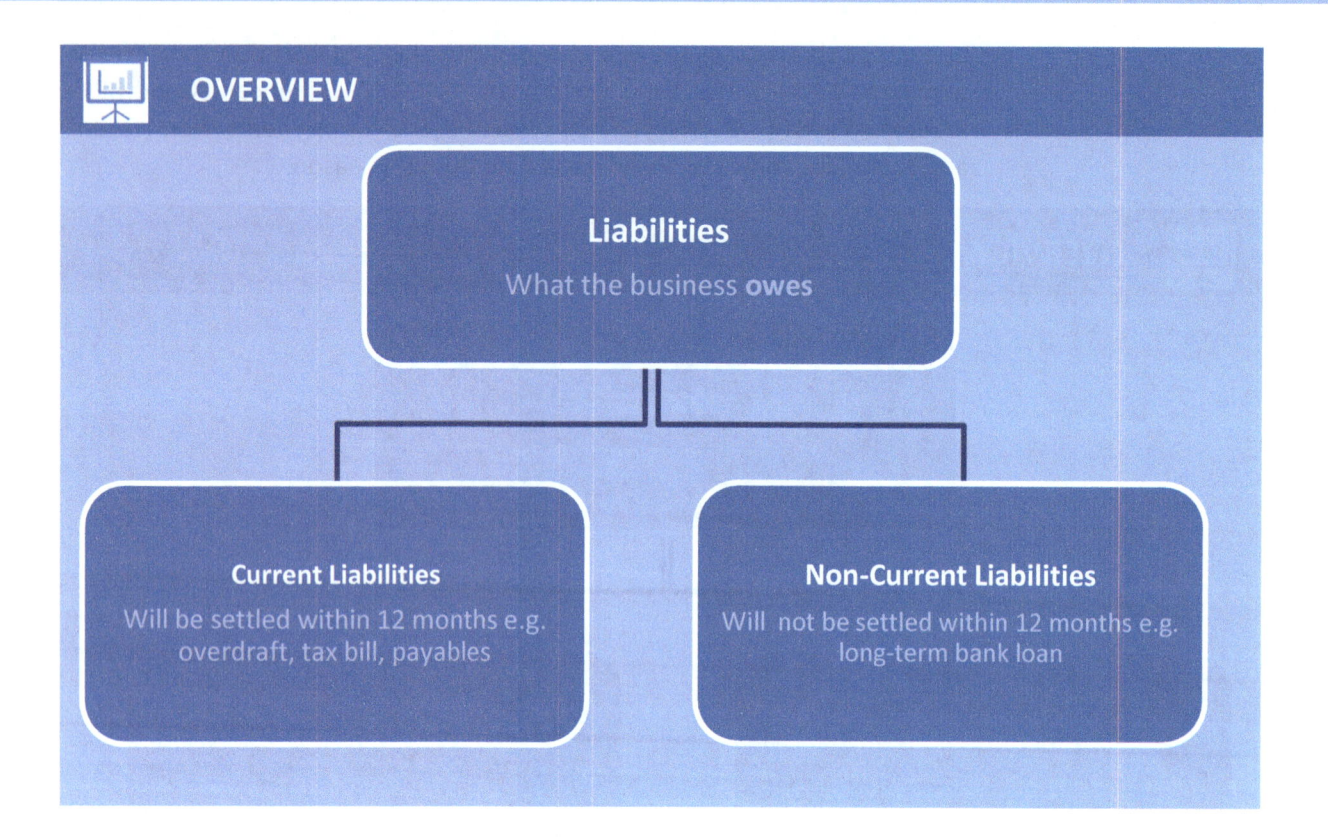

1.15 Equity and the Accounting Equation

> **DEFINITION**
>
> **Formal definition of Equity:** *"The Residual Interest in the assets of the entity after deducting its liabilities"*.
>
> **Put another way:** If you deduct what the business *owes* (its liabilities) away from what it *owns* (its assets) then you are left with what the business is *worth* (its equity). This 'value' belongs to the shareholders as they ultimately own the company and it is known as the 'equity' of the company.

> **KEY POINT**
>
> This simple relationship is summarised in what is known as **'The Accounting Equation'**:
>
> **Equity = Assets - Liabilities**

Simply stated, the **equity** of a company is the **company's worth** … which is equal to the value of everything the company *owns* less everything the company *owes* … and that net worth **belongs to the shareholders** who own the company.

We need to be quite careful when we start to talk about the 'worth' or the 'value' of a company. Ultimately a company is worth what someone is willing to pay for it, and this is best measured by how much a prospective purchaser is willing to pay to buy the shares of the company. In other words, you could only really judge the true worth of a company if the entire company was bought and sold (which can happen but is not a common occurrence).

Our use of the terms 'worth' or 'value' is simply what the business is valued at 'on paper' using all of the accounting principles which were used to originally value each separate asset and liability. So perhaps a better description of equity is the *'accounting value'* of the company (attributable to the shareholders) … which might in reality be more or be less than an actual prospective purchaser is actually willing to pay. This is sometimes referred to as the 'Balance Sheet Value' which neatly makes the point that it's what the company is recorded as being worth on paper.

To summarise … the [accounting] value of the company at a point in time is the value of the assets less the value of the liabilities at that exact point in time. This shows us how that value is **represented** at the given point in time i.e. what is owned and what is owed.

However, we can also reach exactly the same value for equity by considering the **history** of how that value arose. The shareholders originally invested a certain amount of share capital and on 'day 1' of the newly created company the company's value (its equity) was simply equal to the amount of share capital invested (remember the company had not started trading at this stage).

The company then started trading and hopefully making profit. *Some* of that profit will have been passed back to the shareholders by way of dividend payments. However it is unusual for *all* of the profit a company makes to be paid out as dividends. Instead it is more normal for *some* of the profit to be 'retained' within the company to enable the business to grow. The retained profit can be thought of as profit which the shareholders have left invested in the business (i.e. which they have not extracted from the company by way of a dividend). This retained profit means that the company is now worth more than on day 1, and leads us to the second equation for equity, namely:

Equity = Share Capital + Retained Profit

Which represents the 'history' of where the current value of equity arose from i.e. how much is from direct investment in share capital, and how much of it is from retained profit.

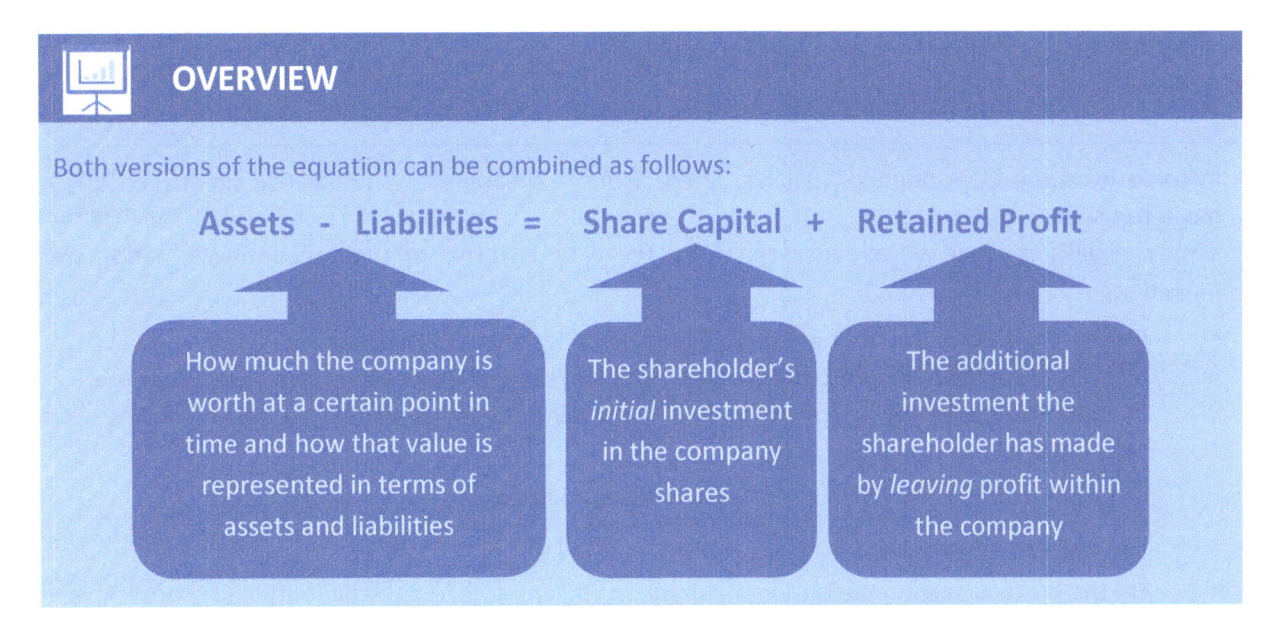

OVERVIEW

Both versions of the equation can be combined as follows:

Assets - Liabilities = Share Capital + Retained Profit

- How much the company is worth at a certain point in time and how that value is represented in terms of assets and liabilities
- The shareholder's *initial* investment in the company shares
- The additional investment the shareholder has made by *leaving* profit within the company

Sole Traders & Partnerships

The term 'equity' specifically refers to the value of a **company** attributable to its shareholders. Obviously sole traders and partnerships are not owned by shareholders as they are simply owned by the sole trader or partners concerned, so in these cases we refer to the owners investment as 'capital', so the accounting equation for a sole trader or partnership would be:

Owner's Capital = Assets - Liabilities

This is the same principle as before … just a slight change in terminology.

1 The Statement of Financial Position

1.16 The Statement of Financial Position (UK Version)

We can now consider the Statement of Financial Position which is nothing more than a visual representation of the Accounting Equation.

This can be presented in more than one way and we'll start by looking at the form traditionally used in the UK.

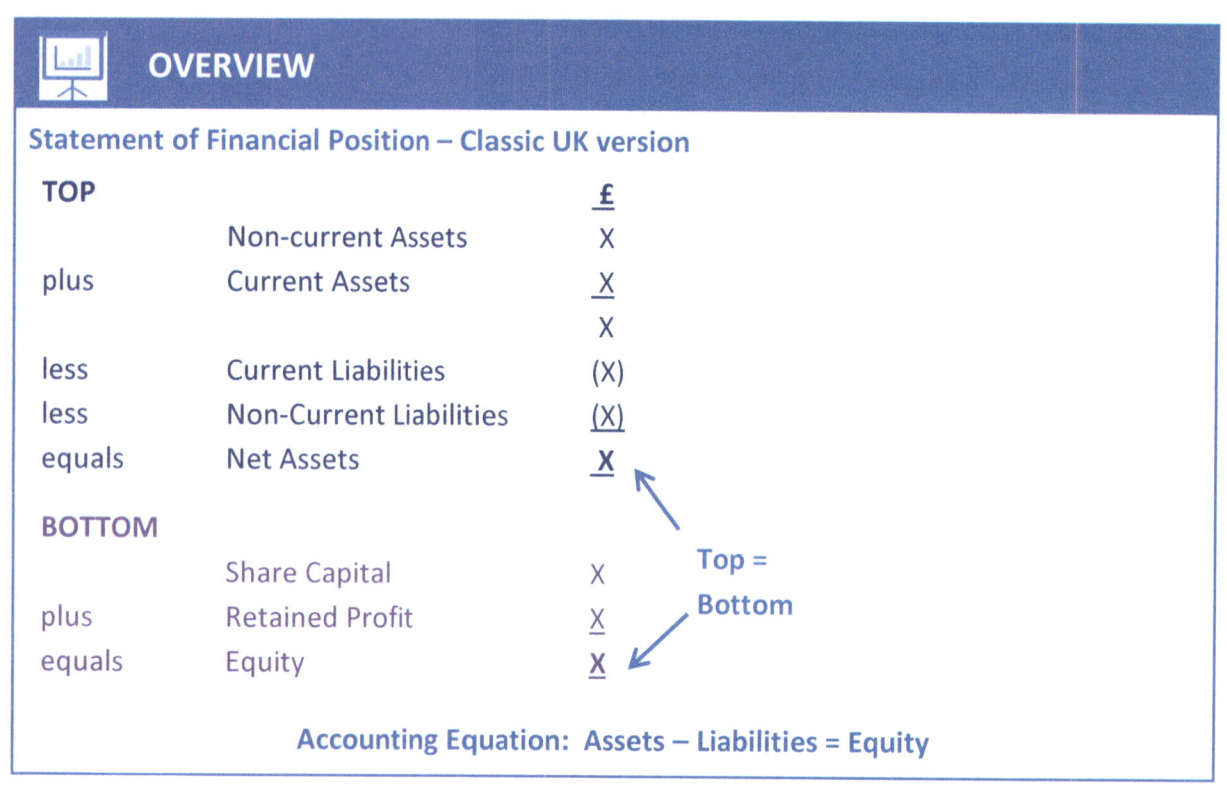

OVERVIEW

Statement of Financial Position – Classic UK version

		£
TOP		
	Non-current Assets	X
plus	Current Assets	X
		X
less	Current Liabilities	(X)
less	Non-Current Liabilities	(X)
equals	Net Assets	X
BOTTOM		
	Share Capital	X
plus	Retained Profit	X
equals	Equity	X

Top = Bottom

Accounting Equation: Assets – Liabilities = Equity

In some ways the older name of 'Balance Sheet' is more meaningful. The balance sheet (i.e. SOFP) has a top section and a bottom section and these should always 'balance' i.e. be equal! The SOFP is simply visualising what we already seen from the various forms of the accounting equation we looked at:

- On the top section the business's assets and liabilities are summarised (in fact they are split down into current and non-current assets, and current and non-current liabilities). The total 'Net Assets' figures for the top of the SOFP is simply the total value of the assets minus the total value of the liabilities:

    Assets - Liabilities

    ... and this figure is of course the worth ('equity') of the business.

- On the bottom section the business's share capital and total cumulative retained profit (since trading commenced) is summarised and the sum of these two figures represents the total investment which the shareholders have made:

    Share Capital + Retained Profit

    ... and this figure is of course also equal to the equity of the business.

- Because the top of the balance sheet always 'balances' with the bottom of the balance sheet we can see that:

    Assets - Liabilities (top) **= Share Capital + Retained Profit** (bottom)

    ... which is simply a version of the accounting equation.

1.17 The Statement of Financial Position (International Version)

Although International Financial Reporting Standards (IFRSs) allow for various different layouts of the Statement of Financial Position, the version below is probably the closest there is to a 'standard' international layout.

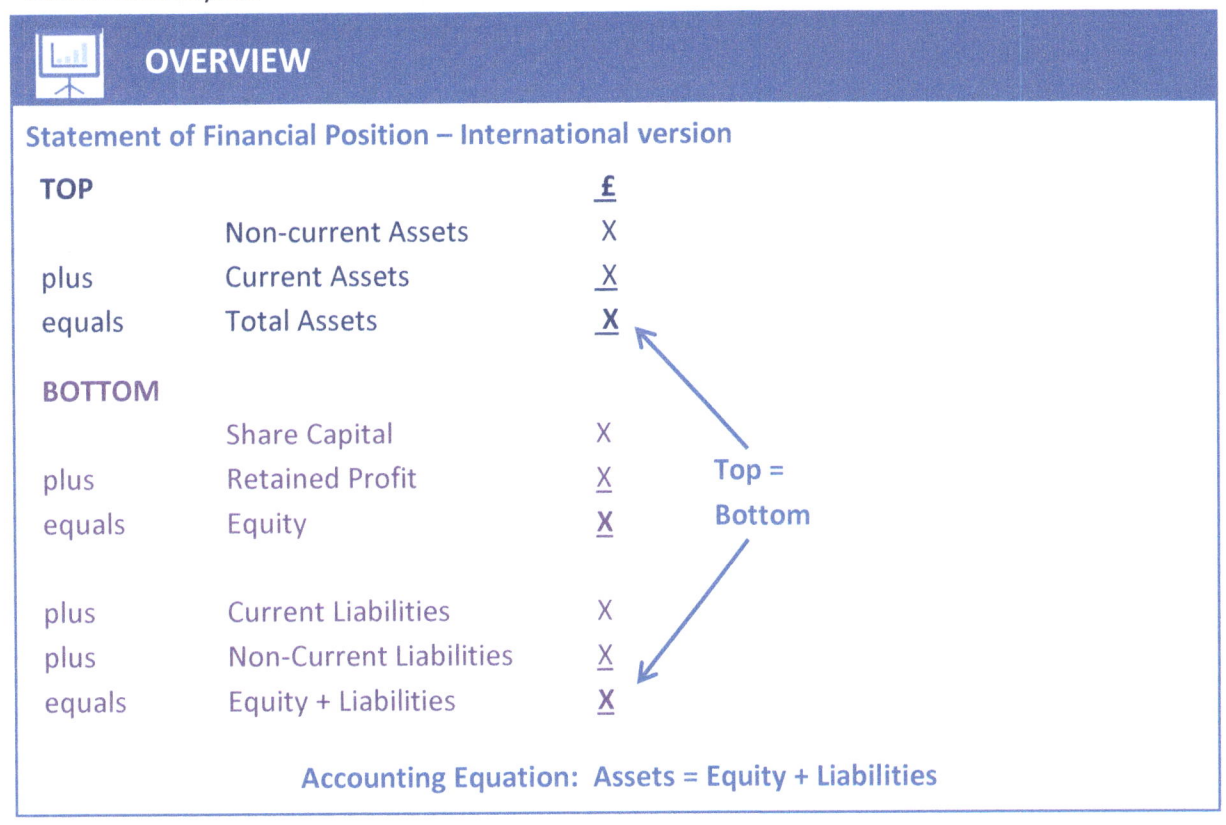

> **OVERVIEW**
>
> **Statement of Financial Position – International version**
>
> **TOP** £
>
> | | Non-current Assets | X |
> | --- | --- | --- |
> | plus | Current Assets | X |
> | equals | Total Assets | X |
>
> **BOTTOM**
>
> | | Share Capital | X |
> | --- | --- | --- |
> | plus | Retained Profit | X |
> | equals | Equity | X |
> | plus | Current Liabilities | X |
> | plus | Non-Current Liabilities | X |
> | equals | Equity + Liabilities | X |
>
> Top = Bottom
>
> **Accounting Equation: Assets = Equity + Liabilities**

This version contains exactly the same elements as before but this time the liabilities have been moved to the bottom of the statement which therefore now mirrors the version of the accounting equation which states:

Assets (top) = [**Share Capital + Retained Profit**] + **Liabilities** (bottom)

1.18 What does the SOFP tell us?

The Statement of Financial Position shows the **position** of a company at a single point in time (often referred to as 'the balance sheet date'). By 'position' we mean:

- The value of its assets
- The value of its liabilities
- The equity of the business and how much of that is share capital and how much is retained profit

All of the figures are based on the appropriate accounting treatment for each item. Some of these are very straightforward and obvious e.g. £10,000 of cash in the bank is valued at £10,000! However, some are less obvious such as valuing non-current assets at their 'Net Book Value' (see next chapter) rather than what their open market value might be worth on the balance sheet date.

This means that all of the values (including the resultant equity figure) are based on accounting principles. These 'book values' might not always correspond to 'real-life' values, which might in fact be either higher or lower.

1 The Statement of Financial Position

The following example illustrates how the SOFP gives a 'snapshot' of a business's assets, liabilities and equity at one specific point in time.

EXAMPLE

Example Company Limited
Statement of Financial Position as at 30th September 2016

ASSETS

	£'000	
Non-Current Assets:		The accounting 'book value' of these assets as at 30th Sept 2016. The company expects to still have them in 12 months so they are 'non-current'.
Land & Buildings	500	
Plant & Machinery	200	
	700	
Current Assets:		The value of inventory, customer debt, and cash held on 30th Sept 2016. These specific items are not expected to still be present in 12 months so they are 'current' (though _different_ inventory, receivables or cash might then be present).
Inventory	50	
Receivables	75	
Cash	25	
	150	
TOTAL ASSETS	**850**	

EQUITY & LIABILITIES

Equity:		The shareholders have invested £10,000 in share capital. Additionally over the entire life of the company up to 30th Sept 2016 there is also £620,000 of profit which has been left invested in the company. Thus the equity (balance sheet value) of the company at this point in time is £630,000.
Share Capital	10	
Retained Profit	620	
	630	
Non-Current Liabilities:		On 30th Sept. 2016 the company owes £100,000 to the bank but it is not repayable in the next 12 months and so it is a non-current liability.
Bank Loan (repayable 2019)	100	
	100	
Current Liabilities:		On 30th Sept. 2016 the company owes £95,000 to suppliers and £25,000 to HMRC. This must be paid within the next 12 months and so it is a current liability.
Payables	95	
Tax Liability	25	
	120	
TOTAL EQUITY & LIABILITIES	**850**	

The Language of Business

TEST YOUR UNDERSTANDING 4

The component parts of a Statement of Financial Position (aka 'Balance Sheet') can be categorised as:

- Non-Current Assets   NCA
- Current Assets   CA
- Non-Current Liabilities   NCL
- Current Liabilities   CL
- Equity   EQ (=share capital + retained earnings)

Allocate each of the following items found on a Balance Sheet into the appropriate category using the above abbreviations.

Cash in Bank	_____
Payables (aka 'Creditors')	_____
Computers (used in head office of a business)	_____
Premises	_____
Share capital	_____
10 Year Mortgage	_____
Inventory (aka 'stock')	_____
Plant & Machinery	_____
Tax owed to HMRC	_____
Receivables (aka 'Debtors')	_____
Retained Profit (aka 'Reserves')	_____
Bank Overdraft	_____
Computers (Held as inventory by a computer retailer)	_____

1 The Statement of Financial Position

⚠ KEY POINTS FROM CHAPTER 1

Different Types of Business Entity

Sole Traders
- No legal distinction between owner and business, therefore unlimited liability
- Simple to set up and administer
- Sole trader pays income tax and NIC on profits

Partnerships
- Two or more individuals working together
- Every partner is jointly and severally liable for the business
- Each partner pays income tax and NIC on their share of the profits
- Relatively simple to set up and administer, but a partnership agreement is advisable

Companies
- A separate legal identity. Managed by Directors. Owned by Shareholders
- Offers limited liability to the shareholders
- Private companies (Ltd) relatively straightforward to set up and administer, but can only trade shares on a private basis
- Public Limited Companies (PLC) complex to set up and administer but can potentially sell shares via a stock exchange (if 'listed')
- Companies pay corporation tax on their profits. Shareholders pay income tax on their dividends

Limited Liability Partnerships (LLP)
- Relatively new concept favoured by professional firms (solicitors, accountants etc.)
- A hybrid between a company and a conventional partnership

   Legally LLPs are corporate bodies and so offer limited liability, but the LLP does not pay corporation tax. Instead the members (i.e. the partners) pay income tax and NIC on their share of profits.

Financial Information

Users of Financial Information include:

- Shareholders — *Invest or divest?*
- Lenders — *Safe to lend?*
- Suppliers — *Safe to offer credit terms?*
- Customers — *Warranty and ongoing support*
- Government — *Tax due and industrial strategy*
- Competitors — *Benchmarking performance*
- Special Interest Groups — *Environmental & pressure groups*
- Employees/Trade Unions — *Wage negotiations*
- Directors/Managers — *Planning, control & decision making*

The Language of Business

To be useful financial information should be:

- Accurate
- Relevant
- Timely
- Understandable
- Comparable

Financial Accounting

- Reporting a 'true & fair' view of the company to external users
- Historic reporting giving broad overview of company's performance & position
- Highly accurate (possibly audited) and regulated by financial reporting standards
- Typically produced annually in the form of published annual accounts

Management Accounting

- Internal use only to assist in planning, control & decision making
- Detailed historic reporting & future forecasting on numerous aspects of the business
- Less accurate but produced very quickly to ensure up to date information

Produced as required (daily, weekly, monthly, annually)

Statement of Financial Position (SOFP)

Reports on a business's 'position' at a point in time by detailing its:

- **Assets** What it owns *(categorised into current and non-current assets)*
- **Liabilities** What it owes *(categorised into current and non-current liabilities)*
- **Equity** The *'book-value'* of the business at that point in time

The SOFP is a visualisation of the Accounting Equation

Accounting Equation

- Equity = Assets – Liabilities

Equity

- Equity = Share Capital + Retained Profit

1 The Statement of Financial Position

Chapter 1: Test Your Understanding Answers

TEST YOUR UNDERSTANDING 1

Single owner and business legally indistinguishable	**ST (sole trader)**
Business is a separate legal entity from owner(s)	**Ltd / PLC / LLP**
Must file accounts at Companies House	**Ltd / PLC / LLP**
May keep finances confidential	**ST / P (partnership)**
Can be set up with £1 share capital	**Ltd**
Requires £50,000+ share capital	**PLC**
Results in owner having unlimited liability	**ST**
Results in owners having 'joint & several' liability	**P**
Gives limited liability to owners	**Ltd / PLC / LLP**
Shares may be traded on London Stock Exchange	**PLC**
Shares may only be traded privately	**Ltd**
Owners directly pay income tax on profits	**ST / P / LLP**
Business pays corporation tax on profits	**Ltd / PLC**
Can employ staff	**All**
Small fledgling businesses	**ST / P (typically)**
Growing businesses wanting limited liability	**Ltd**
Firm of Solicitors wanting to limit liability	**LLP**

TEST YOUR UNDERSTANDING 2

Shareholders	**Invest / Divest?**
Lenders	**Ability to repay loan?**
Customers	**Ongoing future supply / ongoing product support?**
Suppliers	**Credit worthiness / will we get paid?**
Employees / Trade Unions	**Wage negotiation / How much are the Directors earning?!?**
HMRC	**How much tax should be paid?**
Directors / Managers	**Planning, control & decision making**
Competitors	**Market research / bench-marking**
Special Interest Groups	**Fact finding (e.g. Greenpeace & BP)**

TEST YOUR UNDERSTANDING 3

Weekly Sales Reporting	**MA**
Available for public scrutiny	**FA**
Very detailed	**MA**
Only consisting of historic information	**FA**
Consists of historic information + future projections	**MA**
Possibly reviewed by external Auditor	**FA**
Possibly scrutinised by potential suppliers	**FA**
Less accurate	**MA**
Very out of date when first made available	**FA**
Presentation & content highly regulated	**FA**
Typically annually	**FA**
Quick to produce	**MA**
Intended for internal use	**MA**
Filed at Companies House	**FA**
Not regulated	**MA**

TEST YOUR UNDERSTANDING 4

Cash in Bank	**CA**
Payables (aka 'Creditors')	**CL**
Computers (used in head office of a business)	**NCA**
Premises	**NCA**
Share capital	**EQ (part of)**
10 Year Mortgage	**NCL**
Inventory (aka 'stock')	**CA**
Plant & Machinery	**NCA**
Tax owed to HMRC	**CL**
Receivables (aka 'Debtors')	**CA**
Retained Profit (aka 'Reserves')	**EQ (part of)**
Bank Overdraft	**CL**
Computers (held as inventory by a computer retailer)	**CA**

1 The Statement of Financial Position

Chapter 1: End of Chapter Exercises

Section A Questions

Question 1.1
Which one of the following statements regarding sole traders is not true?

- A There is no legal distinction between the individual running the business and the business itself, and therefore the individual has unlimited liability.
- B A sole trader cannot employ staff.
- C A sole trader will pay income tax and national insurance contributions (NIC) based on the profits they make.
- D A sole trader must inform Her Majesty's Revenue & Customs (HMRC) that they have commenced a new business by 5th October in the following tax year.

Question 1.2
Which one of the following statements regarding partnerships is not true?

- A All partners have joint and several liability i.e. each partner can be held legally responsible for the actions of another partner.
- B A partnership is an unincorporated body i.e. the partnership does not have a separate legal identity from that of the partners.
- C Each partner is individually responsible for paying income tax and national insurance contributions (NIC) based on their share of the partnership profits.
- D In order to create a partnership the prospective partners must agree and sign a formal partnership agreement.

Question 1.3
Which one of the following statements regarding companies is not true?

- A A company has a separate legal identity to the various shareholders who own the company (which provides the shareholders with limited liability).
- B A company must register with Companies House and then file an annual return and set of financial accounts each year which will be made publically available online.
- C A company is responsible for paying income tax based on the profits it makes.
- D The Directors of a company are legally responsible for its proper running and are ultimately working on behalf of the shareholders of the company.

The Language of Business

Question 1.4
Which one of the following statements regarding Limited Liability Partnerships (LLPs) is <u>not</u> true?

A   An LLP has a separate legal identity to the various partners (or 'members') who own the LLP (which provides the partners with limited liability).

B   An LLP must register with Companies House and then file an annual return and set of financial accounts each year which will then be made publically available online.

C   The Limited Liability Partnership structure is often popular with large law and accountancy firms who have large numbers of partners ('members').

D   Since the LLP is a corporate body it is responsible for paying corporation tax based on the profits it makes.

Question 1.5
Which one of the following statements regarding the features of private limited companies (Ltd) and public limited companies (PLCs) is <u>not</u> true?

A   If a company achieves PLC status this automatically means that it can be listed on a stock exchange

B   Although the roles of 'director' and 'shareholder' are entirely separate, it is often the case that company directors are also shareholders.

C   A public limited company must have a minimum of £50,000 share capital. There is no corresponding requirement for a private limited company.

D   The financial results of both private and public limited companies are made publically available via the Companies House website.

Question 1.6
Which one of the following statements about management accounting is <u>not</u> generally true?

A   Management accounting information is produced however frequently the business requires it, be that daily, weekly, monthly, quarterly or annually.

B   Because management accounting information is purely produced for use by internal users it is not required to comply with financial reporting standards.

C   Because management accounting information is required promptly *(if it is to remain relevant)* it sometimes contains estimates.

D   The shareholders of a PLC will regularly scrutinise the management accounts of the business.

1 The Statement of Financial Position

Question 1.7
Which one of the following statements about users of financial information is <u>not</u> generally true?

- A Credit rating agencies will study the financial accounts of companies to assess how credit worthy they are.
- B A train operator who is considering the purchase of a fleet of trains might scrutinise the financial statements of the train manufacturer to confirm their long-term viability and thereby ensure that the promised warranties and after-sales service are robust.
- C The only interest the government has in the financial results of large PLCs is to check the amount of corporation tax paid by the company.
- D Companies will examine the financial statements of their competitors to gather as much information about their competitor's activity and performance as possible.

Question 1.8
Which one of the following could <u>not</u> be ascertained by examining the Statement of Financial Position of a company?

- A The 'book value' of the assets owned by the company at that point in time.
- B The profitability of the company over the previous financial period.
- C The level of debt and borrowing which the company has at the balance sheet date.
- D The equity of the company at that point in time.

Question 1.9
Which of the following consists of two correct alternative ways of expressing 'equity'?

- A Equity = Assets + Liabilities   Equity = Share Capital – Retained Profit
- B Equity = Assets + Liabilities   Equity = Share Capital + Retained Profit
- C Equity = Assets – Liabilities   Equity = Share Capital + Retained Profit
- D Equity = Assets – Liabilities   Equity = Share Capital – Retained Profit

Question 1.10
The Statement of Financial Position of a company reveals that at its financial year-end it has:

- Total Assets of £500,000
- Total Liabilities of £290,000
- Share Capital of £20,000

What amount of retained profit does the company have?

- A £190,000
- B £210,000
- C £230,000
- D £810,000

Section B Questions

Question 1.11

The following table includes some examples of the wide range of financial information that could be produced in relation to a particular company.

Which user from the following list would be *most* interested in each type of information:

- **HMRC** (Her Majesty's Revenue & Customs)
- The company's **Sales Director**
- Potential new **shareholders** contemplating investing in the company
- The company's **bank** as it decides whether to extend a significant bank loan to the company
- The **Trade Union** representing the company's employees
- A new potential **supplier** considering whether or not to grant credit terms to the company
- The company's **Purchasing Manager**

Obviously many of the items would be of interest to several different users, but try to think in terms of which user would most find that specific piece of information particularly useful.

Type of Information	Which user might be most interested?
The average number of days the company takes to pay its suppliers.	Potential Suppliers
An analysis of the usage of the various components and raw materials used in production	Purchasing Manager
The dividend payments per share a company has made in recent years.	Shareholders
The amount of cash generated by the company over the past year.	The Bank
The total remuneration of the company's CEO compared to the previous year.	Trade Unions
The amount of profit generated by the company over the past year.	HMRC
A detailed analysis of last month's sales performance analysed by product type and geographical area.	SHAREHOLDERS

1 The Statement of Financial Position

Question 1.12

An individual starting up a new business will have the choice between either simply operating as a sole trader or incorporating the business into a limited company.

What would be the key differences between these two alternatives?

	Sole Trader	Limited Company
Legal liability of business owner?	UNLIMITED	LIMITED
Perceived professionalism of the business?	LESS PROFESSIONAL	MORE PROFESSIONAL
Taxation of business?	LOWER INCOME	HIGHER CORPORATION
Options for raising additional finance to aid future expansion?	CANNOT SUE SHARES	CAN SUE
Confidentiality of finances?	CONFIDENTIAL	PUBLISHED
Administration requirements?	MINIMUM	FURTHER
Ability to employ staff and enter into contracts?	CAN	CAN

Question 1.13

Aspect Ltd has been in existence for a number of years. The company was originally founded with £1,000 share capital and this has remained unchanged. At this point in time Aspect Ltd has the following balances on its Statement of Financial Position:

- A Payables (owed to suppliers)   £10,000
- A Cash in bank   £5,000
- A Plant & Machinery   £25,000
- A Receivables (owed by customers) £8,000
- L Owed to HMRC   £4,000
- L Inventory (stock)   £3,000
- L Outstanding 10 year bank loan   £20,000

List and quantify each of Aspect's assets: £

PAYABLES   10,000
_____   5,000
_____   25,000
_____   8,000

TOTAL ASSETS   48,000

List and quantify each of Aspect's liabilities: £

_____   4,000
_____   3,000
_____   20,000

TOTAL LIABILITIES   27,000

Using the 'accounting equation' calculate Aspect's equity at this point in time?

State the equation linking equity, share capital & retained profit and hence calculate Aspect's retained profit over the entire life of the company (i.e. profit <u>not</u> paid out in dividends)

1 The Statement of Financial Position

Draw up the Statement of Financial Position for this point in time and ensure that it balances!

ASSETS

Non-Current Assets: £ £

PLANT + MACHINERY 25,000
                                       25,000

Current Assets:

RECIEVABLES 8,000
CASH IN BANK 5,000
INVENTORY 3,000
                                       16,000

TOTAL ASSETS   41,000

EQUITY & LIABILITIES

Equity: £

SHARE CAPITAL 1,000
RETAINED PROFIT 6,000
                                       7,000

Non-Current Liabilities:

BANK LOAN 20,000
                                       (20,000)

Current Liabilities:

OWED to HMRC 4,000
PAYABLES 10,000
                                       14,000

TOTAL EQUITY & LIABILITIES   41,000

42

Question 1.14

What are the key differences between management and financial accounting?

	Financial Accounting	Management Accounting
Who are the intended users?	EXTERNAL	INTERNAL
Key purpose of the accounts?	SHAREHOLDERS	DIRECTORS
Relative accuracy of information?	GENERAL	ACCURATE
Relative speed of production of accounts?	SLOW	ANYTIME
Typical frequency of producing information?	ANNUAL	ANYTIME
Historic or future information?	HISTORIC	FUTURE
Relative level of detail?	GENERAL	HIGHER

1 The Statement of Financial Position

Chapter 2

The Statement of Profit or Loss

INTRODUCTION

In the last chapter we introduced the accounting concepts of assets, liabilities and equity and showed how they are represented in the **Statement of Financial Position**.

In this chapter we introduce the accounting concepts of **income, expenditure and profit,** and show how these are represented in the **Statement of Profit or Loss** using the **'accruals concept'**.

We will finish by looking at **The Statement of Changes in Equity**.

OVERVIEW AND OBJECTIVES

By the end of this chapter you should be able to:

- define and illustrate how income, expenses and profit apply to business
- identify the key aspects and uses of The Statement of Profit or Loss
- understand the information which forms The Statement of Changes in Equity

and answer questions relating to these areas.

2 The Statement of Profit or Loss

2.1 The Statement of Profit or Loss

> **DEFINITION**
>
> **The Statement of Profit or Loss** (or *'P&L account'*) reports on a business's **performance** over a **period of time**, by detailing the
>
> - Income
> - Expenses ... and hence
> - the Profit
>
> of a business
>
> ... over that period of time.

Again, let's start by examining each of these new terms in turn.

2.2 Income

> **DEFINITION**
>
> **Income (also known as 'sales', 'sales revenue' or 'turnover')**
>
> **Formal Definition:** *"Income is increases in economic benefit during the accounting period in the form of inflows or enhancements of assets or decreases in liabilities that result in increases in equity, other than those relating to contributions from equity participants."*
>
> **Put more simply:** Income is the inflow of wealth into the **business from its ordinary operations** i.e. sales from trading, **not** from issuing shares or receiving a bank loan.
>
> **Examples:** Sales of goods or services

2.3 Expenses

> **DEFINITION**
>
> **Expenses (also known as 'costs' or 'expenditure')**
>
> **Formal Definition:** *"Expenses are decreases in economic benefits during the accounting period in the form of outflows or depletions of assets or incurrences of liabilities that result in decreases in equity, other than those relating to distribution to equity participants."*
>
> **Put more simply:** Expenses are the outflow of wealth from the business **from its ordinary operations** i.e. the costs involved in trading. They do **not** include the repayment of bank loans or paying dividends to shareholders.
>
> **Examples:** wages, rent, electricity, telephone etc.
>
> We often use the term 'costs' interchangeably with 'expenses'.

2.4 Profit

> **DEFINITION**
>
> **Profit (also known as 'earnings')**
>
> **Formal Definition:** *"Profit is the increase in wealth attributable to the owners of the business that arises through the business operations during a period of time."*
>
> **Put more simply:** The profit of the accounting period is the difference between income earned and expenses incurred.
>
> **Profit = Income - Expenses**

2.5 Accounting period

> **KEY POINT**
>
> When we looked at the **Statement of Financial Position** we were looking at a snap shot of the assets, liabilities and equity of a business **at a single point in time.**
>
> In contrast, when we look at the **Statement of Profit or Loss** we are considering the income, expenses and profit of a business **over a period of time.**

We produce Statements of Profit or Loss for specific accounting periods, and different accounting periods might be used for Financial Accounting and for Management Accounting, as follows:

Financial Accounting

Financial accounts are typically produced for periods of one year. Businesses are free to select whatever financial year-end they choose and advise Companies House of their **Accounting Reference Date**. They then produce their annual accounts (filed at Companies House) for the 12 months leading up to that date (known as the business's **financial year**).

e.g. *"Statement of Profit or Loss for Year Ending 30th September 2018"* would detail the income, expenses and profit for the accounting period 1st October 2017 to 30th September 2018.

Additionally, the same set of accounts filed at Companies House would also include a Statement of Financial Position drawn up for the last day of this period …

e.g. *"Statement of Financial Position as at 30th September 2018"* which would provide a snap shot of the assets, liabilities and equity of the company at the close of trading on the last day of the business's financial year.

Management Accounting

Because management accounting is purely for internal users (i.e. the directors and managers) the business is free to choose whatever accounting periods are most useful to it, and indeed may use different accounting periods for different purposes including daily, weekly, monthly, quarterly and annual reporting. Every business is different, but it is very common for businesses to produce monthly (management) statements of profit or loss for their own internal use, so that identified issues can be tackled sooner rather than later.

2 The Statement of Profit or Loss

The Statement of Profit or Loss shows the performance (i.e. profitability) of the business over a period of time. The exact form it will take depends on whether it is being prepared for financial or management accounting purposes.

2.6 Statement of Profit or Loss – Financial Accounting

Since the financial accounts are intended for external users they must be prepared in accordance with the appropriate financial reporting standards to aid comparability and objectivity. These reporting standards do allow a certain amount of choice for the precise format of the financial statements, but the format below is the one most commonly used by companies.

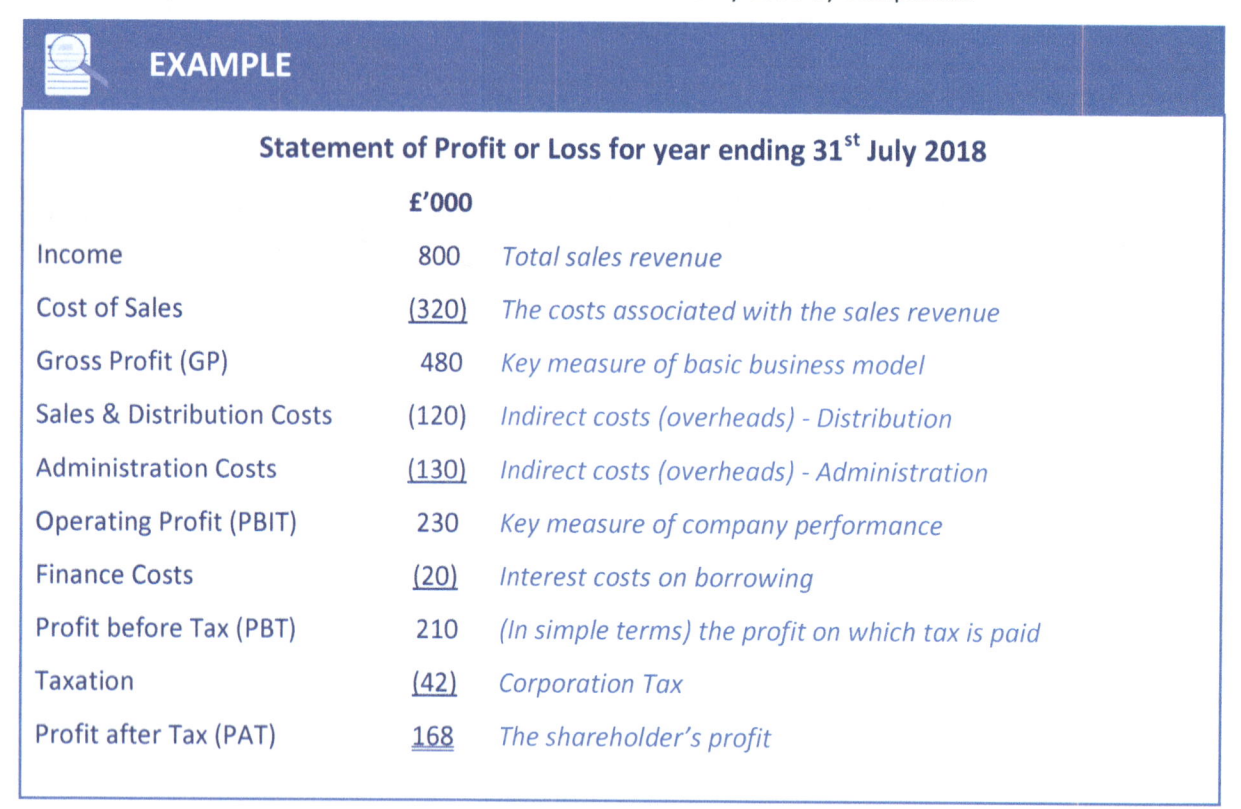

> **EXAMPLE**
>
> **Statement of Profit or Loss for year ending 31st July 2018**
>
> | | £'000 | |
> |---|---|---|
> | Income | 800 | Total sales revenue |
> | Cost of Sales | (320) | The costs associated with the sales revenue |
> | Gross Profit (GP) | 480 | Key measure of basic business model |
> | Sales & Distribution Costs | (120) | Indirect costs (overheads) - Distribution |
> | Administration Costs | (130) | Indirect costs (overheads) - Administration |
> | Operating Profit (PBIT) | 230 | Key measure of company performance |
> | Finance Costs | (20) | Interest costs on borrowing |
> | Profit before Tax (PBT) | 210 | (In simple terms) the profit on which tax is paid |
> | Taxation | (42) | Corporation Tax |
> | Profit after Tax (PAT) | 168 | The shareholder's profit |

Income is sometimes referred to as *'the top line'* or *'top line sales'* ... whilst profit is often referred to as *'the bottom line'* or *'bottom line profit'* (though as we can see above there are in fact several different profit figures!).

> **TUTORIAL NOTE**
>
> In accounting we use brackets to signify a negative number; a single underline to signify a calculation leading to a sub-total; and a double underline to signify a final total. However these rules are far from universal and brackets are frequently omitted with the user just being expected to know that expenses/costs will need to be deducted.

Let us go through the statement from the top ….

Income *(aka 'sales' , 'sales revenue' or 'turnover')*

All of the sales revenue generated from the sales of goods and services during this period.

Cost of Sales *(aka 'COS')*

The cost to the business of the goods or services sold during the period. The exact items which make up this figure will vary depending on the type of business, e.g. :

- For a wholesaler or retailer the cost of sales will largely consist of the purchase price of the goods sold.

- For a manufacturing business the cost of sales will consist of the direct cost of the materials, labour and other expenses used in manufacture, plus a share of any indirect production expenses.

It is also important to note that the cost of sales figure does not include any costs incurred for items which have been purchased or manufactured, but not yet sold. We'll come back to this point shortly.

Gross Profit *(aka 'GP', ' gross margin' … or just 'margin')*

Gross Profit = Sales Revenue - Costs of Sales

The first reported profit figure of 'gross profit' is calculated by deducting the cost of sales figure (associated wth the purchase or manufacture of the goods/services sold) away from the income generated when those goods/services were sold.

From the example above we can see that £800,000 of income was generated by selling goods/services. Those goods/services had a cost of £320,000 i.e. they cost £320,000 for the business to purchase or manufacture. So the business made a gross profit of £480,000, *before any other indirect costs are considered!*

Understanding the Gross Profitability of a company is essential if its basic business model is to be understood. The term 'gross margin', or just 'margin', helps us to appreciate that it is the amount of the original sales revenue left after the initial costs of those sales have been deducted.

Gross Profit % *(aka 'GP%', 'gross margin %' or 'margin %')*

In fact understanding how much gross profit a business makes is so important that it is frequently also quoted as a percentage (of the sales revenue).

$$\text{Gross Profit \%} = \frac{\text{Gross Profit (£)}}{\text{Sales Revenue (£)}} \times 100\%$$

In the above example : Gross Profit % = £480,000 / £800,000 x 100% = 60%. In other words the business made 60p of gross profit for every £1 of sales.

Expressing GP as a percentage helps us to compare how efficiently a business is turning sales into profit, compared to the GP performance achieved *from a totally different level of sales* (e.g. compared to the previous year's performance, or a competitor's performance, or compared to the budgeted performance)

Sales & Distribution Costs / Administration Costs *(aka 'overheads')*

As well as the costs associated with the goods/services actually sold, a business has many other indirect costs ('overheads') such as rent, office salaries, marketing costs, telephone, insurance etc. which in financial accounts are normally categorised into:

- **Selling & Distribution Overheads** e.g. Sales teams, warehousing & transport
- **Administration Overheads** e.g. Finance & Human Resource departments

Operating Profit *(aka 'Profit [or Earnings] before Interest & Tax' i.e. 'PBIT' or 'EBIT')*

Operating Profit = Gross Profit - Sales & Distribution Costs - Administration Costs

When the various overheads have been deducted from gross profit we then get a true picture of the profit the company has made after all general expenses (both direct and indirect) have been deducted.

The Operating Profit figure is one of the most widely used ways of examining the underlying profitability of a company's operations, as it takes all general expenses into account ... but ignores finance costs and taxation.

Operating Profit %

Because of the importance of understanding how much operating profit a business makes, this is also frequently quoted as a percentage (again of the sales revenue).

$$\text{Operating Profit \%} = \frac{\text{Operating Profit (£)}}{\text{Sales Revenue (£)}} \times 100\%$$

In the above example : Operating Profit % = £230,000 / £800,000 x 100% = 28.8%. In other words the business made 28.8p of operating profit for every £1 of sales.

Finance Costs

Having calculated operating profit we then (separately) look at the finance costs a business has incurred i.e. how much interest have they paid on loans and other borrowings to help *finance* the business. Interest costs are **not** costs of the day to day **operations** of the business (in the same way as selling and distribution, or administration costs are) so we do **not** deduct them to calculate the **Operating Profit** figure.

Rather, interest costs concern how the company is *financed* and this may change from year to year (and have nothing to do with the underlying profitability of the company's *operations*). For example, one year a business might borrow heavily to invest in new machinery and incur very high interest costs. A year later it may have paid these loans off and then have low or no interest costs. However, if we want to look at the underlying profitability of the company we do not want our profit figure to shoot up and down depending on how much borrowing there was in a given year. This is why we so often use operating profit (i.e. before interest and taxation) as a simple uncluttered method of looking at company's *operating* performance.

However finance costs such as bank interest are valid expenses which may be deducted in order to reduce the profit figure which is then subject to corporation tax, and they are therefore deducted from operating profit to produce profit before tax.

Profit before Tax *(aka PBT)*

Profit before Tax = Operating Profit - Finance Costs

Deducting the finance costs from the operating profit produces our third different profit figure: Profit before Tax. This (in simple terms) is the profit figure from which the company's tax liability is calculated.

Taxation

Companies in the UK pay corporation tax on their profits (currently at the rate of 19%). Corporation tax operates under a 'self-assessment' regime where the company (or more likely its accountant) calculates its own tax liability. Small companies then have to pay this tax liability to HMRC 9 months after the end of their financial year, whilst large companies are required to pay it in instalments.

The statement of profit or loss shown above makes it look as though the tax liability is simply calculated as a percentage of the profit before tax figure, and indeed for the purposes of our studies we shall assume this to simply be the case. Unfortunately, in reality, tax law and financial reporting standards have two different sets of rules governing how 'profit' should be calculated and therefore many adjustments are made to the final 'tax adjusted' profit figure which is actually used to calculate the corporation tax liability.

For our purposes we shall steer well clear of this added complexity and just assume that we are simply working out the corporation tax liability based on the profit before tax figure. In reality the tax liability of a company might fluctuate wildly from year to year (even if a similar level of PBT has been made) as companies can claim significant tax breaks for certain types of expenditure, such as that on new capital equipment or research & development. This is another reason why we use the operating profit to get an understanding of a company's underlying *operational* performance, as this is also free from any quirks of that year's tax calculation.

Profit After Tax *(aka PAT)*

Profit after Tax = Profit before Tax   - Taxation

The final profit after Tax figure is the [very!] bottom line as this profit figure is after deduction of **all** direct, indirect, interest & tax costs. The profit after tax figure (PAT) is therefore the profit figure attributable to the shareholders (who actually own the company). Typically part of the PAT will be paid out to the shareholders by way of a dividend payment, whilst the remainder will be retained within the company by way of addtional investment which allows the company to grow and therefore be worth more.

The shareholders benefit either way:

- Any profit after tax which is *paid out* as a dividend is obviously then cash in their hands
- Any profit after tax which is *retained* makes their company bigger and hopefully more profitable in the future, and should increase the value of their shares if they wish to sell them in the future.

2 The Statement of Profit or Loss

TEST YOUR UNDERSTANDING 1

Fill in the blanks in the incomplete Statement of Profit or Loss below to both **name** and **calculate** the various types of profit which feature on this financial statement.

		£
	Sales Revenue	232,000
Less	Cost of Sales	154,000
Equals	Gross Profit	(78,000)
Less	Distribution Costs	15,000
Less	Administration Costs	27,000
Equals	Operating Profit	36,000
Less	Interest Costs	5,000
Equals	Profit before Tax	31,000
Less	Taxation	6,000
Equals	Profit after Tax	25,000

The Language of Business

TEST YOUR UNDERSTANDING 2

For each of the different profit figures you identified in Test Your Understanding 1, state a simple defining formula (hint: look at exactly where each profit figure appears in the P&L). Give an example of how it might be used.

The first one (gross profit) is already completed as an example.

Gross Profit

Definition: *Gross Profit = Sales Revenue – Cost of Sales*

Basic Use: *Most businesses trade by making & selling (or by buying & selling). The Gross Profit gives an indication of the business's basic profitability from simply making (or buying) and selling ... before looking at any other 'overhead' expenses of the business. Identifying what 'margin' a business operates on, is a key part of understanding their 'business model' i.e. how they make a profit.*

Operating Profit (PBIT)

Definition: operating profit ÷ income × 100 = %

Basic Use: company profit derived from operations

Profit before Tax (PBT)

Definition: OP – interest costs

Basic Use: company profit after financing has been accounted for

Profit after Tax (PAT)

Definition: interest costs – taxation

Basic Use: final company profit attributable to the share holders

2.7 Statement of Profit or Loss – Management Accounting

Since the management accounts are intended for internal users, they can be prepared in whatever format best suits the directors and managers of the business. Indeed they may produce several versions, each differently formatted to focus on the needs of the separate departments within the company. This is perfectly acceptable since management accounts are not regulated. The only common-sense proviso would be that the different versions should be ultimately consistent with each other so that there is only *'one version of the truth'*!

2 The Statement of Profit or Loss

Every business will decide for itself exactly what format(s) of the Statement of Profit or Loss *(or P&L account as it is more likely to be called within a business)* are required, and the example below is just representative of what a P&L format could look like. These could be prepared for whatever reporting period the business chooses, though monthly accounting is probably the most common.

EXAMPLE

Aardvark Ltd - Profit & Loss – July 2018

	£'000	
UK Sales	80	*Sales & profit performance of UK Sales Dept.*
UK Cost of Sales	(30)	
UK Gross Profit (GP)	**50**	
UK GP%	*62.5%*	
Export Sales	40	*Sales & profit performance of Export Sales Dept.*
Export Cost of Sales	(22)	
Export Gross Profit (GP)	**18**	
Export GP%	*45%*	
TOTAL Gross Profit	**68**	*Total company gross profit for month*
	£'000	
Logistics Dept.	9	*Salaries, pensions, travel etc*
Marketing Dept.	5	*--- Ditto ---*
Finance Dept.	3	*--- Ditto ---*
Human Resource Dept.	2	*--- Ditto ---*
Rent & Rates	5	
Heat & Light	2	*Gas & Electricity*
Telephone & Broadband	8	*Line rental, calls, mobile contracts*
Other Expenses	6	
Bank interest	4	*Overdraft & bank loan costs*
TOTAL	**44**	
Profit before Tax	**24**	

In the example above it is important for the company to understand how their two sales channels (UK & Export) are both performing and so they are reported separately. The company also appears keen to understand how much expense each separate department incurs.

Note that the P&L finishes with Profit before Tax which is very common for management accounts. Calculating the company's tax liability for the year is a major exercise best undertaken by the company's external tax advisers and only once all relevant information for the year is available. It is not something which can be accurately calculated on a month by month basis.

2.8 The Accruals Concept

One of the most fundamental accounting concepts is the accruals concept (aka 'matching concept') which states that:

- **Sales** should be 'recognised' (i.e. included) in the statement of profit or loss when they are **'earned'.**

- **Expenses** should be recognised in the statement of profit or loss when they are **'incurred'.**

Let's illustrate both of these with examples.

> **EXAMPLE**
>
> **When are sales 'earned'?**
>
> **Question:**
> On 5th January 2018 a company receives an order from a customer to supply £10,000 of goods. The goods are despatched to the customer on 10th February 2018 on 30 day credit* (so the customer should pay for these goods no later than 10th March 2018). In actual fact the customer takes nearly 2 months to pay and the company finally receives payment on 8th April 2018.
>
> Assuming the company produces monthly management accounts, in which month (January, February, March or April) should these £10,000 of sales be recorded?
>
> **Answer: February** - The customer received the goods in February and so the sales were *'earned'* in that month. The original date of the customer's order is not relevant and neither is the date when the payment was due or finally received.
>
> *N.B. 30 day credit terms = 1 month, 60 day credit terms = 2 months, etc. ….regardless of how many days there are in each month!*

> **EXAMPLE**
>
> **When are expenses incurred?**
>
> **Question:**
> A company orders and receives £5,000 of advertising brochures in March 2018 but is given 30 day credit terms from their supplier and so does not have to pay for them until April.
>
> Assuming the company produces monthly management accounts, in which month (March or April) should this £5,000 of advertising expenditure be recorded?
>
> **Answer: March.** The expense was *'incurred'* in March as this was when the brochures were ordered and received.
>
> The fact that they were not paid for until a month later is not relevant.

Both of the above cases involve selling or buying on credit terms. However, regardless of whether sales or purchases are on a credit or a cash basis, the sales or expenses are always recognised when they are *earned* or *incurred*, **not** when the money is received or paid.

2 The Statement of Profit or Loss

2.9 Accruals and pre-payments

In addition to selling or buying on credit terms, a business can also pay in advance for goods / services received; or conversely incur expenses which are not immediately charged to the business, as follows:

Pre-payments

If a business pays in advance for something which it does not immediately use, then it is said to have 'pre-paid' for it. In effect, although it might have paid the money, it has not yet 'incurred' (i.e. used) the corresponding expense.

> **EXAMPLE**
>
> **Question:**
>
> A company rents its premises at an annual cost of £12,000 per annum, payable in two equal six-monthly instalments of £6,000, each paid in advance on the 1st January and the 1st July (which the company pays exactly on time).
>
> If the company prepares monthly management accounts what figure should be included in the May P&L account for rent?
>
> **Answer: £1,000.**
>
> Every month that the business is occupying its premises it is *'incurring'* rent … regardless of the actual dates it is paid. An annual rent of £12,000 corresponds to a monthly rent of £1,000 and this amount of rent should be included in every month's P&L account, including May's.
>
> The tricky bit of accounting is deciding how to record the amount of rent that has been paid in advance … but not yet used! That particular problem is solved by recording the rent paid in advance as a 'pre-payment' which is recorded on the statement of financial positon under 'current assets'. If this sounds a little odd, remember that a current asset is something the business owns which it plans to use in the next 12 months. In this case the business 'owns' the right to occupy the building in the next few months (because it has paid for it). It has not yet used this right, but will do so in the coming months.

Accruals

(There is a slight potential for confusion because we are now using the term 'accrual' to describe one specific example of how the general 'accruals' concept might arise!)

The opposite scenario occurs if an expense is incurred but the supplier is late in invoicing for the corresponding amount. Under the accruals concept the expense *must* be recognised because it has been *incurred*. In the absence of an invoice the company must 'accrue' this expense i.e. add it into the P&L expenditure (even though the company hasn't even received an invoice yet).

The Language of Business

EXAMPLE

Question:

A company calls out a maintenance contractor to carry out urgent repairs to manufacturing machinery in April 2018 and is told that there will be a £1,000 cost for these repairs. The corresponding invoice is not received until May and is not paid until June. If the company prepares monthly management accounts when should the £1,000 repair expense be recorded?

Answer: April. The £1,000 expense needs to be recorded in the April P&L account as this is when it was *'incurred'*. The date the money is actually paid is not relevant.

Again the tricky bit of accounting is deciding how to record an expense when the bill hasn't even arrived! The solution this time, is to record the expected expense in the month's P&L when the expense was incurred by entering an 'accrual', and also record the corresponding liability of an invoice which has not yet arrived in the 'current liability' section of the statement of financial position. This is logical because the 'accrual' represents a sum of money which is 'owed' and which will be paid within 12 months (so it is a 'current liability').

TEST YOUR UNDERSTANDING 3

'Baths & Basins Ltd' [BB Ltd] is a medium sized company which retails bathroom fittings. They produce monthly management accounts which (in accordance with good accounting practice) are produced on an 'accruals' basis.

a) BB Ltd sell £3,000 of bathroom equipment to a customer on 15th July 2015. They offer the customer 30 day credit terms and the customer pays the £3,000 on 15th August 2015.

In which month's statement of profit or loss will the £3,000 sale appear?

July

b) During July 2015 BB Ltd receive a £10,000 delivery of bathroom equipment from their supplier which goes into stock (i.e. it forms part of their inventory for resale). This is the only purchase of inventory made during the whole of July.

The corresponding purchase invoice is dated 25th July 2015 and shows that BB Ltd have 60 days credit in which to pay. BB Ltd actually pay the invoice on 25th September 2015.

Into which month is the £10,000 of purchases 'posted' (i.e. accounted for)?

Split over all appropriate months

c) On 1st July 2015 BB Ltd had £20,000 of unsold inventory ('opening stock' for July).

As mentioned in (b) above they purchased £10,000 of inventory in July. On 31st July 2015 BB Ltd had £24,000 of unsold inventory ('closing stock' for July).

What value of inventory (inventory is usually valued at original cost price) did BB Ltd actually sell during July i.e. what was BB Ltd 'cost of sales' figure for July?

2 The Statement of Profit or Loss

2.10 Depreciation of capital expenditure

In accounting we differentiate between two different types of expenditure:

- **Revenue Expenditure:** where there is believed to be no lasting value to the expenditure and it is therefore immediately 'charged' in its entirety to the corresponding accounting period. For example, November's gas bill is charged in full to November's P&L account - there is no ongoing value or benefit that extends into the following months.

and in contrast ...

- **Capital Expenditure:** where it is believed that the expenditure has lasting value and therefore the cost of the capital expenditure is spread out over the entire period which will benefit (economically) from it.

Capital expenditure therefore requires special accounting treatment to ensure that the cost of it is spread out (or 'matched') over the life of the capital asset. This is another example of accrual accounting whereby we deem that the expense is *'incurred'* month by month as the capital asset 'depreciates' and is used up over its working life.

The formula for calculating depreciation is:

$$\text{Annual Depreciation} = \frac{\text{Initial Cost - Residual Value}}{\text{Expected Life}}$$

EXAMPLE

Question:
A business purchases a delivery van for £22,000. It is believed that the van will have a 3 year working life, after which it will be sold for £4,000. How should the cost of the van be accounted for in the company's accounts?

Answer:
The van must be 'depreciated' over its three year life as follows:

$$\text{Annual Depreciation} = \frac{£22,000 - £4,000}{3 \text{ years}} = £6,000 \text{ per annum}$$

Each year's P&L account would therefore be charged with £6,000 of depreciation.

Meanwhile, on the Statement of Financial Positon, the remaining value of the van at the end of each year would be recorded (known as the 'Net Book Value' or NBV). This represents the remaining 'book value' of the van at that point in time, which is yet to be 'written off' (i.e. not yet charged to the P&L).

Profit & Loss Account

	Annual Depreciation Charge
Year One	£6,000
Year Two	£6,000
Year Three	£6,000

Statement of Financial Position

	Net Book Value of Van
End of Year One	£16,000
End of Year Two	£10,000
End of Year Three	£4,000

After three years the van is sold for its Net Book value of £4,000.

The net cost of the van to the business is £22,000 - £4,000 = **£18,000**

And the total cost 'charged' to the business via P&L depreciation charges is 3 x £6,000 = **£18,000**

(If monthly accounts were being prepared then each month would be charged with £500 of depreciation (= £6,000 / 12), and the remaining value of the van recorded on the Statement of Financial Position would be 'written off' by the same £500 per month.)

TEST YOUR UNDERSTANDING 4

A business purchases new manufacturing machinery at a cost of £270,000 on the 1st January 2018. It intends to keep the machinery for four years at the end of which it will have a residual value of £30,000.

Calculate the annual depreciation charge (straight-line depreciation) and then complete the tables below to show:

- How the cost of the machinery will be charged to the business's P&L account
- How the remaining value of the machinery will be recorded on each year-end Balance Sheet

Annual Depreciation Charge *INITIAL COSTS - RESIDUAL VALUE ÷ ANTICIPATED LIFE*

Year Ending:	Depreciation Charge on each P&L Account:
Y.E. 31/12/18	60,000
Y.E. 31/12/19	60,000
Y.E. 31/12/20	60,000
Y.E. 31/12/21	60,000

Balance Sheet Date:	Net Book Value on each Balance Sheet:
As at 31/12/18	
As at 31/12/19	
As at 31/12/20	
As at 31/12/21	

2.11 Cost of Sales

Cost of Sales (COS) are another example of how the accruals concept influences the way in which financial statements are produced. This is best illustrated by considering the purchase of inventory (i.e. stock for resale).

2 The Statement of Profit or Loss

> **EXAMPLE**
>
> **Question:**
> If a business purchases £1,000 of inventory on a cash basis, but has not resold the inventory to a customer by the end of the accounting period, does this represent an 'expense' being incurred which should be recorded in that accounting period's statement of profit or loss?
>
> **Answer:**
> We need to remind ourselves that the definition of an expense referred to an *'outflow of wealth from the business'*. So the question is whether or not paying £1,000 cash in order to buy £1,000 of inventory represents an outflow of wealth. The answer is 'No' …. All the business has done is to change one type of asset (cash, worth £1,000) … into another type of asset (inventory, also worth £1,000). Hence the business is neither richer nor poorer as a result of this purchase, hence an expense has *not* been incurred and it will not therefore be recorded on the P&L account.

However, hopefully at some point in the future this inventory will eventually be sold and will then cease to be an asset of the business. At this stage it will become an expense, but this expense should then be more than balanced by the business also then receiving the sales revenue earned for the sale of the inventory, and hence making some gross profit on the sale.

Gross Profit = Sales Revenue - Cost of Sales

> **KEY POINT**
>
> Inventory is not an expense when it is purchased … but it becomes an expense when it is sold. Put another way, we do *not* 'charge' the cost of **purchases** to the P&L account, we charge the cost of **sales** instead.
>
> In order to calculate the cost of sales (COS) for an accounting period we use the formula below:
>
> **Cost of Sales = Opening Inventory + Purchases - Closing Inventory**
>
> A simple way of looking at this formula is that it [initially] assumes that:
>
> - All the opening inventory has been sold during the accounting period
> - All the new purchases have also been sold during the accounting period
> - All of the closing inventory remains unsold

> **EXAMPLE**
>
> At the beginning of July a business has an opening inventory of £2,000. During July it purchases £5,000 of new inventory, and at the end of July it has a closing inventory of £3,000. What is the cost of sales figure for July?
>
> **Cost of Sales** = Opening Inventory + Purchases - Closing Inventory
>
> = £2,000 + £5,000 - £3,000
>
> = £4,000
>
> The cost of sales is therefore only £4,000…despite there being £5,000 of purchases in the month.

Why? Because £1,000 worth of the new purchases remain unsold. This can be seen because the closing inventory has increased by £1,000 compared to the opening figure at the start of the month. Possibly a slightly over-simplified explanation, but hopefully it makes the point that we do *not* charge the P&L account with what we have *purchased* during the accounting period, but rather with what has been *sold* i.e. the Cost of **Sales**.

2.12 Interaction between Statement of Financial Position, and Statement of Profit or Loss

DEFINITIONS

The Statement of Financial Positon (SOFP) records the **assets and liabilities** (and hence **equity**) of a company at a **point in time** (the 'balance sheet date').

The Statement of Profit or Loss (P&L) records the **income and expenses** (and hence **profit**) over a **period of time** (the accounting period).

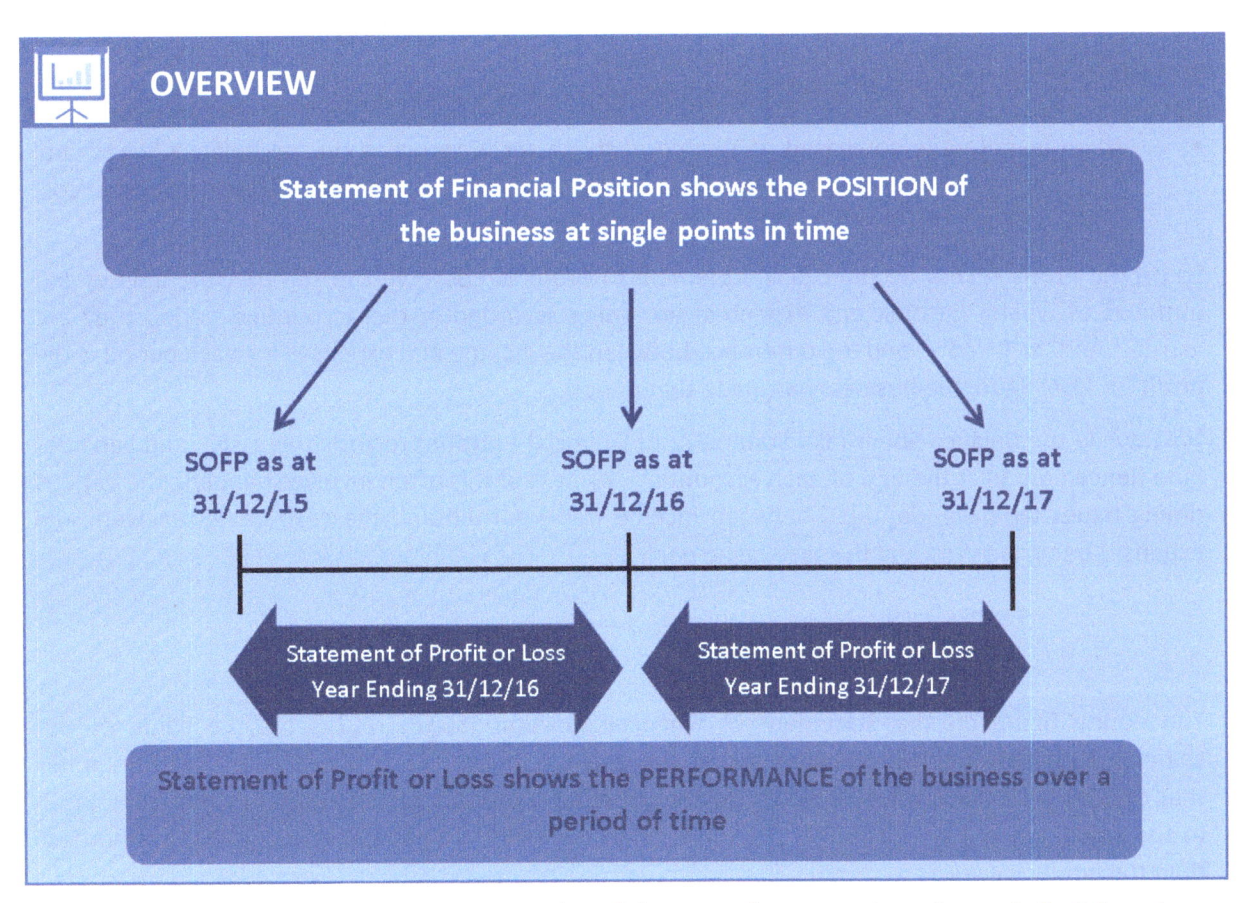

OVERVIEW

Statement of Financial Position shows the POSITION of the business at single points in time

| SOFP as at 31/12/15 | SOFP as at 31/12/16 | SOFP as at 31/12/17 |

Statement of Profit or Loss Year Ending 31/12/16

Statement of Profit or Loss Year Ending 31/12/17

Statement of Profit or Loss shows the PERFORMANCE of the business over a period of time

We have just worked through several examples of the accruals concept in action and all of them have a common theme. In order to record:

- Income when it is **earned** *and not when the corresponding cash is received...* and
- Expenses when they are **incurred** *and not when the corresponding cash is paid...*

2 The Statement of Profit or Loss

... we have been using the Balance Sheet (aka Statement of Financial Position) as a means of handling the timing differences between both 'earned sales' and 'cash received', and between 'expenses incurred' and 'cash paid'.

We have seen examples of all of the following:

- The cost of capital expenditure is not charged to the P&L in one go, but is instead 'depreciated' over a number of accounting periods. Meanwhile its remaining net book value (NBV) is shown on the Balance Sheet as an asset.

- Credit sales made to a customer are immediately shown on the P&L when they are earned even though payment has yet to be received. Instead the customer's unpaid debt to the business is shown on the Balance Sheet as a 'receivables' figure (an asset).

- Credit purchases made from a supplier are immediately shown on the P&L when they are incurred even though payment has yet to be made. Instead the unpaid debt to the supplier is shown on the Balance Sheet as a 'payables' figure (a liability).

- If an expense is incurred and the supplier is late in invoicing it, the business will 'accrue' the corresponding charge on the P&L and show the corresponding liability on the Balance Sheet (under 'accruals' in the 'current liability' section').

- If a payment is made in advance for a service not yet received, it will *not* be shown on the P&L (because the expense has not yet been incurred). Instead the payment will be recorded as a 'pre-payment' on the Balance Sheet (under the current asset section).

- When inventory is purchased, the value of this asset is recorded on the Balance Sheet until such time as it is sold. Only then will it be charged as an expense on the P&L as part of the 'cost of sales' figure.

So on the **Profit & Loss Account** (aka Statement of Profit or Loss) we can see that the inflows and outflows of wealth (income and expenses) are being recorded in the accounting period they are 'earned' and 'incurred' ... and the difference between the income and expenses for each period is the profit (or loss) figure the business has made that period.

Meanwhile the **Balance Sheet** (aka Statement of Financial Position) records the assets and liabilities (and hence equity) at the end of each accounting period and this often involves handling the various timing issues we have identified between income being earned and the cash being received; and expenses being incurred and the cash being paid.

2.13 Statement of Changes in Equity

The equity figure on the Statement of Financial Position (SOFP) represents the value of the shareholder's investment in the company at the balance sheet date. However, we must remember that this 'balance sheet value' is purely derived from accounting principles and may not correspond to the actual amount a prospective purchaser might be willing to pay (which could be more or less than the equity value).

If the company makes a profit during an accounting period then the value of the equity will increase. In fact if (for just a moment) we assume that the shareholders neither take any dividends nor purchase any fresh shares, then the increase in equity (from the start of the accounting period, to the end of the accounting period) would be exactly equal to the profit made during that accounting period (see diagram on the next page).

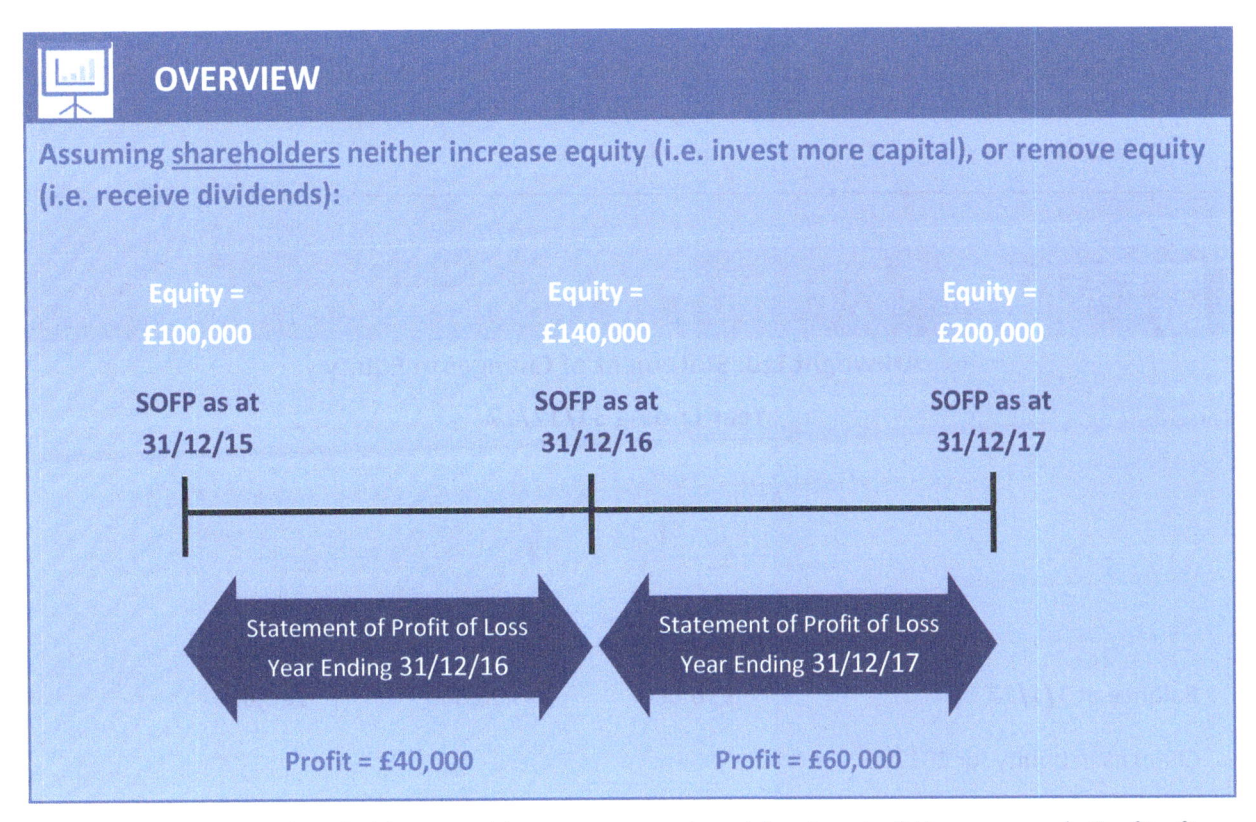

OVERVIEW

Assuming shareholders neither increase equity (i.e. invest more capital), or remove equity (i.e. receive dividends):

```
Equity =              Equity =              Equity =
£100,000              £140,000              £200,000

SOFP as at            SOFP as at            SOFP as at
31/12/15              31/12/16              31/12/17

        Statement of Profit of Loss    Statement of Profit of Loss
        Year Ending 31/12/16            Year Ending 31/12/17

             Profit = £40,000                Profit = £60,000
```

Of course in reality shareholders would expect to receive at least part of the company's Profit after Tax (PAT) in the form of a dividend. This will of course then reduce the equity in the company (as cash is being extracted from it).

Other factors which might also change the amount of equity include:

- Brand new shares being issued in exchange for cash going into the company…..or more rarely, existing shares being 'redeemed' (i.e. bought back by the company) in exchange for cash leaving the company.

- Company assets (such as Land & Buildings) being periodically revalued (which we will not consider further in this book).

In order to help the shareholders understand how the equity value of their company has changed over the accounting period just finished, a 'Statement of Changes in Equity' (SOCE) is included within the annual accounts of a company filed at Companies House.

KEY POINT

The **Statement of Changes in Equity** shows:

i. The **opening position** for equity at the beginning of the accounting period. This is of course exactly the same as the closing positon for equity at the end of the **previous** accounting period. The opening equity is split into its constituent parts of share capital and retained profit, remembering that :

Equity = Share Capital + Retained Profit

ii. Any **changes in equity** during the accounting period, caused by:
- Profit (or loss) made during the accounting period
- Any new share capital issued (or more rarely existing shares redeemed)
- Dividends paid out to shareholders

2 The Statement of Profit or Loss

iii. The **resultant closing position** for equity at the end of the accounting period *(which then becomes next period's opening equity position)*. The closing equity is again split into its constituent parts of share capital and retained profit.

EXAMPLE

Arkwright Ltd: Statement of Changes in Equity
Year Ending 31/12/17

The opening figures for Share Capital, Retained Profit and Total Equity (which appeared on the SOFP as at 31/12/16)

	Share Capital	Retained Profit	Total Equity
Balance at 1/1/17	£50,000	£30,000	£80,000
Changes in equity for 2017:			
Profit for Year		£20,000	£20,000
Issue of Share Capital	£10,000		£10,000
Dividends		(£5,000)	(£5,000)
Balance as at 31/12/17	£60,000	£45,000	£105,000

The closing figures for Share Capital, Retained Profit and Total Equity then appear on the SOFP as at 31/12/17

The Statement of Changes in Equity is primarily for the benefit of the shareholders and is a standard part of the financial accounts, but does not typically feature in the internal management accounts.

TEST YOUR UNDERSTANDING 5

In the year ending 31st December 2017 Weetwood Ltd made a profit after tax of £20,000. They paid out £8,000 in dividends and issued new £10,000 of new share capital.

Complete their Statement of Changes in Equity below to find their Total Equity as at 31st December 2017

Weetwood Ltd - Statement of Changes in Equity

Year Ending 31/12/17

	Share Capital	Retained Profit	Total Equity
Balance at 1/1/17	£50,000	£90,000	£140,000
Changes in equity for 2017:			
Profit for Year		£40,000 *(handwritten)*	£40,000 *(handwritten)*
Issue of Share Capital	_____		_____
Dividends		_____	_____
Balance as at 31/12/17	_____	_____	_____

2 The Statement of Profit or Loss

⚠ KEY POINTS FROM CHAPTER 2

Statement of Profit or Loss (aka Profit & Loss Account)

Reports on a business's performance over a period of time by detailing:

- Income - Inflow of wealth into business from its ordinary operations
- Expenses - Outflow of wealth from the business due to its ordinary operations
- Profit - Increase in wealth due to its ordinary operations

…..over that period of time

$$\text{Profit = Income - Expenses}$$

Financial Accounting Format for Statement of Profit or Loss

Statement of Profit or Loss for year ending 31st July 2018

£'000

Income	800	Total sales revenue
Cost of Sales	(320)	The costs associated with the sales revenue
Gross Profit (GP)	480	Key measure of basic business model
Sales & Distribution Costs	(120)	Indirect costs (overheads) - Distribution
Administration Costs	(130)	Indirect costs (overheads) - Administration
Operating Profit (PBIT)	230	Key measure of whole company performance
Finance Costs	(20)	Interest costs on borrowing
Profit before Tax (PBT)	210	(In simple terms) the profit on which tax is paid
Taxation	(42)	Corporation Tax
Profit after Tax (PAT)	168	The shareholder's profit

Key Ratios

$$\text{Gross Profit \%} = \frac{\text{Gross Profit (£)}}{\text{Sales Revenue (£)}} \times 100\%$$

$$\text{Operating Profit \%} = \frac{\text{Operating Profit (£)}}{\text{Sales Revenue (£)}} \times 100\%$$

Accruals Concept

- Sales should be 'recognised' (i.e. included) in the statement of profit or loss when they are 'earned'.
- Expenses should be recognised in the statement of profit or loss when they are 'incurred'.

The accruals concept means:
- Credit sales are recognised in the statement of profit or loss when the goods or services are supplied to the customer, not when the customer pays
- Credit Purchases are recognised in the statement of profit or loss when the goods or services are received from the supplier, not when the supplier is paid
- 'Accruals' are used to recognise incurred expenses, not yet charged
- 'Pre-payments' are used to delay recognising expenses paid for, but not yet incurred
- Depreciation is used to spread the expense of capital expenditure over the period in which the business will enjoy economic benefit from it
- Gross Profit is calculated after deduction of the 'cost of sales' *(and not the cost of purchases)* from sales revenue

Statement of Changes in Equity

Reports on the changes in equity over a financial period by showing:
- The opening equity at the start of the financial period
- Any changes in equity during the financial period due to:
    - Profit or Loss being made
    - Any share capital being issued (or existing shares redeemed)
    - Dividends paid out to shareholders
- Revaluation of company assets e.g. Land & Buildings
- The closing equity at the end of the financial period.

2 The Statement of Profit or Loss

Chapter 2: Test Your Understanding Answers

TEST YOUR UNDERSTANDING 1

	Sales Revenue	£232,000
Less	Cost of Sales	£154,000
Equals	**Gross Profit**	**£78,000**
Less	Distribution Costs	£15,000
Less	Administration Costs	£27,000
Equals	**Operating Profit**	**£36,000**
Less	Interest Costs	£5,000
Equals	**Profit before Tax**	**£31,000**
Less	Taxation	£6,000
Equals	**Profit after Tax**	**£25,000**

TEST YOUR UNDERSTANDING 2

Gross Profit (GP)

Definition: Gross Profit = Sales Revenue – Cost of Sales

Basic Use: *Most businesses trade by making & selling (or by buying & selling). The Gross Profit gives an indication of the business's basic profitability from simply making (or buying) and selling … before looking at any other 'overhead' expenses of the business. Identifying what 'margin' a business operates on, is a key part of understanding their 'business model' i.e. how they make a profit.*

Operating Profit (PBIT)

Definition: Operating Profit = Gross profit – Overheads

Basic Use: *The Operating Profit figure gives an indication of the underlying profitability of the operations of the business (ignoring both financing costs and tax liabilities). This gives a very comparable measure of profit from one year to another (or from one company to another).*

Profit before Tax (PBT)

Definition: Profit before Tax = Operating profit – Finance Costs

Basic Use:	*Businesses are sometimes partly 'debt-financed' and the 'Profit before Tax' figure reflects the profitability of the business after the cost of this financing. Interest payments are an allowable tax deduction, and therefore are deducted before the final tax figure and Profit after Tax are quoted.*

Profit after Tax (PAT)

Definition:	Profit after Tax = Profit before Tax - Taxation
Basic Use:	*This is the final profit to which the owners of the business (the shareholders) have a claim. They will benefit from their share of the PBT by receiving a cash dividend and/or by owning a share of the larger 'equity' of the company as a result of any profit which the company has retained.*

TEST YOUR UNDERSTANDING 3

a) July: Sales are recorded when **earned** .... not when the cash is received.

b) July: Expenses are recorded when **incurred** ..... not when paid

c) **Cost of Sales** = Opening Stock + Purchases - Closing Stock

                    = £20,000 + £10,000 - £24,000

                    = £6,000

TEST YOUR UNDERSTANDING 4

Annual Depreciation Charge = (Initial Cost – Residual Value) / Anticipated Life

                                   = (£270,000 - £30,000) / 4 = £60,000 pa

Year Ending:	Depreciation Charge on each P&L Account:	Balance Sheet Date:	Net Book Value on each Balance Sheet:
Y.E. 31/12/18	£60,000	As at 31/12/18	£210,000
Y.E. 31/12/19	£60,000	As at 31/12/19	£150,000
Y.E. 31/12/20	£60,000	As at 31/12/20	£90,000
Y.E. 31/12/21	£60,000	As at 31/12/21	£30,000

TEST YOUR UNDERSTANDING 5

Weetwood Ltd – Statement of Changes in Equity. Year Ending 31/12/17

	Share Capital	Retained Profit	Total Equity
Balance at 1/1/17	£50,000	£90,000	£140,000
Changes in equity for 2017:			
Profit for Year		£20,000	£20,000
Issue of Share Capital	£10,000		£10,000
Dividends		(£8,000)	(£8,000)
Balance as at 31/12/17	**£60,000**	**£102,000**	**£162,000**

Chapter 2: End of Chapter Exercises

Section A Questions

Question 2.1
Which of the following do not represent the 'income' of a business?

i   Sales revenue from the sale of goods
ii Cash received from shareholders subscribing for new shares
iii Sales revenue from the provision of services
iv Cash received from the bank for a new loan

Choose the correct answer:

A   i and iii
B   ii and iv
C   ii and iii
D   iii and iv

Question 2.2
A customer places an order with a business in January. The business supplies the ordered goods to the customer and immediately invoices them during February (with the sales invoice requesting payment from the customer before the end of March). In the event, the customer actually pays the invoice in April.

According to the 'accruals concept' in which month should the business 'recognise' (i.e. include) this sale within its monthly accounts?

A   January
B   February
C   March
D   April

Question 2.3
On 31st March a business receives a telephone bill requesting payment for all of the telephone calls made during the previous three months (January, February & March). The bill is paid in April. According to the accruals concept in which month(s) Statement of Profit or Loss should the telephone expense be recorded in within the business's monthly accounts?

A   March
B   April
C   January, February & March
D   January, February, March & April

2 The Statement of Profit or Loss

Question 2.4

On the first day of a new financial year a business buys manufacturing machinery at a cost of £120,000. It intends to use for machinery for 5 years after which it will have a residual value of £20,000. The business depreciates all capital expenditure on a straight-line basis.

What will be the corresponding:

- Deprecation charge in the year-end Statement of Profit and Loss in Year 2?
- Net Book Value in the year-end Statement of Financial Position in Year 2?

	Statement of Profit or Loss	Statement of Financial Position
A	£20,000 Depreciation Charge	£100,000 Net Book value
B	£20,000 Depreciation Charge	£80,000 Net Book value
C	£24,000 Depreciation Charge	£96,000 Net Book value
D	£24,000 Depreciation Charge	£72,000 Net Book value

Question 2.5

On 1st May a business has £25,000 of inventory. During May it purchases £12,000 of new inventory. On 31st May it has £19,000 of inventory remaining. The business records sales revenue of £42,000 during May. What gross profit does the business make during May?

A £24,000

B £30,000

C £36,000

D £42,000

The following incomplete financial statement relates to questions 2.6 to 2.8

Beech Ltd : Statement of Profit or Loss. Year Ending 31st December 2017

Sales Revenue	£900,000
Cost of sales	(£410,000)
Gross Profit (£)	£ ???
Selling & Distribution	(£240,000) Administration (£194,000)
Operating Profit (£) (PBIT)	£ ???
Finance Costs	(£5,000)
Profit before Tax (PBT)	£51,000
Taxation	(£10,000)
Profit after Tax (PAT)	£41,000

Question 2.6

What is the Gross Profit (£) and Gross Profit (%) for Beech Ltd for year ending 31/12/17?

	Gross Profit (£)	Gross Profit (%)
A	£410,000	45.6%
B	£490,000	54.4%
C	£410,000	19.5%
D	£490,000	19.5%

Question 2.7

What is the Operating Profit (£) and Operating Profit (%) for Beech Ltd for year ending 31/12/17?

	Operating Profit (£)	Operating Profit (%)
A	£51,000	5.7%
B	£56,000	6.2%
C	£250,000	27.8%
D	£296,000	32.9%

Question 2.8

Beech Ltd has 36,000 issued shares and pays a dividend of 50p per share in year ending 31st December 2017. What is the retained profit for the year?

A £5,000

B £23,000

C £33,000

D £41,000

2 The Statement of Profit or Loss

Question 2.9

Which of the following represents the final profit figure which is attributable to the shareholders of the company?

- A Profit before Tax
- B Operating Profit
- C Profit after Tax
- D Gross Profit

Question 2.10

The opening balance on a company's Statement of Changes in Equity showed an opening figure for equity of £240,000. During the year the company:

- Received £50,000 for the issue new share capital
- Made £60,000 profit after tax
- Paid dividends of £22,000

What was the corresponding year-end closing figure for equity?

- A £228,000
- B £278,000
- C £328,000
- D £372,000

Section B Questions

Question 2.11

We have now encountered two key financial statements: The statement of profit or loss (aka 'Profit & Loss account') and the statement of financial position (aka 'Balance Sheet') ... but what is the difference between the two?

Briefly state which financial components (e.g. assets, expenses etc.) each statement consists of, what the statement describes, and for what period or instant of time?

Statement of Profit or Loss

Statement of Financial Position

2 The Statement of Profit or Loss

EXAM

Question 2.12

A business purchases new manufacturing machinery at a cost of £130,000 on the 1st January 2019. It intends to keep the machinery for four years at the end of which it will have a residual value of £10,000. Calculate the annual depreciation charge (straight-line depreciation) and then complete the tables below to show:

- How the cost of the machinery will be charged to the business's P&L account
- How the remaining value of the machinery will be recorded on each year-end Balance Sheet

Annual Depreciation Charge **INITIAL COST − RESIDUAL VALUE ÷ LIFE SPAN**
£ 30,000

Year Ending:	Depreciation Charge on each P&L Account:
Y.E. 31/12/19	£ 30,000
Y.E. 31/12/20	£ 30,000
Y.E. 31/12/21	£ 30,000
Y.E. 31/12/22	£ 30,000

Balance Sheet Date:	Net Book Value on each Balance Sheet:
As at 31/12/19	£ 100,000
As at 31/12/20	£ 70,000
As at 31/12/21	£ 40,000
As at 31/12/22	£ 10,000

Question 2.13

The company Alpha Ltd was created on 31st December 2018 when it issued share capital in exchange for cash.

Prepare an opening balance sheet for this date, and then produce month-end P&L accounts and Balance Sheets for the end of January, February & March.

31ST DECEMBER 2018

The company Alpha Ltd was created on 31st December 2018 when £10,000 of share capital was subscribed for in cash. No other transactions occurred on that date.

Complete the Balance Sheet at close of play on 31st December 2018 (i.e. at the end of 'day 1' of the new business) using the format:-

- Assets - Liabilities = Net Assets ……. on the top of the Balance Sheet
- Share Capital + Cumulative Retained Profit = Equity ……. on the bottom of the Balance Sheet

N.B. The top and bottom must always balance i.e. Assets – Liabilities = Share Capital + Retained Profit

Balance Sheet as at 31st December 2018	
ASSETS	
Computer	
Inventory	
Receivables	
Cash	10,000
less	
LIABILITIES	
Payables	
equals	
NET ASSETS	10,000
Share Capital	10,000
Retained Profit	
EQUITY	10,000

Top of Balance Sheet

Assets – Liabilities = Net Assets (aka Equity)

Bottom of Balance Sheet

Share Capital + Retained Profit = Equity

Tutorial Note:

- *The top and bottom of the Balance Sheet must always 'balance' because….*
  ***Assets – Liabilities = Equity**   (The Accounting Equation)*

2. The Statement of Profit or Loss

JANUARY 2019

The company did not start trading immediately. During January 2019 Alpha Ltd:-

- Purchased £2,000 of inventory ('*stock*') on 60 day credit terms
- Purchased an office computer for £1,000 cash

Produce the Balance Sheet at close of play on 31/1/19 and produce a P&L account for the month ending 31/1/19.

P&L – Month Ending 31st Jan 2019	
Sales	
Less Cost of Sales	
Equals Gross Profit	
Less Expenses	
Equals Net Profit	

Balance Sheet as at 31st January 2019	
ASSETS	
Computer	1,000
Inventory	2,000
Receivables	
Cash	9,000
less	
LIABILITIES	
Payables	2,000
equals	
NET ASSETS	10,000
Share Capital	10,000
Retained Profit	0
EQUITY	10,000

Tutorial Note:

- The 'cost of sales' figure on the P&L is the cost of what has been sold, not the cost of what has been purchased.
- The definition of 'expense' refers to an outflow of 'wealth' from the business. If there is no outflow of wealth, then there has not been an expense!

FEBRUARY 2019

On 1st February 2019 Alpha Ltd started trading. During February Alpha Ltd:

- Made cash sales of £2,500
- Incurred £500 of expenses which it paid cash for
- Made no further purchases of inventory ('stock')
- At the end of February Alpha had closing inventory of £1,000 (valued at 'cost')

Produce the Balance Sheet at close of play on 28/2/19 and produce a Profit & Loss account for the month ending 28/2/19.

P&L – Month Ending 28th Feb 2019

Sales	2,500
Less Cost of Sales	1,000
Equals Gross Profit	1,500
Less Expenses	500
Equals Net Profit	1,000

Balance Sheet as at 28th Feb 2019

ASSETS	
Computer	1,000
Inventory	1,000
Receivables	
Cash	11,000
less	
LIABILITIES	
Payables	2,000
equals	
NET ASSETS	11,000
Share Capital	10,000
Retained Profit	10,000
EQUITY	11,000

The month's 'Net Profit' from the P&L is added to the (cumulative) 'Retained Profit' on the Balance Sheet

Tutorial Note:

- Cost of Sales = Opening Stock + Purchases – Closing Stock
- The 'Retained Profit' figure on the bottom of the balance sheet is a **cumulative total** of all the retained profit the business has ever made since its inception ('retained' means that it has not been distributed to the shareholders via dividend payments)

2 The Statement of Profit or Loss

MARCH 2019

In March 2019 Alpha Ltd:

- Paid the supplier for the £2,000 of inventory purchased in January on credit
- Made sales of £3,000 (£2,000 of these were cash sales, whilst £1,000 were on 45 days credit)
- Incurred £700 of expenses which it paid cash for
- At the end of March Alpha had closing inventory of £300 (valued at 'cost')

Produce the Balance Sheet at close of play on 31/3/19 and produce a P&L account for the month ending 31/3/19.

P&L – Month Ending 31st March 2019

Sales	3,000
Less Cost of Sales	700
Equals Gross Profit	2,300
Less Expenses	700
Equals Net Profit	1,600

Balance Sheet as at 31st March 2019

ASSETS	
Computer	1,000
Inventory	300
Receivables	1,000
Cash	10,300
less	
LIABILITIES	
Payables	–
equals	
NET ASSETS	12,600
Share Capital	10,000
Retained Profit	1,600
EQUITY	12,600

*The month's 'Net Profit' from the P&L is **added** to the (cumulative) 'Retained Profit' on the Balance Sheet*

Tutorial Note:

- Cost of Sales = Opening Stock + Purchases – Closing Stock
- You will need to work out the various cash inflows and outflows to establish how much cash there is on 31st March

Question 2.14

The Statement of Financial Position (aka 'Balance Sheet') records the assets and liabilities of a business at a single point in time, and hence the 'book value' of the business, known as the 'Equity'. This statement is simply a visual representation of the 'Accounting Equation' which states:

- Equity = Assets - Liabilities

The Statement of Profit or Loss (aka 'P&L Account') records the income (sales) and expenditure of the business over a period of time, and hence the profit that the business has made during that period:

- Profit = Income - Expenditure

Typically the P&L is formatted to show several different profit figures, each having their own specific use. The following figures relate to a business on their financial year-end date of 31st December 2018 and should be used to complete the year-end Statement of Profit or Loss, and the Statement of Financial Position.

- 2018 sales revenue: £500,000
- Opening inventory on 1st January 2018: £45,000
- Purchases (of inventory) made during 2018: £209,000
- Closing inventory on 31st December 2018: £39,000
- Receivables on 31st December 2018: £42,000
- Payables on 31st December 2018: £18,000
- Outstanding balance on 10 year bank Loan as at 31st December 2018: £180,000
- Interest payments made during 2018: £2,000
- 2018 Premises Costs (rent, rates, heat & light etc): £90,000
- Net Book Value of land & buildings as at 31st December 2018: £200,000   NC
- 2018 Staff costs (salaries, wages, Employer's NIC etc.): £115,000
- Other 2018 Expenses (depreciation, advertising, accountancy fees etc.): £28,000
- Bank Overdraft as at 31st December 2018: £5,000   A
- 2018 Corporation Tax: £10,000
- Net Book Value of plant & machinery as at 31st December 2018: £40,000   NC
- Share Capital as at 31st December 2018: £1,000
- Retained Profit as at 1st January 2018: £77,000

Tutorial Note:

- *Assets, Liabilities or Equity (on the balance sheet date) → will relate to the Balance Sheet*
- *Sales Revenue or Expenses → will relate to the P&L Account (some additional calculations will be required)*

2. The Statement of Profit or Loss

Statement of Financial Position as at 31/12/18

Non-Current Assets:

VALUE OF LAND — 200,000

VALUE OF MACHINERY — 40,000

Current Assets:

INVENTORY — 39,000

RECIEVABLES — 42,000

TOTAL ASSETS £ 159,000

Current Liabilities:

PAYABLES — 18,000

OVERDRAFT — 5,000

Non-Current Liabilities:

BANK LOAN — 180,000

TOTAL LIABILITIES 313,000

NET ASSETS 474,000

Equity

SHARE CAPITAL — 1,000

RETAINED PROFIT 77,000 +

TOTAL EQUITY

Tutorial Note:

- *The 'retained profit' is a cumulative total of all the retained profit over the entire life of the business*

$$E = A - L$$

Statement of Profit or Loss – Year Ending 31/12/18

Sales Revenue	500,000
Cost of Sales 45,000 + 209,000 – 39,000	215,000
GROSS PROFIT	285,000
Expenses:-	
PREMISES	(90,000)
COST OF STAFF	(115,000)
OTHER	(28,000)
Total Expenses	40,000
OPERATING PROFIT	52,000
Finance Costs	(2,000)
PROFIT BEFORE TAX	50,000
Taxation	(10,000)
PROFIT AFTER TAX	40,000

Tutorial Note:

- *Cost of Sales = Opening Stock + Purchases – Closing Stock*
- *The term 'Purchases' has a specific meaning in accounting which is the purchase of inventory (aka 'stock'). The purchases figure is therefore used in the calculation of 'cost of sales' and is not treated as a general expense of the financial period*

2 The Statement of Profit or Loss

Question 2.15

In the year ending 31st December 2018 Bolton Ltd made a profit after tax of £50,000. They paid out £20,000 in dividends and issued new £5,000 of new share capital.

Complete their Statement of Changes in Equity below to find their Total Equity as at 31st December 2018.

Bolton Ltd - Statement of Changes in Equity
Year Ending 31/12/18

	Share Capital	Retained Profit	Total Equity
Balance at 1/1/18	£30,000	£80,000	£110,000
Changes in equity for 2018:			
Profit for Year		50,000	50,000
Issue of Share Capital	5,000		5,000
Dividends		20,000	20,000
Balance as at 31/12/18	5,000	70,000	75,000

Question 2.16

You are the owner of a small business specialising in website design. It is the end of your financial year (Y.E. 31/12/18) and you are preparing your year-end accounts which you understand should be prepared on the 'accruals basis'.

a) Your business is operating from rented premises and your rent is £3,000 per quarter (paid in advance). The last rent invoice you paid was dated 1/12/18 and was for the period 1/12/18 to 28/2/19.

How much of this £3,000 should be charged to your statement of profit or loss for the Y.E. 31/12/18?

£1000

Which period's statement of profit or loss should the remainder be charged to and why?

DEC – FEB

In the meantime, where should the balance of the rent paid be recorded?

PRE PAYMENT

What name is given to the process of accounting for payments made in advance?

b) You also pay for the telephone and broadband usage on a quarterly basis but this time in arrears. The last invoice you paid was dated 1/11/18 and was the quarter 1/8/18 to 31/10/18 and it totalled £900.

As you prepare your year-end accounts you realise that you have not yet received an invoice for Novembers & December telephone & broadband usage.

What charge should be added into the statement of profit or loss for Y.E. 31/12/18 to correct this omission?

What corresponding adjustment do you also need to make to another financial statement?

What name is given to the process of accounting for expenses which haven't yet been invoiced?

2 The Statement of Profit or Loss

Question 2.17

The statements of profit or loss for 'Harmer Ltd' for two successive years are shown below:

		Y.E. 31/12/17	Y.E. 31/12/18
	Sales Revenue	£500,000	£600,000
Less	Cost of Sales	(£250,000)	(£320,000)
Equals	Gross Profit	£250,000	£280,000
Less	Distribution Costs	(£70,000)	(£80,000)
Less	Administration Costs	(£60,000)	(£80,000)
Equals	Operating Profit	£120,000	£120,000
Less	Interest Costs	(£20,000)	£Nil
Equals	Profit before Tax	£100,000	£120,000
Less	Taxation	(£22,000)	(£23,000)
Equals	Profit after Tax	£78,000	£97,000

a) Calculate the Gross Profit % and Operating Profit % for both years

	Y.E. 31/12/17	Y.E. 31/12/18
Gross Profit %	_____	_____
Operating Profit %	_____	_____

Comment on the relative Gross Profit and Operating Profit performance for the two successive years in both % and £ terms:

_____

_____

_____

b) Comment on the Profit before Tax performance for the two successive years. Is the higher figure in the later year because of better operating performance?

_____

_____

Question 2.18

On 1st January 2019 a high street baker introduces a new service whereby employees of local businesses can telephone through orders for lunchtime sandwiches in the morning and the baker will then deliver them to the desk.

On 1st January 2019 the baker pays £13,000 cash for a suitable small delivery van. It is anticipated that this van will be used for 5 years at which point it will then be worth £3,000.

The baker is concerned that a £13,000 charge will appear on coming year's P&L and make it look like the bakery hasn't performed very well. The baker emails their accountant about this and receives the following email back from their accountant:

Please complete the blanks.

Email

To   Charlie Choux (Baker)

From   Gordon Figures (Accountant)

Date   15th January 2018

Re. Purchase of Van

I understand that you are concerned that the £13,000 van you have just purchased will appear as a £13,000 expense on your statement of profit or loss for Y.E. 31/12/19 and therefore reduce your reported profit by £13,000 for this year.

In actual fact the van is an example of a _____ asset which it is intended to retain and use in the business for longer than 12 months (in your case, you plan to use it for 5 years). To ensure that we produce meaningful information we will prepare your accounts in accordance with the _____ concept. This means that we will _____ the cost of the van over the 5 years in which you will use it to generate new sales income.

Over its five year life the total effective cost to the business of the van will be _____. We will therefore charge a 'depreciation' figure of _____ to each statement of profit or loss for the next five years.

On each corresponding Statement of Financial Position (SOFP) we will record the remaining value of the van at each year end (we call this the 'Net Book Value'). Thus over the next five years the van's value will be recorded on each successive SOFP as:

2 The Statement of Profit or Loss

	Net Book Value of Van
SOFP as at 31/12/19	_____
SOFP as at 31/12/20	_____
SOFP as at 31/12/21	_____
SOFP as at 31/12/22	_____
SOFP as at 31/12/23	_____

If we did not 'depreciate' the van over five years in this fashion, then the first year would have a £13,000 charge (reducing profit by £13,000 in that year), followed by 4 years of no charge (and hence higher reported profit), followed (at the start of the 6th year) by the sale of the second-hand van giving £3,000 income and hence increasing the reported profit in year 6! This would clearly produce a series of statements of profit or loss which distorted the underlying performance of your bakery, and this highlights why depreciation is used to match the annual cost of the van, over the same time period from which your business benefits from the van.

I hope this helps.

Gordon Figures ACCA

Chapter 3

Long term finance for the business – debt versus equity

INTRODUCTION

Virtually all businesses require some form of financing to allow them to commence trading in the first place, and to then expand their operations as their business grows,

The required funding can come from either short-term sources of finance or long-term sources of finance, and we will consider these separately.

The funding and optimisation of short-term 'working capital' (which allows day to day trading) will be returned to in chapter 11. In this chapter we will focus on the long-term financing requirements of a business and the two main ways this may be achieved via **borrowed funds ('debt')** or via **shareholder investment ('equity')**.

The balance between how much long-term finance a business derives from debt (as opposed to equity) leads us to an important concept known as **'gearing'**.

OVERVIEW AND OBJECTIVES

By the end of this chapter you should have developed an understanding of:

- Capital Investment options for companies
- The difference between debt finance and equity finance
- Gearing

and be able to answer questions relating to these areas.

3 Long term finance for the business – debt versus equity

3.1 The need for investment

Virtually all businesses require some form of financial investment to help them get off the ground and commence trading. Moreover a new business rarely immediately generates a profit, and might actually run at a loss for some time. Funds (i.e. cash) will be needed to keep the operation going through its initial stages of setting up and early trading.

Furthermore, the need for funding does not disappear after the initial period, but instead it typically increases as the business grows and wishes to fund its expansion into larger premises with more delivery vehicles etc.

Obviously different businesses will have different requirements, but typically businesses will need to invest in both (long-term) non-current assets, as well as (short-term) current assets.

Investment in Non-Current Assets

Non-current assets (aka 'Fixed Assets' or 'Capital Assets') include anything which the business owns and intends to keep for the long-term, such as:

- Land & Buildings
- Machinery
- Vehicles
- Computers
- Office Furniture etc.

Of course a business can *reduce* the amount required to be invested in long-term assets by (say) renting premises or leasing cars. However most businesses will still need purchase at least some non-current assets.

In chapter 9 we will look at various capital investment appraisal techniques which should be used to evaluate any proposed outlay in non-current assets.

Investment in Current Assets

Current assets include anything which the business owns and intends to 'use up' (such that it will then cease to exist) in the next 12 months, such as:

- Inventory - stock which it is hoped will be sold in the near future
- Receivables - owed by credit customers who will hopefully soon pay
- Cash – which is being spent (and hopefully replenished!) on a daily basis

The important point to realise is that such current assets *also* need to be funded. In practice, this is partly achieved by a business offsetting its current *liabilities* against this funding requirement. For example, the funding requirement for 'receivables' *(amounts owed to the business by its credit customers)* can in effect be part-funded by the 'payables' *(amounts owed by the business to its credit suppliers)*.

Such use of current liabilities is an example of short-term financing as *(by definition)* a current liability will need to be paid within 12 months. However most businesses are still then left with a remaining 'funding gap' which is known as 'Working Capital' and is defined as:

Working Capital = Current Assets less Current Liabilities

We shall study working capital in depth in chapter 11 (particularly how to reduce the corresponding funding requirement for it) but for now just note that in addition to requiring some form of long-term finance for *non-current assets*, a business also typically requires some form of long-term finance for its *working capital* requirements.

The Language of Business

> **TUTORIAL NOTE**
>
> There is a story of a budding businessman who scraped together the money required to take over a petrol filling station, only to discover that the supplying oil company insisted on cash in advance for the first supply of petrol. The individual had no funds left to actually purchase his stock of fuel (which is an element of Working Capital) and therefore never got as far as opening for business!

Capital Investment

We can therefore see that both new and established businesses require some level of long-term investment to allow them to start trading, and then to grow. The name given to this long-term investment is **'capital investment'** or just **'capital'**.

For the remainder of this chapter we will restrict ourselves to looking at how companies obtain the *long-term* capital investment they require. We will return to the various techniques for reducing working capital requirements by use of *short-term* finance in chapter 11.

So the question we now need to consider is exactly where this long-term capital investment comes from. In the case of companies (which this chapter will focus on) there are two main sources of long term capital investment:

- **Equity Finance**   i.e. Shareholder Investment
- **Debt Finance**   i.e. Borrowings

Before we look in detail at both equity and debt finance, it is useful to realise that everything mentioned so far in this chapter can be derived from the basic 'Accounting Equation' we met in Chapter 1.

> **DEFINITIONS**
>
> The 'Accounting Equation' simply states:
>
> **Assets – Liabilities = Equity**
>
> And we know that both assets and liabilities can be categorised into (short-term) 'current', and (long-term) 'non-current' components, so:
>
> **Non-Current Assets + Current Assets – Non-Current Liabilities – Current Liabilities = Equity**
>
> Taking Non-Current Liabilities to the right hand side we get:
>
> **Non-Current Assets + Current Assets – Current Liabilities = Equity + Non-Current Liabilities**

Finally we now know that Current Assets – Current Liabilities is in fact called 'Working Capital' (the funding required to allow day to day trading in a business); and we need to recognise that Non-Current Liabilities essentially represent long-term debt (such as mortgages and bank loans). The equation thus becomes:

Non-Current Assets + Working Capital = Equity + Debt

Which very neatly summarises what we have covered so far:

- The business needs to fund Non-Current Assets and Working Capital *(on left hand side)*
- This funding can come from Equity or Debt *(on right hand side)*

*(In fact the Balance Sheet can also be formatted in such a way as to exactly show this relationship ...... with **what is being funded** (non-current assets and working capital) on the top; and **how it is being***

3 Long term finance for the business – debt versus equity

funded (equity and long-term debt) on the bottom. Unfortunately the modern international standard format for the balance sheet does not use this particular format!)

3.2 Equity finance

The first source of finance is from the shareholders who actually own the company and who have invested in shares in the company **('share capital').**

The shareholders' investment will comprise of the original money they paid when the company first issued the shares, plus any profits the company has since made which have been retained within the company **('retained profits')** i.e. profits **not** paid out to the shareholders as dividends. The shareholders own the company, and any (of their) profit retained by the company represents an **increase** in the investment the shareholders are making.

The term 'equity' can be used to describe either the total value of a company, or the value associated with one individual investor. In both cases equity is comprised of share capital plus retained profit as seen in Chapter 1.

> **TUTORIAL NOTE**
>
> **Equity Finance = Share Capital + Retained Profit**
>
> **The total equity** in a company is the **total** amount of share capital that the company has received when it has issued shares, plus the *total* amount of retained profit throughout the whole life of the company i.e. all the cumulative profit that the company has ever made which has *not* been returned to the shareholders by way of dividends.
>
> **An individual's equity** in a company is the amount of initial share capital that particular individual invested in buying new shares, plus the total amount of cumulative retained profit that relates to those shares.

Generally shares are issued by a company on a permanent basis (occasionally a company might 'buy back' (aka 'redeem') its own shares, but this is not standard practice). Once an individual has subscribed for (i.e. bought *newly issued*) shares they must normally either retain the shares themselves, or sell them to a third party.

Because companies do not normally redeem (i.e. buy back) their own shares, share capital can usually be regarded as being permanent, at least from the company's perspective. From the shareholder's perspective each individual investor has the option of selling his/her shares to another investor, but this leaves the share capital invested in the company (from the original subscription) unchanged.

It is therefore important not to confuse brand new shares being first issued by a company, with the possible subsequent resale of these 'second-hand' shares to a third party investor.

- When an investor buys brand new shares from a company they are said to *'subscribe'* for the shares, and the transaction is between the company (who receive cash in exchange for the newly issued shares) and the investor (who receives the shares in exchange for cash).

- In contrast, if such an investor later decides that they no longer want the shares then they have the option of selling them on to a new investor. This transaction does not directly involve the original company. It is simply a sale and purchase of second-hand shares between two third party investors, and the company does not receive any cash in the process. The company does however need to update its register of shareholders so that it knows who to pay dividends to, and who to invite to the company's Annual General Meeting (AGM) etc.

The Language of Business

> **TEST YOUR UNDERSTANDING 1**
>
> An Investor Rachel subscribes for 1,000 newly issued shares in Halifax Ltd at a cost of £2 per share.
>
> How much cash does Halifax Ltd receive? _____
>
> Sometime time later Rachel sells all of her 1,000 Halifax shares to a 3rd party investor Tony for £2,500.
>
> How much money does Halifax then receive? _____
>
> What administration must Halifax Ltd undertake when the shares are transferred from Rachel to Tony, and why?

Reasons why investors purchase shares

When an investor purchases shares in a company they potentially have three different expectations from their ownership of the shares:

1) **Voting Power**

    Each share normally carries the right to a single vote on various matters raised at the Company's Annual General Meeting (AGM) so (in theory at least) ownership of the share confers some power over decision making in the company. How much 'power' an individual shareholder has in practice obviously very much depends on their percentage ownership of the company. A 51% shareholding gives effective control, whilst a 1% shareholding (in isolation) provides little or no power.

2) **Expectation of Dividends**

    Ownership of a 'share' of the company should also result in the shareholder receiving a share of the company's profits via a dividend payment. If the company has made a large profit the shareholders might expect higher dividends, whilst if the company has not performed well (or even made a loss) then shareholders' expectation will probably be for low (or even no) dividends to be paid that year.

    Regardless of the shareholder's expectations, it is up to the Directors to propose the level of dividends and they typically retain part of the company's profit for ongoing reinvestment and therefore only distribute some of the available profit to the shareholders via dividend payments.

    At the AGM the shareholders will then vote on whether to accept the proposed dividends, or whether to *reduce* them. They cannot vote to increase them! Under company law dividends can only be paid out of retained profit and not out of the share capital itself! So even if the company makes a loss in a particular year, the Directors *could* still propose a dividend payment out of the cumulative retained profit of previous years.

    It is important to appreciate that dividends are *not* tax deductible from profit. They are not an 'expense' of the business which can be set off against profit, *they are the profit* (or at least, the share of the profit which being distributed to the shareholders).

3 Long term finance for the business – debt versus equity

3) Possible Capital Gain

Shareholders will also hope (in addition to receiving some ongoing dividend income) that the market value of their shares will increase so that they can (if they wish) sell their shares to a third party and make a capital gain i.e. sell shares for more than they bought them for. As already stated, a shareholder selling shares to a third party has no immediate cash consequence for the company. The transaction was simply a sale and purchase agreement between two external parties (often via a stock market), and the company's involvement is limited to updating their 'register' of shareholders.

> **TUTORIAL NOTE**
>
> Both points 2 and 3 above are entirely dependent on how well the company is performing and how its future prospects are perceived. A highly profitable company with good growth prospects will be able to pay a good level of dividend and its share price should increase.
>
> Unlike the providers of debt finance (see later), the shareholders have a strong vested interest in the performance of the company because if the company does well, they do well (in terms of higher dividends and increased share price). In other words, their investment stands or falls depending on the performance and prospects of the company!

In the event of the company failing, the shareholders will find themselves last in line to receive any compensation after the company's assets have been liquidated (i.e. sold for cash). The 'pecking order' for claims in the event of a liquidation is:

1) Secured creditors (including secured bank loans)
2) Unsecured creditors (including unsecured bank loans, suppliers, employees & HMRC)
3) Shareholders

The shareholders will therefore often emerge from a liquidation having lost all of their investment, but then that is what their 'limited liability' was i.e. limited to the value of their share capital.

> **TEST YOUR UNDERSTANDING 2**
>
> An Investor Peter subscribed for 10,000 newly issued £1 ordinary shares in Norfolk Ltd when it was first incorporated at a cost of £1 each.
>
> Some years later Sarah subscribes for 10,000 newly issued £1 ordinary shares in Norfolk Ltd at a cost of £2 each (£1 nominal value + £1 share premium).
>
> In both cases these are the only shares in Norfolk Ltd that they hold.
>
> **Which investor has the greater voting power & why?**
>
>
>
> **Which investor will receive the higher dividend & why?**

3.3 Debt finance

The second source of finance for a company is for it to simply borrow funds. The most obvious examples are bank loans and mortgages, though large companies will often take a proactive approach and issue 'bonds' (aka 'corporate bonds') which are simply a form of loan initiated by the company requiring the funds, as opposed to the taking the more reactive route of approaching a bank to apply for a bank loan.

Bonds are often sold by the company through stock markets (such as the London Stock Exchange) where both private and institutional investors (such as pension funds) can purchase them. Bonds can be traded in much the same way as shares, so that an investor who has purchased say a 10 year bond (one which will be repaid by the borrowing company in 10 years' time) can actually get their money back earlier by selling the second-hand bond to another investor on an appropriate stock exchange.

Following the normal principles of 'risk versus return', the higher the perceived level of risk (*i.e. of the company not ultimately repaying the loan*), the higher will be the rate of interest required to compensate for this risk.

⚠ KEY POINT

Both bank loans and bonds (and indeed any other type of *'debt instrument'* as they are collectively known) can be categorised by:

- **The Principal** - How much money is initially paid across to the company by way of a loan (or the purchase of a bond)

- **The Term** - How many years will pass before the loan must be repaid or the bond must be 'redeemed' (i.e. paid back by the company)

- **The Interest Rate** – Which might be a **fixed** rate of interest (i.e. set at the outset and not changing) or **variable** rate of interest which varies according to (say) the Bank of England Base rate e.g. *"2% over Base Rate"*

- Whether the debt is **secured** or **unsecured**

  A **secured** loan gives some level of protection *to the lender* by giving them the legal right to claim company assets if the debt is not repaid. For instance a bank loan might be secured on the company's premises – meaning that the lender would have the legal right to force the sale of the company's premises to recover their money if the loan is not repaid on time!

  Conversely an **unsecured** loan gives no such protection if the borrower defaults. The fact that a loan is secured is mainly a benefit to the lender as it offers them greater protection. However, because the level of risk is then lower, the interest rate charged should then also be lower (*risk versus reward*) which is then of benefit to the borrower!

- **Capital Repayment Terms** – When must the 'principal' sum be repaid? Bonds and some commercial loans are repaid in full at the end of their term (with no interim repayments of the capital sum). Alternatively, the capital sum might be repayable in instalments (quarterly? monthly?) over the term of the loan such that the amount actually owed is reducing at the loan goes on.

- **Interest Payment Terms** - Is the interest paid monthly, quarterly, annually etc.? If regular capital repayments are being made throughout the term of loan, then the corresponding interest charges on the (reducing) remaining balance should decrease with time.

3 Long term finance for the business – debt versus equity

The nature of debt finance

Debt Finance is perhaps more straightforward to understand than equity finance as it is simply a form of contract between the lender and the borrower (i.e. the company) as follows:

- The **Lender** agrees to lend a certain sum of money, for a certain length of time, for a certain rate of interest (which might be either a fixed or a variable rate). If the lender has the added comfort of the loan being 'secured' against the company's assets then they will typically receive a lower rate of interest than if the loan is 'unsecured', as they are exposing themselves to less risk.

- From the **Borrowers** perspective the company has received the funds they required and all they have to do now is to pay the interest on time, and make capital repayments of the actual principal sum borrowed when due. The borrower is contractually obliged to make these payments regardless of the company's performance i.e. whether it has made a profit or loss.

- From the **Lender's perspective** they are merely interested in receiving the interest payments and capital payments on time. So long as both of these happen the lender has no particular interest in the performance of the company over the term of the debt. It makes no difference to the lender whether the company is making massive profits or no profits ...... *so long as the interest is paid and the ultimate repayment of the loan is assured!*

- The **Lender** generally has no influence within the company (*though banks will sometimes impose various stipulations on the company known as 'Banking Covenants' as a condition of lending*). They do not have any voting rights and their relationship with the company is limited to the right to receive interest and capital repayments when due.

- The **interest** which the company will pay over the term of the loan represents an *expense* to the company (recorded on the Statement of Profit and Loss) and assuming that the loan has been taken out to support the trading activities of the company, then it is a tax-deductible expense. This means that the fact the company is paying (tax deductible) interest will reduce reported profits and therefore result in the company's corporation tax liability being based on a smaller profit figure. Though reducing the company's profits might not immediately sound like a good thing to achieve, reducing the company's tax liability definitely is!

- In contrast, the **capital repayments** are not an expense. They are merely the repayment of a liability. The capital repayments are therefore *not* recorded as expenses, and they are *not* tax deductible.

> **TUTORIAL NOTE**
>
> Remember, expenses represent outflows of wealth from the business.
>
> Making (say) a £500 capital repayment on a bank loan does not mean wealth has left the business. Certainly, the business's assets (i.e. cash) have now reduced by £500; but the business's liabilities (i.e. outstanding bank loan) have also reduced by £500!

3.4 Bond versus equity: The Investor's Perspective

The decision between whether a potential investor should invest in bonds (debt finance) or shares (equity finance) in a company is a choice between accepting different levels of risk and hence expecting different levels of potential return on the investment.

Risk Adverse Investors

A 'risk averse' investor might be more tempted by investing in bonds as these will typically pay a fixed rate of interest of (say) 5% regardless of how well or how poorly the company performs, as the company is contractually obliged to pay 5% interest ... *even if it makes a loss!* Unless the company completely fails the investor will receive 5% interest, and at the end of the 'term' of the debt will have the original sum 'redeemed' by the company.

The worst case scenario would be that the company failed and was put into administration. The loaned funds would then be at risk and (along with the various other creditors owed money by the company) the lender would have to join the queue to share in whatever funds could be salvaged from the failed company. If the debt was 'secured' then this might put the lender in a stronger position (further up the queue), but regardless of whether the lender had invested in secured or unsecured debt one fact would remain.......he/she would be paid out (in whole or in part) *before* the shareholders received anything at all!

Risk Seeking Investors

Conversely a 'risk seeking' investor might be more tempted by investing in shares (equity finance) in the hope of higher returns via the dividends, plus capital growth in the share price. A company can only pay dividends out of its ultimate net profit *after* it has paid debt interest and taxation, but if it has performed well it could pay a level of dividends that exceeded the level of return achieved by those who invested in bonds instead. Then again ... if the company performance was not that spectacular then it is possible that the return on the dividends could be less than that on the bonds..... or even zero!!!

Furthermore if the company failed (i.e. went into administration and was ultimately 'wound up') then the shareholders will not receive a penny until every other creditor has been paid in full. This often means that the shareholders will get nothing at all back from their original investment in the shares.

> **TUTORIAL NOTE**
>
> As an investor, you pay your money ... and you take your choice! If you want lower risk but potentially lower returns, invest in bonds. However if you are prepared to accept a higher level of risk with the prospect of potentially higher returns, invest in shares.

3 Long term finance for the business – debt versus equity

OVERVIEW

The differences between equity finance and debt finance

	Equity Finance	Debt Finance
Power within company	A right to vote at AGM	No voting power
Duration of Finance	Typically permanent investment	Fixed term investment
Investor Return	Expectation of dividends	Guaranteed interest paid
Strong company performance	Possibly higher dividends	Same interest paid regardless
Weak company performance	Lower or no dividends	Same interest paid regardless
Nature of Payment	Share of company profit	Tax deductible interest payment
Risk of Company Failure	Shareholders last in line	Repaid before shareholders
Investor Risk versus Return	Higher Risk / Higher Potential Return	Lower Risk / Lower Potential Return

3.5 Gearing

Both a new company in search of *initial* investment, and an established company looking for *additional* investment to facilitate expansion, have the choice between seeking long-term funding from either equity finance, or from debt finance, or indeed from both.

Of course slow and steady growth can be funded by simply retaining a greater proportion of the business's profits for reinvestment, rather than paying generous dividends to the shareholders. This is of course equity finance *(since Equity = Share Capital + Retained Profit)* but is a slow route to growth. We will instead focus on the scenario of a company in a hurry to grow, and with expansion plans that require fresh funds to be injected into the business.

Although both debt finance and equity finance provide funds for the company, they have very different characteristics and will ultimately give rise to a different 'risk profile' for the company. The more a company relies on debt financing, the more highly 'geared' it is said to be and we shall now explore the concept of gearing in some detail.

> **DEFINITION**
>
> There is not a single agreed definition of 'gearing' and so it is possible that you will see alternative definitions of it. The one below is perhaps the easiest to understand and therefore arguably the most useful.
>
> The gearing of a company is the percentage of the company's <u>total</u> capital investment that comes from debt finance (such as bank loans taken out, or bonds issued)
>
> **Gearing %** = $\dfrac{\text{Debt Finance (£)}}{\text{Total Capital Employed (£)}}$ x 100%
>
> Where 'Total capital Employed' is simply the sum of: long-term Debt Finance + Equity Finance.
>
> **So, if you prefer:**
>
> **Gearing %** = $\dfrac{\text{Debt Finance (£)}}{\text{(Debt + Equity) (£)}}$ x 100%

What is considered to be a normal or appropriate level of gearing will be different for individual companies depending on the sector they operates in, the prevailing state of the economy at the time, and their own specific circumstances.

However as a very general guideline:

- **Less than 25% gearing** - would generally be regarded as 'low gearing'
- **25%-50% gearing** - is fairly typical for an established company
- **Over 50% gearing** - (that is more than half of the company's capital base coming from borrowings) would generally be regarded as 'high gearing'.

3 Long term finance for the business – debt versus equity

EXAMPLES

1. No Gearing

A company has £50,000 of equity (made up of £5,000 share capital and £45,000 of retained profits), and no long-term debt.

Gearing % = $\dfrac{\text{£ nil}}{\text{£nil + £50,000}}$ x 100% = 0%

The company's capital base is not reliant on borrowing at all.

2. Low Gearing

A company has £90,000 of equity (made up of £10,000 share capital and £80,000 of retained profits), and £10,000 long-term debt.

Gearing % = $\dfrac{\text{£10,000}}{\text{£10,000 + £90,000}}$ x 100% = 10%

A modest 10% of the company's total capital employed comes from borrowing.

3. Medium Gearing

A company has £200,000 of equity (made up of £20,000 share capital and £180,000 of retained profits), and £90,000 long-term debt.

Gearing % = $\dfrac{\text{£90,000}}{\text{£90,000 + £200,000}}$ x 100% = 31%

31% of the company's total capital employed comes from borrowing.

4. High Gearing

A company has £30,000 of equity (made up of £1,000 share capital and £29,000 of retained profits), and £300,000 long-term debt.

Gearing % = $\dfrac{\text{£300,000}}{\text{£300,000 + £30,000}}$ x 100% = 91%

Only 9% of the company's capital is provided by shareholder funds (equity), the remaining 91% is derived from long-term debt.

3.6 Options to increase the capital invested

In order for a business to grow it will normally need to increase its capital base *(aka Total Capital Employed)* in order to allow the funding of a larger scale operation, which might include some or all of the following:

- Additional (or just larger) premises
- Additional (or just more modern) manufacturing machinery
- Increased distribution network (warehousing, trucks etc.)
- Office equipment (computer infrastructure, office furniture etc.)
- Increased levels of inventory (to support higher sales)
- Increased customer receivables (bigger credit customer base)
- Increased cash requirements (to ensure ongoing liquidity)
- Investment in research & development (with little or no immediate return)
- Increased marketing spend (with delay before corresponding increase in demand)

Of course there is no point investing in any of the above unless the business is reasonably certain that they will enjoy a corresponding worthwhile return on this investment! In particular, can their business model be scaled up? Will increasing capital investment actually promote a corresponding growth in profitability?

We will examine capital expenditure appraisal techniques in chapter 9 (which might be used to appraise expenditure on premises, plant & machinery etc.). Whilst in Chapter 11 we will look at the efficient management of working capital (including inventory, receivables & cash).

For now we will focus on *where* a business will get this extra capital investment from?

There are three main funding routes it could consider:

1. **Retained Profits**
2. **New Share Issue**
3. **Borrowing (increasing gearing)**

Let us look at each one in turn.

1. Retained Profits

The company could choose to simply grow 'slowly but surely' by retaining some of the profits it makes, so that sometime *in the future* the company will have increased the level of capital employed. The company would *not* have increased its gearing (i.e. its borrowing) as retained profits are equity finance (i.e. the funding comes from the shareholders 'leaving' their profits invested in their company).

The trouble is that by the time the company has accumulated sufficient retained profits, the window of opportunity might have gone whilst their more 'bullish' competitors (who had quickly financed themselves for growth) might have overtaken them!

3. Long term finance for the business – debt versus equity

2. New Share Issue

Alternatively the company could aim to raise more equity finance by offering additional new shares in the company in the hope of gaining more (permanent) equity investment. They could aim to achieve this from either their existing shareholders buying more shares, or by attracting completely new investors.

We'll explore the options for raising equity finance further in the next section, but for now let's just recognise the general effects of issuing more shares:

- The new share capital received from 'subscribers' (in exchange for the new shares) will increase the level of equity finance in the company.
- The level of debt finance will be unchanged.
- Therefore the proportion of the total capital employed that derives from debt will in fact reduce i.e. the gearing% will lower as a result.
- The level of interest payments that the company needs to make (on existing borrowings) will be unchanged as there are no new borrowings.
- The number of shareholders (or at least the number of shares in circulation) will have increased.
- If, as hoped, profits increase as a result of the expansion, then these profits will need to be shared among more shareholders (or at least between more shares).
- If the hoped for increase in profits does not arise, then whatever profit *is* made will still need to be shared among more shareholders (or at least between more shares) so the shareholder's returns might even go down!

3. Borrowing

Alternatively the company could simply borrow funds (via bank loan or by issuing corporate bonds etc.) and this would be a form of debt finance. Again, let's just recognise the general effects of taking on more debt:

- The level of equity in the company will be unchanged.
- The level of debt finance will increase.
- Therefore the proportion of the total capital employed that derives from debt will increase i.e. the gearing% will increase as a result.
- The level of interest payments that the company needs to make will increase (as there are new loans or more bonds to pay interest on).
- The number of shares in circulation will be unchanged.
- If the final profits (i.e. after the debt interest has been paid) increase as a result of the expansion, then these profits will be shared among *the same number* of shareholders i.e. the individual shareholder returns will increase.
- However if the operating profits do not increase (or worse still the company makes a loss), then unfortunately the debt interest must still be paid. This might the mean that the final profits (i.e. after the debt interest has been paid) will decrease as a result of the expansion and so the shareholder's returns might go down.

We will shortly examine scenarios 2 and 3 more closely, so that we can understand the various effects of both strong and weak profit performance, in a company which has either low or high gearing.

However, let's first quickly deal with how a company might increase its share capital via a 'Rights Issue'.

3.7 Rights Issues

A common starting point for a company wishing to increase its share capital is to first try to sell the newly issued shares to *existing* shareholders via what is known as a 'Rights Issue' Not only is this likely to meet with a higher success rate (as presumably the existing shareholders are already convinced that the company is a sound investment), but it also avoids upsetting existing shareholders by potentially 'diluting' their percentage ownership of the company, which might happen if new shares are offered to new investors.

Consider a small company that was founded when ten investors each subscribed for 500 £1 nominal shares. The total (initial) share capital would be £5,000 and each investor would own 10% of the company. The company trades successfully for several years and accumulates £45,000 of retained profit. The total equity is now £50,000 (£5,000 share capital + £45,000 retained profit).

Each £1 nominal share now has a theoretical value of £10 (£50,000 company equity shared between 5,000 shares).

If the company now wishes to raise additional share capital it could of course issue new £1 shares (at the price of £1 each) to new subscribers. However, that would have two adverse consequences:

1) Since the original £1 nominal shares are now worth £10 each, issuing new £1 nominal shares at a cost of £1 would be failing to appreciate their current value, and hence devaluing the original shares in the process. Remember, all shares (of the same class, in the same company) give their holders an equal right to vote and equal right to receive a dividend. For this reason any new £1 nominal shares should sold for ~£10 each (£1 nominal value + £9 share premium = £10)

2) Secondly, if shares were offered to new shareholders (even at £10 each) this would have the effect of reducing the original subscribers' percentage ownership of the company. If for instance 5,000 new £1 shares were issued for £10 each then the company would end up with 10,000 shares in issue, meaning that each original subscriber would now only own 5% of the company (=500 / 10,000 x 100%). Of course the company itself would now be worth twice as much (£50,000 equity before new issue + £50,000 new share capital raised = £100,000). So each original subscriber would still have the same theoretical share value of £5,000 (5% x £100,000 ... instead of 10% x £50,000). Despite not losing any monetary value in their shareholding, existing shareholders might still resent the loss of voting power (10% down to 5%) caused by this dilution of their percentage ownership.

The solution to both of these potential problems is to issue new shares at a premium price to the existing shareholders only. This is called a 'Rights Issue' as each existing shareholder has the 'right' to buy new shares in proportion to their existing shareholding (it's a 'right', not an obligation!). For instance a '1 for 1 Rights Issue' gives existing shareholders the right to buy one new share for each existing share they own. If all the original shareholders exercised this right then their percentage ownership would remain unchanged.

Rights issues are usually offered at a discount compared to what new shares might be sold for on the open market, to encourage existing shareholders to exercise their right. You can't force shareholders to buy more shares, but an existing shareholder who did not exercise their right would have effectively 'diluted' their % shareholding.

3 Long term finance for the business – debt versus equity

EXAMPLE

Question:

A company currently has 10,000 £1 nominal shares in issue. The company has £900,000 of retained profit and hence the total equity of the company is £910,000 (valuing each share at £91 each).

The company now wishes to raise additional capital (via equity finance) and so makes a 1 for 4 rights issue at an offer price of £85 per share (£1 nominal + £84 share premium).

If 70% of the shareholders exercise their right how much additional capital will the company raise?

Solution:

A '1 for 4' rights issue means that each existing shareholder has the right to buy 1 new share for every 4 shares currently held.

Additional capital raised = 70% x 10,000 x ¼ x £85 = £148,750.

TEST YOUR UNDERSTANDING 3

The private limited company Beta Ltd has total issued share capital of 50,000 £1 ordinary shares. The current equity value of the company ('balance sheet' value) is £200,000.

What is the theoretical current market value of each share?

_____

Beta Ltd now wish to raise additional long-term finance via a '1 for 2' Rights Issue and decide to offer the shares at a 10% discount on their theoretical market value

At what price will the new shares be offered?

_____

If all of the existing shareholders took up their 'rights' what amount of additional finance would be raised from the 'Rights Issue'?

_____

3.8 Chapter 2 Recap & Interest Cover

Statement of Profit or Loss

To fully understand the effects of gearing we must first revisit our basic P&L statement (from Chapter 2) so that we can see exactly at which stage the interest payments of the debt finance will be charged, and at which stage the shareholders can claim a right to the company's profit.

The basic format of the Statement of Profit or Loss is as follows:

	Income
Less	Cost of Sales
Equals	**Gross Profit**
Less	Overheads
Equals	**Operating Profit**
Less	Finance Costs *(i.e. debt interest costs)*
Equals	**Profit before Tax**
Less	Taxation
Equals	**Profit after Tax** *(attributable to the Shareholders)*

By way of a quick recap on The Statement of Profit or Loss:

- The **Operating Profit** figure is used as a key measure of company performance because it takes into account all of the operational income and expenditure, but *excludes* non-operational items such as interest paid on borrowing, and taxation (which does not always directly correspond to the accounting profit figure and can therefore lead to a misleading Profit after Tax figure).

- By putting finance costs (i.e. interest paid) after operating profit, we are effectively drawing a line between how well their company is operating in its given sector ….. and how it is actually financed (equity finance or debt finance) which is a separate matter.

- The final profit figure is **Profit after Tax** and this is the profit which 'belongs' to the shareholders i.e. after all other expenses (including interest & tax) have been paid. Each company will have to decide how much of the profit after tax to return to the shareholders as dividends, and how much to retain to re-invest in the company (retained profits forming part of equity finance).

Return on Capital Employed (ROCE)

One of the key operating measures we use to examine the operating performance of a company is known as **'Return on Capital Employed' (ROCE)** defined as:

$$\text{Return on Capital Employed (ROCE)} = \frac{\text{Operating Profit (£)}}{\text{Total Capital Employed (£)}} \times 100\%$$

(Remembering that 'Total Capital Employed = Equity Finance + Debt Finance)

It is sometimes useful to estimate how much operating profit a company would make (at a certain % ROCE) if more capital were pumped into the business (either via equity or debt financing). The above equation can be simply re-arranged to show this:

$$\text{Operating Profit (£)} = \text{Total Capital Employed (£)} \times \text{ROCE (\%)}$$

Return on Equity (ROE)

One of the key operating measures we use to examine the returns enjoyed by the shareholders on their investment is known as **'Return on Equity' (ROE)** defined as:

Return on Equity (ROE) = $\dfrac{\text{Profit after Tax (£)}}{\text{Equity (£)}} \times 100\%$

Return on Equity purely focuses on what the shareholders 'get out' (Profit after Tax) compared to what they 'put in' (Equity). It is important to understand that just equity *(and not debt!)* is on the denominator of the equation. The shareholders did <u>not themselves</u> provide any debt finance (even if they have enjoyed bigger profits as the result of a bigger company financed partly from borrowings!)

Interest Cover

As well as looking at the gearing % itself, another key financial indicator which potential lenders will look at is the 'interest cover' of the company, which is the ratio of how many times over the company can pay its current interest charge from the operating profit it has made (look at the format of the Statement of Profit or Loss above)

Interest Cover = $\dfrac{\text{Operating Profit}}{\text{Debt Interest}}$

> #### EXAMPLE
>
> If a company had an operating profit of £100,000 and interest payments of £2,000 then its interest cover would be:
>
> Interest Cover = $\dfrac{£100,000}{£2,000}$
>
> = **50 times**
>
> *(Interest Cover is not a percentage, it is a pure number)*

Obviously the higher the interest cover, the safer any new potential lenders will feel about the company's ability to be able to pay its debt interest. In the above example the interest cover of 50 times is very safe *(and chances are that this is at least partly due to the company having a low gearing)*.

If however a bank was approached for a new loan by a company with an interest cover of (say) 1.5 then they might well decline the loan request. The company is just too close to being unable to pay its current interest payments (in relation to the size of the profit it makes) let alone take on any more debt!

3.9 Is gearing good or bad?

The answer is 'It depends'….. *on how well the company then performs:*

- If the company delivers a strong performance (high ROCE) then its operating profit will increase
- If the company increases its gearing, then the amount of debt interest it must pay (regardless of its performance) will increase
- If the company has expanded via equity finance then any additional profit will need to be shared across an expanded shareholding

- If the company has expanded via debt finance then any additional profit will be shared across the same original number of shareholders

This is best illustrated with a series of different scenarios to see what the actual end results are for each scenario. In each case we will consider the fictitious company "Ambitious Ltd".

3.10 Ambitious Ltd: an example of gearing

The next four examples will be based on the fictitious company 'Ambitious Ltd which has been trading for a number of years.

The following information on Ambitious Ltd is provided:

- It currently has £5,000 of share capital and £95,000 of retained profits, so it currently has i.e. £100,000 of equity (Because Equity = Share Capital + Retained Profits)

- It has an existing £10,000 bank loan (interest rate = 10% pa)

- Ambitious Ltd now wish to raise an additional £90,000 of capital to fund their expansion plans which they can either achieve by issuing new shares (equity finance route), or by further borrowing at a 10% interest rate (debt finance route).

- The company is currently making a 15% return on capital employed (ROCE) and *hopes* to continue to deliver 15% ROCE when the company is expanded. However the worst case scenario for a downturn in the company's performance *might* result in only achieving a 7% ROCE.

- For simplicity we will assume that the company pays 20% corporation tax on its Profit before Tax (PBT) figure.

We will now explore what happens to Ambitious Ltd in four different scenarios:

1) If they borrow an additional £90,000 and make a 15% ROCE
2) If they borrow an additional £90,000 but only make a 7% ROCE
3) If they instead issue £90,000 of new share capital and make a 15% ROCE
4) If they instead issue £90,000 of new share capital but only make a 7% ROCE

In each scenario Ambitious Ltd has expanded to have a total capital employed of £200,000. For each case we will examine both the final Profit after Tax (PAT) the company makes, and the corresponding return the shareholders enjoy on their investment (ROE).

(The recap of some basics covered in Section 3.8 might prove useful).

3 Long term finance for the business – debt versus equity

EXAMPLE

Initial Starting Position

Ambitious Ltd are making 15% ROCE on a £110,000 capital base.

Capital Structure

Equity Finance = £100,000

Debt Finance = £10,000

Total Capital Employed = £110,000

Gearing = 9%   *Gearing = Debt / Total Capital Employed x 100%*

Profitability
Bottom half of Statement of Profit or Loss (starting at operating profit)

Operating Profit	£16,500	= £110,000 Capital Employed x 15% ROCE
Less interest	(£1,000)	= 10% interest on £10,000
Profit before Tax	£15,500	
Less Tax	(£3,100)	= £15,500 PBT x 20% corporation tax
Profit after Tax	£12,400	

Interest Cover

Interest cover   16½ times   = £16,500 / £1,000

Return on Equity

Return on Equity   12.4%   = £12,400 / £100,000 x 100%

TUTORIAL NOTE

This is the starting position at Ambitious Ltd before any expansion plans are undertaken, and as such is the benchmark against which all four expansion scenarios should be judged. The company has low gearing and the interest costs are easily affordable (16½ times over). The shareholders are enjoying a 12.4% return on their investment. In other words for every £100 they have invested in equity their company is making £12.40 back in Profit after Tax. A key question for the shareholders is how their return (ROE) will be affected by the company's expansion plans.

EXAMPLE

Scenario One: High Gearing and Strong Performance

Ambitious Ltd borrow an additional £90,000 and make a 15% ROCE

Capital Structure

Equity Finance =	£100,000	
Debt Finance =	£100,000	*including £10,000 original borrowing*
Total Capital Employed =	£200,000	
Gearing = 50%		*Gearing = Debt / Total Capital Employed x 100%*

Profitability

Bottom half of Statement of Profit or Loss (starting at operating profit)

Operating Profit	£30,000	*= £200,000 Capital Employed x 15% ROCE*
Less interest	(£10,000)	*= 10% interest on £100,000*
Profit before Tax	£20,000	
Less Tax	(£4,000)	*= £20,000 PBT x 20% corporation tax*
Profit after Tax	£16,000	

Interest Cover

Interest cover	3 times	*= £30,000 / £10,000*

Return on Equity

Return on Equity	16%	*= £16,000 / £100,000 x 100%*

TUTORIAL NOTE

Ambitious have now nearly doubled their capital base (from £110,000 to £200,000) and have increased their gearing from a very modest 9% to a substantial 50% in the process i.e. Half of their capital base now comes from borrowed funds. As a result of this expansion Ambitious Ltd's operating profit has increased from £16,500 to £30,000. Unfortunately all the extra borrowing has resulted in their interest costs increasing ten-fold to £10,000 pa, which reduces their interest cover to only 3 times i.e. 1/3 of their operating profit is used to pay the loan interest! However the shareholders' Return on Equity has increased from 12.4% to 16%, so the returns the shareholders are receiving have increased without them having to invest any more funds into the business. The company has borrowed and successfully invested funds, and the shareholders have benefited!

3 Long term finance for the business – debt versus equity

EXAMPLE

Scenario Two: High Gearing and Poor Performance

Ambitious Ltd borrow an additional £90,000 and make a 7% ROCE

Capital Structure

Equity Finance =	£100,000	
Debt Finance =	£100,000	*including £10,000 original borrowing*
Total Capital Employed =	£200,000	
Gearing = 50%		*Gearing = Debt / Total Capital Employed x 100%*

Profitability

Bottom half of Statement of Profit or Loss (starting at operating profit)

Operating Profit	£14,000	*= £200,000 Capital Employed x 7% ROCE*
Less interest	(£10,000)	*= 10% interest on £100,000*
Profit before Tax	£4,000	
Less Tax	(£800)	*= £4,000 PBT x 20% corporation tax*
Profit after Tax	£3,200	

Interest Cover

Interest cover	1.4 times	*= £14,000 / £10,000*

Return on Equity

Return on Equity	3.2%	*= £3,200 / £100,000 x 100%*

TUTORIAL NOTE

A downturn in the company's performance means that they are now only making a modest 7% ROCE which produces £14,000 operating profit. Unfortunately most of this is then used to pay the £10,000 pa interest charge on their large borrowings. The desperate nature of this is revealed by the fact that they could only pay the interest costs 1.4 times over. In effect the company is largely operating just to pay bank interest! Having paid the loan interest there is only a modest residual Profit after Tax and hence the shareholder's return on equity has plummeted to 3.2% (at which level they could probably get a better risk free return for their investment elsewhere).

> ## EXAMPLE
>
> ### Scenario Three: Low Gearing and Strong Performance
>
> **Ambitious Ltd issue an additional £90,000 of share capital and make a 15% ROCE**
>
> **Capital Structure**
>
> Equity Finance =   £190,000
>
> Debt Finance =   £10,000   *just £10,000 original borrowing*
>
> Total Capital Employed = £200,000
>
> Gearing = 5%   *Gearing = Debt / Total Capital Employed x 100%*
>
> **Profitability**
> Bottom half of Statement of Profit or Loss (starting at operating profit)
>
> | | | |
> |---|---|---|
> | Operating Profit | £30,000 | *= £200,000 Capital Employed x 15% ROCE* |
> | Less interest | (£1,000) | *= 10% interest on £10,000* |
> | Profit before Tax | £29,000 | |
> | Less Tax | (£5,800) | *= £29,000 PBT x 20% corporation tax* |
> | Profit after Tax | £23,200 | |
>
> **Interest Cover**
>
> Interest cover   30 times   *= £30,000 / £1,000*
>
> **Return on Equity**
>
> Return on Equity   12.2%   *= £23,200 / £190,000 x 100%*

> ## TUTORIAL NOTE
>
> The company's gearing has decreased because the newly issued shares mean that an even greater percentage of their total capital employed comes from equity finance (and hence an even *smaller* percentage comes from debt finance). The very modest interest charges are highlighted by the very high interest cover figure which shows that the company could pay this level of interest 30 times over. The strong ROCE performance means that the company delivers £23,200 profit after tax (PAT). This is higher than the corresponding PAT from the scenario 1 (strong performance/high gearing) because of the absence of high interest costs.
>
> However, despite making more actual £ profit after tax, the Return on Equity is *lower* than the highly geared company in Scenario 1 *because the profit has to be shared across a greater shareholding!*

3 Long term finance for the business – debt versus equity

> **EXAMPLE**
>
> ### Scenario Four: Low Gearing and Poor Performance
>
> **Ambitious Ltd issue an additional £90,000 of share capital and make a 7% ROCE**
>
> **Capital Structure**
>
> Equity Finance = £190,000
>
> Debt Finance = £10,000   *just £10,000 original borrowing*
>
> Total Capital Employed = £200,000
>
> Gearing = 5%   *Gearing = Debt / Total Capital Employed x 100%*
>
> **Profitability**
> Bottom half of Statement of Profit or Loss (starting at operating profit)
>
> | | | |
> |---|---|---|
> | Operating Profit | £14,000 | = £200,000 Capital Employed x 7% ROCE |
> | Less interest | (£1,000) | = 10% interest on £10,000 |
> | Profit before Tax | £13,000 | |
> | Less Tax | (£2,600) | = £13,000 PBT x 20% corporation tax |
> | Profit after Tax | £10,400 | |
>
> **Interest Cover**
>
> Interest cover   14 times   *= £14,000 / £1,000*
>
> **Return on Equity**
>
> Return on Equity   5.5%   *= £10,400 / £190,000 x 100%*

> **TUTORIAL NOTE**
>
> The poor performance only delivers £14,000 operating profit. However, unlike Scenario 2, they only have modest interest charges and hence most of this profit is passed down to the shareholders (after the corporation tax has been paid!). Despite the poor performance the interest costs are easily covered (14 times over) because the company has such low gearing. The final profit after tax figure of £10,400 is better than the poorly performing / highly geared company in Scenario 2 because of the lack of high interest charges, and despite having to share this profit out over a larger shareholding, the return on equity of 5.5% is still better than that achieved in the equivalent performing highly geared company in Scenario 2.

3.11 The impact of gearing

The preceding example of Ambitious Ltd can be summarised as follows:

Highly geared company with a strong performance

If a company borrows cash to invest in the company, and then makes a good return (ROCE) on this capital (which is *more than sufficient* to pay the interest costs) then the shareholders will benefit as a result.

The important point to appreciate is that the company has expanded and increased its profitability *without* the shareholders having to invest any more money themselves! So the additional final Profit after Tax can be shared amongst the same original number of shareholders. This means that the shareholders Return on Equity (ROE) will increase.

Highly geared company with a poor performance

If a company borrows cash to invest in the company, and then makes a poor return (ROCE) on this capital (*insufficient* to pay the interest costs) then the shareholders will lose out as a result.

The interest charges on the borrowing must be paid *regardless* of the company's performance. If the additional profit which results from the additional investment is barely sufficient to pay the interest costs of the borrowing, then the final Profit after Tax figure will be lower and the Return on Equity will fall

As seen, the same company could instead expand via the equity finance route by issuing more shares. This higher equity will result in the gearing going down.

Low geared company with a strong performance

If a company issues more shares, and then makes a good return (ROCE) on this capital then the company will benefit as a result. In fact (if all other factors are the same) a low geared company will make more profit than the high geared equivalent company because it has no additional interest costs!

However from the shareholders' perspective, it must be appreciated that this extra profit will then need to be shared between more shareholders so the actual Return on Equity (ROE) will be lower than for the (equivalent) highly geared company.

Low geared company with a poor performance

If a company issues more shares, and then makes a poor return (ROCE) on this capital then the shareholders will obviously lose out as a result. However because the company has not incurred any extra interest costs, they will not lose out as much as the (equivalent) poorly performing highly geared company.

We can now see where the name 'gearing' derives from. It is the concept of a relatively small equity base driving (and benefitting from) a proportionally bigger total capital base (whose larger size derives from borrowing) to allow higher levels of operating profit which will ultimately be enjoyed by the relatively small number of shareholders (once the interest charges are paid!). This additional borrowing will only benefit the shareholders (i.e. increase their Return on Equity) whilst the company's returns (ROCE) are higher than the cost of borrowing the funds.

In summary, a highly geared company consists of a smaller shareholding, driving a much bigger capital base (from taking on debt), in order to make more profit (even after paying debt interest) for the benefit of the smaller number of shareholders.

3 Long term finance for the business – debt versus equity

OVERVIEW

Gearing

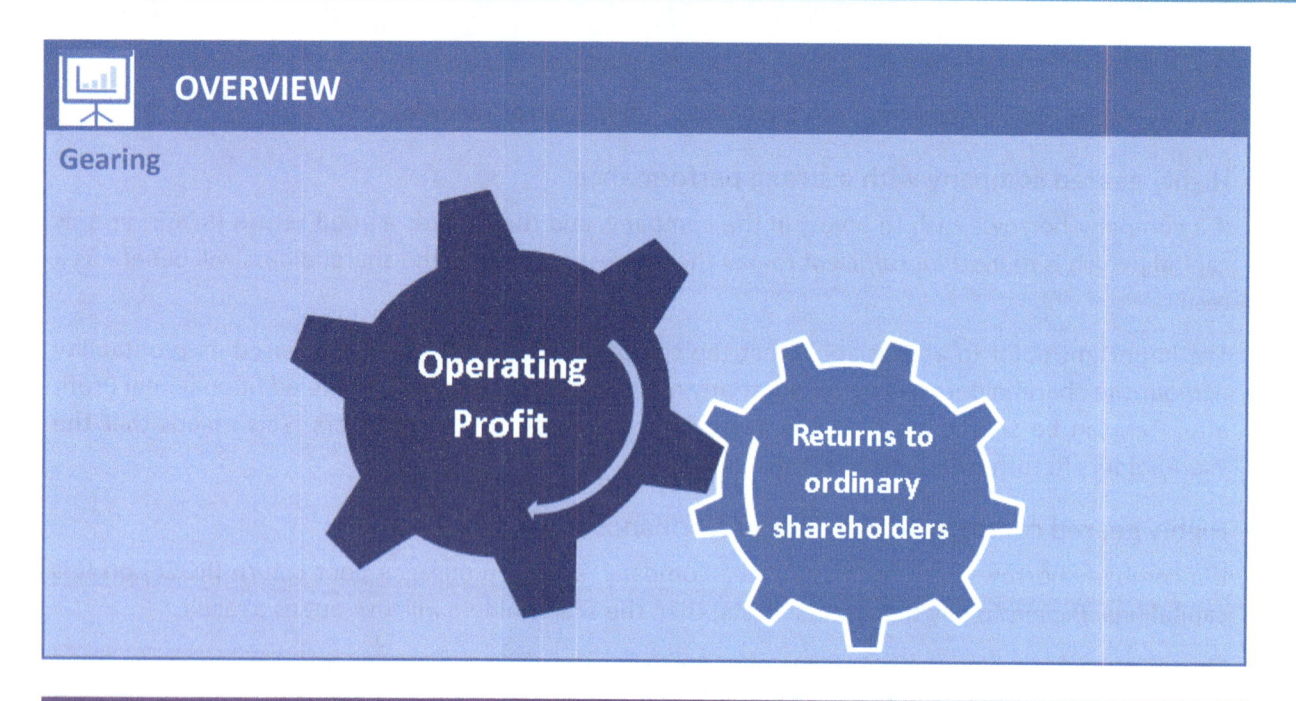

TEST YOUR UNDERSTANDING 4

Indicate whether each of the following statements is more typically applicable to debt financing ("D") or equity financing ("E")

Which type of finance …………..

- Results in a cost which must be paid regardless of profit performance _____

- Is typically permanent finance _____

- Represents a tax deductible cost _____

- Might be actioned via a 'Rights Issue' _____

- Can generally be raised more quickly _____

- Will increase 'gearing' _____

- Will not dilute existing shareholder's voting power _____

- Is typically for a fixed term _____

- Automatically arises from retaining profit _____

- Leads to the final profit being shared amongst more shareholders _____

- Delivers the highest Return on Equity (ROE) if the company performs well _____

- Delivers the lowest Return on Equity (ROE) if the company performs poorly _____

- Represents a higher potential risk to the company _____

3.12 'To gear or not to gear'... that is the question!

There is no point in raising more funds to invest in the company (either by issuing more shares or via debt) unless the company is certain that it can produce an increased net return as a result of that additional investment. In fact the whole question of whether *'to gear or not to gear'* largely depends on how much additional profit the company believes can be earned from the extra investment compared to the additional cost of that borrowing (i.e. interest payments).

If the additional borrowing is successfully invested in the company and produces a financial return which is *greater* than the cost of the debt (i.e. the interest payments) then the exercise will have been worthwhile and the existing shareholders will enjoy an increased return on *their existing* investment as a result of the increase in gearing.

However, if the investment of the additional borrowing in the company does not meet expectations and produces a financial return which is *less* than the cost of the debt (as the interest payments must be paid regardless) then the exercise will have been to the detriment of the existing shareholders who will see a decreased return on their existing investment as a result of the increase in gearing.

So long as the company Directors are confident that they can continue to borrow cash at a (say) 10% interest rate, invest it and make (say) 15% ROCE, then this will benefit the shareholders. In fact, whilst times are good, the higher the gearing, the higher the returns the shareholders will receive (without having to make any additional investment themselves).

Either way the shareholders have benefitted by the company taking on debt i.e. by increasing its gearing. The idea is that the shareholders are benefitting from the profit which has been achieved by borrowing cash…..instead of being asked to invest more themselves! Any movement in the large 'profit gear' has an amplified effect on the small 'shareholder-returns gear'.

So from the company's perspective is it best to raise new Capital Investment via Equity Finance or Debt Finance?

If the company is completely confident that it take on debt finance (i.e. it can borrow money) and make a **bigger** return on it than the cost of borrowing, then this will benefit the shareholders who will see an increase in the return they make on their [share] investment. In other words, under these circumstances the increase in gearing will actually *increase* the return to shareholders.

However if the returns are *less* than the cost of borrowing then the people who will be immediately affected are the shareholders themselves, since in these circumstances the increase in gearing will actually *decrease* the return to the shareholders.

So in order to answer the question of whether or not to take on debt (i.e. increase gearing) an honest assessment needs to be made of whether or not the anticipated returns from the extra capital are realistic or not…. factoring in all the unknowns of an uncertain future!

In the absence of a crystal ball no company director knows for sure what surprises the future will hold *(general economic downturn, failure of a major customer, increased competitor activity)* and it is therefore a high risk strategy to over-gear a company beyond a certain level (which will vary from one company and business sector to another).

The key point is that interest on debt finance must be paid regardless of company performance. Failure to pay interest when due could expose the company to legal action from the bank or other lender and place the company's future at risk. By comparison, the dividends which shareholders might hope to receive will depend entirely on the company's performance. If the company does not perform well and no (or low) dividends are paid the shareholders might be unhappy and the market value of the shares might fall as a result… but there will not be an *immediate* threat to the company since there was never an obligation to pay dividends in the first place!

Moreover debt must be ultimately repaid at the end of its 'term' and this involves valuable cash being taken out of the company, whereas shares do not need repaying as they are a permanent source of capital investment in the company *(at least they are permanent from the company's perspective, even if the individual shareholder* investor sells his/her shares onto a third party).

3.13 A potential lender's perspective on gearing

A bank or any other potential lender of funds will also look closely at the level of gearing a company already has, and how much further stretched it would be by lending it even more money.

We have already said that a bank's key aim is to be certain of receiving interest payments when due and eventual repayment of any loan made. It does not receive any direct additional benefit if a company has increased profitability, as it is the shareholders who will benefit from this.

So from the bank's perspective there is no 'upside' to high gearing ... it merely increases their risk if a company has large interest payment commitments and the bank's new loan is just one of many examples of debt that the company has to service.

The Language of Business

⚠ KEY POINTS FROM CHAPTER 3

- Both new companies and existing companies require long-term finance to allow them to invest in the assets they need to start or expand their business, and to fund various overheads as they wait for the subsequent anticipated profitability to come through.

- There are two major sources of long-term finance available to a company: equity finance and debt finance. When added together they give the total capital employed in that company.

    Total Capital Employed = Equity Finance + Debt Finance

- The equity finance comprises the original amount the company was paid when it first issued the shares (the 'share capital') plus any profits which the company has not paid out in dividends but has chosen to keep for reinvestment in the company (the 'retained profit').

    Equity = Share Capital + Retained Profits

    The sale and purchase of second-hand shares between one investor and another does not have any effect on the company's equity.

- The debt finance comprises any borrowing the company has made either by taking out bank loans, or any 'bonds' issued to the market (which are just a form of loan stock which can be traded).

- Equity and Debt are very different concepts. Equity is a share in the ownership of the company and therefore a share of the profits (if any). From the company's perspective it is a permanent investment (though individual investors can sell their shares to a 3rd party). In contrast, debt is a commercial loan in exchange for guaranteed interest payments regardless of the profitability of the company. Unlike equity, at some stage the debt will have to be repaid.

- If a company has an immediate need for more long-term funding it can try to issue more shares to existing shareholders (typically via a 'Rights Issue') or issue new shares to new investors (a 'Share Issue' via a stock market). However, these can be expensive and slow to administer. A quicker solution to raising finance is to simply borrow funds i.e. take on debt finance.

- The concept of gearing is used to describe what proportion of the company's total capital employed is derived from debt finance.

    $$\text{Gearing \%} = \frac{\text{Debt Finance (£)}}{\text{Debt Finance (£) + Equity Finance (£)}} \times 100\%$$

- The performance of a company is assessed by looking at how much return (measured by operating profit) it makes from its long term capital investment.

    $$\text{Return on Capital Employed (ROCE)} = \frac{\text{Operating Profit (£)}}{\text{Total Capital Employed (£)}} \times 100\%$$

- The benefit a shareholder receives from their investment is:

    $$\text{Return on Equity (ROE)} = \frac{\text{Profit after Tax (£)}}{\text{Equity (£)}} \times 100\%$$

- A company can increase its profitability by simply borrowing in order to expand the scale of its operations. If the ROCE it makes on the total capital is higher than the cost of debt then the shareholders will see an increase in their ROE

- However, if the ROCE it makes on the total capital is lower than the cost of debt then the shareholders will see a decrease to their ROE

3 Long term finance for the business – debt versus equity

- Highly geared companies (>50% gearing) might be considered high risk. If their performance suffers a downturn then the debt interest must still be paid, leaving little or nothing for the shareholders.
- A company with low gearing (<25%) could be accused of not optimising its shareholder returns if it had the potential to grow profits by expanding but chose not to do so to avoid debt!
- An existing or potential investor might welcome a degree of gearing as this might result in their shares producing bigger returns, as borrowed funds are used to 'gear up' the performance of the company without any further investment being required from the shareholders themselves.
- Conversely banks and other lenders would typically be wary of lending further to already highly geared companies as this indicates a higher level of risk for the lender. The bank might decline to lend … or increase their interest rate to compensate for the extra risk.
- Banks and other lenders often assess the lending risk by looking at the 'interest cover' of the company, as this indicates how 'stretched' a company is in terms of the interest payments it is obliged to make.

Interest Cover = $\dfrac{\text{Operating Profit}}{\text{Debt Interest}}$

Chapter 3: Test Your Understanding Answers

TEST YOUR UNDERSTANDING 1

How much does Halifax receive when Rachel first subscribes for the shares?   **£2,000**

How much money does Halifax receive when the shares are sold to Tony?   **None**

What administration must Halifax Ltd undertake when the shares are transferred from Rachel to Tony?

Halifax Ltd must update its register of shareholders so that it knows who is entitled to attend and vote at the Annual General Meeting (AGM) and who is entitled to Dividend payments.

TEST YOUR UNDERSTANDING 2

Which investor has the greater voting power & why?

Both investors own 10,000 shares and therefore both have 10,000 votes.

Which investor will receive the higher dividend & why?

Dividends are declared as a fixed amount (quoted in pence) per share … regardless of how much those shares were purchased for. So both investors will receive the same dividend.

TEST YOUR UNDERSTANDING 3

Theoretical current market value of each share?

£200,000 / 50,000 shares = £4 per share (i.e. 400p)

At what price will the new shares be offered?

£4 x 90% = £3.60 (i.e. 360p)

Additional finance raised from the 'Rights Issue'?

50,000 shares x ½ x £3.60 = £90,000

3 Long term finance for the business – debt versus equity

TEST YOUR UNDERSTANDING 4

Which type of finance ....

- Results in a cost which must be paid regardless of profit performance — **D**
- Is typically permanent finance — **E**
- Represents a tax deductible cost — **D**
- Might be actioned via a 'Rights Issue' — **E**
- Can generally be raised more quickly — **D**
- Will increase 'gearing' — **D**
- Will not dilute existing shareholder's voting power — **D**
- Is typically for a fixed term — **D**
- Automatically arises from retaining profit — **E**
- Leads to the final profit being shared amongst more shareholders — **E**
- Delivers the highest Return on Equity (ROE) if the company performs well — **D**
- Delivers the lowest Return on Equity (ROE) if the company performs poorly — **D**
- Represents a higher potential risk to the company — **D**

Chapter 3: End of Chapter Exercises

Section A Questions

Question 3.1
Which of the following represent long-term sources of finance to a business?

i   Bank overdraft facilities

ii   Cash received from shareholders subscribing for new shares

iii   Retained Profit

iv   Supplier credit terms on purchases

Choose the correct answer from the options provided:

A   i and iii

B   ii and iv

C   ii and iii

D   iii and iv

Question 3.2
Which of the following is a shareholder <u>not</u> automatically entitled to?

A   The right to attend the company's Annual General Meeting

B   The right to attend the company's Board Meetings

C   The right to a share of any declared dividend

D   The right to vote on re-appointment of the Directors

Question 3.3
A company wishes to raise £100,000 of additional equity finance via a 1 for 2 Rights Issue. It has 100,000 £1 (nominal value) shares issued. Assuming an 80% take-up of the rights issue, at what price must the new shares be offered?

A   £0.625

B   £1.00

C   £2.00

D   £2.50

3 Long term finance for the business – debt versus equity

Question 3.4

A corporate bond is decribed as a *"£100 2030 5% bond"*.

Which one of the following statements is **not** true?

A   The bond will pay an additional 5% terminal bonus when redeemed in 2030

B   The bond will be redeemed for £100 in the year 2030

C   The bond will pay 5% interest on its nominal £100 value each year.

D   The bond may be sold to a new investor for more or less than its nominal £100 value

Question 3.5

A company's statement of financial position reports it as having:-

- 50,000 issued £0.50 shares
- £220,000 of retained profit
- A £50,000 10 year bank loan
- A £5,000 overdraft

What is the gearing of the company?

A   17%

B   19%

C   20%

D   22%

Question 3.6

Which of the following statements about debt finance are correct?

i   At some point debt finance must be repaid

ii   If a company makes larger than expected profits it should pay more interest on debt

iii If a company makes a loss then it may withhold debt interest payments

iv   Debt interest payments are tax deductible for corporation tax purposes

Choose the correct combination of statements:

A   i and iii

B   i and iv

C   ii and iii

D   iii and iv

The following information relates to questions 3.7 & 3.8:

A company's statement of financial position shows that it has £500,000 of equity and £200,000 of long-term debt, whilst its statement of profit or loss reports an operating profit (PBIT) of £56,000 and a profit after tax (PAT) of £30,000.

Question 3.7
What is the company's Return on Capital Employed (ROCE)?

A   4%

B   8%

C   11%

D   28%

Question 3.8
What is the company's Return on Equity (ROE)?

A   4%

B   6%

C   11%

D   15%

Question 3.9
Which of the following statements about low geared companies is **not** true?

A   Gearing of below 20% would usually be regarded as relatively low

B   Low geared companies are usually regarded as being lower risk

C   A poorly performing low geared company will probably deliver a higher return on equity than a correspondingly poor peforming more highly geared company

D   A low geared poorly performing company might have lower interest payment commitments, but will still be committed to pay a certain level of dividends to its shareholders

Question 3.10
Which of the following statements about high geared companies is **not** true?

A   Gearing of above 50% would usually be regarded as relatively high

B   High geared companies are usually regarded as being higher risk

C   A strongly performing highly geared compnay will probably deliver a higher return on equity than a correspondingly strong performing more lowly geared company

D   Increasing gearing dilutes the ownership of existing shareholders

3 Long term finance for the business – debt versus equity

Section B Questions

Question 3.11

Complete the following summary of Long Term Finance using the words from the following list (some words are used more than once) :

directors	debt finance	loan interest	ROCE
rights issue	equity finance	shareholders	ownership
permanent	non-current assets	higher	working capital
geared	share capital	lower	total capital employed

Sources of Long Term Finance

If a business wishes to expand its operations it will often need to raise additional long term finance. This additional capital may be used to invest in additional _____ (e.g. land & buildings, plant & machinery etc.) and/or to fund increased _____ (e.g. cash, inventory, receivables etc.). The two alternative sources of long term finance for a business are _____ (e.g. bank loans or issuing corporate bonds) or _____ (comprising of both share capital and retained profits).

The sum of both of these sources of long term finance is known as the Total Capital Employed, hence: **Total Capital Employed = Equity Finance + Debt Finance**. The greater the proportion of the total capital employed that comes from debt finance, the more highly _____ the business is said to be. The level of borrowing a business take on can be expressed in percentage terms, by dividing the level of _____, by the _____ and expressing the answer as a percentage i.e. **Gearing% = Debt Finance / Total Capital Employed x 100%**

Of the two alternatives equity finance is _____ risk and normally involves issuing additional _____. Bringing new shareholders into a business can dilute the ownership of existing shareholders and for this reason a company will often choose to offer new shares via a _____ where existing shareholders are offered the opportunity to buy new shares and hence maintain their percentage _____ of the company. Although shareholders may have the expectation of regular dividends, these are not guaranteed, but are at the discretion of the _____ of the company. If the company has a poor year then low (or even possibly no) dividend payments will be made.

In contrast, debt finance is considered to be _____ risk because regardless of the company's performance _____ payments must be made. If a business borrows to fund a planned expansion and then delivers a lower _____ on that expansion than the cost of the _____, then the business will suffer reduced profitability and the _____ will lose out as a result. Conversely, if the planned expansion performed well (and more than covered the cost of the borrowing) then the company will increase its profitability. This will have benefitted the shareholders without them having had to invest any additional funds into the business!

When increasing the gearing of a company it must always be remembered that regardless of the business's performance the _____ payments must always be made, and ultimately the _____ will need to be repaid to the original lender. In contrast equity finance is typically more _____ in nature as once issued, companies do not typically redeem (i.e. 'buy back') shares from shareholders.

Question 3.12

Omega Ltd: Statement of Financial Position as at 31st December 2018

Non-Current Assets		
Land & Buildings	£100,000	
Plant & Machinery	£50,000	
		£150,000
Current Assets		
Inventory	£15,000	
Receivables	£25,000	
Cash	£10,000	
		£50,000
TOTAL ASSETS		**£200,000**
Equity		
Share Capital	£50,000	
Retained Profit	£100,000	
		£150,000
Non-Current Liabilities		
10% Corporate Bond (repayable 2025)	£20,000	
		£20,000 *Debt*
Current Liabilities		
Payables	£20,000	
Tax Liability	£10,000	
		£30,000
TOTAL EQUITY & LIABILITIES		**£200,000**

3. Long term finance for the business – debt versus equity

What is the shareholder's total investment (equity finance)? _____

What is the level of debt finance? _____

What is the Total Capital Employed (long-term debt + equity)? _____

What is the level of gearing? *(=Debt / Total Capital Employed x 100%)* _____

What is the current annual cost of Omega's debt finance? _____

Omega Ltd: Statement of Profit or Loss. Year Ending 31st December 2018

Complete the Omega's SOPL to find the Profit after Tax

Sales Income	£100,000
Cost of sales	(£30,000)
Gross Profit	£70,000
Selling & Distribution	(£20,000)
Administration	(£24,500)
Operating Profit (PBIT)	£25,500
Finance Costs (purely comprises of 10% corporate bond)	(£2,000)
Profit before Tax (PBT)	£23,500
Taxation (assume 20% of PBT)	£4700
Profit after Tax	£18,500

The Language of Business

For Year Ending 31/12/18 evaluate the Omega's overall performance by calculating its Return on Capital Employed (ROCE); and evaluate the returns the shareholders have enjoyed by calculating its Return on Equity (ROE):

Omega's Return on Capital Employed

Total capital employed   180,000

Operating Profit   25,500

ROCE   14.16%

Omega's Return on Equity

Total Equity   150,000

Profit after Tax   18,800

ROE   12.53%

The Board of Omega Ltd believe that with additional £100,000 long-term investment they could 'scale' up their operation and profits. The additional investment could be achieved either:

a) By borrowing an additional £100,000 at an interest cost of 10% (in addition to their existing £20,000 borrowing)

.... or

b) By issuing £100,000 more share capital (and just retaining the existing £20,000 borrowing)

In order to make an informed decision as whether Omega should expand via debt finance or equity finance you are required to explore what would happen in both scenarios (additional borrowing and additional share capital) if:

a) Omega maintained a strong performance with a ROCE of 15%

b) Omega suffered a downturn in its performance with a ROCE of 5%

In particular we are trying to examine the two options from the perspective of **existing** shareholders. Would they rather their company borrow money to expand, or would they rather their company issue more shares which will possibly lead to a dilution of their existing ownership (and hence any future profit having to be shared between more shareholders).

We therefore need to need to calculate FOUR different Returns on Equity (ROE), as follows:

Scenario A - High Gearing

1) Omega borrows an additional £100,000 at a cost of 10% and delivers a 15% ROCE

2) Omega borrows an additional £100,000 at a cost of 10% but delivers a 5% ROCE

Scenario B – Lower Gearing

3) Omega issues £100,000 additional share capital and delivers a 15% ROCE

4) Omega issues £100,000 additional share capital but delivers a 5% ROCE

We know that ......   **ROCE = Operating Profit / Total Capital Employed**

So if we know the Total Capital Employed .... and we know the ROCE (i.e. the return the company is making on that capital) ...... then we can re-arrange the equation to estimate the Operating Profit they will make:

Operating Profit = Total Capital Employed x ROCE

3 Long term finance for the business – debt versus equity

Scenario A: Additional £100,000 of 10% Debt Finance (Higher Gearing)

Omega's New Capital Structure

- Equity: £150,000
- Debt: £120,000
- Total Capital: £270,000
- Gearing {=D/(D+E)}: 44%

1) **Assuming Omega make 15% ROCE**

   Complete the statement of profit or loss starting from Operating Profit

   (Remember ….. Operating Profit = Capital Employed x ROCE)

Operating Profit (PBIT)	£40,500
Finance Costs (£120,000 @ 10%)	£12,000
Profit before Tax (PBT)	£28,500
Taxation (assume 20% of PBT)	5,700
Profit after Tax (PAT)	22,800

   What will Omega's ROE now be?
   (ROE = PAT / EQUITY x 100%) — 15.2%

2) **Assuming Omega make 5% ROCE**

   Complete the statement of profit or loss starting from Operating Profit

   (Remember ….. Operating Profit = Capital Employed x ROCE)

Operating Profit (PBIT)	£13,500
Finance Costs (£120,000 @ 10%)	£12,000
Profit before Tax (PBT)	£1,500
Taxation (assume 20% of PBT)	£300
Profit after Tax (PAT)	£1,200

   What will Omega's ROE now be?
   (ROE = PAT / EQUITY x 100%) — 0.8%

The Language of Business

Scenario B: Additional £100,000 of Share Capital (Lower Gearing)

Omega's New Capital Structure

Equity	250,000
Debt	20,000
Total Capital	270,000
Gearing {=D/(D+E)}	7.4%

3) Assuming Omega make **15% ROCE**

   Complete the statement of profit or loss starting from Operating Profit
   (Remember ..... Operating Profit = Capital Employed x ROCE)

Operating Profit (PBIT)	£40,500
Finance Costs (£20,000 @ 10%)	2,000
Profit before Tax (PBT)	38,500
Taxation (assume 20% of PBT)	7,700
Profit after Tax (PAT)	30,800
What will Omega's ROE now be? (ROE = PAT / EQUITY x 100%)	12.32%

4) Assuming Omega make **5% ROCE**

   Complete the statement of profit or loss starting from Operating Profit
   (Remember ..... Operating Profit = Capital Employed x ROCE)

Operating Profit (PBIT)	£13,500
Finance Costs (£20,000 @ 10%)	2,000
Profit before Tax (PBT)	11,500
Taxation (assume 20% of PBT)	2,300
Profit after Tax (PAT)	9,200
What will Omega's ROE now be? (ROE = PAT / EQUITY x 100%)	3.68%

3. Long term finance for the business – debt versus equity

Summarise your findings from each scenario by summarising the previously calculated Returns on Equity for each of the four scenarios:

Return on Equity %	Higher Gearing	Lower Gearing
Weaker Performance	0.8 %	3.68 %
Stronger Performance	15.2 %	12.32 %

If Omega Ltd deliver a strong performance (15% ROCE) which gearing scenario *(lower gearing or higher gearing)* delivers more Profit after Tax and why?

If Omega Ltd deliver a strong performance (15% ROCE) which gearing scenario *(lower gearing or higher gearing)* delivers a higher Return on Equity for the Shareholders and why?

Explain the apparent discrepancy between the two answers above

If you were an Omega shareholder and were fairly confident that the company could deliver a high ROCE would you want the company to increase its gearing? Explain you reasoning.

If you were an Omega shareholder and were less confident that the company could deliver a high ROCE would you want the company to increase its gearing? Explain you reasoning.

The Language of Business

Question 3.13 *Exam*

Surrey Ltd arranges a £500,000 bank loan to fund an expansion programme. The bank loan has a 10 year term, and is at an 8% per annum fixed rate of interest. The principal sum is to be repaid in 40 equal quarterly payments (each being payable on the last day of each quarter). The interest is also payable on the last day of each quarter, and is calculated on the outstanding capital balance during the preceding quarter.

Complete the table below to show the quarterly capital repayment and interest payments for the first two years.

Quarter	Opening Balance	Capital Repayment	Closing Balance	Interest Payment
1	£500,000	12,500	£487,000	10,000
2	487,000		475,000	9,750
3	475,000		462,500	9,500
4	462,500		450,000	9,250
5	450,000		437,500	9,000
6	437,500		425,000	8,750
7	425,000		412,500	8,500
8	412,500		400,000	8,250

Should each quarter's capital repayment appear on the Statement of Profit or Loss *i.e. is it an expense?*

_____

Should each quarter's interest payment appear on the Statement of Profit or *Loss i.e. is it an expense?*

_____

Should each quarter's capital repayment appear on the Statement of Cashflows *i.e. does it represent a cash outflow from the business?*

_____

Should each quarter's interest payment appear on the Statement of Cashflows *i.e. does it represent a cash outflow from the business?*

_____

3 Long term finance for the business – debt versus equity

Question 3.14

A company wishing to rapidly expand their business has the choice between: borrowing additional funds (Debt Finance, which leads to higher gearing), or issuing additional shares (Equity Finance, which results in lower gearing).

What would be the key differences between these two alternatives?

	Debt Finance	Equity Finance
Nature of the investor's returns Are the investor returns simply interest on a commercial loan, or are they a share of the company profits (i.e. dividends)?		
What determines the level of the returns investors enjoy? Are they a pre-determined rate of interest, or discretionary dividends set by the Directors?		
Potential tax relief on the cost of the finance Can the company claim tax relief on loan interest and/or dividend payments?		
Duration of the Finance Is the finance for a pre-defined fixed period of time, or is it a potentially permanent source of finance?		
Perceived Risk Which form of finance might a prospective investor regard as being higher risk?		

Chapter 4

Pricing and profitability

INTRODUCTION

Your study of marketing will have covered alternative pricing strategies and we start by quickly recapping these. This leads us onto the perpetual quandary that **as we increase prices we typically decrease demand** … but by how much?

We then look at how to **assess profitability** at different price levels by introducing the concepts of **'mark-up'** and **'margin'**.

Finally most businesses are required to add VAT to their selling prices, and so we will learn how to **calculate VAT** inclusive prices.

OVERVIEW AND OBJECTIVES

By the end of this chapter you should be able to:

- describe and assess different pricing strategies
- calculate profitability
- understand the concept of Price Elasticity of Demand
- understand how Value Added Tax (VAT) is calculated and applied

and be able to answer questions relating to these areas.

4 Pricing and profitability

4.1 Sales volume, selling price and sales revenue

The 'Marketing Mix' aims to identify the key elements for the successful marketing of a product or service and is often summarised by the 4 P's:

- Product
- Place
- Promotion
- Price

In this chapter we will explore the 'Price' element and in particular the link between price and profitability.

> **DEFINITIONS**
>
> **Sales Volume:** refers to the number of units of a particular product which have been sold
>
> e.g. 42 electronic tablets were sold during November.
>
> **Selling Price:** refers to the price that each individual unit was sold for
>
> e.g. each electronic tablet was sold for £288.
>
> **Sales Revenue (aka 'Sales Value' or just 'Sales'):** the total sales amount for all of the units sold
>
> e.g. the total sales revenue for the sale of electronic tablets during November was £12,096.
>
> This is very simply calculated from the equation below:
>
> **Sales Revenue = Sales Volume x Selling Price**
>
> i.e. 42 x £288 = £12,096

It is not uncommon for the selling price of the same item to vary for a whole range of reasons such as:

- Change in purchase or manufacturing cost
- General annual price increase
- Promotional price to encourage sales
- Discount given to a valued customer or for a large order.

> **EXAMPLE**
>
> During July twelve lawnmowers were sold for a total of £912.
>
> Some were sold at full list price whilst others were discounted.
>
> The average selling price was £912 / 12 = £76.

4.2 Different pricing strategies

OVERVIEW

- Penetration Pricing
- Price Skimming
- Competitive Pricing
- Cost Plus Pricing
- **PRICING STRATEGIES**
- Bundle Pricing
- Psychological Pricing
- Premium Pricing
- Optional Pricing

DEFINITIONS

Many different pricing strategies exist. Those included in the diagram are defined here:

Penetration Pricing: Initially setting a low price to gain a foothold in an established market.

Price Skimming: Initially setting a high price for a newly launched product in the belief that keen / loyal consumers are willing to pay a higher price to access the new product.

Competitive Pricing: Basing selling prices on what the competition are selling similar products or services for.

Bundle Pricing: Selling several products together as part of an attractively priced sales package.

Optional Pricing: Encouraging consumers to purchase optional extras together with their main purchase by offering attractive prices

Premium Pricing: Selling at an artificially high price to convey the impression of a premium product.

Psychological Pricing: To convey the impression of a lower price e.g. £1.99 instead of £2.00

Cost Plus Pricing: Setting selling prices by first calculating the base cost of a product or service, and then adding the required profit margin.

4.3 Effects of pricing strategies

One of the biggest competitive 'tools' a company has at its disposal is the ability to alter its selling prices and hence immediately change its competitive offering. Unfortunately what is often *not* appreciated is how many other factors are then also affected by pricing strategy, as shown in the diagram on the following page.

4 Pricing and profitability

OVERVIEW

Pricing strategy can affect...
- Staff costs
- Sales revenue (£)
- Gross profit
- Infrastructure costs
- Market share (%)
- Sales volume (units)

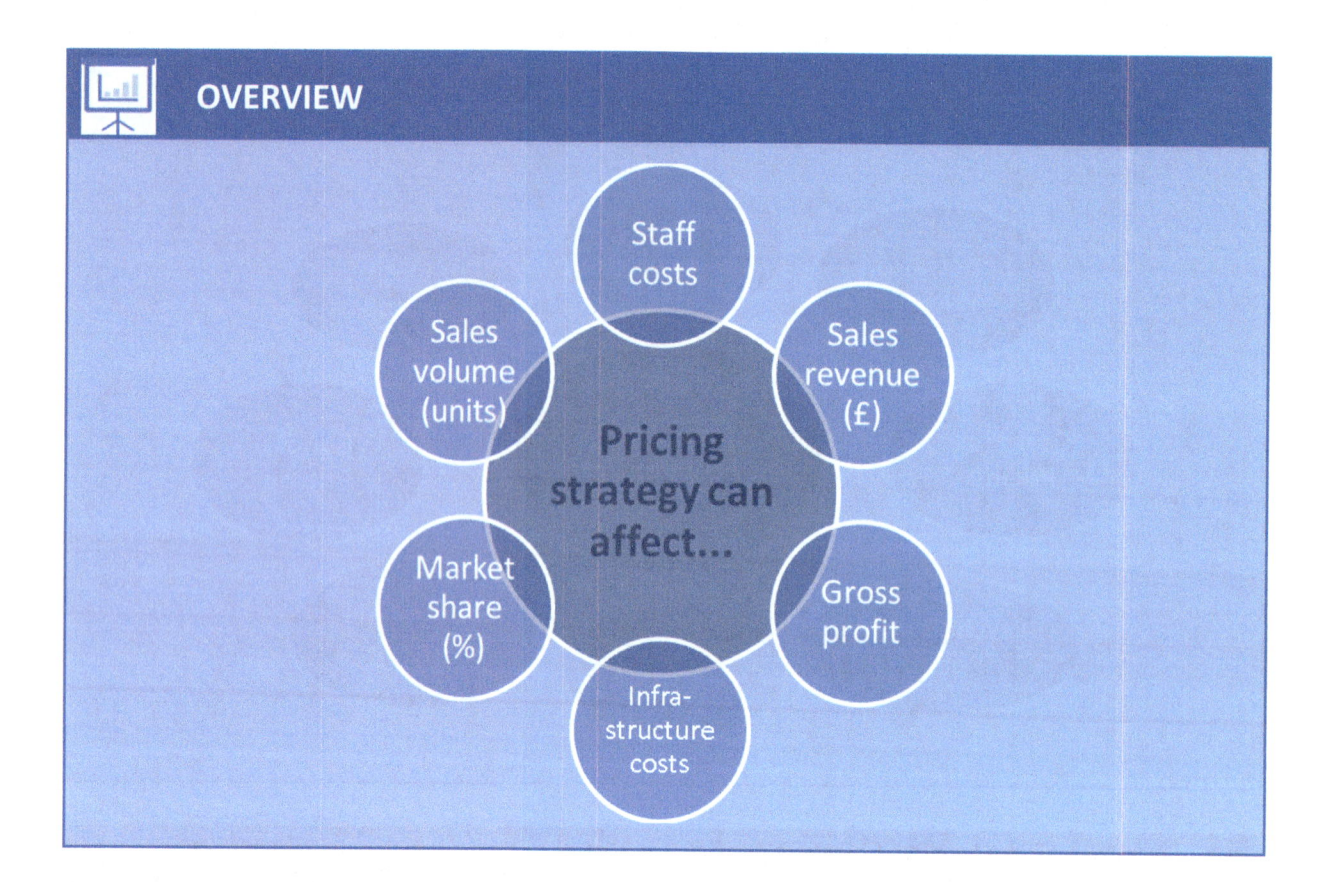

EXAMPLE

A **decrease** in selling price will have the following potential effects:

Sales Volume: Decreasing the selling price tends to *increase* the sales volume.

Sales Revenue: A decrease in selling price will have the *immediate* effect of decreasing sales revenue (after all less is being received for each item sold)..... unless a corresponding increase in sales volume compensates for this.

Market Share (%): Market share is usually calculated by comparing sales revenues to the size of the entire market (though sales volumes can also be used if the data is available) and what happens to sales revenue (see above) will also determine the change (down or up) in market share.

Gross Profit (£): A decrease in selling price will result in less Gross Profit (£) *per unit* being made. However the question then is whether any increase in the sales volume will more than compensate for this in terms of the *total* Gross Profit made.

Gross Profit (%): A decrease in selling price will always reduce the Gross Profit (%).

Infrastructure Costs: If a decrease in price leads to a significantly higher sales volume, then this might in turn lead to an increase in infrastructure costs as larger premises etc. are required to handle the increased sales demand.

Staff Costs: Similarly if a decrease in price led to a significantly higher sales volume then this might also lead to an increase in staff costs as more people are required to handle the increased sales demand.

Whilst in general increasing selling prices will have the opposite effects.

4.4 Profitability calculations

At this stage we shall assume that every product or service has a simple cost which can be used to calculate profitability. In later chapters we will then consider alternative ways of costing products, and what happens when costs vary, but for now we will assume that all products have a simple cost which remains constant!

We will repeatedly use the concept of gross profit:

sometimes in relation to selling one item:

Gross Profit (for one item) = Selling Price (of one item) – Cost (of one item)

and sometimes as a total for the sale of multiple items …

Gross Profit (for all items) = Sales Revenue (for all items) – Cost (of all items)

… which is not really any different to how gross profit was calculated on a statement of profit or loss for *all* sales revenue for the *whole* accounting period.

> ⚠️ **KEY POINT**
>
> The above equations can be quickly re-arranged depending on whether we are trying to calculate: Gross Profit, Selling Price or Cost.
>
> The formulae are so close that we only need to remember one version, and then re-arrange it when required:
>
> **Gross Profit (£) = Selling Price (£) – Cost (£)**
>
> **Selling Price (£) = Cost (£) + Gross Profit (£)**
>
> **Cost (£) = Selling Price (£) – Gross Profit (£)**

The fact that all of the terms above are monetary terms has been emphasised by the use of the £ symbol. We will now start to consider percentage profitability and it is important for us to distinguish between Gross Profit (£) and Gross Profit (%).

It is very common to quote the level of profitability in percentage terms and there are two different ways of stating percentage profitability: Gross Profit % or Mark Up %.

Gross Profit % (aka GP %)

$$\text{Gross Profit (\%)} = \frac{\text{Gross Profit (£)}}{\text{Selling Price (£)}} \times 100\%$$

With Gross Profit % the monetary gross profit figure is expressed as a percentage of the **selling price** *i.e. the selling price represents 100%.*

Mark Up % (aka MU %)

$$\text{Mark Up (\%)} = \frac{\text{Gross Profit (£)}}{\text{Cost (£)}} \times 100\%$$

With Mark Up % the monetary gross profit figure is expressed as a percentage of the **cost** *i.e. the cost represents 100%.*

4 Pricing and profitability

TUTORIAL NOTE

Both 'Gross Profit %' and 'Mark Up %' use the **same** Gross Profit (£) figure. The difference is how that is then expressed as a percentage:

- **Gross Profit %** → Expressed as a percentage of the *selling price*

    and so the selling price = 100%

- **Mark Up %** → Expressed as a percentage of the *cost price*

    and so the cost price = 100%

From these simple equations we can solve a whole range of day to day pricing and profitability queries, albeit a bit of re-arranging and 'detective work' might be needed as can be seen from the following examples.

EXAMPLES

Scenario 1

A product costs £1.35 to manufacture and it sells for £3.95.

What gross profit (£) and gross profit (%) is made?

Answer:

Gross profit (£) = Selling Price (£) – Cost (£) = £3.95 - £1.35 = **£2.60**
Gross Profit (%) = Gross Profit (£) / Selling Price x100% = £2.60 / £3.95 x100% = **65.8%**

Scenario 2

A product costs £160 and a 70% mark-up is required.

What price will the product sell for and how much gross profit (£) will it achieve?

Answer:

When dealing with Mark Up % we know that the cost represents 100%, so
Selling Price (%) = Cost Price (100%) + Mark-Up (70%) = 170% (i.e. 1.7)
Selling Price (£) = £160 x 1.7 = **£272**
Gross Profit (£) = Selling Price (£) – Cost Price (£) = £272 - £160 = **£112**

Scenario 3

Market research suggests that a new product should be sold for £28 and a minimum 65% GP% is required.

What is the maximum cost for this product to ensure that the target GP% is achieved?

Answer:

The question quotes GP% so the selling price is 100%. If the GP% is 65% the cost % must be 35%.
i.e. Selling Price (100%) = Cost Price (35%) + Gross profit (65%)
A useful intermediate step is often to find 1% and work from there.
In this case we know that 100% = £28, so 1% = £28/100 = £0.28.
The maximum cost is 35% i.e. 35 x £0.28 = **£9.80**
Check: GP (£) = £28 - £9.80 = £18.20; GP% = £18.20/£28 x 100% = 65%.

The Language of Business

> ## TEST YOUR UNDERSTANDING 1
>
> When we use Gross Profit % we are simply expressing how much profit is required *as a percentage of the Selling Price* i.e. we regard the Selling Price as representing 100%.
>
> **Product A:** Costs £4.27 and sells for £12.50. What Gross Profit (%) is achieved?
>
> _____
>
> **Product B:** Costs £25.69. What selling price is required to achieve 57% Gross Profit?
>
> _____
>
> **Product C:** Sells for £110.60 and achieves 43% Gross Profit. How much does it cost?
>
> _____
>
> When we use Mark Up % we are simply expressing how much profit is required *as a percentage of the Cost Price* i.e. we regard the Cost Price as representing 100%.
>
> **Product D:** Costs £9.60 and has a 100% mark-up. What price is the product sold for?
>
> _____
>
> **Product E:** Sells for £120 after a 50% mark-up. What is the cost of the Product?
>
> _____
>
> **Product F:** Costs £4.50 and sells for £10.00. What Mark-Up % is achieved?
>
> _____

4.5 Price Elasticity of Demand

Intuitively we would expect …

- the sales demand for a product to decrease if its selling price was increased …

and conversely….

- the sales demand for a product to increase if its selling price was decreased

…. and this is usually borne out in practice.

However the question is then by *how much* will sales demand change compared to a change in selling price. In other words how price sensitive is the sales demand?

4 Pricing and profitability

The **Price Elasticity of Demand (PED)** measures the responsiveness of demand after a change in price, thus:

Price Elasticity of Demand = % Change in Demand / % Change in Price

Since changes and price usually move in opposite directions we do not need to include the minus sign

The PED is a pure number (i.e. has no units) and its value indicates how sensitive that product's sales demand is to changes in price, as follows:

- Intuitively it might be expected that (say) a 5% increase in price would lead to a 5% fall in sales demand, and if this was indeed the case then **PED = 1** and we would describe it as **'unit elastic'**
- If the % change in demand is greater than the % change in price then the **PED >1** and we describe the demand as being **'elastic'** i.e. the demand is sensitive to a change in price
- If the % change in demand is less than the % change in price then the **PED <1** and we describe the demand as being **'inelastic'** i.e. the demand is not very sensitive to a change in price
- If the demand does not change at all when the price changes (rare!) then **PED=0** and we describe the demand as being **perfectly inelastic**.

Having used test data to establish what the PED for a certain product is, this could then in theory be used to predict what the effect on sales will be of future proposed price changes.

However it must be emphasised that Price Elasticity of Demand is nothing more than an economic model which helps us to understand and categorise the behaviour of products to price changes. It is not an infallible method of sales forecasting, but it might help a business to understand its products and markets a little better.

> ### EXAMPLE
>
> A petrol station increased the price of petrol from £1.00 to £1.02 and found that their daily sales of petrol fell from 5,000 litres to 4,700 litres.
>
> **What is the PED of petrol?**
>
> *% Change in demand = 300 / 5,000 x 100% = 6%*
>
> *% Change in Price = £0.02 / £1.00 x 100% = 2%*
>
> ***PED** = % Change in Demand / % Change in Price = 6% / 2% = 3*
>
> The change in demand is three times as great as the change in price, so petrol appears to be very price sensitive i.e. it has an elastic demand. For every 1% change in price (up or down) we would expect an opposing 3% change in sales. This should make the petrol retailer very wary of increasing prices, but perhaps curious to carry out some sales volume versus gross profit forecasts based on a potential lowering of their prices.

4.6 Factors affecting Price Elasticity of Demand

There are a number of potential reasons why a product might display elastic or inelastic behaviour:

Close Substitutes

If a product has close substitutes such that customers can easily switch to an alternative product (such as the petrol example above) then the more elastic demand will be.

High Switching Costs

If changing to an alternative product would involve incurring high switching costs then the customer would be more likely to simply accept a price increase and stick with the original product. i.e. tends to exhibit inelastic demand.

Prestige Brands

The sales of sought after brands are more resilient to price increase i.e. tend to be inelastic. If someone really wants a Rolex watch they probably won't be put off by a price increase!

Peak Time Demand

Goods and services which are in high demand in peak season or the peak time of day (e.g. train tickets at rush hour) can withstand higher prices i.e. tends to exhibit inelastic demand.

Off Peak Demand

When the demand is naturally lower in off-peak times, customers will tend to be even more resistant to price increases ... because they have the option of making alternative arrangements (e.g. catching a later cheaper train) i.e. tends to exhibit elastic demand.

Luxury Goods

Goods which customers do not absolutely need to buy are discretionary purchases (e.g. Cola) and the customer has the option of simply not buying them if the price is perceived as being too high i.e. tends to exhibit elastic demand.

Necessity Goods

Goods which customers do in fact really need (e.g. milk) will still be purchased even if the price increases i.e. tends to exhibit inelastic demands.

4 Pricing and profitability

TEST YOUR UNDERSTANDING 2

Price Elasticity of Demand = % Change in Demand / % Change in Price

a) A supermarket drops the price of its 'own brand' cola from £1.20 per litre to £1.00, and weekly sales increase from 500 litres to 800 litres

   Calculate & comment on the Price Elasticity of Demand.

b) 'Ditsy & Gullible' is a well-known manufacturer of Italian designer handbags who sold 2,500 handbags per month at £575 each. They decided to increase the price to £595 each and the monthly sales dropped to 2,495 hand bags per month.

   Calculate & comment on the Price Elasticity of Demand.

c) A petrol station sold petrol for £1.20 and enjoyed sales of 100,000 litres per month. However the owner of the petrol station was not satisfied with the very low gross profit margin he was achieving and so decided to increase his selling price to £1.25. Petrol sales then fell to 91,000 litres per month.

   Calculate & comment on the Price Elasticity of Demand.

4.7 Discounting and profitability

Every business should have a good understanding of the market they operate in and this includes an understanding of the general PED behaviour of their products (or better still, exact PED calculations based on empirical evidence). However before an over-zealous sales person starts heavy discounting they should first look at the potential profitability effects of their proposals.

Increasing sales is quite easy - you simply reduce your prices and more people buy your products. The harder challenge is to increase profitability as it is the 'bottom line' which should be of interest to those in business. This is best illustrated with an example.

EXAMPLE

Scenario

The manager of a city centre bar is keen to take a bigger slice of the Friday night 'circuit' trade and knows that drinks sales are quite 'elastic' i.e. if he reduced selling prices by a certain percentage, then the sales volume will increase by an even larger percentage.

Currently the bar sells 1,000 drinks on a Friday night (average £3 selling price each) and makes a 60% gross profit margin on them. The Manager introduces a Buy One Get One Free (BOGOF) offer and is delighted that sales volume of the bar immediately triples!

Has the Manager hit on a really smart promotion or are they actually damaging their business?

Solution

Pre-BOGOF Performance

Sales Revenue = 1,000 drinks @ £3 each = £3,000

Gross Profit = £3,000 x 60% = **£1,800**

Just to help understand this, remember that before the BOGOF promotion the drinks make 60% gross profit when they were sold at £3 each.

That is for one average drink:

- Sales Revenue = £3.00 each
- Gross Profit = £1.80 each (60% of sales revenue)
- Cost = £1.20 each (40% of sales revenue)

Post-BOGOF Performance

Sales Revenue = 3,000 / 2 x £3.00 = £4,500

(1,500 drinks sold + 1,500 'free' drinks = 3,000 drinks)

Total Cost = 3,000 x £1.20 = £3,600

Gross Profit = £4,500 - £3,600 = **£900**

So despite the number of drinks being sold tripling as a result of the promotion (elastic demand) the gross profit achieved has halved... and that is even before the cost of employing bar staff to handle the increased level of sales is taken into account.

4 Pricing and profitability

> **TUTORIAL NOTE**
>
> It's an old adage but nonetheless remains true that
>
> *"Sales are Vanity .... Profit is Sanity!"*
>
> Businesses should always sense check what effect discounting and promotions might have on their bottom line profitability rather than waiting until after the event to see what actually happened.

TEST YOUR UNDERSTANDING 3

A company sells the single product it manufactures (the *'z-gadget'*) to a range of retailers. The standard wholesale selling price (i.e. price to the retailers) for the z-gadget is £200 and at this price it makes 75% gross profit.

The company employs two sales representatives (*'Prudence'* and *'Reckless Eric'*) who are both allowed to negotiate whatever discounts they believe are required to secure sales contracts within their own sales territory.

Both sale representatives have exactly the same number of potential customers of equal size within their respective territories, so both have an equal opportunity to generate business.

Over the course of 2017 'Prudence sells' 1,000 z-gadgets for a total sales value of £190,000; whilst 'Reckless Eric' sells 1,150 z-gadgets for a total sales value of £195,500.

What is the cost of the z-gadget? _____

2017 Performance	Prudence	Reckless Eric
Sales Revenue (£)	_____	_____
Sales Volume	_____	_____
Average Selling Price (£)	_____	_____
Average Discount (%)	_____	_____
Total Cost (£)	_____	_____
Gross Profit (£)	_____	_____
Gross Profit (%)	_____	_____

Which sales representative is providing the most benefit to their company?

4.8 VAT registration and VAT returns

VAT was introduced in 1973 when the UK first entered the European Union. Unfortunately since it raises approximately £100 billion of revenue for the UK government each year it will no doubt remain even after the UK leaves the European Union!

Once a business's 'taxable' sales exceed £85,000 per annum they must become VAT registered and charge VAT ('output tax') on any sales they make, which in due course they must pass onto the UK taxman (HMRC). Different rates of VAT exist for different types of sales but most goods and services fall into the 'standard rated' category which carries a 20% rate of VAT.

However it's not all bad news for a business forced to register for VAT. As a VAT registered business they are now able to reclaim any VAT ('input tax') they have to pay to their (VAT registered) suppliers, which was previously an irrecoverable cost to the business.

Businesses usually have to account for VAT on a quarterly basis by sending a VAT return to HMRC which summarises:

- The sales they have recorded over the past three months and the amount of (output) VAT collected from their customers …. *which now needs to be paid across to HMRC*

- The purchases they have made over the past three months and the amount of (input) VAT they have paid to their suppliers …. *which can now be reclaimed from HMRC.*

The net difference between output tax (collected from customers) and input tax (paid to suppliers) represents the net amount of VAT to be paid to HMRC.

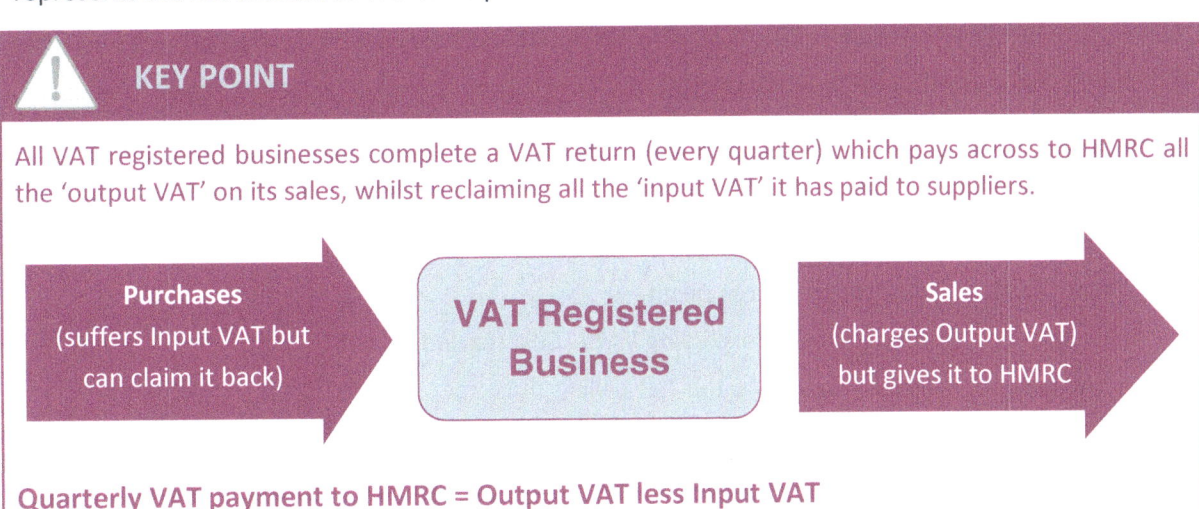

KEY POINT

All VAT registered businesses complete a VAT return (every quarter) which pays across to HMRC all the 'output VAT' on its sales, whilst reclaiming all the 'input VAT' it has paid to suppliers.

Purchases (suffers Input VAT but can claim it back) → **VAT Registered Business** → **Sales** (charges Output VAT) but gives it to HMRC

Quarterly VAT payment to HMRC = Output VAT less Input VAT

TUTORIAL NOTE

As shown above, the business is merely acting as an unpaid tax collector for HMRC and **does not actually pay VAT itself.**

It is the end customer (who is not VAT registered) who ultimately suffers the VAT i.e. VAT is a consumer borne tax.

4 Pricing and profitability

4.9 Where does VAT appear in the accounts?

The simple truth is that VAT hardly appears in the accounts of a VAT registered business.

Statement of Profit or Loss

VAT does not appear anywhere on the P&L account of a VAT registered business because:

- The output VAT is *not* included as part of the business's sales revenue. It is simply collected by the business on behalf of HMRC and paid across to them at the end of each VAT quarter.

- The input VAT is *not* included in the business's expenses because it will be reclaimed from HMRC at the end of the next VAT quarter. It is not therefore ultimately an expense.

Statement of Financial Position

At any point in time a VAT registered business will probably have a certain amount of net VAT (output tax less input tax) they owe HMRC at that point in time. Each Statement of Financial Position will include the net amount of VAT owed at that balance sheet date (under "Tax Liability" in the "Current Liabilities" section). At the end of each VAT quarter the liability at that point in time is actually paid across to HMRC.

4.10 Sales and profitability calculations and VAT

The good news is that VAT should be ignored in all calculations right up until dealing with retail prices where end-consumers (who cannot reclaim VAT) need to know what the full retail price is (including VAT).

So …..

- Ignore VAT in cost prices (as the input VAT can be reclaimed and therefore is not a real expense). In fact Business to Business (B2B) trading normally quotes VAT exclusive prices for this reason.

- Ignore VAT when calculating gross profit

    i.e. gross profit = selling price (excluding VAT) - Cost (excluding VAT)

- Add 20% (standard rate VAT) to the net selling price (i.e. exc. VAT price) of most goods and services to final consumers, to produce a retail price which includes VAT.

- If presented with a VAT inclusive sales figure you must remove the VAT (to produce a VAT exclusive sales figure) before any further calculations are performed.

The simplest way of converting sales including VAT (inc. VAT) to sales excluding VAT (exc. VAT) is to use the formulae below:

$$\text{Sales (inc. VAT)} = \text{Sales (exc. VAT)} \times 1.2$$

$$\text{Sales (exc. VAT)} = \text{Sales (inc. VAT)} \div 1.2$$

It is also useful to remember that it is the VAT Exclusive price which represents 100%:

$$\text{Sales exc. VAT (100\%)} + \text{VAT (20\%)} = \text{Sales inc. VAT (120\%)}$$

EXAMPLES

Scenario 1

A shop has 'retail' sales (i.e. including VAT) of £100,000 in July and makes a 55% gross profit margin.

How much gross profit (£) does the shop make in July?

Answer:

Sales exc. VAT = £100,000 ÷ 1.2 = £83,333

Gross Profit = £83,333 x 55% = **£45,833**

Scenario 2

A product costs £150 and needs to be sold at a price which achieves a 70% gross profit margin.

What retail price (inc. VAT) does the product need to be sold for?

Answer:

GP% = 70% → so Cost % = 30%

Cost = £150 = 30% → so 1% = £150 ÷ 30 = £5

So selling price (exc. VAT) = 100% = 100 x £5 = £500

(We are given a GP% so this means that selling price (exc. VAT) is 100%)

So retail price (inc. VAT) = £500 x 1.2 = **£600**

4 Pricing and profitability

TEST YOUR UNDERSTANDING 4

VAT Exc. Price (100%) + VAT (20%) = VAT inc. Price (120%)

For each of the following complete the missing fields. *Hint ... Find 1% first!*

All products are liable to the standard 20% rate of VAT.

Product	VAT Exc. Price (£)	VAT (£)	VAT Inc. Price (£)
Q	£10		
R			£120
S	£8		
T			£24
U	£1,220		
V		£9	
W	£15		
X			£72
Y		£150	
Z			£150

KEY POINTS FROM CHAPTER 4

Sales Volume, Selling Price, Sales Revenue
- **Sales Volume**   The number of items sold
- **Selling Price**   The price each individual unit was sold for
- **Sales Revenue**   The total sales amount for all units sold
- **Sales Revenue** = Sales Volume x Selling Price

Pricing Strategies
- **Penetration Pricing:** Initial low price to gain foothold in established market
- **Price Skimming:** Initial high price relying on loyalty of past customers
- **Competitive Pricing:** Basing selling prices on competitors' prices
- **Bundle Pricing:** Several products sold as a discounted package
- **Optional Pricing:** Promoting optional extras with the main purchase
- **Premium Pricing:** High price to convey premium image
- **Psychological Pricing:** To convey the impression of a lower price
- **Cost plus Pricing:** Selling prices set by reference to cost

The strategy chosen can have knock-on effects to: Sales Volume, Sales Revenue, Market Share, Gross Profit (£), Gross Profit (%), Infrastructure Costs and Staff Costs.

Profitability Calculations
- **Gross Profit (one item)** = Selling Price (one item) – Cost (one item)
- **Gross Profit (all items)** = Sales Revenue (all items) – Cost (all items)

Both of which can be re-arranged as required:
- **Gross Profit (£)** = Selling Price (£) – Cost (£)
- **Selling Price (£)** = Cost (£) + Gross Profit (£)
- **Cost (£)** = Selling Price (£) – Gross Profit (£)

Gross Profit (%) and Mark Up (%)
(Gross Profit is also known as 'margin' or 'gross margin')

- **Gross Profit (%)** = $\dfrac{\text{Gross Profit (£)}}{\text{Selling Price (£)}} \times 100\%$

- **Mark Up (%)** = $\dfrac{\text{Gross Profit (£)}}{\text{Cost (£)}} \times 100\%$

Both 'Gross Profit %' and 'Mark Up %' use the <u>same</u> Gross Profit <u>(£)</u> figure. The difference is how that is then expressed as a percentage:
- Gross Profit % → Expressed as a percentage of the <u>selling price</u> and so the selling price = 100%
- Mark Up % → Expressed as a percentage of the <u>cost price</u> and so the cost price = 100%

Price Elasticity of Demand (PED)
Measures the responsiveness of demand after a change in price, thus:

Price Elasticity of Demand = $\dfrac{\%\text{ Change in Demand}}{\%\text{ Change in Price}}$

4 Pricing and profitability

The PED is a pure number which indicates how sensitive a product's sales demand is to changes in the price of the product, as follows:

- PED = 1   Unit elastic
- PED >1   Elastic Demand i.e. price sensitive
- PED < 1   Inelastic demand i.e. price insensitive
- PED = 0   Perfectly inelastic i.e. demand does not vary with price change (rare)

Valued Added Tax (VAT)

- Businesses must register for VAT once their taxable supplies exceed £85,000 pa. The standard rate of VAT is 20%.
- **'Output VAT'** - Added by a VAT registered business to sales of goods and services
- **'Input VAT'** - VAT Suffered on purchases of goods and services
- **Quarterly VAT Return:** VAT registered businesses must pay across to HMRC all output VAT levied on sales, less input VAT suffered on purchases
- Sales exc. VAT (100%) + VAT (20%) = Sales inc. VAT (120%)
- Sales (inc. VAT) = Sales (exc. VAT) x 1.2
- Sales (exc. VAT) = Sales (inc. VAT) ÷ 1.2

Chapter 4: Test Your Understanding Answers

TEST YOUR UNDERSTANDING 1

Product A   Gross Profit (£) = £12.50 - £4.27 = £8.23

Gross Profit (%) = 8.23/12.50 x 100 = 65.8%

Product B   Cost (%) = 100% - 57% = 43% and Cost = £25.69

So, 1% = £25.69 / 43 = £0.5974

So, selling price (100%) = £0.597 x 100 = £59.74

Product C   Selling Price (100%) = £110.60 so 1% = £110.60 / 100 = £1.1060

Cost % = 100% - 43% = 57%   so cost = £1.106 x 57 = £63.04

Product D   Gross Profit = £9.60 x 1 = £9.60

Selling Price = Cost + Gross Profit = £9.60 + £9.60 = £19.20

Product E   Cost Price = 100%   Gross Profit = 50% (of cost)

Selling Price = 150% (of cost) so 1% = £120 / 150 = £0.80

So cost (100%) = £80.00

Product F   Gross Profit = £10.00 - £4.50 = £5.50

Mark Up % = Gross Profit / Cost x 100% = £5.50 / £4.50 x 100 = 122%

TEST YOUR UNDERSTANDING 2

a)   % Change in demand = (800-500) / 500 x 100% = 60%

% Change in Price = (£1.20 - £1.00) / £1.20 x 100% = 16.7%
PED = 60 / 16.7 = 3.6   (Highly Elastic)

b)   % Change in demand = (2,500-2,495) / 2,500 x 100% = 0.2%

% Change in Price = (£595 - £575) / £575 x 100% = 3.5%
PED = 0.2 / 3.5 = 0.06   (Nearly Inelastic)

c)   % Change in demand = (100,000 – 91,000) / 100,000 x 100% = 9%

% Change in Price = (£1.25 - £1.20) / £1.20 x 100% = 4.2%
PED = 9 / 4.2 = 2.1   (Very Elastic)

4 Pricing and profitability

TEST YOUR UNDERSTANDING 3

Z-Gadget   Cost% = 100% - 75% = 25%   Cost (£) = £200 x 0.25 = £50.00

2017 Performance	Prudence	Reckless Eric
Sales Revenue (£)	£190,000	£195,500
Sales Volume	1,000	1,150
Average Selling Price (£)	£190 (£10 discount)	£170 (£30 discount)
Average Discount (%)	£10/£200 x 100% = 5%	£30/£200 x 100% = 15%
Total Cost (£)	1,000 x £50 = £50,000	1,150 x £50 = £57,500
Gross Profit (£)	(£190,000 - £50,000) = £140,000	(£195,500 - £57,500) = £138,000
Gross Profit (%)	£140,000/£190,000 x 100% = 73.7%	£138,000/£195,500 x 100% = 70.6%

Despite having lower sales, Prudence is actually delivering more profit to the company.

TEST YOUR UNDERSTANDING 4

Product	VAT Exc. Price (£)	VAT (£)	VAT Inc. Price (£)
Q	£10	£2	£12
R	£100	£20	£120
S	£8	£1.60	£9.60
T	£20	£4	£24
U	£1,220	£244	£1,464
V	£45	£9	£54
W	£15	£3	£18
X	£60	£12	£72
Y	£750	£150	£900
Z	£125	£25	£150

Chapter 4: End of Chapter Exercises

Note: VAT may be ignored in all exercises unless specifically referred to.

Section A Questions

Question 4.1

A product costs £2.60 (excluding VAT) to manufacture and it sells for £11.20 (excluding VAT) and £13.44 (including VAT). How much gross profit (£) and gross profit (%) does this product make?

	Gross Profit (£)	Gross Profit (%)
A	£2.24	20%
B	£8.60	64%
C	£8.60	77%
D	£10.84	97%

Question 4.2

A product costs £0.45 (excluding VAT) to manufacture and it sells for £2.00 (excluding VAT) and £2.40 (including VAT). How much gross profit (£) does this product make and what percentage mark-up does this represent?

	Gross Profit (£)	Mark Up (%)
A	£1.55	78%
B	£1.55	344%
C	£1.95	78%
D	£1.95	81%

Question 4.3

A petrol station sold 10,000 litres of petrol per week at a price of £1.20 per litre. It then increased its selling price to £1.22 per litre and its weekly sales fell to 9,500 litres.

Based on these figures what is the price elasticity of demand for petrol?

A 0.2
B 0.3
C 2
D 3

4 Pricing and profitability

Question 4.4

A product costs £55 to manufacture. If the manufacturer wishes to make a 73% gross profit margin what retail price (including standard rate VAT) must the product be sold for (answer to the nearest £)?

A £95

B £114

C £204

D £244

Question 4.5

Which two of the following statements correctly state the treatment of VAT within a VAT registered business?

i. The statement of profit or loss will include output VAT in its sales revenue figures, and input VAT within its expenditure figures
ii. VAT will not be included within any of the figures on the statement of profit or loss
iii. The statement of financial position will (typically) record the amount of VAT owing to HMRC within its current liabilities
iv. Gross profit is calculated by deducting cost of sales (inclusive of VAT) from sales revenue (inclusive of VAT)

Choose the most appropriate combination of statements:

A i & iv

B i & iii

C ii & iii

D ii & iv

Question 4.6

If the selling price of an item is increased which one of the following statements is then true?

A Gross Profit % will increase but demand will tend to decrease

B Gross Profit % will increase and demand will also tend to increase

C Gross Profit % will decrease but demand will tend to increase

D Gross Profit % will decrease and demand will also tend to decrease

Question 4.7

A retailer normally sells a particular item for £120 and makes 70% gross profit at this selling price. If the retailer holds a "50% off everything" sale, what gross profit % will they now make on this item? (Ignore VAT)

A 30%

B 35%

C 40%

D 45%

Question 4.8

A retailer normally sells a particular item for £80 and makes 60% gross profit at this selling price. If the retailer holds a sale event and now only makes 20% gross profit on the item, by what percentage have they discounted the selling price? (Ignore VAT)

A   30%

B   33%

C   40%

D   50%

Question 4.9

When a product is sold at a selling price of £120 it makes £32 gross profit.

If the selling price is discounted by 10%, by how many percent will the gross profit (£) reduce? (Ignore VAT)

A   10.0%

B   37.5%

C   45.0%

D   60.0%

Question 4.10

A retailer company launches a new product which costs £6.70 to purchase. At what retail selling price *(including 20% VAT)* must they sell for the product if they wish to make 75% gross profit?

A   £11.73

B   £14.07

C   £26.80

D   £32.16

4 Pricing and profitability

Section B Questions

Question 4.11 (VAT)

Complete the missing fields from the following table of selling prices (assume that 20% VAT applies). The completed first row is included as an illustration.

Price (excluding VAT)	VAT	Price (including VAT)
£50.00	£10.00	£60.00
£10		
		£132
	£1	
£15		
		£42
	£17	

Question 4.12 (Gross Profit aka 'Margin')

Remember, when we quote percentage profitability in terms of **Gross Profit %**

- Cost Price (£) + Gross Profit (£) = Selling Price (£)
- Gross Profit (%) = Gross Profit (£) / Selling Price (£) x 100%
- Gross Profit % is calculated as a % of the Selling Price (£) *i.e. Selling Price = 100%*
- Cost Price% + GP% = 100% Selling Price

(The term 'margin' is often interchanged with 'gross profit' i.e. 'Margin £' = 'Gross Profit £' and 'Margin %' = 'Gross Profit %')

Fill in the blanks in the following table

(Tutorial Hint: When working with Gross Profit % ……the Selling Price will always be 100%)

Item	Cost Price (£)	Gross Profit (%)	Gross Profit (£)	Selling Price (£)
A	£100			£250
B	£20		£80	
C		65%		£80
D			£16.50	£62.75
E	£635	57.8%		
F		47%	£1.35	

4 Pricing and profitability

Question 4.13 ('Mark-Up')

Remember, when we quote percentage profitability in terms of **Mark Up %**

- Cost Price (£) + Gross Profit (£) = Selling Price (£)   (Exactly the same as Question 1)
- Mark Up (%) = Gross Profit (£) / Cost Price (£) x 100%
- Mark-Up % is calculated as a % of the Cost Price (£)   i.e. Cost Price = 100%
- 100% Cost Price + Mark-Up% = Selling Price%

(Mark-Up £ is just an alternative name for Gross Profit £. The distinction only arises when we use percentages. Mark-Up % is calculated as a % of the cost price, whereas gross profit % is calculated as a % of the selling price).

Fill in the blanks in the following table

(Tutorial Hint: When working with Mark-Up% ……the Cost Price will always be 100%)

Item	Cost Price (£)	Mark-Up (%)	Gross Profit (£)	Selling Price (£)
G	£200			£320
H	£50		£40	
I		65%		£132
J			£1.25	£6.25
K	£32.00	57%		
L		67.5%	£111.38	

158

Question 4.14 (Price Elasticity of Demand - PED)

Tutorial Note:
Price Elasticity of Demand (PED) = % Change in Demand / % change in Price
(PED is a pure number ... no need to multiply by 100%)

A petrol station previously sold 38,000 litres of petrol per week at a selling price of £1.20 per litre. The petrol station then increased it selling price to £1.22 per litre and their sales volume dropped to 36,500 litres per week.

Calculate the PED for petrol based on the above figures and state whether it is elastic or inelastic.

3.9 ÷ 1.7 = 2.232 — elastic (more than 1)

If instead of increasing the selling price of petrol, it had instead been reduced to £1.17 per litre, what would the resultant weekly sales have increased to, based on the calculated PED?

4 Pricing and profitability

Question 4.15 ('BOGOF')

A supermarket sells 200 jars of mayonnaise per week at a selling price of £2.50 each and makes a 75% Gross Profit.

At this same selling price the mayonnaise is then put onto a 'Buy One Get One Free' promotion.

What Gross Profit (%) is now achieved, and how what sales volume (individual jars of mayonnaise – including both 'sold' and 'free') is now required to make the same Gross Profit (£) per week on this product? Does this promotion make commercial sense?

Tutorial Hint: During the promotion regard the sales unit as being two jars, and think in terms of: selling price (for 2 jars), cost price (for 2 jars) and gross profit (for 2 jars)

(GP = SP - Cost)

price per jar - 0.625p | price = £2.50 | 75% of £2.50 = 67p
GP per jar - £1.875 | cost = £1.25 | 75% = 1.88
cost per jar - £2.50 | GP = 1.25
total gross profit - £375 (2 × 0.625)
200 × 1.875 = £375 | 1.25 ÷ 2.50 × 100 = 50%

Question 4.16 ('Three for Two')

A high street chemist sells 100 bottles of suntan lotion per week at a selling price of 3.50 and makes a 75% Gross Profit.

The suntan lotion is then put onto a 'Three for Two' promotion (i.e. 3 bottles for £7.00).

What Gross Profit (%) is now achieved? Assuming that customer now only buy suntan lotion as part of the three for two promotion, how many promotional sales (of three bottles) does the chemist need to make to result in the same Gross Profit (£) per week on this product? Does this promotion make commercial sense?

Tutorial Hint: During the promotion regard the sales unit as being three bottles, and think in terms of: selling price (for 3 bottles), cost price (for 3 bottles) and gross profit (for 3 bottles)

GP = 75% = 3.50 = 0.875 | 262.50 ÷ 4.375 = 60
SP = £7
cost = £2.625
GP = 7 - 2.625 = £4.375
4.375 ÷ £7 = 0.625 × 100 = 62.5% GP

Question 4.17 (VAT Returns)

A retail business is VAT registered and only buys and sells 20% standard rated products. In the last VAT quarter it purchases stock at a cost of £100,000 (exc. VAT); and makes retail sales of £250,000 (exc. VAT).

(We shall ignore any variations in opening & closing stock and regard 'purchases' as being the same as 'cost of sales')

What was the total amount (inc. VAT) paid to the suppliers?	£120,000
How much 'Input Tax' did this contain?	
What was the total amount (inc. VAT) received from customers?	
How much 'Output Tax' did this contain?	
What 'Sales Revenue' is shown in the quarterly statement of profit or loss?	
What 'Purchases' is shown in the quarterly statement of profit or loss?	
What 'Gross Profit' is shown in the quarterly statement of profit or loss?	
What amount of VAT must be paid to HMRC (Taxman!) this VAT Quarter?	
How much VAT does the company itself ultimately pay?	
Who does ultimately pay the VAT?	

4 Pricing and profitability

Question 4.18 (VAT)

Tutorial Note:

In business we largely ignore VAT except when looking at the final retail selling price. Most businesses are VAT registered and do not therefore ultimately 'suffer' VAT themselves. They claim back any 'input tax' they suffer on purchases from HMRC, and pay over any 'output tax' they have levied on their sales, to HMRC. They typically quote all cost prices and selling prices exclusive of VAT and all profitability calculations (including P&Ls) are based on VAT exclusive figures. The only time we need to consider VAT is when prices are quoted inclusive of VAT, which is typically when quoting retail selling prices for end-consumers (who cannot reclaim VAT).

Remember (for the 20% 'standard rated' sales):

- VAT Exclusive Price (100%) + VAT (20%) = VAT Inclusive Price (120%)
- VAT Inclusive Price = VAT exclusive Price x 1.2
- VAT Exclusive Price = VAT Inclusive Price / 1.2

A clothing retailer buys designer jeans for £30 per pair (excluding VAT) and wishes to make 60% gross profit on them. What retail price (i.e. including 20% VAT) should the retailer sells the jeans at?

The same clothing retailer sells T-Shirts for £24.00 each (inc. VAT). These also make a 60% gross profit margin. What is the cost price (exc. VAT) of a T Shirt?

The Language of Business

Question 4.19 (£ Margin versus % Margin)

Tutorial Note:

The same gross profit margin formulae we used earlier for single items can be equally applied to a business on a larger scale. We may amend the terminology e.g. 'sales revenue' instead of 'selling price' to show that we are considering multiple items, but the mathematical form remains the same.

- *Cost of Sales (£) + Gross Profit (£) = Sales Revenue (£)*
- *Gross Profit (%) = Gross Profit (£) / Sales Revenue (£)   x 100%*
- *Gross Profit % is calculated as a % of the Sales Revenue (£)   i.e. Sales Revenue = 100%*
- *Cost of Sales % + Gross Profit % = 100% Sales Revenue*

A restaurant records the following costs & sales revenues for its various categories of income over a particular month. Complete the blanks (including the Total row) and briefly comment on the relative profitability of the different categories.

Category	Sales Revenue(£)	Cost of Sales (£)	Gross Profit (£)	Gross Profit (%)
Starters	£6,800	£2,040	£4,760	70%
Main Courses	£10,000	£4,000	£6,000	60%
Desserts	£4,000	£800	£3,200	80%
Wine	£7,200	£2,520	£4,680	65%
Teas & Coffees	£2,000	£200	£1,800	90%
TOTAL	£30,000	£9,560	£20,440	68.13%

4 Pricing and profitability

Chapter 5

Introduction to Costing and Marginal Costing

INTRODUCTION

In the last chapter we looked at setting the selling price, which is one half of the profit equation (Profit = Selling Price – Cost). We now need to look at the other half of the equation (cost).

Up to this point we have simply been told the cost of a particular product or service, but now we must start to explore **'costing'** a little more closely and actually understand how the 'cost' of a product is actually calculated.

In this chapter we will look at **'marginal costing'** which only takes **variable costs** into account. In the next chapter we will look at **'absorption costing'** which also includes a fair share of the fixed costs within a product's cost.

Only when we know the cost of whatever it is we are selling, can we properly decide on how much we need to sell it for to make the required level of profit.

OVERVIEW AND OBJECTIVES

At the end of this chapter you should have a good understanding of the following key concepts and how to apply them to a business:

- Cost Classifications
- Marginal Costing & Contribution
- Cost Volume Profit (CVP) Calculations

and answer questions on these subjects.

5 Introduction to Costing and Marginal Costing

5.1 The importance of costing

Profitability depends on two factors: income and expenses, since:

Profit = Income - Expenses

(Remembering from Chapter 2 that in accordance with the accruals concept, income is recognised when it is 'earned' whilst expenses are recognised when they are 'incurred')

The last chapter considered the influence of pricing on income and profitability. In this chapter we will start to consider the second factor affecting profitability, namely expenses or 'costs' as they are commonly known.

Costing falls very much in to the 'management accounting' side of things (see chapter 1) and by its nature management accounting is a very practical and pragmatic discipline. The real world of business is often hopelessly complex because of the numerous factors which are involved in every decision and situation. Making business decisions often requires us to simplify complex real world situations into more basic models which can be used to make informed decisions.

Therefore you must become 'comfortable' with making simplifying generalisations which might not be true 100% of the time, but which are far preferable to the alternative of not even trying to understand a problem at all because it appears too complex!

5.2 Cost classifications

> **DEFINITION**
>
> **Definition of an accountant?**
>
> *It has been said that an accountant is someone who knows the cost of everything and the value of nothing!*
>
> As sad as it may seem, accountants regard costs as being a big deal and with good reason. If companies do not understand the costs involved in their business they cannot hope to succeed commercially. Generating sales by itself will not guarantee profitability....you have to be aware of both factors in the profit equation: Sales **and** Costs.

Accountants have devised several different ways of classifying costs and some accountants (imaginatively known as 'cost accountants') specialise in this field. We will focus on arguably the two most important methods of classification:

- Whether costs are Fixed or Variable (or a hybrid of the two)
- Whether costs are Direct or Indirect

....and will then briefly mention some of the other different ways of describing costs.

Cost Objects / Cost Units

A common requirement is to establish the cost of a particular product or service which is being offered for sale. Before a selling price can be set for this 'cost object' it is first necessary to calculate the unit cost of one cost object i.e. the 'cost unit'

The choice of cost objects will vary depending on the business in question but common examples might include:

- The cost of manufacturing one product e.g. the cost of manufacturing one smart phone
- The cost of providing one service e.g. the cost of flying one airline passenger from London to New York.

5.3 Variable/fixed costs

Costs can be classified according to whether they change with the level of activity:

- Variable Costs increase as the level of activity increases
- Fixed costs remain constant despite increased levels of activity

The first question is what do we mean by 'activity', and the simple answer is that 'activity' is a measure of how busy a business is, in doing whatever it does :

- 'Activity' in the manufacturing sector might refer to the number of products which have been produced.
- 'Activity' in the service sector might refer to how much of a particular service has been delivered.

It is important to identify exactly what the activity is in a particular scenario before trying to consider whether the various costs involved are variable or fixed. There are sometimes several different possible measures of activity and a choice needs to be made as to which one is most appropriate for the situation being considered. This choice is important.

Variable costs

A variable cost is signified where its **total** value increases with activity and there is no cost at zero activity.

> **EXAMPLE**
>
> A manufacturing company makes stainless steel saucepans. The major raw material is (unsurprisingly) stainless steel. The total cost of the stainless steel used for different level of production is shown on the accompanying graph. We can immediately see from the graph that the total cost of stainless steel varies with the level of activity (i.e. number of saucepans manufactured) and that for example:
>
> - £280 of stainless steel is required to manufacture 200 saucepans
> - £700 of stainless steel is requires to manufacture 500 saucepans
>
> …. and importantly that producing *no* saucepans requires *no* expenditure on stainless steel!
>
> It is **not** simply the case that if the **total** cost increases with activity then it *must* be a variable cost (as we will shortly see with 'semi- variable' costs).
>
> The only way to definitely identify a cost as being a variable is either:
>
> - Look at a graph of its behaviour which proves that there is nil expenditure at nil activity (i.e. the graph goes through the 0-0 origin)
> - Or to work out the 'unit cost' of one unit of activity and showing that this unit cost is constant regardless of the overall level of activity

5 Introduction to Costing and Marginal Costing

[Graph showing Total Cost (£) of Stainless steel on y-axis against Activity (No of saucepans) on x-axis. A straight line passes through the origin (0,0), through (200, £280), and (500, £700).]

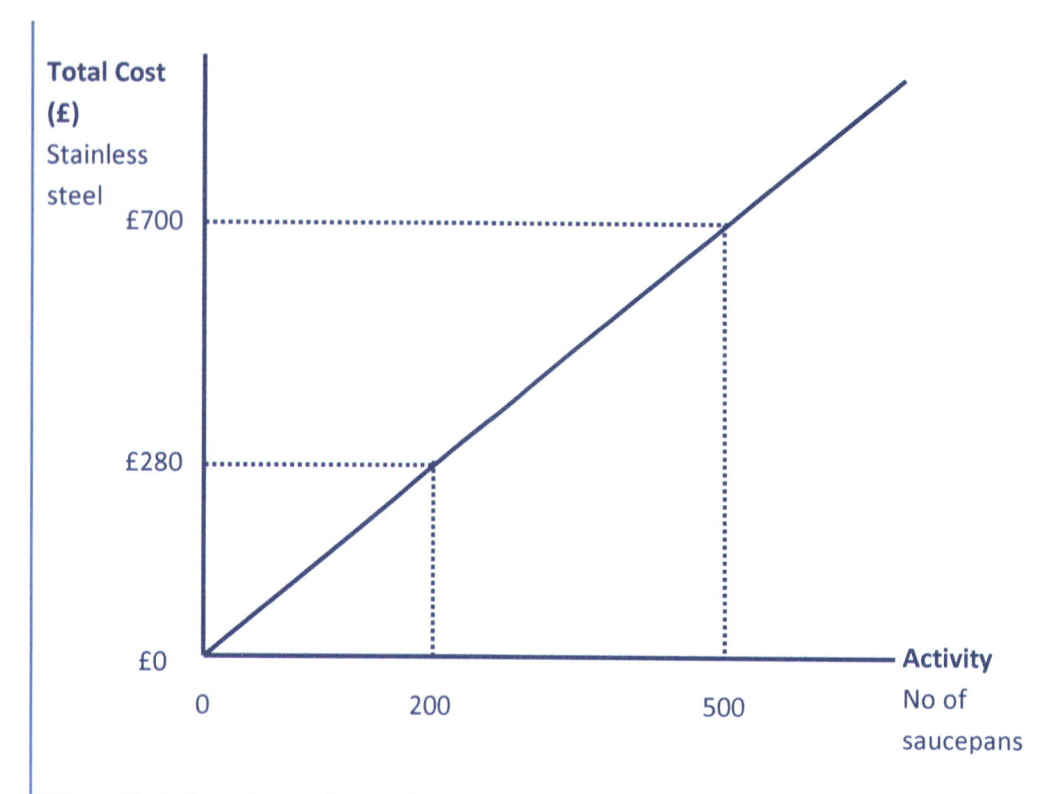

The table below shows that each saucepan requires £1.40 of stainless steel (this is known as the 'unit cost')... regardless of whether it the 1st or 500th saucepan being manufactured.

Activity (No. of Saucepans)	Total Cost of Stainless Steel	Unit Cost of Stainless Steel (= Total Cost / Activity)
100	£140	£1.40
200	£280	£1.40
300	£420	£1.40
400	£560	£1.40
500	£700	£1.40

TUTORIAL NOTE

Tell-Tale Sign of a Variable Cost

We do not always have the luxury of seeing cost information displayed graphically (and seeing that the line goes through 0-0 signifying a variable cost). However, variable costs can still be spotted by identifying the presence of **both** of these tell-tale signs:

   i. The **total** cost **increases** with activity
   ii. The **unit** cost remains **constant** at different levels of activity

…. as show in the table above.

Fixed costs

A fixed cost is signified where its **total** value remains constant regardless of the level of activity and there *is* a cost at zero activity.

Continuing the example of the manufacturing company making stainless steel saucepans, a major cost to the company is the £1,000 per week rent it pays for its factory.

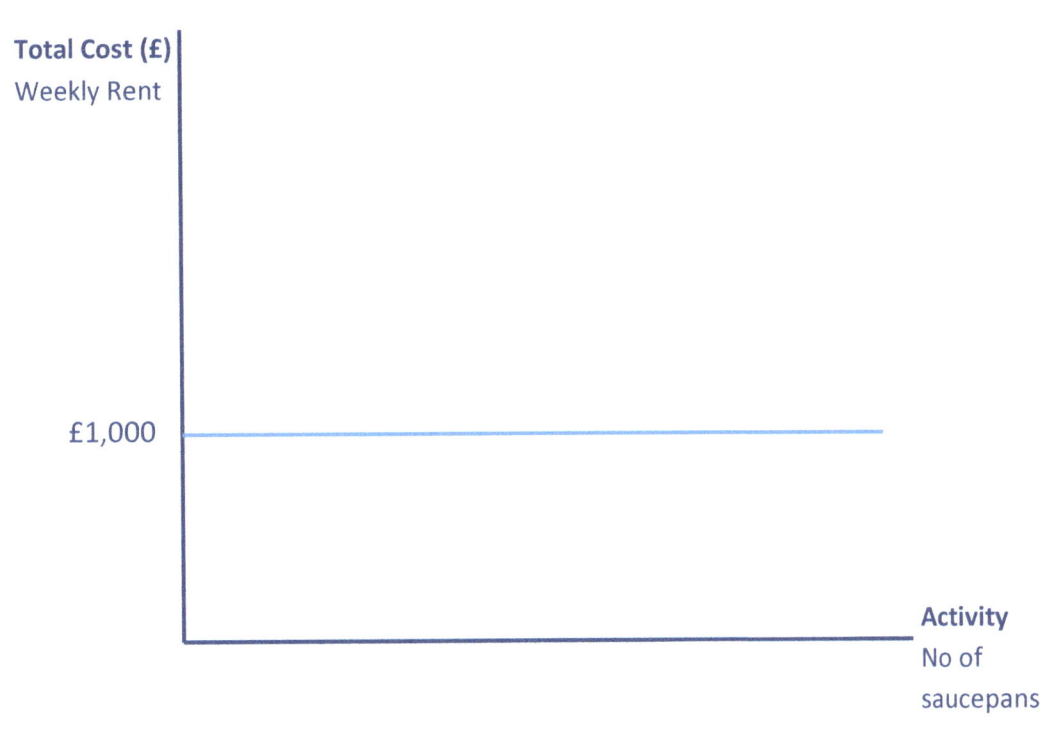

Total Cost (£)
Weekly Rent

£1,000 ─────────────────────────────

Activity
No of saucepans

The accompanying graph shows how the amount of rent paid per week changes according to the level of activity in the factory (which is measured by how many saucepans have been produced that week) …. and it can immediately be seen that the rent does **not** change with different levels of activity!

Clearly the amount of rent the manufacturing company has to pay has nothing to do with how busy they are manufacturing saucepans i.e. the rent is fixed at £1,000 per week regardless of whether the company is working flat out to meet peak demand, or whether the factory is closed down for Christmas!

TUTORIAL NOTE

The way to identify a cost as being fixed is either:

- Look at a graph of its behaviour which proves that there is a fixed level of expenditure (i.e. a horizontal line) regardless of the level of activity.
- By simple inspection of the figures identifying that the level of expenditure does not change with different levels of activity.

Tell-Tale Sign of a Fixed Cost

Fixed costs are the easiest type of cost to identify because they are clearly fixed:

The **total** cost remains constant despite the level of activity changing.

5 Introduction to Costing and Marginal Costing

5.4 Semi-variable costs

Let's now consider a brand new example.... the cost of a business's telephone bill which comprises both a £100 monthly fixed line rental cost, plus an additional charge of £0.10 per minute call charge.

If we plotted the total telephone charge against the level of activity (which is taken to be minutes of telephone usage) we get the graph shown. We can see that at zero activity we still have the £100 per month fixed cost for line rental. However, as the activity increases (i.e. people start making telephone calls!) a variable expense of £0.10 per minute also adds in.

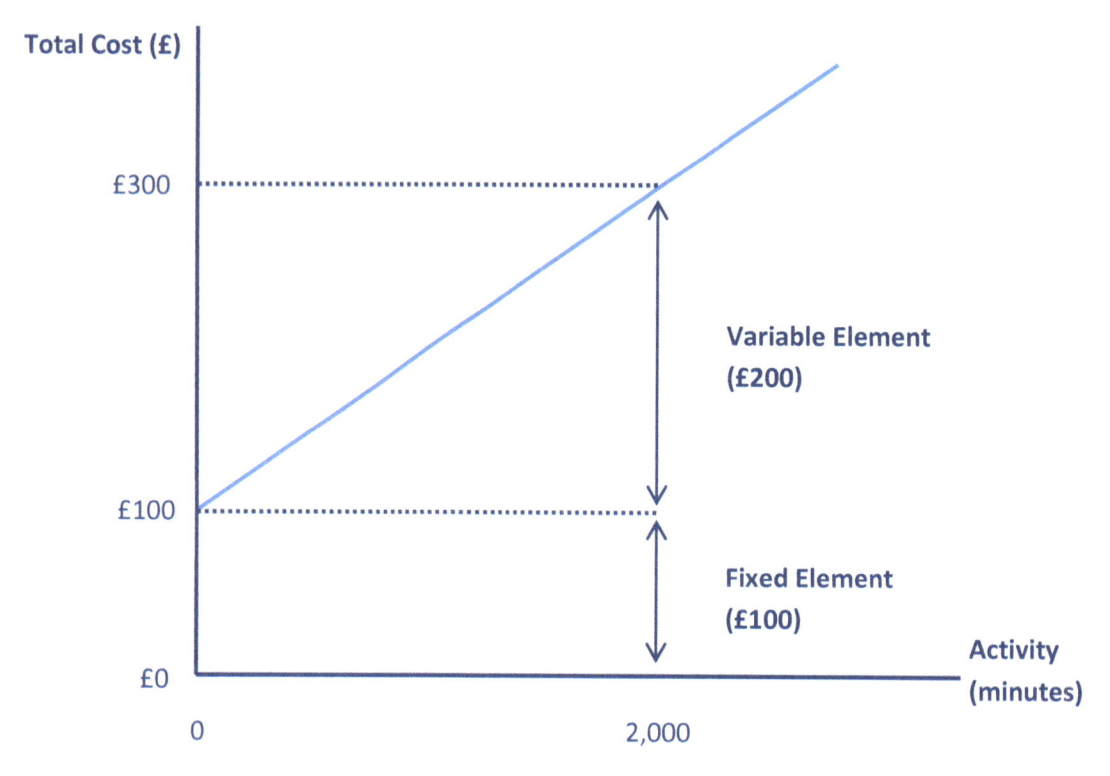

As an example (see graph above) at the 2,000 minute level of activity the total cost is made up of two parts:

- Fixed cost of £100
- Variable Cost of 2,000 minutes x £0.10 per minute = £200
- Total Cost = £300

We call such costs 'semi-variable' costs as they have both fixed and variable elements of cost.

The telephone example is shown in tabular form below but with more levels of activity included.

Activity (Minutes of telephone calls per month)	Total Cost of Telephone Bill	Total Unit Cost of Telephone calls per minute (= Total Cost / Minutes)
500	£150	£0.30 per minute
1,000	£200	£0.20 per minute
2,000	£300	£0.15 per minute
3,000	£400	£0.133 per minute
4,000	£500	£0.125 per minute

The Language of Business

> ### TUTORIAL NOTE
>
> **Tell-Tale Sign of a Semi-Variable Cost**
>
> Again, we do not always have the luxury of seeing cost information displayed graphically and seeing something akin to the previous graph which immediately identifies the cost as being semi-variable i.e. total cost increasing with activity, but NOT zero when there is no activity.
>
> Instead we often just have some numerical data showing the total costs at a number of different levels of activity. We then have to look for two tell-tale signs to confirm that these costs are in fact semi-variable:
>
> i. The **total** cost **increases** with activity (which is the same as for a variable cost)
>
> ii. The **unit** cost **reduces** at higher levels of activity (which is NOT the case for a variable cost)

TEST YOUR UNDERSTANDING 1

Using the figures from the telephone example above verify each of the figures above to prove that you understand where they came from by completing the table below.

The first row is completed for you …..

Activity (Minutes of telephone calls per month)	Fixed Cost	Variable Cost	Total Cost of Telephone Bill (= Fixed + Variable Costs)	Total Unit Cost of Telephone calls per minute (= Total Cost / Minutes)
500	£100	500 minutes x £0.10 = **£50**	£100 + £50 = **£150**	£150 / 500 minutes = **£0.30 per minute**
1,000				
2,000				
3,000				
4,000				

As mentioned, the slightly quirky thing to note is that the total unit cost of telephone calls per minute appears to be reducing as the level of activity increases, and hopefully you can see why this is the case. The fixed cost of £100 per month is fixed regardless of how many calls are made. So when we work out the total unit cost *per minute* for a higher level of activity the fixed cost has been shared out between more minutes and therefore appears smaller … per minute!

5 Introduction to Costing and Marginal Costing

5.5 Hi-Lo method

A common challenge in business is to try and understand how a certain cost behaves, merely starting with some historical examples of that cost, as follows:

Fixed costs

The **total** cost is fixed and does not change with different levels of activity. Fixed costs are usually immediately obvious and the simplest to identify and quantify.

Variable Costs

The **total** cost **increases** with higher levels of activity, but when we calculate the **unit** cost we see that this remains **constant** (both proving it to be a variable cost, and quantifying it at the same time).

Semi-Variable Costs

The **total** cost **increases** with higher levels of activity, but when we calculate the **unit** cost we see that this reduces for higher levels of activity. However, in order to actually identify what both the fixed cost element and the variable costs elements are from a sample of numerical data we must first use the **Hi-Lo method.**

> **DEFINITION**
>
> The **Hi-Lo method** is used to analyse a cost *(which is known to be a semi-variable cost)* into its fixed and variable components.

To illustrate the method we will look at a fresh example.

> **EXAMPLE**
>
> A business has a fleet of delivery vans and has collected the following total costs for running this fleet of vans over the last four months. It also has records of how many miles the vans have travelled in total for each of these months (i.e. their level of activity).
>
> It now wishes to estimate how much the vans will cost to run next month (May) when the vans are expected to travel 54,000 miles.
>
> | Month | Total Cost of Operating Fleet | Total Miles Travelled |
> |---|---|---|
> | January | £16,000 | 46,000 miles |
> | February | £16,750 | 49,000 miles |
> | March | £12,000 | 30,000 miles |
> | April | £13,750 | 37,000 miles |
>
> Our challenge is to identify what type of cost this (fixed, variable or semi-variable), and to then describe the cost behaviour in a quantitative fashion (i.e. put some numbers to it).
>
> Once we have done this we can then quickly estimate what May's total van expense will be....

Step One: Identify the Cost Type

We can immediately see that the total cost varies with different levels of activity so it's immediately obvious that the expense of running the fleet of vans is *not* a fixed cost. That leaves two possibilities: either it is a variable cost, or it is a semi-variable cost.

To make matters clearer it helps to rearrange the above data in order of increasing activity *(not essential but useful)* and we also need to work out the unit cost per mile (as this will confirm whether the cost is variable or semi-variable.

So, in order, from lowest number of miles travelled to greatest number of miles travelled:

Month	Total Cost of Operating Fleet	Total Miles Travelled	Unit Cost per mile
March	£12,000	30,000 miles- **Lo**	£0.40 per mile
April	£13,750	37,000 miles	£0.37 per mile
January	£16,000	46,000 miles	£0.35 per mile
February	£16,750	49,000 miles- **Hi**	£0.34 per mile

We can now confirm that this cost is a semi-variable cost, because:

i. The total cost increases with the level of activity …. **and**

ii. The unit cost decreases with the level of activity

Step Two: Analyse the cost into fixed and variable elements (Hi-Lo Method)

We identify the month with the lowest activity (March) and the month with the highest level of activity (February). We base our analysis on just these two months and ignore the other months.

We have already ascertained that these are semi-variable costs and therefore have a fixed component of cost and a variable element of cost. The mathematical 'trick' which the Hi-Lo method uses is to recognise that both the March and the February totals have exactly the *same* fixed cost included within them, because the fixed cost is fixed! So any **difference in total cost** between March and February is *purely* as a result of different variable costs (caused by **different level of activity**).

Let's spell that out, step by step:

a) February's total cost is £4,750 more than March's (£16,750 - £12,000 = £4,750)

b) February's activity is 19,000 miles more than March's (49,000 - 30,000=19,000 miles)

c) The £4,750 increase in cost is purely as a result of the 19,000 additional miles. Each of those additional miles must have cost £0.25 (i.e. £4,750 / 19,000). The fixed cost played no part in this £4,750 increase in cost, because regardless of how much the fixed cost is (we'll work it out shortly) it is already in both March's and February's figures

d) Therefore the variable cost element is £0.25 per mile.

5. Introduction to Costing and Marginal Costing

Having calculated the variable element it is now a simple process to substitute this into (either) the March or February total and thereby calculate how much the fixed element of cost must be. Using March's total (we could have used either month):

a) Total variable cost in March = 30,000 miles x £0.25 per mile = £7,500

b) But we know that the total cost in March is actually £12,000

c) The £4,500 difference (i.e. £12,000 - £7,500) must be the fixed cost

In summary, the van expenses have been shown to be a semi-variable cost with:

- A fixed element of £4,500 per month (*insurance, maintenance etc.*)
- An additional variable element of £0.25 per mile (*driver's wages, diesel etc.*)

Let's use this to answer the original question …. how much expense will be incurred by the fleet of vans in May when they are expected to travel 54,000 miles? The answer is found simply by adding the monthly fixed cost to 54,000 lots of variable cost!

Van Fleet Costs (May) = £4,500 + (54,000 x £0.25) = £4,500 + £13,500 = **£18,000**

… which we can 'sense-check' by seeing that it is in the right vicinity compared to the other months.

TUTORIAL NOTE

For those who like to memorise equations:

$$\text{Variable Cost Element} = \frac{\text{Total Cost (Hi)} - \text{Total Cost (Lo)}}{\text{Total Activity (Hi)} - \text{Total Activity (Lo)}}$$

… and then substitute the calculated cost into either the Hi or Lo total cost to reveal the additional fixed cost.

These methods are based on the mathematical concept of subtracting 'simultaneous equations' followed by a substitution which you may well have encountered before. The Hi-Lo method simply presents the same principle in a more intuitive way.

The Language of Business

TEST YOUR UNDERSTANDING 2

A business rents a photocopier for its own office use. The rental terms consist of a fixed monthly rental sum, plus a charge for every copy made. The total cost and activity for the last three months are shown

	July	August	September
No. of Copies	1,500	1,200	2,200
Total Cost	£95	£89	£109

What is the fixed monthly rental sum for the photocopier and what is the charge for every copy made?

_____
_____
_____

Now estimate the total costs for the next three months:

	October	November	December
No. of Copies	900	1,900	2,400
Total Cost	_____	_____	_____

5.6 Assumptions and simplifications

In the real business world we have to simplify complex and imperfect situations in order to allow us to derive simple mathematical models which can be utilised to better run our businesses.

For example:

- Variable costs such as labour costs based on someone being paid (say) £10.00 per hour might not always be accurate for various reasons, including paying higher overtime rates, or unproductive hours (which still must be paid for) .. to say nothing of annual wage increases.

- Purchasing costs of raw materials might not always be the same constant price of (say) £2 per Kg. If the raw material in question was in short supply the cost per Kg might increase. Conversely a business might buy in bulk to receive a discounted cost per Kg.

- Fixed costs such as the rent paid on a premises are not fixed forever. At some point there will be a rent review and the rent will typically increase.

These are just a few examples of the complexities faced in the real business world. It is realised and accepted that the assumptions used have limitations, but it is still preferable to base our business decisions on less than perfect analysis, than on no analysis at all!

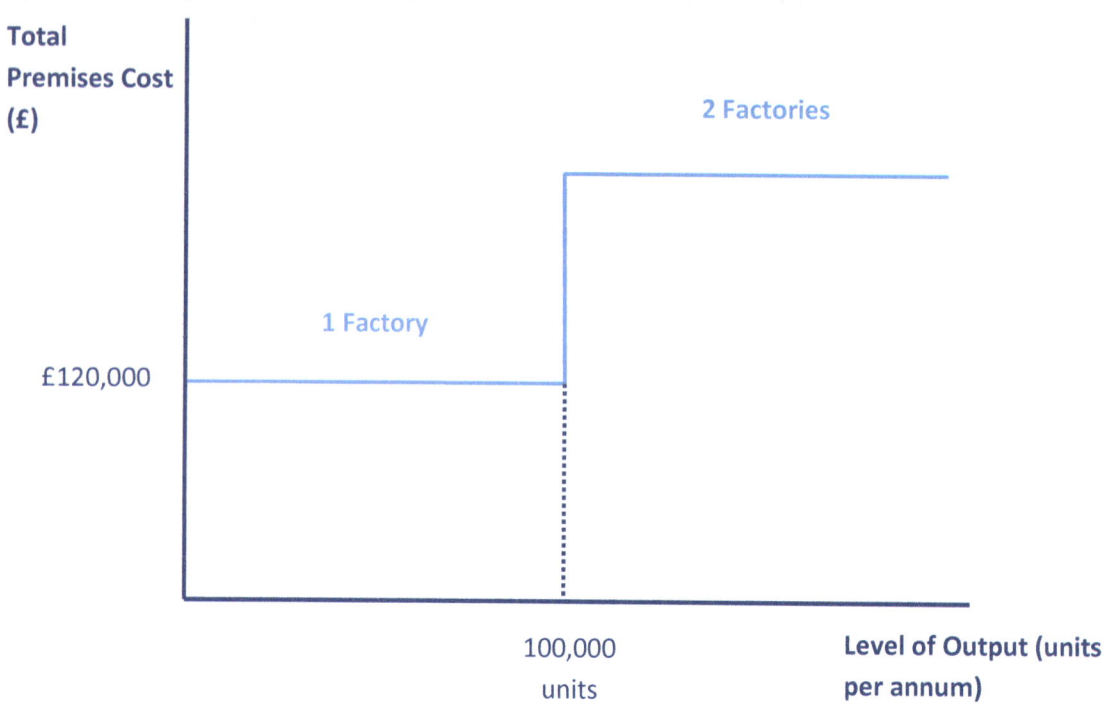

5 Introduction to Costing and Marginal Costing

One example often encountered is illustrated in the graph below which shows the premises costs for a manufacturing business.

[Graph: Total Premises Cost (£) vs Level of Output (units per annum). Step cost function showing £120,000 for 1 Factory up to 100,000 units, then stepping up to a higher level for 2 Factories.]

The immediate assumption is that premises costs (rent, business rates, heat & light, insurance etc.) would be fixed in nature regardless of the level of activity (in this case measured by annual units of production). However this is only true to the point where the factory is working at absolute full capacity and simply cannot produce any more output.

At this stage if the business still requires more capacity then it presumably needs a new second factory and the premises cost 'steps' up until the second factory is also working at full capacity. We call such costs **'step costs'** and they are often really just a recognition that fixed costs are not fixed for *all* levels of production.

In the graph above, the business concerned would regard their premises costs as being a fixed £120,000 pa whilst their production output ranges from nil to 100,000 units pa. If more than 100,000 units of production are required in a year then the premises fixed cost will suddenly not be fixed anymore and will step up. Similarly the £120,000 fixed cost pa is also only valid until the rent or heat & light costs etc. are affected by inflation or rent reviews.

In summary, all of our costing assumptions are only approximations made *within certain ranges of activity and certain periods of time*. If the business needs to understand what will happen outside those ranges then fresh analysis will be required.

5.7 Direct costs

Having looked at classifying costs as either fixed or variable (or a hybrid of the two as semi-variable), we can now consider the second major way of classifying costs, namely as either **Direct or Indirect Costs**.

We have already introduced the idea of 'cost objects' being an activity for which we are trying to ascertain a cost. For example, in a car manufacturing business each model of car would be a cost object as the producer would need to know how much it cost to produce each type of car. How can the car manufacturer know at what price to market the car until they know how much it costs to produce?

Similarly, in a service business, such as a garage, the cost of servicing a car would be a cost object. How can the garage know how much to charge for servicing a car until it knows how much the service costs to perform?

> **DEFINITION**
>
> A **Direct Cost** is any cost that **can** be directly and exclusively linked to a particular cost object.

> **EXAMPLES**
>
> i. **Direct Labour** – Labour costs that are directly and exclusively identified with a particular cost object
>
> ii. **Direct Materials** – Any component parts or raw materials that are directly and exclusively identified with a particular cost object
>
> iii. **Direct Expenses** – Any other costs that are directly and exclusively identified with a particular cost object
>
> The total of these three expenses are sometimes referred to as the Prime Cost of a product or service i.e. the total direct expenses that can be directly and exclusively identified with that product or service.
>
> **Prime Cost = Direct Labour + Direct Materials + Direct Expenses**

5.8 Indirect costs

> **DEFINITION**
>
> An **Indirect Cost** is any cost that **cannot** be directly and exclusively linked to a particular cost object.

A cost could be regarded as being indirect because it is shared between more than one cost object, or sometimes because it is not practical to identify how much of a certain cost has been used for each different cost unit. In either case the end result is that we have costs that have been incurred by the business but where we cannot readily identify which cost objects they relate to.

Such costs are known as Indirect Costs or by their alternative name of 'Overheads'.

> **EXAMPLES**
>
> - Premises costs (rents, rates, heat & light etc.) because the premises are typically used for different products/services (and each product or service is a different cost object).
> - The cost of managers who supervise multiple staff working on different cost objects.
> - The depreciation costs arising from past capital expenditure, where the plant & machinery in question is used across several different cost objects.

5 Introduction to Costing and Marginal Costing

Indirect costs (overheads) are often categorised into three different classifications:

1. **Production Overheads:** Which are indirect costs involved in the manufacture of products (e.g. factory rent, machinery depreciation, factory manager etc.)

2. **Selling & Distribution Overheads:** Any indirect costs involved in the storage, distribution and selling of goods (e.g. warehousing and delivery van costs etc.)

3. **Administration Overheads:** Any other general indirect costs incurred by the business (e.g. finance or HR department, or the cost of the annual audit etc.)

Financial accounting (i.e. producing financial statements for external users) is strictly regulated by various financial reporting standards which dictate exactly how the statements should be compiled. One of those reporting standards states that the value of inventory (i.e. unsold goods) should include a fair share of the production overheads incurred. Additionally, the standard format for the statement of profit or loss requires the non-production overheads to be categorised into Selling & Distribution Overheads and Administration overheads. For these (financial accounting) reasons we often tend to categorise overheads into the three groupings above.

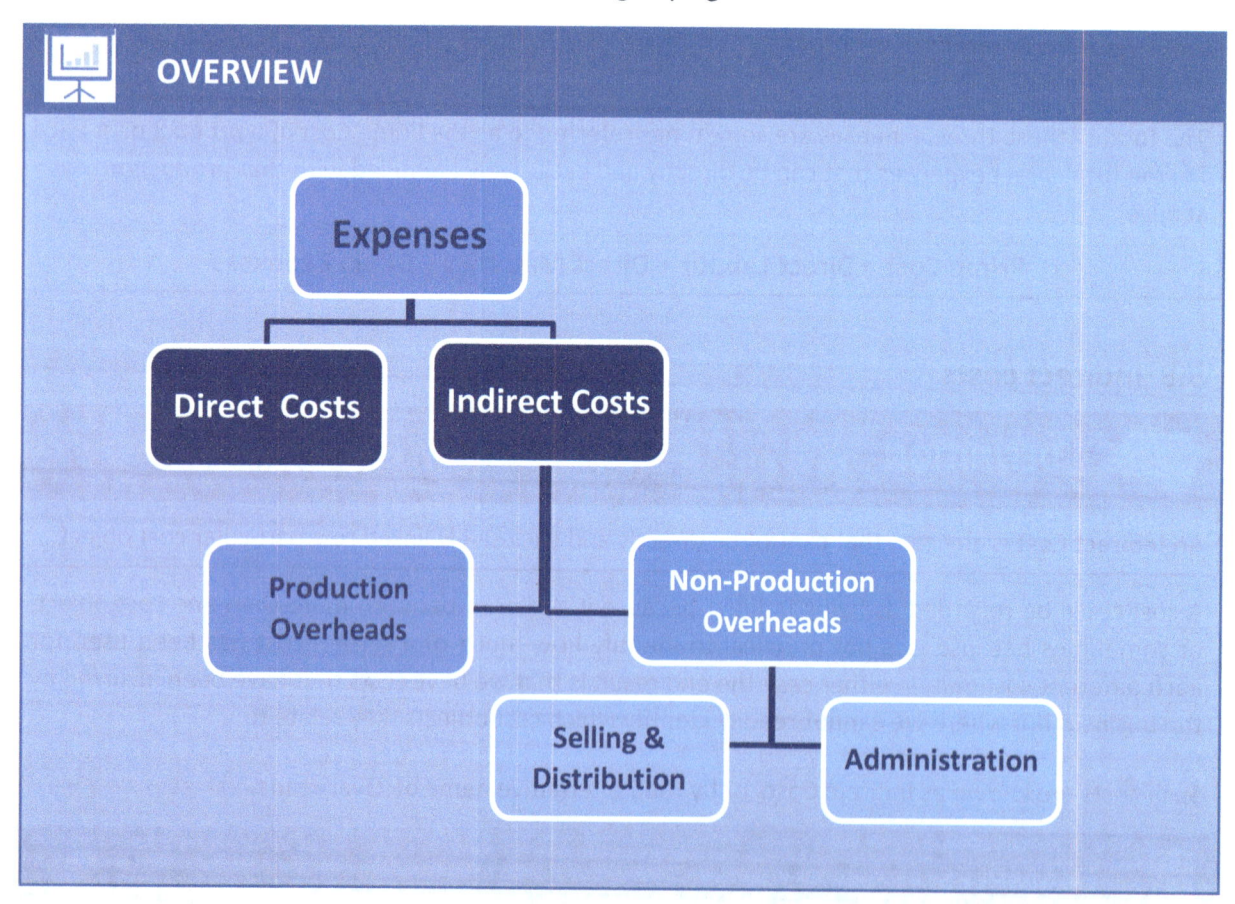

OVERVIEW

Expenses
├── Direct Costs
└── Indirect Costs
    ├── Production Overheads
    └── Non-Production Overheads
        ├── Selling & Distribution
        └── Administration

EXAMPLES

Direct and Indirect Costs

A garage carries out servicing of cars and needs a way of recording the costs which have been incurred in each service so that they can invoice the customer accordingly. The various expenses of the garage include: mechanic's wages, supervisor wages, premises costs, depreciation charges for the diagnostic equipment and hydraulic ramps etc., new parts and consumables (e.g. engine oil) and sundry expenses (for protective plastic seat covers, cleaning materials, greases etc.).

The first challenge is to categorise these costs into:

- **Direct Costs** – which relate directly to a particular service for a particular car (this is our cost object) and should therefore be directly charged to that cost object

- **Indirect Costs** - which are used by multiple cost objects and therefore need to be shared between these different cost objects in some fair way

Let's look at each cost in turn:

- **Mechanic wages = Direct :** If a mechanic works on a particular car for (say) two hours then those two hours of labour are directly attributable to that car service (i.e. that cost object)

- **Supervisor wages = Indirect :** Assuming the supervisor is responsible for over-seeing the work of several different mechanics (all working on different cars) then the supervisor's time cannot be directly linked to a particular cost object

- **Premises Costs = Indirect :** The premises are used for numerous car services over the year and therefore a rent invoice (for example) cannot be associated with a particular car service

- **Depreciation Charges = Indirect :** The plant & machinery in question is again used for numerous car services over the year and therefore cannot be associated with a particular car service

- **Spare Parts, Oil etc. = Direct :** If a car requires an oil change then the cost of (say) 10 litres of engine oil and a new oil filter should be charged to that particular car service. The expense of the parts was directly linked to a particular cost object

- **Sundry Expenses = Indirect :** Although you could argue that the cost of a plastic protective seat cover, a few squirts of grease and a few millilitres of brake cleaning fluid could be identified and therefore charged to a particular cost object, this is rarely done. The amount of each used on one particular car service represents a fairly trivial expense and it is simply not worth the effort to track down where (say) every single squirt of grease (from a 50 gallon drum of grease) ended up!

5 Introduction to Costing and Marginal Costing

> ## EXAMPLES
>
> ### Variable and fixed costs
>
> Using exactly the same garage example above, let's now classify each of the costs according to the alternative categorisation of whether they are fixed or variable. Remember, it is always important to specify how 'activity' is being measured. In this case activity is measured by the number of car services which are undertaken over (say) a year.
>
> - **Mechanic wages = Variable:** If (say) it takes a mechanic 2 hours to perform each car service, then we can see that the more services are undertaken the more mechanic labour hours will be needed…. and if absolutely no car services were undertaken then no mechanic hours would be required. In our simple model we do *not* concern ourselves with what happens if we employ mechanics and then have no work for them. Instead we regard the supply of mechanics' time as a commodity we can turn off and on (like a tap!) as required. This is another example of the sort of simplification we make in management accounting to simplify a complex real world into a manageable model.
>
> - **Supervisor wages = Fixed:** Assuming that the garage employs one supervisor, this is a fixed cost regardless of how many car services are being undertaken. Of course, if the level of activity became very high then maybe a second supervisor might be required – in which case it would become a 'stepped cost'. However, within our normal range of activity we could regard the supervisor's wages as being fixed.
>
> - **Premises Costs = Fixed:** Regardless of how many car services are undertaken the same amount of rent, rates, insurance, heat & lighting costs need to be paid. You might argue that very high levels of activity would result in (say) a higher electricity bill, but this is a trivial effect and is therefore ignored for our analysis. Again, we are making the assumption that the range of activity (i.e. number of car services) can always be accommodated within the current size of the premises.
>
> - **Depreciation Charges = Fixed:** If the business had invested £100,000 in plant and machinery (with a ten year life & no residual value thereafter) then this would equate to a £10,000 annual depreciation regardless of how many services the garage carries out in a particular year i.e. a fixed cost.
>
> - **Spare Parts & Oil etc. = Variable:** The more car services are carried out then the more oil and oil filters etc. the business will have to purchase. In theory, if no services were carried out then no oil or oil filters would need to be purchased.
>
> - **Sundry Expenses = Variable:** The more car services are carried out then the more sundry materials the business will have to purchase. In theory, if no services were carried out then no sundry materials would need to be purchased.

In an ideal world, we would at this stage show how the two alternative cost classifications of variable/fixed and direct/indirect were linked together by some over-reaching 'unifying cost theory'. Regrettably this is *not* the case and it is usually best to simply regard the variable/fixed classification and direct/indirect classification as being two entirely separate methods of cost analysis which are not to be mixed.

On some occasions (such as in 'marginal costing') we will focus on whether costs are variable or fixed; whilst on other occasions (such as in 'absorption costing' – next chapter) we will focus on whether costs are direct or indirect. Resign yourself to the fact that the two alternative systems of classification do not always neatly meet up, and instead regard them as two alternative systems of cost classification, where we will use *one* or *the other* in a given situation.

5.9 Comparison of fixed/variable and direct/indirect classification

To reinforce the point that the two classifications do not always perfectly align with each other, let's quickly look at the previous garage example and 'plot' all of the costs into a matrix which categorises the costs into both cost classification systems (variable/fixed and direct/indirect):

	Variable Costs	Fixed Costs
Direct Costs	- Mechanics' Wages - Spare Parts & Oil	
Indirect Costs	- Sundry Expenses	- Supervisor Wages - Premises Costs - Depreciation

Having (quite correctly) stated that the two systems of cost classification are entirely separate and should be generally kept apart, let us nonetheless see if we can glean any general traits from this one (very limited) example:

- **Top Row:** All of the Direct Costs appear to be Variable. This is in fact generally largely true. Direct labour, direct materials and direct expenses all (generally) increase with activity i.e. they are also variable. Occasionally you might encounter an example of a direct cost which is fixed, but such examples are the exception. For our purposes we generally make the assumption that direct costs are in fact also variable costs.

- **Bottom Row:** Although Indirect Costs often appear to be Fixed (e.g. supervisor wages, premises costs and depreciation)…..this is not always the case (e.g. sundry expenses).

- **Left Hand Column:** Variable costs can be either direct or indirect.

- **Right Hand Column:** Fixed Costs appear to always be Indirect Costs. For the purposes of this book we will take this as a general rule …. but in the real world you may encounter exceptions.

Having covered variable/fixed and direct/indirect classifications in detail we will now take a quick look at some other cost classifications.

TEST YOUR UNDERSTANDING 3

A large town centre Bar incurs a number of different costs. In general terms how would you classify the following costs in terms of being Variable (V), Fixed (F) or Semi-Variable (SV), and Direct (D) or Indirect (I)?

Consider the operation of the Bar over different days (e.g. quiet Mondays compared to busy Saturdays etc.). The Bar's 'activity' will be measured by the value of drinks sold on a given day.

Remember….. Management Accounting simplifies real-life down to simple models to allow us to make valid (though not 100% accurate) decisions. We simplify and approximate cost behaviour based on certain assumptions and within a certain 'range of activity' or time period. Your answers will quite possibly depend on the assumptions you make!

5 Introduction to Costing and Marginal Costing

	V / F / SV	D / I
Rent for Premises	_____	_____
Bar Staff Wages	_____	_____
Manager's salary	_____	_____
Purchase cost of drinks	_____	_____
Telephone Bill	_____	_____
Premises Insurance	_____	_____
Heat & Light	_____	_____
Depreciation on Furniture	_____	_____
Staff Supervisor's Salaries	_____	_____
Building Maintenance	_____	_____
Bar Consumables (straws etc.)	_____	_____

5.10 Product and period costs

A method of cost classification that is particularly useful for manufacturing industry is to state whether a cost should be treated as a 'product cost' or a 'period cost'.

Product Costs

Product costs are costs which are 'attached' to the value of the manufactured items (i.e. added into the value of the manufactured item). They are known as product costs since they are effectively 'charged' to the products themselves.

Period Costs

Period costs are costs which are **not** attached to the value of manufactured items, but are instead simply charged directly to the statement of profit and loss (P&L) as an expense in the period they were incurred.

Direct costs (e.g. direct labour, direct materials, direct expenses) will always appear as **product costs** since they are inextricably linked to the cost of manufacturing the item.

However certain **indirect costs** (specifically production overheads) may *either* be treated as product costs *or* period costs, depending on the accounting treatment adopted, as follows:

- **Financial accounting information** for external use *must* comply with financial reporting standards, which dictate that the cost of inventory must include any appropriate amount of the production overhead cost (based on a 'normal' level of activity). In other words financial reporting standards dictate that certain production overheads *must* be treated as product costs.
- **Management accounting information** (which is purely for internal use) can choose whether or not to include production overheads in the cost of manufactured items (as product costs) or, whether to simply charge them as a general expense to the P&L (as period costs).

The issue of whether to not to include production overheads as period costs or product costs is important because this then immediately affects the cost of sales figure on the P&L because including production overheads as product costs will increase the valuation of inventory, which affects the cost of sales figure thus:

Cost of Sales = Opening Inventory + Purchases - Closing Inventory

In turn, the cost of sales figure on the P&L then immediately affects the gross profit figure, because:

Gross Profit = Sales Income – Cost of Sales

The end result is that if the amount of inventory (i.e. items manufactured, but not yet sold) increases or decreases between the beginning and the end of a financial period, then the business will report different levels of profitability depending on whether they have treated certain overheads as product costs or period costs.

- **'Period costs'** are immediately charged to the P&L when they are incurred and will therefore immediately reduce reported profitability.
- **'Product costs'** will only effectively be charged to the P&L when the manufactured products are actually sold. Until then the corresponding value of the production overheads will remain attached to the unsold inventory and be represented by a higher closing inventory valuation.
- **If the level of production exceeds the level of sales** (i.e. manufactured stock remains unsold and the level of inventory *increases* over the period) then treating overheads as product costs will result in higher profits being reported.
- **If the level of sales exceeds the level of production** (i.e. inventory levels *decrease* as items manufactured in previous periods are now sold) then treating overheads as product costs will result in lower profits being reported.

5.11 Avoidable and unavoidable costs

Businesses should constantly be aware of all the costs which they are incurring (i.e. their 'cost base') since these will directly and immediately affect their profitability. Wherever possible they should seek to reduce their cost base as far as possible (without jeopardising their strategic aims), but there will always be certain costs which they can do nothing about.

Very simply, **avoidable costs** are those which can be avoided, or at least reduced, by adopting a certain course of action, and it is these costs which should be scrutinised to ensure that they are being incurred for reasons which are beneficial to the business.

5 Introduction to Costing and Marginal Costing

A simple tool to ensure that such expenditure represents value for money for the business is to assess it against the three E's:

- **Effectiveness** – Does the expenditure support the strategic aims of the business? If not, why is it being incurred?

- **Economy** – Is the resource being purchased at the lowest possible price, or could a re-tendering exercise result in cost savings on this particular expenditure

- **Efficiency** – Is the business getting the maximum *output* (i.e. benefit) compared to the financial *input* from this expenditure (getting *'more bang for your buck'*!)

> **EXAMPLE**
>
> A manufacturing company producing agricultural fertilizer purchases a certain chemical as a raw material for its production process and is now carrying out a value for money audit on this expenditure:
>
> - **Effectiveness** – Is the expenditure necessary for the company's strategic aims? The answer is clearly 'yes' as it is being used to produce a key product being sold.
>
> - **Economy** – Is the chemical being purchased at the cheapest price per tonne possible? The business should put its annual requirements for this product out to tender across all available suppliers to ensure that it is paying the lowest possible price. Furthermore, it should possibly maintain two ongoing suppliers of the chemical to ensure security of ongoing supply and maintain a stronger negotiating position (consider Porter's Five Forces from your other studies).
>
> - **Efficiency** - Is the company maximising the output volume of agricultural fertilizer compared to the input of this particular chemical, by reducing wastage at all stages of the process i.e. How many tonnes of finished fertilizer is it managing to produce per tonne of this chemical used ? Can this be increased?

By comparison, **unavoidable costs** are those which cannot be avoided or reduced. There is therefore no point in wasting time analysing them, if ultimately there is nothing which can be done about them.

> **EXAMPLE**
>
> The manufacturing company producing agricultural fertilizer (above) incurs a premises cost of £50,000 of business rates per annum payable to the local authority:
>
> - The payment of £50,000 business rates per annum is clearly a major expense to the business and one which it would dearly like to avoid. They have already employed the services of a chartered surveyor to challenge the local authority's rates assessment but without success. On the assumption that the business would not consider relocating to a cheaper premises/area at this stage, then the £50,000 of business rates represents an unavoidable cost. They may as well stop wasting time thinking about something which they cannot change, and instead focus on other avoidable costs which they can reduce or avoid.

The Language of Business

5.12 Relevant and irrelevant costs (and revenues)

When making a business decision it is important to focus on what the direct consequences of that decision will be i.e. what will change as a result of a decision to either follow or not follow a certain course of action. Put the other way around ... it is unhelpful, and potentially confusing, to bring into the debate issues which will *not* be affected as they are ultimately irrelevant to the decision. Although we are specifically looking at costs in this chapter, the same relevant/irrelevant classification can be applied to revenues (i.e. income).

Relevant Costs and Revenues are those which will be affected by a certain decision or course of action.

Special cases of relevant costs include:

- **Opportunity Costs:** which are the loss of a potential revenue as a result of a certain decision
- **Opportunity Benefits:** which are the loss of a potential cost as a result of a certain decision

Irrelevant Costs and Revenues are those which will *not* be affected by a certain decision or course of action.

Special cases of irrelevant costs can include:

- **Sunk Costs** – where the expenditure has already been spent and regardless of any decision now made cannot be 'unspent'. This can include ongoing depreciation charges still being incurred for past capital expenditure.
- **Committed Costs** – where (say) a legal obligation exists to incur a certain future cost which regardless of any decision now made, cannot be avoided.

> **EXAMPLE**
>
> A business has spent £50,000 on market research into the viability of a new product to address falling demand for its current product range. Although a final decision on whether or not to launch the new product had not yet been made, the business nonetheless committed itself to £20,000 of advertising space on prime billboard locations to support any future launch.
>
> - If the new product launch does not go ahead then some of the workforce will have to be made redundant at a cost of £100,000.
> - If the product launch does go ahead the business can use an empty building they currently own from which to distribute the new product. Alternatively they can rent this empty building out to a tenant and receive £20,000 of rental income pa.
> - Estimated incremental annual sales revenues are £200,000, whilst estimated incremental annual costs are £80,000 pa.
> - If the product launch proceeds then existing warehouse equipment (hi-bay racking, forklift trucks etc.) which is currently surplus to requirements can be utilised. The depreciation on this capital equipment is £10,000 pa.
>
> The managers of this business run the very real risk of 'not being able to see the wood for the trees' unless they can sort out which of the above figures are relevant to the decision and which are not.
>
> - **£50,000 Market Research** – is a **sunk cost**. Regardless of the decision now made this figure cannot be unspent. It is therefore **irrelevant**
> - **£20,000 Billboard advertising** – is a **committed cost**. Regardless of the decision now made this figure cannot be unspent. It is therefore **irrelevant.** (However this assessment might change if the billboard space could be utilised for advertising other products and save money elsewhere).

5 Introduction to Costing and Marginal Costing

> - **£100,000 Redundancy** – is an **opportunity benefit**. If the product launch goes ahead the £100,000 savings in redundancy payments are equivalent to £100,000 of additional revenue from the project. It is therefore **relevant** to the decision
>
> - **£20,000 Rental Income** – is an **opportunity cost**. If the product launch does go ahead then the business will forego £20,000 of revenue pa which is equivalent to an additional £20,000 cost pa. It is therefore **relevant** to the decision.
>
> - **£200,000 Incremental sales revenue** – definitely **relevant**.
>
> - **£80,000 Incremental costs** – definitely **relevant**.
>
> - **Ongoing £10,000 depreciation pa** – This is **irrelevant**. The original capital expenditure for the warehouse racking and forklift trucks was made some time ago and is therefore a sunk cost. All that remains is the **non-cash** depreciation charges for the remaining net book value of the surplus equipment, which must be accounted for … but which do not represent a cash flow.
>
> **Having disregarded all irrelevant items the business can now consider the financial viability of the proposed product launch by purely focussing on the relevant costs and revenues.**

5.13 Costing methods

Having introduced some basic costing concepts we can now start to explore the two main methods of costing products and services. Whilst this may not appear to be the cutting-edge of business, remind yourself that a business will only survive if it remains both competitive and profitable within its market sector.

To achieve these dual aims of being both competitive and profitable, a business must accurately know how much its products and services cost to make and deliver, and how low they can (or should) take their selling prices to remain attractive to their customers, whilst ultimately delivering a bottom line profit. Businesses who fail to properly understand the true cost of their products and services run the very real risk of failing as a direct result.

We shall consider two main costing methods. In this chapter we will look at marginal costing (which just focuses on the variable costs of cost objects), whilst in the next chapter we will look at absorption costing (which aims to absorb a fair-share of fixed production overheads into cost objects).

5.14 Marginal costing

> **DEFINITION**
>
> **The marginal cost** of a product is the cost of producing *one more* of that item.

This definition is worth committing to memory as it can frequently simplify and clarify problems which at first appear quite complex.

Imagine that a business produces 100 units of a certain product (cost object) each year and incurs a whole range of fixed and variable costs along the way. The marginal cost of that product is *not* the cost of producing the very first item, *nor* is it the average cost of producing one item. It is simply how much it would cost to make *one more* single item i.e. the cost of producing the 101st item.

The Language of Business

Once this is appreciated, the task of calculating the marginal cost become immediately easier as the only question is *"what costs will be involved purely in making item number 101 ?"* .... which stated another way is simply *"what incremental costs will be incurred if one more item is now made?"*

- There is no need to even consider any of the fixed costs relating to the cost object ... because they are fixed and will not increase if one more item is produced.
- The only costs that need to be considered are the variable costs because these will indeed vary when one more item is produced.

> **KEY POINT**
>
> The marginal cost of a cost object simply comprises its variable costs.

Marginal costing is a very useful and fairly simple technique which is frequently used in business to make operational decisions. A key idea in marginal costing is the concept of 'profit contribution', which we will now introduce.

> **EXAMPLE**
>
> A business manufactures a product 'the cappit' which has the following cost structure:
>
> Direct Labour   £5 per unit
>
> Direct Material   £2 per unit
>
> Variable Overhead   £1 per unit
>
> Fixed Overhead   £200 per week
>
> **If the business produces and sells 50 cappits per week, what is the marginal cost of one unit?**
>
> - The marginal cost is simply the cost of producing one more item and hence only consists of variable costs. Fixed costs can be ignored because they will not change if one more item is made.
> - Direct costs can be assumed to variable costs and this is confirmed by them being quoted "per unit".
> - So the marginal cost simply consists of the direct labour, direct materials and the variable overhead (all of which are variable costs). The fixed overhead is ignored.
> - **Marginal cost of one cappit = £5 + £2 + £1 = £8**

5 Introduction to Costing and Marginal Costing

5.15 Profit contribution

> **DEFINITION**
>
> **Profit Contribution** (or just 'contribution') is the profit that is left over after all variable (i.e. marginal) costs have been deducted.
>
> **Contribution = Sales Revenue - Variable Costs**

So as a measure of profit we can see that contribution has *not* taken into account any of the fixed costs which might be present, and this is why it is called 'contribution'. It is a *'contribution towards'* covering the fixed costs of a business and (once these are covered at the 'breakeven' point) towards the net profit.

> **EXAMPLE**
>
> Following on from the last example… if each cappit is sold for £13, how much contribution does each cappit make?
>
> **If 50 cappits are sold per week, what is total contribution made per week?**
>
> - Contribution = Sales Revenue – Variable Costs (i.e. Marginal Cost)
> - Contribution of one cappit = £13 - £8 = £5 per unit
> - Total contribution per week = 50 x £5 = £250 per week

5.16 Breakeven point

> **DEFINITION**
>
> The breakeven point is the point at which profit contribution equals the fixed costs i.e. there is neither a net profit nor a net loss
>
> **At Breakeven: Profit Contribution = Fixed Costs**

> **EXAMPLE**
>
> Following on from the previous example… with weekly fixed costs of £200 how many cappits must be sold each week to breakeven?
>
> - The sale of one cappit produces £5 contribution
> - The weekly fixed costs are £200
> - At breakeven : Total Profit Contribution = Fixed Costs
> - Therefore: breakeven units x £5 = £200
> - So breakeven units = £200 / £5 = 40 units

This idea can be shown graphically by plotting the (increasing) amount of contribution as the sales volume increases and seeing where this intercepts the amount of fixed costs. Where the two lines cross identifies the breakeven sales volume.

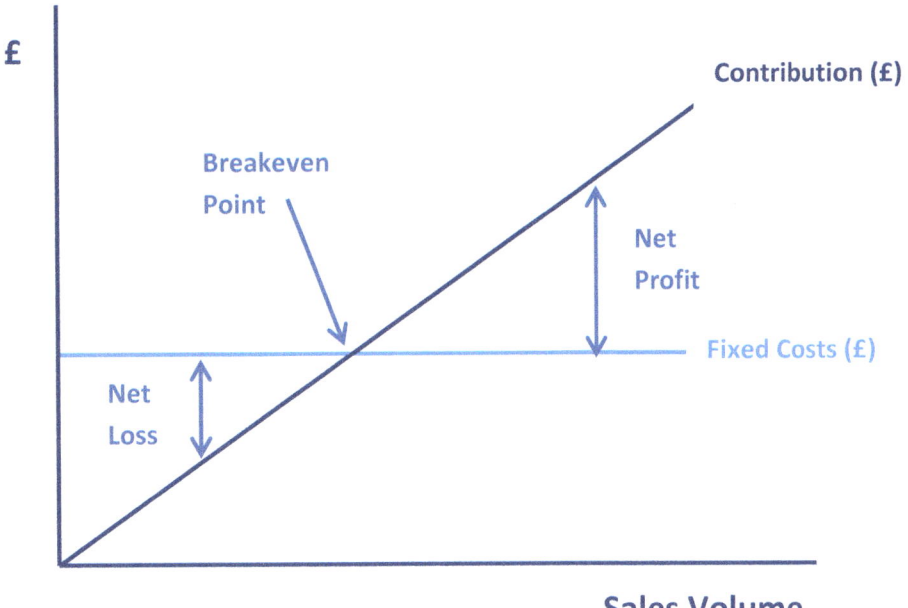

5.17 Marginal costing statement

We have already seen that the format of a normal statement of profit or loss takes the form shown below (albeit with variations depending on its intended use):

Standard Format for Statement of Profit or Loss

		£
	Income	X
less	Cost of Sales	(X)
equals	Gross Profit	X
less	Expenses	(X)
equals	Net Profit	X

However, when we are using marginal costing techniques we use the slightly different format shown below:

Standard Format for Marginal Costing Statement

		£
	Income	X
less	Variable Costs	(X)
equals	Contribution	X
less	Fixed Costs	(X)
equals	Net Profit	X

5 Introduction to Costing and Marginal Costing

> **EXAMPLE**
>
> Following on from the previous example… with weekly sales volume of 50 cappits and fixed costs of £200 per week, how much net profit is made per week?
>
> **Cappit Marginal Costing Statement**   *Workings:*
>
> | | | | |
> |--------|----------------|---------|------------------------------|
> | | Income | £650 | 50 units x £13 selling price |
> | less | Variable Costs | (£400) | 50 units x £8 marginal cost |
> | equals | Contribution | £250 | £650 - £400 |
> | less | Fixed Costs | (£200) | |
> | equals | Net Profit | £50 | £250 - £200 |
>
> [Of course, having already calculated that each cappit delivers £5 contribution, the same net profit figure could have been more quickly calculated thus:
>
> Total weekly contribution = 50 x £5 = £250 … less £200 fixed costs → Net profit = £50]

5.18 Cost Volume Profit calculations

We have already seen how relatively simple marginal costing calculations can aid a business's operational decision making. It is often useful to relate the problem in hand to the breakeven graph above, which visually describes how many units must be sold to produce sufficient contribution to cover the fixed costs. If this model is fully understood many of the problems become fairly simple to tackle.

In addition to the net profit and breakeven calculation we have already looked at, we can also use marginal costing to examine:

- Margin of safety calculations
- Target profit calculations
- Limiting factor calculations

These calculations are often referred to as 'cost volume profit' (CVP) calculations, as they are all variations on the same basic principles of calculating costs, sales volumes and profit levels.

A good starting point for any of these calculations is to first calculate the contribution per unit. If in doubt, start by doing this and the next step may then become more obvious.

5.19 Margin of Safety

We have already seen how to calculate a breakeven sales volume, but in practice businesses do not wish to merely breakeven, but to make a net profit and will therefore set their budget targets somewhat higher than the breakeven point. The margin of safety expresses by how many units (or by what percentage) the budgeted sales volume could be missed and *still* breakeven.

> Margin of Safety (units) = Budgeted Sales Volume - Breakeven Sales Volume
>
> Margin of Safety % = Margin of Safety (units) / Budgeted Sales Volume x 100%

Sometimes the budgeted sales volume is replaced by the actual sales volume to show the margin of safety between the current actual sales performance and the breakeven point.

> **EXAMPLE**
>
> From the previous example we saw that 40 'cappits' needed to be sold each week in order to breakeven, but that in fact 50 units were being sold weekly.
>
> **Margin of safety (units)** = Actual Sales Volume − Breakeven Sales Volume
>
> = 50 units − 40 units
>
> = 10 units
>
> **Margin of Safety %** = Margin of Safety (units) / Actual Sales Volume x 100%
>
> = 10 units / 50 units x 100%
>
> = 20%
>
> **Thus sales of the cappit could drop by 10 units per week (which is 20% of the current sales level) and the cappit would still (just) breakeven.**

Obviously the larger the margin of safety is (either in unit or % terms) the better for the business. The aim of a business is to make a profit, not simply to breakeven!

5.20 Target profit

Another requirement might be to calculate the sales volume required to achieve a certain target level of net profit. Again, a good starting point is to understand the contribution made when a single item is sold.

> **EXAMPLE**
>
> Following on from the previous example … with weekly fixed costs of £200, how many cappits must be sold each week to make a net profit of £600?
>
> Let's start by reminding ourselves of the contribution made per Cappit sold:
>
> Marginal cost = £8, Selling Price = £13 , Contribution per unit = £5   (£13- £8)
>
> It is useful to use the breakeven graph to help visualise the problem.
>
> [Breakeven graph showing Contribution (£) line rising with Sales Volume, Fixed Costs line at £200, £600 Net profit above fixed costs, Total Contribution Required = £200 + £600 = £800, £200 Fixed Costs]
>
> So to produce £800 total contribution, we must make and sell
> £800 ÷ £5 = 160 cappits.

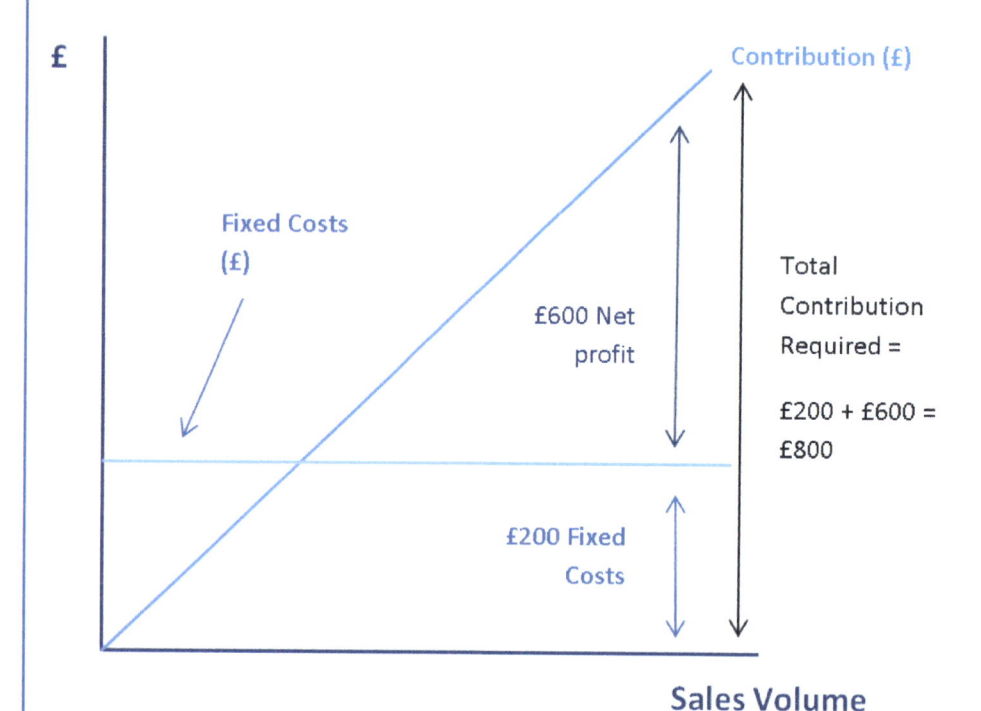

The Language of Business

> **TEST YOUR UNDERSTANDING 4**
>
> A coffee bar has the following costs per month:
>
> - Salaries   £1,000
> - Rent, Heat & Light £500
> - Coffee Beans   £1,200
> - Milk   £200
> - Sugar   £100
>
> They expect to sell 2,000 coffees at £2.50 each, exactly using the above ingredients.
>
> **What is the contribution per cup of coffee?**
>
> _____
>
> **What is the total expected contribution?**
>
> _____
>
> **What is their expected net profit for the month?**
>
> _____
>
> **How many coffees must they sell to breakeven?**
>
> _____
>
> **How many coffees must they sell to make a net profit of £3,000?**
>
> _____

5.21 Limiting Factor calculations

It is sometimes the case that a business is unable to produce and sell as many items as it would like because either labour or a certain raw material is in short supply. The scarce resource is then said to be a limiting factor on production. If the business in question makes several different products (which each use the scarce resource) then the questions arises of how to choose which products to prioritise in order to maximise profitability i.e. how to best use however much of the scarce resource is actually available.

Again, the starting point is to calculate the contribution **per unit** for each different product, but we then need to put in the additional step of calculating the contribution **per unit of the limiting factor** for each product. This is best illustrated with an example.

5 Introduction to Costing and Marginal Costing

> ## EXAMPLE
>
> A company makes three products as shown below:
>
> | Product | X | Y | Z |
> |---|---|---|---|
> | Selling Price | £200 | £120 | £160 |
> | Direct Materials | £30 | £25 | £40 |
> | Direct Labour | £50 | £20 | £30 |
> | Monthly Sales Demand | 300 | 400 | 250 |
>
> Direct Labour is paid at £10 per hour. Fixed costs are £25,000 per month
>
> Due to staff holidays there are only 2,000 hours of direct labour available this month, which is insufficient to meet full sales demand.
>
> Produce a production plan that maximises profitability for the labour hours available and calculate the net profit that this will deliver.
>
> A good starting point is to calculate the contribution per unit for each product. Remember, we can assume that direct costs are always variable costs, and we ignore fixed costs when calculating contribution:
>
> | Product | X | Y | Z |
> |---|---|---|---|
> | Selling Price | £200 | £120 | £160 |
> | Direct Materials | £30 | £25 | £40 |
> | Direct Labour | £50 | £20 | £30 |
> | Contribution per unit | £120 | £75 | £90 |
>
> So our initial thought might be that product X is the most profitable, followed by product Z, with product Y being least profitable. However we have not yet taken into consideration the fact that there are insufficient labour hours to produce enough of these products to meet full sales demand.
>
> The next step therefore is to calculate how many hours of labour (paid at £10 per hour) each product takes to make, and then to calculate the contribution **per hour of labour** that each product delivers.
>
> | Product | X | Y | Z |
> |---|---|---|---|
> | Direct Labour (£) | £50 | £20 | £30 |
> | Direct Labour (Hours) | 5 hours | 2 hours | 3 hours |
> | Contribution per unit | £120 | £75 | £90 |
> | Contribution per hour of labour | £24.00 | £37.50 | £30.00 |
> | Ranking (based on limited labour) | 3rd | 1st | 2nd |

194

We can now see that although product X made the highest contribution per unit, it also used more precious labour hours than the other products, and in fact made the lowest contribution per labour hour.

Conversely, although product Y produces the lowest contribution per unit, it in fact delivers the highest contribution per hour of labour. Having ranked the products 1st, 2nd & 3rd according to the contribution per unit of limiting factor we can then devise a production plan which prioritises the products which make most profit contribution per unit of the scarce resource… in this case labour hours.

Production Plan

1st **Product Y 400 units** (max. demand) x 2 hours each = 800 labour hours

This leaves 2,000 – 800 = 1,200 labour hour remaining

2nd **Product Z 250 units** (max. sales demand) x 3 hours each = 750 labour hours

This leaves 1,200 – 750 = 450 labour hours remaining. There are insufficient labour hours left to make the full 300 demand for product X, but the remaining hours will be used to make as many as possible.

3rd **Product X 90 units** (450 remaining hours / 5 hours per X = 90 units)

Profit Forecast

Contribution:

Product Y	400 x £75	=	£30,000
Product Z	250 x £90	=	£22,500
Product X	90 x £120	=	£10,800
Total Contribution			£63,300
Less Fixed Costs			(£25,000)
Net Profit			**£38,300**

5 Introduction to Costing and Marginal Costing

> ⚠️ **KEY POINTS FROM CHAPTER 5**

Variable, Fixed & Semi-Variable Costs

- **Variable Costs** are recognised by the total cost increasing with the level of activity, but the unit cost remaining constant

- **Fixed costs** are easily recognised as total cost remaining constant despite level of activity changing

- **Semi-Variable costs** are recognised by total cost increasing with activity, but unit cost falling

- **Hi-Lo method** used to split semi-variable costs into variable and fixed components

Direct and Indirect Costs

- **Direct Costs** are those costs which can be directly and exclusively linked to a particular cost object.

- **Indirect Costs** (aka overheads) are those costs which cannot be directly and exclusively identified with a particular cost object

- Indirect Costs are often categorised into:
    - Production Overheads
    - Selling and Distribution Overheads
    - Administration overheads

- Financial reporting standards stipulate that (for financial accounting purposes) 'Cost of Sales' must include an appropriate share of production overheads.

- Although 'fixed/variable' and 'direct/indirect' are alternative cost classifications which should be used separately, it is worth noting that 'direct costs' are typically 'variable'.

Other Cost Classifications

- **Product Costs** are those cost which are 'charged' to a cost object; whereas **Period Costs** are costs which will simply be charged directly to the P&L instead in the period they were incurred.

- **Avoidable Costs** are those which can be avoided or at least reduced by adopting a certain course of action; whereas **Unavoidable Costs** are those which cannot be avoided or reduced.

- **Relevant Costs and Revenues** are those which will be affected by a certain decision or course of action; whereas **Irrelevant Costs and Revenues:** are those which will *not* be affected by a certain decision or course of action.

- Special cases of relevant costs include:
    - **Opportunity Costs**: which are the loss of potential revenue as a result of a certain decision
    - **Opportunity Benefits:** which are the loss of potential cost as a result of a certain decision

Marginal Costing

- The marginal cost of a product is the cost of producing one more of that item.

- The marginal cost of a cost object therefore simply comprises its variable costs.

Profit Contribution

Profit Contribution (or just 'contribution') is the profit that is left over after all variable (i.e. marginal) costs have been deducted.

Contribution = Sales Revenue - Variable Costs

Contribution has *not* taken into account any of the fixed costs which might be present. It is a *'contribution towards'* covering the fixed costs of a business and (once these are covered at the 'breakeven' point) towards the net profit.

Breakeven Point

The breakeven point is the point at which profit contribution equals the fixed costs i.e. there is neither a net profit nor a net loss

At Breakeven: Profit Contribution = Fixed Costs

Standard Format for Marginal Costing Statement

		£
	Income	X
less	Variable Costs	(X)
equals	Contribution	X
less	Fixed Costs	(X)
equals	Net Profit	X

Margin of Safety (MOS)

- **Margin of Safety (units) = Budgeted Sales Volume - Breakeven Sales Volume**
- **Margin of Safety % = Margin of Safety (units) / Budgeted Sales Volume x 100%**

(Budgeted sales volume can be replaced by the actual sales volume)

Cost Volume Profit (CVP) Calculations

The concepts of marginal costing and profit contribution can be used to perform various useful business calculations, usually commencing with the calculation of 'contribution per unit'. Uses include calculation of **breakeven point** and also:

- **'Target Profit'** – calculation of how many units must be sold to achieve a certain target net profit (where the required total contribution = fixed costs + target net profit)
- **'Limiting Factor'** problems caused by scarce resources (e.g. labour or materials). Having calculated 'contribution per unit', you must then calculate contribution per unit of the limiting factor for each product to enable their planned production to be ranked.

5 Introduction to Costing and Marginal Costing

Chapter 5: Test Your Understanding Answers

TEST YOUR UNDERSTANDING 1

Activity (Minutes of telephone calls per month)	Fixed Cost	Variable Cost	Total Cost of Telephone Bill (= Fixed + Variable Costs)	Total Unit Cost of Telephone calls per minute (= Total Cost / Minutes)
500	£100	500 minutes x £0.10 = £50	£100 + £50 = £150	£150 / 500 minutes = £0.30 per minute
1,000	£100	1,000 minutes x £0.10 = £100	£100 + £100 = £200	£200 / 1,000 minutes = £0.20 per minute
2,000	£100	2,000 minutes x £0.10 = £200	£100 + £200 = £300	£300 / 2,000 minutes = £0.15 per minute
3,000	£100	3,000 minutes x £0.10 = £300	£100 + £300 = £400	£400 / 3,000 minutes = £0.133 per minute
4,000	£100	4,000 minutes x £0.10 = £400	£100 + £500 = £500	£500 / 4,000 minutes = £0.125 per minute

TEST YOUR UNDERSTANDING 2

Hi-Lo Method (Sept & Aug)

$$\frac{£109 - £89}{2,200 - 1,200} = \frac{£20}{1,000} = £0.02 \text{ per copy variable cost.}$$

Substitute £0.02 per copy into (say) September figures:-

Fixed Cost = £109 − (2,200 x £0.02) = £109 - £44 = **£65 each month**

	October	November	December
No. of Copies	900	1,900	2,400
Fixed Cost	£65	£65	£65
Variable Cost (£0.02 per copy)	£18	£38	£48
Total Cost	£83	£103	£113

TEST YOUR UNDERSTANDING 3

	V / F / SV	D / I
Rent for Premises	F	I
Bar Staff Wages	SV	D
Manager's salary	F	I
Purchase cost of drinks	V	D
Telephone Bill	F (mostly fixed)	I
Premises Insurance	F	I
Heat & Light	F	I
Depreciation on Furniture	F	I
Staff Supervisor's Salaries	SV (Additional supervisors?)	D
Building Maintenance	F (mostly)	I
Bar Consumables (straws etc)	V	D

TEST YOUR UNDERSTANDING 4

Contribution per Cup of Coffee	Variable Costs = (£1,200 + £200 + £100) / 2,000 = £0.75 per cup
	Contribution = £2.50 - £0.75 = £1.75 per cup
Total Expected Contribution	2,000 x £1.75 = £3,500
Expected Net Profit	£3,500 - £1,000 - £500 [i.e. less fixed costs] = £2,000
Breakeven Sales Volume	= Fixed Costs / Contribution per cup = £1,500 / £1.75 = 858 cups
Sales Volume for £3,000 net profit	= (Fixed Costs + Net Profit) / Contribution per cup = (£1,500 + £3,000) / £1.75 = 2,572 cups

5 Introduction to Costing and Marginal Costing

Chapter 5: End of Chapter Exercises

Section A Questions

Question 5.1

Which two of the following statements about variable costs are true?

  i. As activity increases the total cost of a variable cost also increases
  ii. At zero activity the total cost of a variable cost is £nil
  iii. As activity increases the unit cost of a variable cost also increases
  iv. Variable costs can 'step-up' to a higher cost at certain levels of activity

Select the correct answer:

A   i & ii
B   i & iii
C   ii & iii
D   ii & iv

Question 5.2

Which of the following statements correctly describes cost X in the table below?

	Month 1	Month 2	Month 3
Cost X	£525	£480	£615
Activity (units)	350	320	410

A   Semi-variable: Fixed element of £105 per month and variable element of £1.20 per unit
B   Variable cost of £0.67 per unit of activity
C   Semi-variable: Fixed element of £96 per month and variable element of £1.20 per unit
D   Variable cost of £1.50 per unit of activity

Question 5.3

Which two of the following statements about costs are true?

  i. 'Period costs' are charged in full to the P&L account in the period they were incurred.
  ii. 'Product Costs' are charged to the P&L when the corresponding product is manufactured.
  iii. 'Sunk costs' are relevant to future decision making
  iv. 'The loss of potential revenue as the result of a certain decision would be described as an 'opportunity cost'.

Select the correct answer:

A   i & ii
B   i & iv
C   ii & iii
D   ii & iv

The Language of Business

Question 5.4

A factory manufactures large quantities of a product known as the Thingamabob.

Which of the following statements correctly describes the marginal cost of a Thingamabob?

- A   The cost of producing the first Thingamabob
- B   The average cost of producing Thingamabobs
- C   The unit cost of producing Thingamabobs including a fair share of fixed production overheads
- D   The cost of producing one more Thingamabob

Question 5.5

A company car is hired under a lease rental agreement for a fixed monthly sum and an additional cost per mile the car is used each month.

The total lease rental cost for each of the last three months are shown below, together with the mileage the car travelled each month.

	Month 1	Month 2	Month 3
Total Monthly Lease Rental Cost	£555	£480	£510
Monthly Mileage	1,200 miles	700 miles	900 miles

Based on this data calculate the fixed monthly sum and the additional cost per mile charged by the lease rental company.

	Fixed Monthly Sum	Additional Fee per Mile
A	£483	£0.06
B	£447	£0.09
C	£375	£0.15
D	£255	£0.25

Question 5.6

The entire trade of a coffee shop consists of selling coffee at £2.20 per cup. Each cup of coffee costs £0.40 to produce. The fixed costs of the shop are £360 per week.

How many cups of coffee does the shop need to sell each week to breakeven?

- A   164 cups
- B   180 cups
- C   200 cups
- D   900 cups

5 Introduction to Costing and Marginal Costing

Question 5.7

A small manufacturing business makes a single product which it sells for £45.50 each. The product has variable costs of £15.50 per unit, and the business has fixed costs of £2,000 per week.

What is the required weekly sales volume if the business wishes to make £700 profit per week?

A   23 units

B   67 units

C   90 units

D   95 units

Question 5.8

Which of the following statements about the 'break-even' point is incorrect?

A   At breakeven total contribution = total fixed costs

B   At breakeven neither a net profit nor a net loss is made

C   At breakeven total sales revenue = total costs

D   At breakeven the margin of safety has been achieved.

Question 5.9

A business manufactures and sells a single product which costs £5.00 each to produce, and is sold for £13.00 each. The business has fixed annual costs of £20,000.

What level of sales revenue should be included in the business's annual budget if it wishes to have a 25% margin of safety?

A   £32,500

B   £40,625

C   £43,333

D   £56,875

Question 5.10

A company produces three products Alpha, Beta & Gamma with financial details as below:

Per Unit	Alpha	Beta	Gamma
Selling Price	£120	£90	£170
Direct Labour	£36	£9	£45
Direct Materials	£32	£45	£40
Variable Overheads	£12	£14	£10
Maximum Monthly Demand	150	300	200

All labour is paid at £9.00 per hour. There are only 1,500 labour hours available this month.

What is the maximum profit contribution that can be achieved this month with this limited number of labour hours?

A £20,000

B £21,600

C £23,600

D £24,600

5 Introduction to Costing and Marginal Costing

Section B Questions

	January	February	March
Activity (units)	100	150	200
Cost A	£1,500	£2,250	£3,000
Cost B	£500	£500	£500
Cost C	£250	£375	£500
Cost D	£300	£400	£500

For each cost identify whether:

- The total cost remains constant or varies
- The unit cost remains constant or varies

Use this information to:

- State what category (variable, fixed, semi-variable) the cost falls into
- To describe the cost behaviour numerically (using appropriate analysis)

Cost A

VARIABLE

Consistent - 1.5 everytime

£1,500 ÷ 1.5   £2,250 ÷ 1.5   £3,000 ÷ 1.5

Cost B

FIXED COST

Cost is always the same

Cost C

VARIABLE COST

Cost D

SEMI-VARIABLE

inconsistent activity both unit cost and fixed costs change

Based on your findings, now estimate the costs for April, May and June:

	April	May	June
Activity (units)	250	300	400
Cost A	3,750	4,500	3,000
Cost B	500	500	500
Cost C	625	750	1000
Cost D	500	600	800

Semi Variable

Total cost is equal to variable × units + fixed cost

High low method — change in £ ÷ change in units = VC

→ £800 − £500

→ fixed cost

TOTAL COST = £ × unit + FC

D → FC = 300 − 200 = 100

5 Introduction to Costing and Marginal Costing

Question 5.12

A Toy manufacturer is considering launching a new product which it hopes to sell for £9 per unit. Launching production of the new toy will result in the following costs:

- Production Labour (per unit)   £1.00
- Direct Materials (per unit)   £2.00
- Packaging Expenses (per unit)   £0.50
- Variable Overhead (per unit)   £1.50

In addition it is anticipated that there will be £100,000 of additional fixed costs as a result of the product launch and it is anticipated that 45,000 of the toys will be manufactured and sold in the first year.

What are the total variable costs per unit?

£5 = £1 + £2 + 0.50 + £1.50

What will be the contribution per unit? revenue − variable costs

£9 − £5 = £4

What is the breakeven volume?

100,000 ÷ 4 = 25,000

What is the Margin of Safety between the breakeven volume and the budgeted annual sales (in both units and as a percentage)?

45,000 − 25,000 = 20,000 units

20,000 ÷ 45,000 × 100 = 44.4%
           (Budget)

How much net profit will be made if the budgeted sales are achieved?
                                        contribution ×
£9 × 45,000 = 405,000

45,000 × 4 − 100,000 = £80,000

How many would need to be sold to achieve a net profit of £95,000?

15,000 ÷ 4 = 3,750

45,000 + 3,750 = 48,750

206

The Language of Business

Question 5.13

If a business increases its selling price it will increase its profit margin% ...... but probably decrease its sales volume! The trick is to establish the selling price at which profit (measured in £) is maximised. A company has conducted marked research to establish the likely sales volume it will achieve when its sells a new product at various different selling prices. The product has a variable cost of £20 each.

Assuming that the market research is accurate at what selling price will the contribution be maximised?

Selling Price Per Unit (£)	Predicted Sales Volume at Price (units)	Sales Revenue (£)	Variable Costs (£)	Contribution (£)
£120	500	60,000	10,000	60,000
£110	600	66,000	(20x600) 120,000	66-12 54,000
£100	650	65,000	13,000	52,000
£90	700	63,000	14,000	49,000

Question 5.14

A company makes three types of product X, Y & Z. Extract from the budget for next year are as follows:

	X	Y	Z
Demand & Production (units)	1,000	1,500	2,000
Per Unit	X	Y	Z
Selling Price (per unit)	£87	£170	£154
Materials (per unit)	£15	£40	£30
Labour (per unit)	£20	£50	£40
Variable Overhead (per unit)	£12	£30	£24

Labour will be paid at £5 per hour.

Total fixed overheads are expected to be £120,000.

It has been realised that only 30,000 labour hours are available for next year.

You are required to calculate a production plan that will maximise profit within the constraints of the available labour hours, and thereby prepare a marginal profit forecast based on this production plan.

Tutorial Note: The first stage is to calculate the profit contribution per unit of each product, and then to additionally calculate the profit contribution for each product per unit of limiting factor (which in this case is labour hours). This will then allow the three products to be ranked (1st, 2nd, 3rd) in terms of how much profit each makes per hour of labour.

5 Introduction to Costing and Marginal Costing

	Product X	Product Y	Product Z
Selling Price (per unit)	£87	£170	£154
Total Variable Costs (per unit)	£47	£120	30+10+24 £94
Profit Contribution per unit (per unit)	£40	£50	£60
No. of hours labour required (per unit)	4	10	8
Profit Contribution per labour hour (i.e. the limiting factor)	£10	£5	£7.5
Profitability Ranking (1st, 2nd or 3rd) per unit of limiting factor	1st	3rd	2nd

Tutorial Note: Having determined the optimum order in which to produce these three products (in order to maximise the profit possible from the available hours), the next step is to see how many of each product should be manufactured. There is no point in manufacturing more of any of the products than the business has sales demand for, but at some point the available hours will prove insufficient (so we will need to keep a running total of how many labour hours we have used so far.

Ranking	Product	Production Volume	Labour Hours used for this product	Total Labour Hours used	Labour Hours Remaining	Profit Contribution from this product
1st Product	X	1000	4	4000	26000	40,000
2nd Product	Z	2000	8	16,000	10000	120,000
3rd Product	Y	1000	10	10,000	0	50,000
Total Contribution						210,000
Fixed Costs						120,000
Net Profit						90,000

The Language of Business

Question 5.15

A café uses a simple marginal costing system to set the selling prices for all of their menu items. They only take into account the costs of the food ingredients and aim to make a 77% gross profit margin.

Complete the following cost card for a ham & cheese omelette with fries, and hence calculate the required minimum selling price (inc. VAT) to achieve their required margin.

COST CARD – Ham & Cheese Omelette with Fries			
Item	Unit Cost Price	Amount Required	Cost
Eggs	£1.80 per dozen	3 eggs	0.45p
Butter	£1.60 per 250g	25g	0.16p
Cheese	£2.00 per 400g	50g	0.25p
Ham	£2.00 per 150g	30g	0.40p
French Fries	£1.60 per kg	200g	0.32p
		Total Cost of Ingredients	£1.58
		Selling Price (exc. VAT) – to achieve 77% margin	£6.87
		Selling Price (inc. VAT)	£8.24

MARGIN = PRICE 100%

COST   23   23% = 1.58
profit 77   100% = £6.87

5 Introduction to Costing and Marginal Costing

Question 5.16

A company requires a margin of safety of 20%. It has annual fixed costs of £100,000. The company produces only one product with a variable cost of £4 per unit.

Tutorial Note: There is a lot of information provided and it is not immediately obvious how to tackle this problem! In such cases it is often advisable to make a first tentative step with the hope that the next step may then become clearer. 'Margin of Safety' relates to how many of a product a business must sell to break-even and so this might be a good place to start!

Step One:

If the estimated sales are 20,000 units, but this includes a 20% margin of safety, then how many units of the product need to be sold to (just) break-even?

16,000 units

Step Two:

Using this break-even sales volume, derive an equation (which includes the term 'SP' as the unknown selling price) which is based on the fact that at break-even : *Total Contribution = Total Fixed Cost*.

And .... **Total Contribution (at break-even) = Contribution of <u>one unit</u> x break-even sales volume**

SP =

Step Three:

Simply solve the equation to find the unknown term 'SP' which represents what the selling price should be.

210

Chapter 6

Absorption Costing

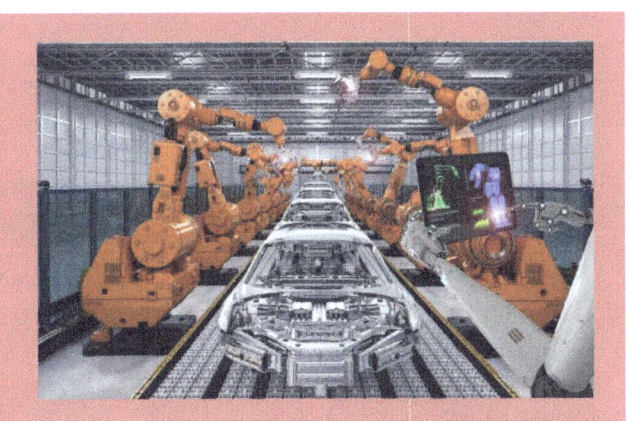

INTRODUCTION

In the last chapter we introduced 'marginal costing' where only variable costs were assigned to the 'Cost Object' (i.e. whatever product or service we are considering). All fixed costs were simply deducted later from the total 'contribution'. This is a very simple and very powerful technique which is widely used in industry (largely because it is so easy to understand and quick to use).

However a major drawback of marginal costing is that because we have (initially) ignored the fixed costs, we may believe that the 'cost' of a product is less than maybe it should be, because not all of the costs have been included. This could result in the product being sold for less than it should be, and possibly even ultimately at a loss!

Absorption costing aims to avoid this danger by including a **'fair share'** of the fixed costs in each cost unit. For this reason it is often referred to as 'Total Costing' or 'Full Costing'.

OVERVIEW AND OBJECTIVES

At the end of this chapter you should understand and be able to apply:

- the mechanics of Absorption Costing
- the concept of Traditional Absorption Costing
- Activity Based Costing methods.

This chapter does not contain any 'Test Your Understanding' questions. Instead you should work through the comprehensive example used throughout the chapter to demonstrate absorption costing.

211

6 Absorption Costing

6.1 Recap of Marginal Costing

In Chapter 5 we saw that the *marginal cost* of a cost object is the cost of making one more of that item, and that *contribution* is the additional profit generated from making and selling one more unit of that cost object.

Marginal costing therefore just focusses on the variable costs associated with a cost object as these will increase with every additional unit. The variable costs consist of all the direct costs plus any variable production overheads.

> **TUTORIAL NOTE**
>
> We are making the assumption that the direct costs we encounter will always be variable. We will *not* concern ourselves with the rarer instance of a direct cost which is also fixed.

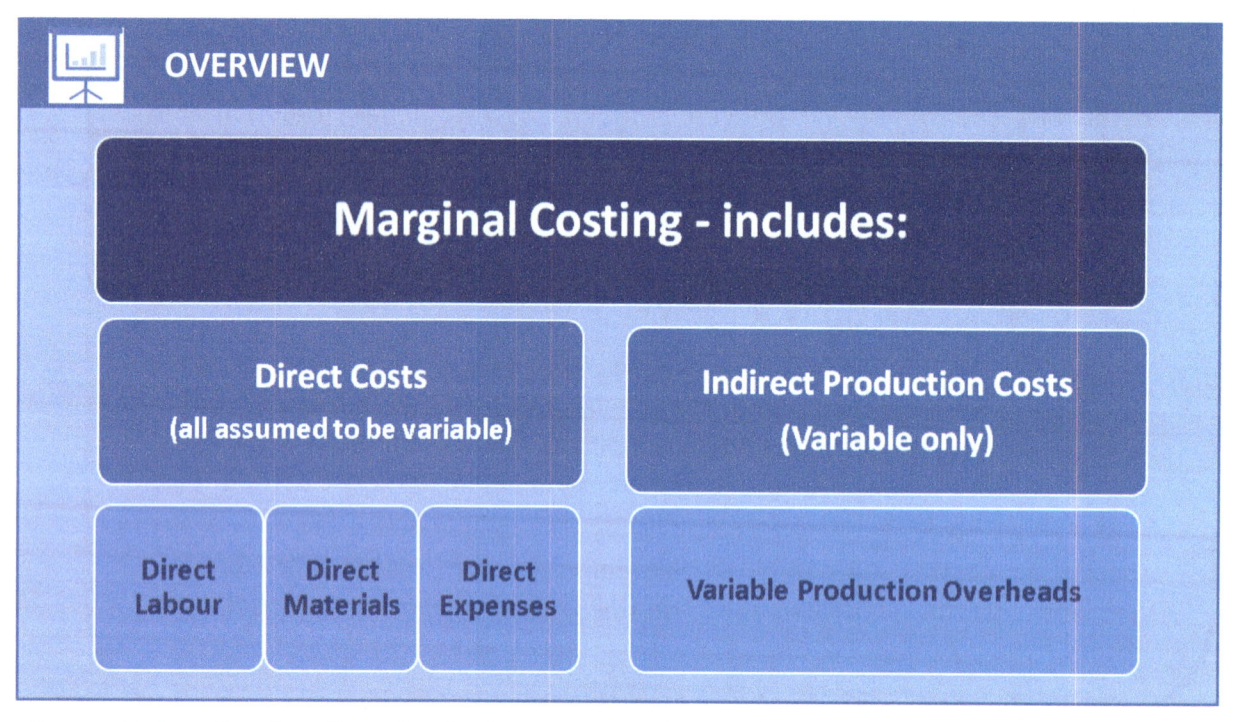

OVERVIEW

Marginal Costing - includes:

- **Direct Costs** (all assumed to be variable)
  - Direct Labour
  - Direct Materials
  - Direct Expenses
- **Indirect Production Costs** (Variable only)
  - Variable Production Overheads

In marginal costing therefore, the fixed costs are *not* included within the cost object itself, but are instead subtracted from total contribution figure to leave the final net profit figure as shown below in the standard format for a marginal costing statement:

Standard Format for Marginal Costing Statement

		£	
	Income	X	
less	Variable Costs	(X)	(aka marginal costs)
equals	Contribution	X	
less	Fixed Costs	(X)	
equals	Net Profit	X	

Whilst this simplicity makes marginal costing very simple to use and understand, it does have the major disadvantage that it can potentially lead to fixed costs being ignored (at least initially). This is commercially dangerous because if a business does not cover its fixed costs then ultimately it will make a net loss.

6.2 Overview of Absorption Costing

In comparison, absorption costing aims to not only include the variable costs of a cost object, but also to include a fair share of the fixed production costs incurred. For this reason absorption costing is often referred to as **'total costing'** or **'full costing'** as it contains both variable and fixed costs.

You will recall that marginal costs already include any variable production overheads (see above). The extra step in absorption costing is that a 'fair share' of any *fixed* production overheads are also included.

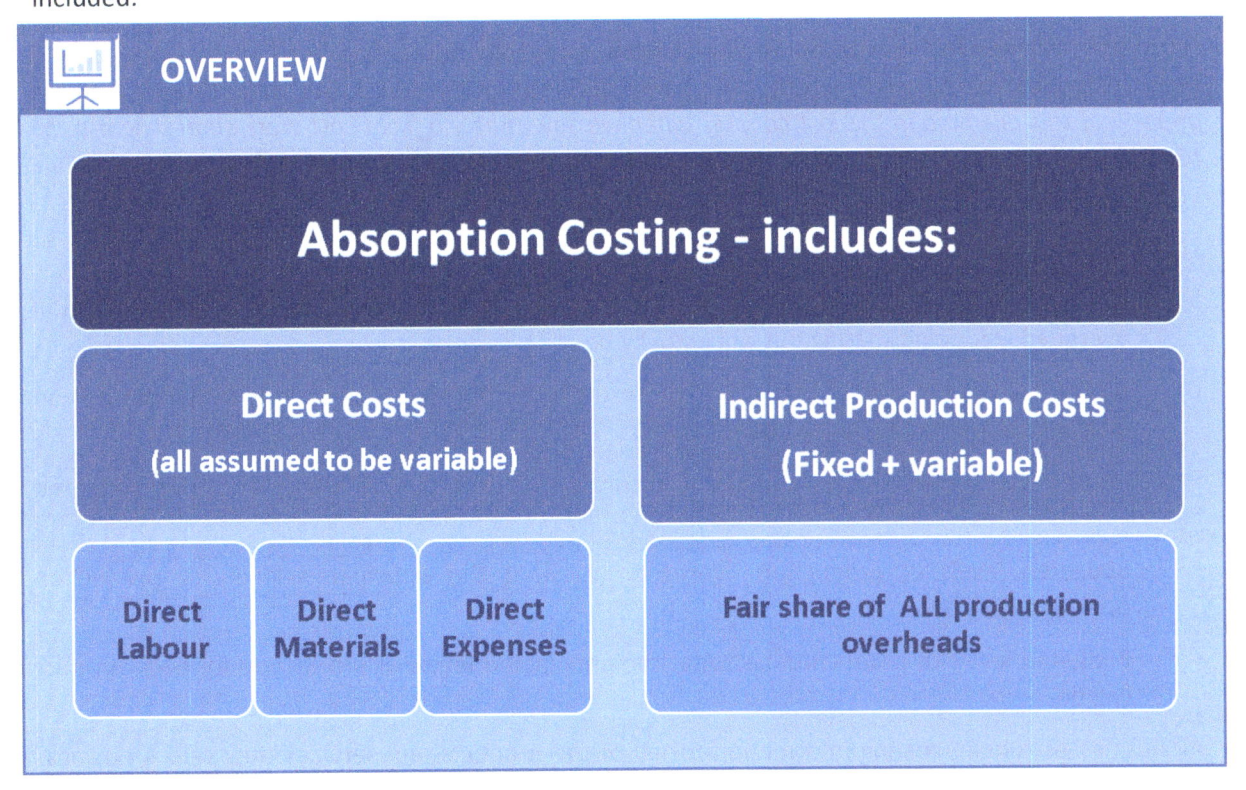

OVERVIEW

Absorption Costing - includes:

- **Direct Costs** (all assumed to be variable)
  - Direct Labour
  - Direct Materials
  - Direct Expenses
- **Indirect Production Costs** (Fixed + variable)
  - Fair share of ALL production overheads

TUTORIAL NOTE

Other indirect costs (overheads) such as administration overheads or selling & distribution overheads are *not* part of the product cost (regardless of whether they are variable or fixed in nature). It is only the **production** overheads which need to be considered.

You may sometimes see references to the effect that absorption costing means including a fair share of simply *'overheads'*. This is actually a shortened, slightly lazy version of the precise definition, which is that absorption costing means including a fair share of any **production** overheads.

In summary, marginal costing has already included **variable** production overheads within each cost unit. Absorption costing goes one step further and **also** includes a fair share of the **fixed** production overheads within each cost unit.

6 Absorption Costing

The first challenge when using absorption costing is devising a method that spreads the cost of any fixed production overheads over all the different cost objects involved (remembering that the definition of an overhead is a cost which *cannot* be readily traced back to *one single* cost object). There are a multitude of variations in the exact method used to share out the fixed production overheads (sometimes including completely bespoke methods for a particular scenario) but they can be roughly divided into two main methods known as:

1. **Traditional Absorption Costing** – where the fixed production overheads of a business are analysed and shared across the relevant **production departments**.

2. **Activity Based Costing (ABC)** – where the fixed production overheads of a business are analysed and shared across the different **activities** of a business.

6.3 Use of budgeted data

A further challenge for absorption costing is knowing exactly *how much* fixed production cost will need to be shared out over exactly *how many* different cost objects. *We actually saw a sneak preview of this dilemma in the last chapter when we saw that if a fixed cost were shared across the total level of production, then the higher the level of production … the smaller share each individual unit would need to absorb.*

There are actually two separate sides to this issue:

a) A business will not always know in advance exactly what the level of fixed production overheads requiring sharing out will actually be

b) A business will not always know in advance the exact number of cost units which these fixed production overheads can be shared across

For both of these reasons both methods of absorption costing (Traditional & ABC) use **budgeted** figures, namely:

- Budgeted levels of production overhead i.e. what the anticipated levels of production overheads will be

- Budgeted levels of production i.e. what the anticipated levels of production for each product will be

All businesses require costing information for all of the products and services they sell. A business simply cannot set an *informed* selling price for a product until it has an idea of how much it cost to produce. Similarly it also cannot value unsold inventory for accounting purposes. Neither of these can wait until the end of the financial year (when *actual* costs and *actual* levels of activity are known). The costing information is needed right from day one and so the best which can be achieved is to use the budgeted overhead costs and budgeted production levels in order to calculate how exactly to share out fixed production overheads across cost objects.

6.4 Traditional Absorption Costing

Traditional Absorption Costing shares out the value of fixed production overheads to cost objects as they pass through **production departments**. The process comprises of the following stages:

Stage One

Calculating how much of the total fixed factory overhead should be borne by each department within the factory (*both production departments and service departments*).

> **DEFINITION**
>
> **Production Departments** include any department that works directly on the products being manufactured e.g. Machining, Assembly, Finishing etc.
>
> **Service Departments** include any department that does not work directly on products, but which indirectly supports production e.g. Quality Control, Canteen, Engineering Support, Purchasing etc.

The various factory overheads should either be:

- **Allocated** to a department if the overhead is purely associated with that particular department
- **Apportioned** across departments on some fair basis if the overhead is associated with several departments.

The end result of Stage One is that the entire fixed factory overhead has now been assigned across all of the departments within the factory.

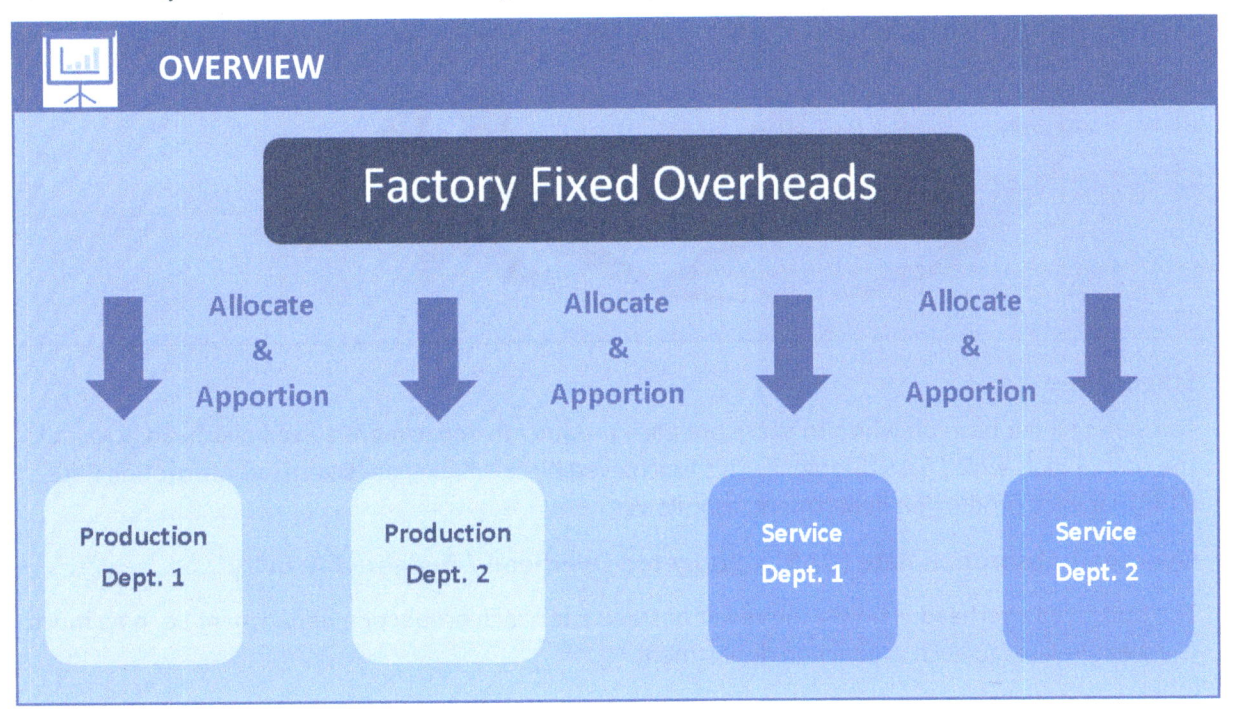

> **OVERVIEW**
>
> **Factory Fixed Overheads**
>
> Allocate & Apportion → Production Dept. 1
> Allocate & Apportion → Production Dept. 2
> Allocate & Apportion → Service Dept. 1
> Allocate & Apportion → Service Dept. 2

Stage Two

Re-assigning the service department overhead into (just) the production departments. An estimate needs to be made as to what extent each production department uses each service department. These estimates are then used to recharge the overheads which were assigned to the service departments (in stage one) to the production departments.

The end result of Stage Two is that the entire fixed factory overhead has now been assigned across just the production departments within the factory.

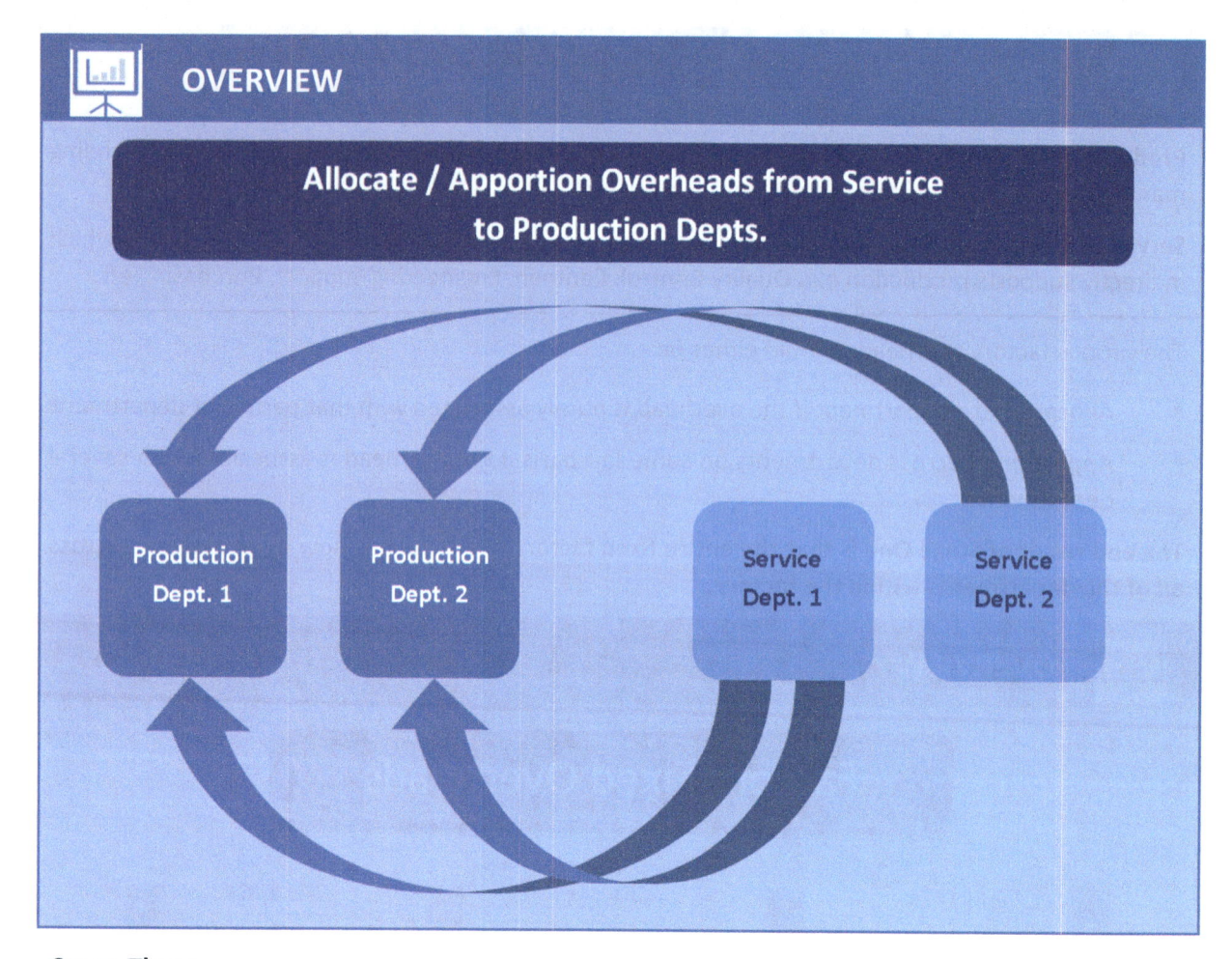

6 Absorption Costing

OVERVIEW

Allocate / Apportion Overheads from Service to Production Depts.

Production Dept. 1 | Production Dept. 2 | Service Dept. 1 | Service Dept. 2

Stage Three

Calculating a fair basis on which to share out each production department's fixed overhead across all the cost objects which pass through it. This is achieved by calculating an 'Overhead Absorption Rate' (OAR) for each production department, as follows:

Overhead Absorption Rate (OAR) = Budgeted Overhead / Budgeted Activity

The **budgeted overhead** is simply the result of stage 2 for each production department i.e. how much overhead relates to each production department.

The **budgeted activity** is simply how much of that department's key activity is expected to occur over the next year e.g. a machining department may be budgeted to be operating its machines for 10,000 hours in the next 12 months i.e. 10,000 machine hours.

Stage Four

Calculating the **full** cost of products by first adding together their various variable costs:

1. Direct labour*
2. Direct materials*
3. Direct expenses*
4. Variable overheads

… and then adding an appropriate share of the fixed costs of *each* production department the product has passed through, using the Overhead Absorption Rate and an estimate of the extent to which the product used that department (e.g. how many machine hours are used).

(*Direct Costs are typically variable).

The end result of this stage is that (by the end of the financial year) all of the fixed production overhead that had been allocated/apportioned to each production department will have been 'absorbed' into the various cost objects that have passed through that department.

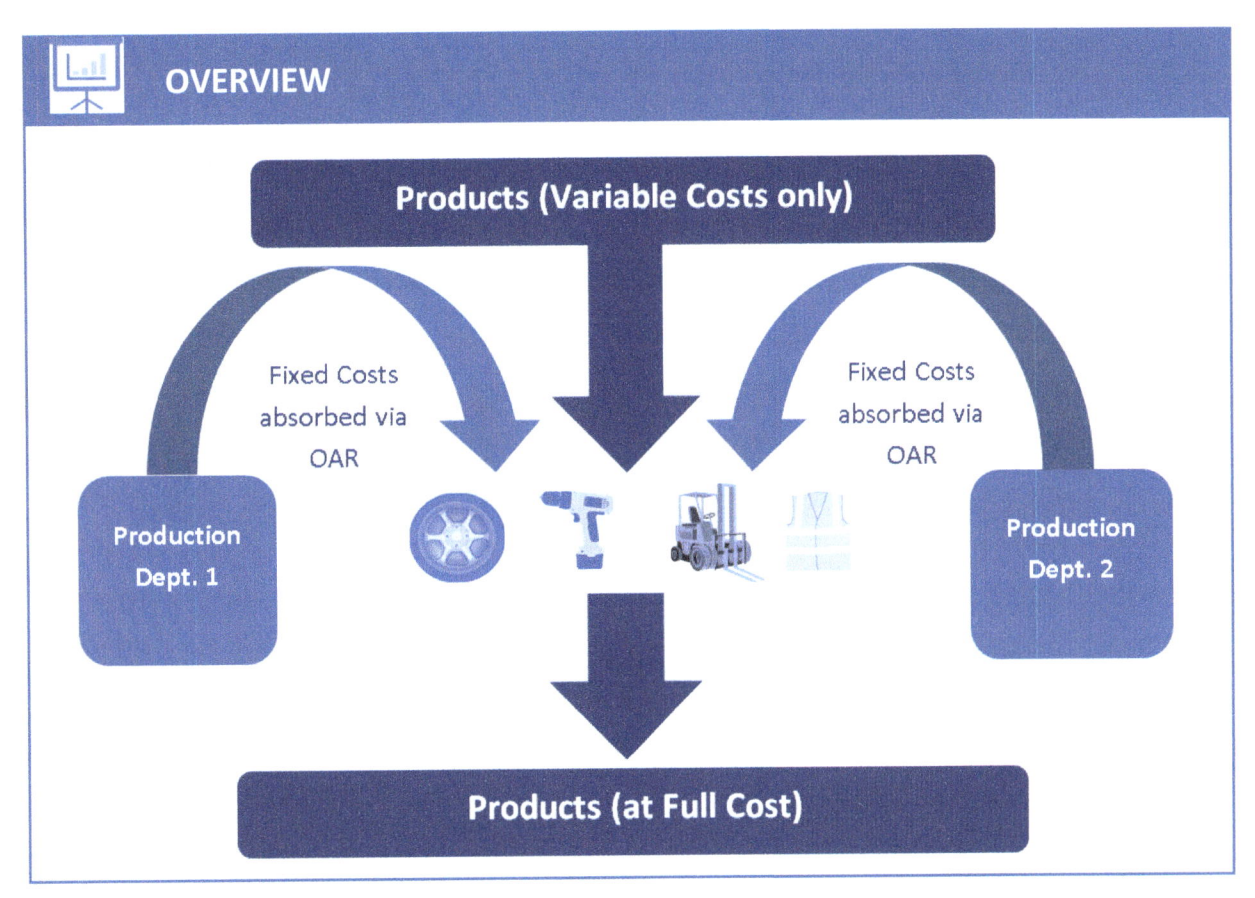

OVERVIEW

Products (Variable Costs only)

Fixed Costs absorbed via OAR — Production Dept. 1

Fixed Costs absorbed via OAR — Production Dept. 2

Products (at Full Cost)

The only way to ensure that you really understand the above overview is to follow through a complete worked example. It's quite long but at the end you should have 'nailed' traditional absorption costing. Grab yourself a coffee and your calculator, and double-check every calculation in the following example!

EXAMPLE

Stage One: Apportion fixed production overheads across all departments

A factory consists of four separate departments:

1. Machining   (production department)
2. Assembly   (production department)
3. Engineering   (service department)
4. Quality Control   (service department)

The factory has the following **budgeted** annual fixed overheads:

- Premises costs (rent, rates, heat & light etc.)   £100,000
- Machine Dept. Manager   £40,000
- Assembly Dept. Manager   £25,000
- Engineering Dept. Manager   £45,000
- Quality Control Dept. Manager   £30,000
- Equipment Depreciation   £60,000
- TOTAL   £300,000

6 Absorption Costing

The floor space taken up by each department, and the value of machinery in each department is given below:

	Floor Space	Value of Machinery
Machining Dept.	3,000 m²	£60,000
Assembly Dept.	4,000 m²	£15,000
Engineering Dept.	2,000 m²	£20,000
Quality Control Dept.	1,000 m²	£5,000
TOTAL	10,000 m²	£100,000

Using a Traditional Absorption Costing approach (i.e. allocation and apportionment) calculate how much fixed overhead should be assigned to each of the four departments (known as 'cost centres').

TUTORIAL NOTE

Absorption costing is by necessity based on *budgeted* overheads and *budgeted* activity levels.

EXAMPLE

Stage One Solution

Allocation: Any costs which purely belong to specified departments can simply be allocated to those departments (e.g. managers' salaries)

Apportion: Any costs which belong to more than one department (e.g. premises costs and depreciation) need to be apportioned (i.e. shared out) between all relevant departments on some fair basis.

Premises Costs

The £100,000 of premises costs should be apportioned according to what proportion of the total floor space each department occupies, so that the departments which occupy a larger floor area bear a correspondingly larger share of the cost.

Machining	(3,000 m² / 10,000 m²) x £100,000	= £30,000
Assembly	(4,000 m² / 10,000 m²) x £100,000	= £40,000
Engineering	(2,000 m² / 10,000 m²) x £100,000	= £20,000
Quality Control	(1,000 m² / 10,000 m²) x £100,000	= £10,000
	TOTAL	£100,000

Equipment Depreciation

The £60,000 of depreciation charges should be apportioned according to the value of equipment used within each department, so that the departments which contain more equipment bear a correspondingly larger share of the depreciation figure.

Machining	(£60,000 / £100,000) x £60,000	= £36,000
Assembly	(£15,000 / £100,000) x £60,000	= £9,000
Engineering	(£20,000 / £100,000) x £60,000	= £12,000
Quality Control	(£5,000 / £100,000) x £60,000	= £3,000
	TOTAL	£60,000

TUTORIAL NOTE

Always 'sense check' calculations whenever possible. In these two cases we are adding up the separate apportioned elements of both the premises cost and depreciation charges to ensure that they add back to the original totals.

All of the above figures are entered onto a summary table on the following page (laid out to facilitate rapid understanding) and the total overhead for each of the four departments found.

This is the end of stage one as we have now established how much of the total £300,000 fixed factory overhead should be borne by each department.

Note that the total overhead spread across the four departments is still £300,000. It has neither grown nor shrunk. It has merely been split across the four departments on a fair basis. The calculations above are included for clarification only and could in fact be performed on a calculator and entered straight into the table below.

OVERVIEW

End of Stage One

	Total	Assignment Basis	Cost Centres			
			Machining	Assembly	Engineering	Quality Control
Premises Costs	£100,000	Apportioned according to Floor Space	£30,000	£40,000	£20,000	£10,000
Machining Manager	£40,000	Allocated	£40,000			
Assembly Manager	£25,000	Allocated		£25,000		
Engineering Manager	£45,000	Allocated			£45,000	
Quality Control Manager	£30,000	Allocated				£30,000
Equipment Depreciation	£60,000	Apportioned according to Equip. Value	£36,000	£9,000	£12,000	£3,000
TOTAL	£300,000		£106,000	£74,000	£77,000	£43,000

6 Absorption Costing

> **TUTORIAL NOTE**
>
> Again, be methodical and check calculations wherever possible. Here we check that the overheads for the four departments combined adds back to the total factory overhead i.e. £106,000 + £74,000 + £77,000 + £43,000 = £300,000..... Correct!

> **EXAMPLE**
>
> **Stage Two: Re-assign Service Department Overhead into Production Department**
>
> Continuing with the example above, now re-assign the <u>service</u> department overheads (from Engineering & Quality Control) into the <u>production</u> departments (Machinery and Assembly).
>
> The factory estimates that the two production departments use the two service departments as follows:
>
> | | Machining | Assembly | Total |
> |---|---|---|---|
> | **Engineering** | 75% | 25% | = 100% |
> | **Quality Control** | 40% | 60% | = 100% |
>
> The Engineering Service Department had a total overhead of £77,000.
>
> This needs to be reassigned between Machining and Assembly in the ratio 75:25.
>
> The Quality Control Department had a total overhead of £43,000.
>
> This needs to be reassigned between Machining and Assembly in the ratio 40:60.
>
> **Stage Two workings**
>
> | | Machining | Assembly | Engineering | Quality Control | Total |
> |---|---|---|---|---|---|
> | Overhead at end of Stage 1 | £106,000 | £74,000 | £77,000 | £43,000 | £300,000 |
> | Re-assign Engineering overhead to Production Depts. | £57,750 [1] | £19,250 [2] | (£77,000) | | £nil |
> | Re-assign Quality Control overhead to Production Depts. | £17,200 [3] | £25,800 [4] | | (£43,000) | £nil |
> | Overhead at end of Stage 2 | £180,950 | £119,050 | £nil | £nil | £300,000 |

Workings (remember in accounting, brackets signify a negative figure):

1. £77,000 x 75% = £57,750
2. £77,000 x 25% = £19,250
3. £43,000 x 40% = £17,200
4. £43,000 x 60% = £25,800

At the end of stage 2 we have removed all of the overhead from the two service departments and via a two-stage process have assigned all of the overhead into just the two **production** departments.

> **TUTORIAL NOTE**
>
> Again, check that the final two overhead figures still add up to the original total overhead to ensure that we have not lost or gained anything along the way! *£180,950 + £119,050 = £300,000... Correct!*

> **EXAMPLE**
>
> **Stage Three: Derive Overhead Absorption Rates (OAR)**
>
> Continuing with the above example, we now need to calculate an Overhead Absorption Rate (OAR) for each production department which can then be used to allow that department's overhead to be progressively 'absorbed' by the products which pass through that department over the course of the year *(so that by the end of the year, all of the overhead will have been 'absorbed' into the cost objects which have passed through that department)*.
>
> The OAR should be based on some measure which is representative of that department's principal activity.
>
> - The **machining department** is obviously machine intensive and so an appropriate measure would be **"machine hours"**
> - The **assembly department** is labour intensive and so an appropriate measure would be **"labour hours"**
> - The machining department's budgeted activity is 10,000 machine hours for the coming year
> - The assembly department's budgeted activity is 50,000 labour hours for the coming year
>
> **Stage Three: Derive Overhead Absorption Rates (OAR)**
>
> **Machining Department OAR** = Budgeted Overhead ÷ Budgeted Activity
>
> = £180,950 ÷ 10,000 = **£18.10 per machine hour**
>
> **Assembly Department OAR** = Budgeted Overhead ÷ Budgeted Activity
>
> = £119,050 ÷ 50,000 = **£2.38 per labour hour**

6 Absorption Costing

TUTORIAL NOTES

1. The OARs are rounded to the nearest penny which is completely appropriate (businesses don't waste their time chasing fractions of a penny!). However this means that small discrepancies may become apparent if you reverse the calculations e.g. 10,000 hours x £18.10 per hour = £181,000 and not the original £180,950 (a £50 difference). As we shall see, since the OARs are based on estimates (i.e. budgeted overheads and budgeted activity) this £50 difference is of no consequence!

2. Always state the units when quoting an OAR (e.g. *'per machine hour'*). Not only is an OAR a bit meaningless without the units, but it will also help keep you focussed on what you have just calculated and what to do with it next!

At the end of stage 3 we have calculated Overhead Absorption Rates for each production department that can now be used to add an appropriate amount of overhead cost to any products ('cost objects') that pass through either department *…..in addition to the direct costs of those products!*

EXAMPLE

Stage Four: Full (Absorption) Costing of Products

Continuing with the above example, the factory only produces two products (Alpha & Beta) for which the following information is available.

	Alpha	Beta
Direct materials	£65	£40
Direct labour	£135	£160
Total Direct Costs	£200	£200
Machining time required	4 hours	1 hour
Assembly time required	10 hours	15 hours

What is the <u>full</u> cost of these two products?

KEY POINT

The term 'full cost' (or 'total cost') infers that the cost needs to include a fair share of fixed production overheads as well as the variable costs (which in this example are just the direct costs, but which could also include variable overheads in other examples).

EXAMPLE

Stage Four Solution

We calculate the full cost of these products by including a share of the fixed overhead (utilising the Overhead Absorption Rates (OAR) calculated in stage 3).

	ALPHA	BETA
Direct Materials	£65.00	£40.00
Direct Labour	£135.00	£160.00
TOTAL DIRECT COSTS	**£200.00**	**£200.00**
Machine Dept. Overhead	£72.40 [1]	£18.10 [2]
Assembly Dept. Overhead	£23.80 [3]	£35.70 [4]
TOTAL OVERHEADS	**£96.20**	**£53.80**
Total Cost	£296.20	£253.80

So according to the Traditional Absorption Costing method product Beta is a considerably cheaper than product Alpha!

Workings

Machine Dept. OAR = £18.10 per machine hour

Assembly Dept. OAR = £2.38 per labour hour

1. Absorbed Machine Dept. Overhead = £18.10 per machine hour x 4 hours = £72.40
2. Absorbed Machine Dept. Overhead = £18.10 per machine hour x 1 hour = £18.10
3. Absorbed Assembly Dept. Overhead = £2.38 per labour hour x 10 hours = £23.80
4. Absorbed Assembly Dept. Overhead = £2.38 per machine hour x 15 hours = £35.70

In the unlikely event that both the budgeted level of overhead and the budgeted level of activity proved to be 100% accurate, then over the course of a year:

- The 10,000 machine hours in the machine department would exactly absorb the £180,950 of machine department overhead (at the rate of £18.10 per machine hour)
- The 50,000 labour hours in the assembly department would exactly absorb the £119,050 of assembly department overhead (at the rate of £2.38 per labour hour)

… and the 'costs' of the products which had passed through either or both of these departments would be 'total costs' which not only reflected the direct costs involved in their manufacture (materials & labour etc.) but also a fair share of any overheads relating to those departments, both variable overheads **and** fixed overheads.

6 Absorption Costing

> **TUTORIAL NOTE**
>
> We'll revisit what happens if the budgeted overheads and/or activity are not accurate later *(pace yourself!)*. In the meantime it's important to grasp the distinction between the marginal cost and the absorption cost of manufacturing a cost object:
>
> **Marginal Cost**
>
> Includes all of the variable costs relating to its manufacture, namely:
>
> - All direct costs (labour, materials, expenses) which are (invariably) variable costs
> - Any variable production overheads
>
> The marginal cost is therefore the cost of producing one more of that item. Fixed costs would *not* alter if one more item were produced and are therefore excluded.
>
> **Absorption Cost**
>
> Includes all of the variable costs (as above) PLUS a fair share of any <u>fixed</u> production overheads, namely:
>
> - All direct costs (labour, materials, expenses) which are (invariably) variable costs
> - Any variable production overheads
> - An absorbed amount of fixed production overhead
>
> Because the absorption cost aims to also include an appropriate share of the fixed production overhead (in addition to the variable costs) it is also known as the 'full cost' or 'total cost'.

6.5 Activity Based Costing (ABC)

A more modern alternative to Traditional Absorption Costing is Activity Based Costing (ABC) which analyses overhead costs by reference to the 'activities' which cause them (rather than trying to simply allocate them into the various production departments).

> **DEFINITION**
>
> The basic mantra of ABC is:
>
> 'Activities cause costs, and products consume activities'.

The six basic steps in the ABC process are:

1. Identify the activities within the business (the 'cost pools')
2. Calculate the total overhead associated with each activity
3. Identify what actually causes the cost to arise (the 'cost driver')
4. Calculate the cost associated with the cost driver activity (the 'cost driver rate')
5. For each product (cost object) calculate the direct costs
6. Using the cost driver rate add the appropriate overhead to the direct costs

Now right at outset its worth stating that in many way the principles of Traditional Absorption Costing and Activity Based Costing are very similar. This means that at times you might find yourself getting confused because the two methods appear so similar *("I don't get it, what's the actual difference!")*.

The thing to hold onto is that:

Traditional Absorption Costing used a two-step process to *ultimately* assign overheads into **production departments**, and then used an **overhead absorption rate** (for each different department) to add overhead to cost objects as they passed through that particular production department.

Activity Based Costing (ABC) instead assigns overhead into different **activities**, and then use a **cost driver rate** (for each different activity) to add overhead to cost objects depending on which activities that product has consumed.

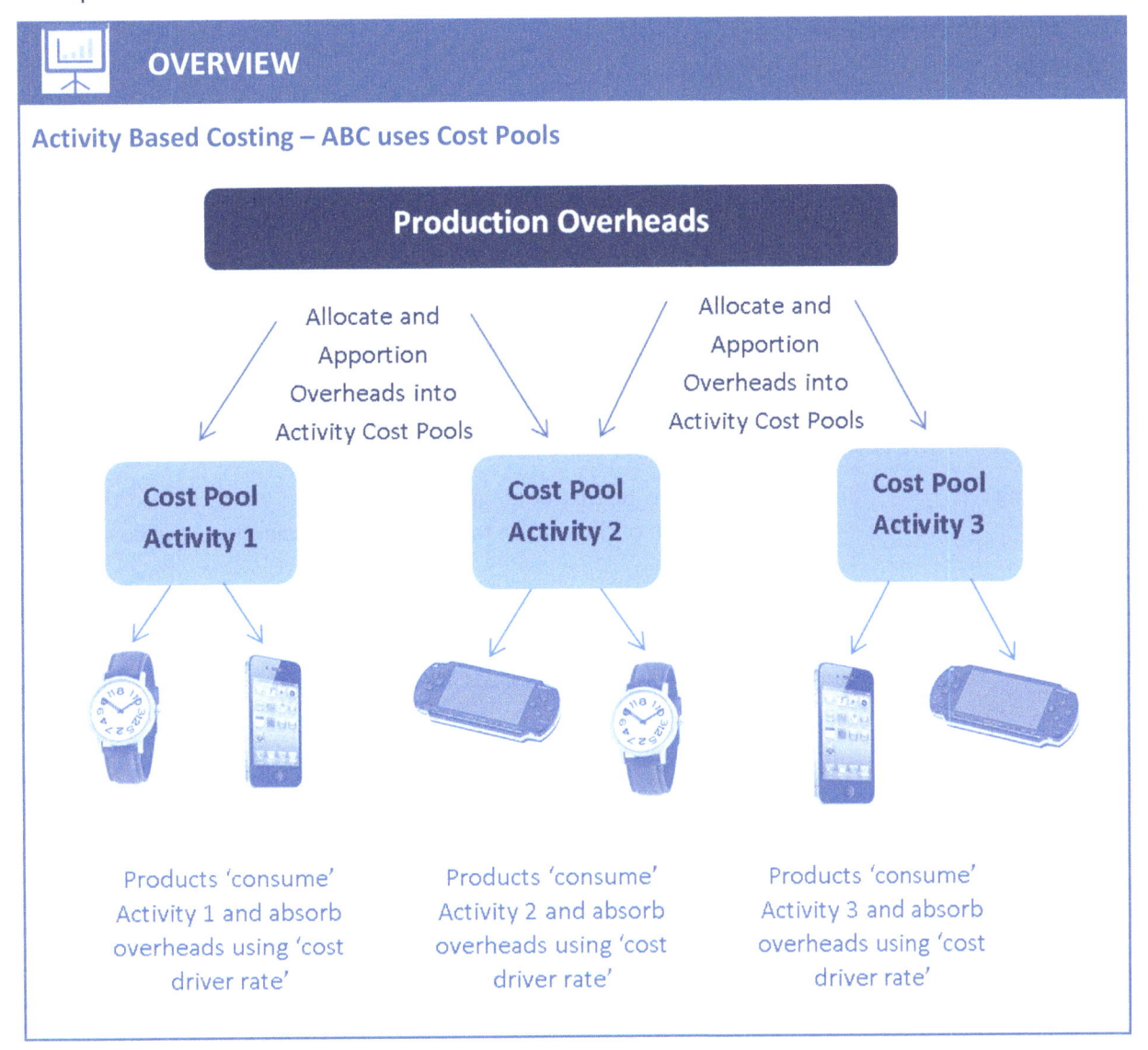

OVERVIEW

Activity Based Costing – ABC uses Cost Pools

Production Overheads

Allocate and Apportion Overheads into Activity Cost Pools

- **Cost Pool Activity 1**
- **Cost Pool Activity 2**
- **Cost Pool Activity 3**

Products 'consume' Activity 1 and absorb overheads using 'cost driver rate'

Products 'consume' Activity 2 and absorb overheads using 'cost driver rate'

Products 'consume' Activity 3 and absorb overheads using 'cost driver rate'

To really grasp the difference between Traditional Absorption Costing and Activity Based Costing we will return to the same factory encountered earlier, which makes just two products (Alpha and Beta) and will this time 'cost' them using ABC.

Step 1 - Identify the activities within the business (the 'cost pools')

The first stage is to identify the activities within the business, which are:

Machining	*activity = manufacture & machining of new components*
Assembly	*activity = assembly of component parts*

6 Absorption Costing

Engineering Support   *activity = maintenance of production equipment*

Quality Control (QC)   *activity = QC Inspection of products*

These are the same four departments originally identified and this should be no surprise. The departments of a company are normally based "on what they do" i.e. their specific activity. Some of those activities will be production activities (e.g. machining and assembly), whilst some will be support activities (e.g. engineering and quality control), but they are *all* activities.

Step 2 - Calculate the total overhead associated with each activity

We have already allocated / apportioned the businesses fixed overheads into these four departments in Step 1 of the traditional absorption costing method. This is no different from allocating / apportioning overheads for ABC purposes:

Machining   £106,000 per annum

Assembly   £74,000 per annum

Engineering   £77,000 per annum

Quality Control   £43,000 per annum

However this time *we do not then need* to re-apportion the service department costs to the production departments (as we did for traditional absorption costing). With ABC the cost pools represent the different *activities* within the business.

Step 3 - Identify what actually causes the cost to arise (the 'cost driver')

For each activity we now need to identify what causes the cost i.e. what is the 'cost driver':

Machining   In a similar fashion to traditional absorption costing we recognise that the costs arise because of time taken to machine components, so the cost driver is **'machine hours'**.

Assembly   In a similar fashion to traditional absorption costing we recognise that the costs arise because of time taken to assemble components, so the cost driver is **'labour hours'**.

Engineering   The engineering department's costs arise because of the engineering support needed to keep production lines running, so the cost driver is **'number of Engineering call-outs'**.

Quality Control   The quality control (QC) department's costs arise because of the need to undertake quality inspections on different batches of products (with some products requiring more quality testing than others), so the cost driver is **'number of QC checks'**.

Step 4 - Calculate the cost associated with the cost driver activity (the 'cost driver rate')

This could be calculated over any period but it is normally convenient to consider the annual cost and annual activity.

Machining   We have already seen that there are 10,000 budgeted machine hours in the coming year.

The cost driver rate is therefore £106,000 / 10,000 = £10.60 per machine hour

Assembly	We have already seen that there are 50,000 budgeted labour hours in the coming year.
	The cost driver rate is therefore £74,000 / 50,000 = £1.48 per labour hour
Engineering	We now need some additional information about the level of activity within the Engineering department, and this is that over a full year they attend 110 breakdowns or maintenance issues i.e. 110 call-outs
	The cost driver rate is therefore £77,000 / 110 = £700 per call out
Quality Control	Again, we need some additional information about the level of activity within the quality control department, and this is that over a full year they perform 500 quality inspections
	The cost driver rate is therefore £43,000 / 500 = £86 per inspection

> **TUTORIAL NOTE**
>
> The ABC cost driver rates for machining and assembly are *not* the same as the OAR calculated under traditional absorption costing (despite at a cursory glance appearing similar) because under ABC the service department's overheads were <u>not</u> re-apportioned to the production departments.

Step 5 - For each product (cost object) calculate the direct costs

There is no difference in this stage between ABC and traditional absorption costing. Both methods need to know what the direct costs are. As before, the following direct materials and labour costs were given:

	Alpha	Beta
Direct materials	£65	£40
Direct labour	<u>£135</u>	<u>£160</u>
Total Direct Costs	£200	£200

Step 6 - Using the cost driver rate add the appropriate overheads to the direct costs

Because some of the activities are not quoted on a 'per item' basis we might need to introduce an additional step to get overhead costs down to an individual item level. For example the engineering cost driver rate is per engineering call-out, whilst the quality control cost driver rate is per inspection. We therefore have to know how many call-outs and inspections both products require each year and how many products these need to be shared across.

Alpha

- Engineering call-outs = 20
- Quality control inspections = 100
- Production volume = 2,000

Beta

- Engineering call-outs = 90
- Quality control inspections = 400
- Production volume = 2,000

6 Absorption Costing

By way of a reminder:

	Alpha	Beta
Machining time required	4 hours	1 hour
Assembly time required	10 hours	15 hours

EXAMPLE

Comparing Alpha and Beta using ABC

We can now work out the overheads under ABC and hence the full cost per unit for both Alpha & Beta.

	ALPHA	BETA
Direct Materials (per item)	£65.00	£40.00
Direct Labour (per item)	£135.00	£160.00
TOTAL DIRECT COSTS	**£200.00**	**£200.00**
Machining (per item)	4 machine hours x £10.60 = £42.40	1 machine hour x £10.60 = £10.60
Assembly (per item)	10 labour hours x £1.48 = £14.80	15 labour hours x £1.48 = £22.20
Engineering (per item)	(20 call-outs x £700) / 2,000 = £7.00	(90 call-outs x £700) / 2,000 = £31.50
Quality Control (QC) (per item)	(100 QC checks x £86) /2,000 = £4.30	(400 QC checks x £86) /2,000 = £17.20
TOTAL OVERHEAD ABSORBED	**£68.50**	**£81.50**
Total Cost (per item)	£268.50	£281.50

So according to ABC costing, Alpha is now the cheaper product!

6.6 Traditional Absorption Costing versus ABC method

It is important to understand *why* the two products appear to have different costs depending on which costing method is used.

We can see that the direct costs are exactly the same for both methods. However the different method of assigning overheads between the two methods results in different final costs.

EXAMPLE

For Alpha, the ABC costing method produces a lower total cost whilst the traditional costing method produces a higher total cost:

ALPHA	Traditional Absorption Costing	Activity Based Costing
Direct Costs	£200.00	£200.00
Overheads	£96.20	£68.50
TOTAL COST	£296.20	£268.50

Conversely for Beta, the ABC method produces a higher total cost whilst the traditional absorption costing method produces a lower total cost:

BETA	Traditional Absorption Costing	Activity Based Costing
Direct Costs	£200.00	£200.00
Overheads	£53.80	£81.50
TOTAL COST	£253.80	£281.50

Before we examine what is causing this anomaly let's first restate some of the basics:

- Both products have the same level of production and the same direct costs *(to keep things simple!)*
- Regardless of which costing method is used the same £300,000 of overhead is being absorbed into the same quantity of production (2,000 Alpha & 2,000 Beta)
- ABC goes into more depth by identifying exactly what *activities* (machining, assembly, engineering, quality control) *cause costs*, and then looking at how much of those activities have been *consumed* by each *product*.

   (Remember the ABC mantra: 'Activities cause costs, and products consume activities')

- Conversely, traditional absorption costing simply 'lumps' all of the overhead into just the production departments and makes the assumption that all of the overhead can be absorbed based on how long each product spends in each department.

TUTORIAL NOTE

This last point is vital *(understand this and you 'get' the difference between the two costing methods).....*

Just because the machining department is estimated to use 75% of the engineering call-outs *does not mean* that these were incurred strictly according to how many hours each product spent being machined - which is the exact assumption traditional absorption costing makes.

If this were so then product Alpha would indeed have had four times as many engineering call-outs because it has four times as much machining time. However the ABC method goes one level deeper and realises that (despite Alpha's being machined for far longer than Beta's) that in actual fact it is the Beta's which are always requiring engineering support .... So ABC assigns (quite correctly!) more of the engineering cost to Beta then to Alpha.

6 Absorption Costing

Similarly, despite the quality control split between machining and assembly being estimated at 40:60 (used by the traditional absorption costing method) the ABC method goes one step deeper and finds out which product requires more QC checks. This is in fact Beta which has four times as many checks as Alpha and therefore (quite correctly) under the ABC system Beta carries four times as much of the quality overhead as Alpha does.

⚠ KEY POINTS

- The traditional absorption costing method makes 'broad brush' assumptions about how the costs of certain activities should be shared between different products and these can sometimes be quite arbitrary

- The ABC method actually looks at where each and every activity is being used and then correctly shares out the cost of each separate activity based on this.

- To achieve this requires an in-depth examination of all the activities within the business and exactly where those activities are used. Such a detailed examination is time consuming and expensive and this is a potential criticism of ABC.

- However, despite the expense, such a close examination of costs and activities can highlight waste and inefficiencies. If their subsequent eradication is a side effect of the implementation of ABC then this is clearly a useful bonus.

EXAMPLE

If you really need convincing that there has been no 'sleight of hand' in the sharing of these overheads then convince yourself that they have all been accounted for by following through the table below.

	Traditional Costing	ABC
No. of Alphas	2,000	2,000
Overhead absorbed per Alpha	£96.20	£68.50
Total Overhead absorbed by Alphas	£192,400	£137,000
No. of Betas	2,000	2,000
Overhead absorbed per Beta	£53.80	£81.50
Total Overhead absorbed by Betas	£107,600	£163,000
Total Overhead Absorbed	**£300,000**	**£300,000**

In both cases the same £300,000 overhead has been absorbed into the same 2,000 Alphas and 2,000 Betas. The differences are purely down to the ABC method carrying out this exercise in a more accurate and objective way, whilst the traditional method carried it out in a less accurate and more arbitrary fashion.

The Language of Business

> ## TUTORIAL NOTE
>
> *But, why does this matter?*
>
> It is tempting to believe that so long as the business has covered its fixed overheads (whether this be more via Alphas or more via Betas) then the company should be able to ensure profitability knowing that both its variable and fixed production costs are covered. The argument goes, that so long as the company sells both products for more than their total costs (whether these were calculated using traditional or ABC costing) then the fixed costs are known to be covered and profitability will follow.
>
> However this reasoning takes no account of the competitive market place in which businesses operate. It is sometimes necessary to see just how low selling prices can be taken to be able to compete with a competitor's aggressive pricing, but not so low that the company is actually making a loss on the transaction.
>
> The key requirement is to have *accurate* cost prices which exactly reflect the costs incurred whenever a certain product is made and sold, and in this respect ABC gets one step closer to the truth than traditional costing.

> ## KEY POINTS
>
> - If ABC costing reveals a *lower* cost price (than traditional costing) then this identifies where the business can become more competitive (if necessary!) to secure sales in a competitive environment.
>
> - If ABC costing reveals a *higher* cost price (than traditional costing) then this might reveal that certain products were in fact previously being sold at a loss under traditional costing (which had underestimated the real cost of producing them).

Accuracy

Back in Chapter 1 we stated that one of the desirable qualities of financial information was 'accuracy'. ABC aims to provide more accurate costs to enable better informed management decisions to be taken. The question is whether the greater accuracy of the ABC method, outweighs the additional cost involved in implementing and running it. The answer to that question will depend on the nature of each individual business:

- **Traditional Manufacturing Industry:** Typically the production costs of these businesses mostly comprised direct costs (direct materials and direct labour etc.) with the overheads accounting for a smaller proportion of the total costs. In these cases the introduction of an expensive ABC system might be of limited value.

- **Modern Manufacturing and Service Industries:** Increasing automation means that the production costs of these businesses tends to have a greater proportion of fixed overheads and so the need for accurate assignment of these fixed costs via ABC becomes far greater.

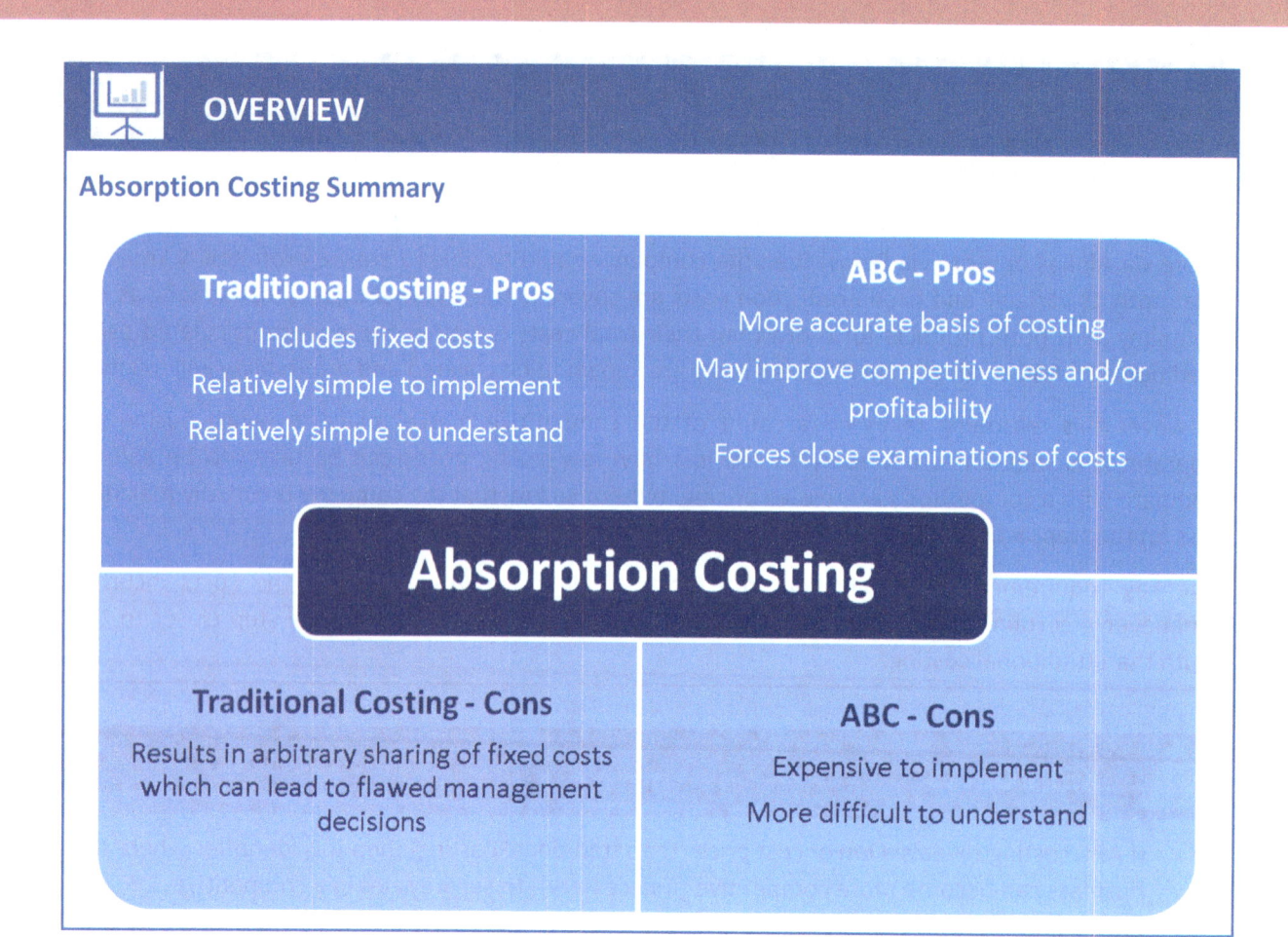

6 Absorption Costing

OVERVIEW

Absorption Costing Summary

Traditional Costing - Pros
- Includes fixed costs
- Relatively simple to implement
- Relatively simple to understand

ABC - Pros
- More accurate basis of costing
- May improve competitiveness and/or profitability
- Forces close examinations of costs

Absorption Costing

Traditional Costing - Cons
- Results in arbitrary sharing of fixed costs which can lead to flawed management decisions

ABC - Cons
- Expensive to implement
- More difficult to understand

6.7 Under and over absorption of overheads

Both traditional absorption costing and activity based costing rely on the **budgeted** figures for both the levels of overhead and the level of activity expected. It is these budgeted figures which are then used to calculate:

- Overhead Absorption Rates (in traditional absorption costing)
- Cost Driver Rates (in ABC)

If *both* the budgeted levels of overhead *and* the budgeted levels of activity are exactly accurate then, over the course of the year, the actual overheads will be exactly absorbed into the cost objects produced.

However, in the real world budgets are seldom 100% accurate and it is therefore quite possible that the total amount of fixed production overhead absorbed into the manufactured products will be either higher *(over-absorption)* or lower *(under-absorption)* than the actual level of overheads incurred, as follows:

- If the **actual overheads** are *higher* than originally budgeted, then potentially *not enough* overhead will have been absorbed by the year-end → **Under- Absorption**

- If the **actual overheads** are *lower* than originally budgeted, then potentially *too much* overhead will have been absorbed by the year-end → **Over-Absorption**

- If the **actual level of activity** is *lower* than originally budgeted, then potentially *not enough* overhead will have been absorbed by the year-end → **Under- Absorption**

- If the **actual level of activity** is *higher* than originally budgeted, then potentially *too much* overhead will have been absorbed by the year-end → **Over-Absorption**

Both under-absorption and over-absorption will need to be corrected by the Finance Department at the end of the financial period (normally the year-end). This ensures that ultimately the correct (i.e. actual) overhead has been charged to the manufactured inventory and hence to 'cost of sales' in the statement of profit or loss; and that the closing inventory has been accurately valued on the statement of financial position.

6.8 Variants of Absorption Costing

This chapter has tried to describe the key features of the two main methods of absorption costing (traditional & ABC) but in reality there exist many variants and hybrids of both methods, for example:

- Some variants of traditional absorption costing immediately allocate/apportion all fixed overheads directly to the production departments (without first allocating/apportioning them to service departments, followed by a re-allocation).

- A mixture of cost drivers may be used including some which appear to be 'activity based' (more complex but more accurate?) and some which appear more arbitrary (simpler but less accurate?)

- Different companies will choose to analyse their business in different ways, some by departments, some by activity (where the activity may or may not also represent a physical department), and some by a combination of both. One example of this is the extreme case of a business regarding itself as consisting of one single department ('production'!) and absorbing overheads on this basis, as illustrated in the following example.

> **EXAMPLE**
>
> ### Scenario
> A small manufacturing company has previously used marginal costing to set its selling prices i.e. by simply looking at all of the variable costs incurred in manufacturing its products and then adding the required mark-up. The company now realises that it should also recognise the fixed production overheads in the calculated product cost, but do not have the skills or experience at this stage to implement a complex absorption costing system. They produce 5,000 items per annum and have fixed production overheads of £20,000 per annum.
>
> **What very simple solution could they immediately implement and what would be the pros and cons of this proposed solution?**
>
> ### Solution
> Treating the company as a 'one-department' business quickly reveals that on average each product needs to absorb £4 of fixed production overhead.
>
> **Overhead Absorption Rate = Overhead ÷ Activity = £20,000 ÷ 5,000 = £4 per item**
>
> This would be a 'quick-fix' solution so that the sales teams etc. were aware that in addition to each individual product's marginal cost, an additional £4 needs to be added to ensure that the business's fixed costs were covered. It is quick to implement and simple to understand, but takes no account of the fact that different products will lead to different fixed costs being incurred. The proposed solution is a stop-gap measure, but ultimately the company needs to better understand the exact details of its own operation.

6 Absorption Costing

6.9 Inventory valuation

The valuation of inventory has two effects on the financial statements of a business:

i. It determines the value of closing inventory on the statement of financial position

ii. It determines the 'cost of sales' figure on the statement of profit or loss

(Cost of Sales = Opening Inventory + Purchases – Closing Inventory)

Financial statements for external users (i.e. financial accounting) must be prepared in accordance with financial reporting standards and these stipulate that inventory must be valued to include an appropriate amount of both variable and fixed production overhead (based on a 'normal' level of production) i.e. absorption costing.

Conversely financial statements for internal users (i.e. management accounting) can be prepared in any way the business sees fit, as they are not governed by financial reporting standards.

This means that absorption costing (either traditional costing or ABC) *must* be used for financial accounting purposes, whereas for management accounting purposes a business may choose for itself whether to use marginal costing or absorption costing.

Businesses may sometimes choose to use marginal costing for their own management accounting because it is simpler (both to prepare and to understand), and also because it means that fixed costs such as rent, rates and insurance are then treated as 'period costs' and therefore simply charged to the P&L in the month they are incurred.

Despite the fact the financial reporting standards stipulate that such expenses should be absorbed into the value of inventory, some businesses remain suspicious of treating (say) factory rent as a 'product cost'. This is especially true when the inventory levels are increasing or decreasing between the beginning and the end of (say) a monthly financial period, thus:

- If the levels of inventory increase then some of this month's factory rent will *not* be charged to the statement of profit or loss, but instead be held as part of the increased inventory valuation of the statement of financial position, and then effectively be charged to a *future* month.

- Conversely, if the levels of inventory decrease then some of the factory rent from *previous* months (which was being held as part of the increased inventory valuation of the statement of financial position) is now charged to the statement of profit or loss for *this* month.

6.10 Marginal Costing versus Absorption Costing

Having now studied marginal costing (in the last chapter) and absorption costing (in this chapter) we can now compare the two costing methods.

Marginal Costing is based on the cost of making *'one more'* item and therefore only includes variable costs. It is an incredibly quick and simple method of decision making in the real world, where you might need to make a quick *'back of an envelope'* calculation to decide whether or not you can match a potential competitor's price and secure a sales order. The problem is that because it (initially) ignores fixed costs it can potentially promote the belief that fixed costs are not that important. This is commercially dangerous and can lead to loss-making contracts.

Absorption Costing (both traditional & ABC) is an attempt to recognise all of the production costs of the business and produce a 'total cost' which includes both variable and (a fair share of) fixed costs. It is a more time consuming method that is harder for staff to comprehend, but is ultimately a safer way to run a business because if pricing decisions are based on a mark-up on a full cost then the business is more likely to ultimately achieve profitability.

Once again it is impossible to make blanket statements about which costing method is superior as this will depend on the precise circumstances involved, as the following examples illustrate.

EXAMPLE

Scenario 1

A newly formed business is in the process of calculating proposed selling prices for its new product range. Should it use marginal or absorption costing?

Solution 1

Using marginal costing would be dangerous as the business has not explicitly recognised the fixed production costs which must be covered to ensure ultimate profitability. The business needs to make some prudent estimates of what those fixed overheads might be, and what production/sales volumes they might achieve, to at least make an estimate of how much fixed cost needs to be absorbed by each product.

EXAMPLE

Scenario 2

An established business (consistently operating at a net profit) now has the opportunity to tender for a one-off large contract but this will mean having to aggressively bid against their competitors. Should it use marginal or absorption costing?

Solution 2

We know that the business has already covered its fixed costs because it is operating at a net profit. So assuming that the fixed costs would remain fixed if the new contract were won (i.e. with the increased level of activity) then marginal costing might be the appropriate costing method. The business wants to know how low it can go on price and has the luxury of knowing that the fixed costs are covered. Any selling price greater than the marginal cost will result is a positive contribution and hence increased net profit; whereas use of a full cost for the product might price them out of the market.

6 Absorption Costing

OVERVIEW

Absorption Costing versus Marginal Costing Summary

Marginal Costing - Pros
Relatively simple to implement.
Relatively simple to understand.
Useful for decision making.

Absorption Costing - Pros
A more accurate basis of costing.
Consistent with financial reporting standards.

Absorption Costing versus Marginal Costing

Marginal Costing - Cons
Fixed costs not captured.
Inconsistent with financial reporting standards.

Absorption Costing - Cons
More difficult to implement.
More difficult to understand.

The Language of Business

> ⚠️ **KEY POINTS FROM CHAPTER 6**

Absorption Costing
- Includes an appropriate share of all production overheads (both fixed and variable) within the cost object, in addition to all direct costs
- Also known as 'total costing' or 'full costing'
- Calculated using budgeted overheads and budgeted levels of activity
- Traditional Absorption Costing assigns fixed production overheads by reference to the production departments within a business
- Activity Based Costing (ABC) assigns fixed production overheads by reference to the activities within a business

Traditional Absorption Costing – Basic Steps

1. Calculate how much of the total fixed factory overhead should be borne by each department within the factory (*both production departments and service departments*).
2. Now re-assign the service department overhead into just the production departments.
3. Calculate a fair basis on which to share out each production department's fixed overhead across all the cost objects which pass through, by calculating an 'Overhead Absorption Rate' (OAR) for each production department, as follows:

   $$\text{Overhead Absorption Rate (OAR)} = \frac{\text{Budgeted Overhead}}{\text{Budgeted Activity}}$$

4. Calculate the full cost of products by first adding together their various variable costs (direct costs + variable overheads) and then using the OAR to add an appropriate share of the fixed costs of each production department the product has passed through.

Activity Based Costing

The mantra of ABC is: *'Activities cause costs, and products consume activities.'*

The six basic steps in the ABC process are:

1. Identify the activities within the business (the 'cost pools')
2. Calculate the total overhead associated with each activity
3. Identify what actually causes the cost to arise (the 'cost driver')
4. Calculate the cost associated with the cost driver activity (the 'cost driver rate')
5. For each product (cost object) calculate the direct costs
6. Using the cost driver rate add the appropriate overhead to the direct costs

Traditional Absorption Costing versus Activity Based Costing

Traditional Absorption Costing: Relatively simple to implement and understand. Achieves the aim of assigning fixed production overheads to cost objects, but in a potentially arbitrary fashion

Activity Based Costing: More difficult to implement and understand, but forces close examination of all activities and associated costs and should result in more accurate costing

Absorption Costing versus Marginal Costing

Marginal Costing: Relatively simple to implement and understand. A quick and useful technique for decision making, but does not take fixed costs into account. Does not comply with financial reporting standards and so cannot be used in financial accounting.

6 Absorption Costing

Absorption Costing: More difficult to implement and understand. Produces a 'full cost' which takes fixed costs into account. Complies with financial reporting standards and so must be used for financial accounting purposes.

Chapter 6: End of Chapter Exercises

Section A Questions

Question 6.1
'Absorption costing' is also referred to as 'Total Costing' because…

- A   It includes the total variable costs of a product or service
- B   It includes the total variable costs of a product or service plus a fair share of all company overheads
- C   It includes all of the direct costs of a product or service plus a fair share of production overheads
- D   It comprises of the total costs of the business

Question 6.2
The mantra of Activity Based Costing is…

- A   "If activities are reduced, products will be cheaper"
- B   "Products cause costs, and activities consume products"
- C   "Base your costs on your activities"
- D   "Activities cause costs, and products consume activities"

Question 6.3
Which of the following comments regarding absorption costing is untrue?

- A   Absorption costing complies with financial reporting standards
- B   Absorption costing results in lower corresponding costs than marginal costing
- C   Absorption costing is also known as 'total costing'
- D   Absorption costing ensures that production fixed costs are accounted for in the cost of a product

Question 6.4
The cost of equipment insurance should be apportioned between the various production departments of a manufacturing company according to:

- A   The value of equipment in each department
- B   The number of different products each produces
- C   The number of staff each employs
- D   Their respective floor space

6 Absorption Costing

Question 6.5

A factory has total floor space of 30,000 metres². The machining department occupies 4,500 metres².

If the rent & rates for the whole factory totals £125,000 per annum, how much of this should be apportioned to the machining department?

A   £16,500

B   £18,750

C   £21,250

D   £24,900

Question 6.6

As part of the budgeting process the assembly department of a factory has been assigned a total production fixed cost of £66,000 and is also budgeted to have 40,000 labour hours in the coming year.

What should the corresponding overhead absorption rate (OAR) be?

A   £0.61 per labour hour

B   £1.61 per labour hour

C   £1.61 per labour hour

D   £1.65 per labour hour

Question 6.7

A firm of Solicitors quotes for legal work based on the estimated time a qualified solicitor will take to complete the task, plus absorbed office fixed costs at a rate of £15.00 per solicitor-hour. Qualified solicitors are paid £25 per hour and a 150% mark-up is added to the calculated total cost.

How much will a customer be quoted for a legal task estimated to take 10 hours?

A   £400

B   £600

C   £1,000

D   £1,400

Question 6.8

A company has previously used a marginal costing system but is now considering changing to an absorption costing system. Under the old marginal costing system a certain product had total direct costs of £15.00 per unit. However under the alternative absorption costing system it also absorbs fixed production costs at the rate of £2.00 per unit.

If, in a certain month, the production of this product exceeded the sales of the product by 200 units what would be the reported difference in net profit between the two costing systems?

A   No reported difference in profit

B   Marginal costing would report £400 higher profit than absorption costing

C   Absorption costing would report £400 higher profit than marginal costing

D   Marginal costing would report £3,400 higher profit than absorption costing

Question 6.9

The 'under-absorption' of overheads might occur as a result of which of the following:

  i. Actual overheads being higher than budgeted
  ii. Actual overheads being lower than budgeted
  iii. Actual activity being higher than budgeted
  iv. Actual activity being lower than budgeted

Choose the answer which shows the correct statements from those provided:

A   i & ii
B   ii & iii
C   iii & iv
D   i & iv

Question 6.10

Which of the following are benefits of Activity Based Costing (ABC) compared to Traditional Absorption Costing?

  i. ABC is cheaper to implement
  ii. ABC is easier for the workforce to understand
  iii. ABC ultimately provides more accurate costing
  iv. The detailed analysis required in the implementation of ABC might reveal areas of potential cost saving

Select the most appropriate statements from those provided:

A   i & ii
B   ii & iii
C   iii & iv
D   i & iii

6 Absorption Costing

Section B Questions

Question 6.11 – Traditional Absorption Costing (AAA)

Botanical Ltd manufacture a large range of different gardening tools and use a 'cost-plus' system to set their selling prices. The company is keen to ensure that the set prices cover all the costs of the business and not just the direct costs which relate to individual products, and has therefore decided to implement an absorption costing system for the company's product range.

The factory consists of three production areas:

1. **Machining**

    Where certain components are actually manufactured 'in house'. This department is heavily dependent on machines.

2. **Assembly**

    Where both components manufactured in-house, and bought in components are assembled into finished products. The work in this department largely comprises of manual labour.

3. **Finishing**

    In the finishing department the finished goods have any required safety labels fixed and are packaged complete with a set of instructions where required. Despite the diversity of the product range it has been noted that each product requires approximately the same time in the finishing department.

Use traditional absorption costing techniques and the supplied information to calculate a 'total cost' for two of the company's products: a garden fork, and an electric strimmer. This will require three distinct stages:

1. Since this is a multi-department company the first stage is to apportion (or simply allocate) each of the total budgeted factory overheads across (or into) the appropriate production departments.

2. The second stage is to calculate an Overhead Absorption Rates (OAR) for each Department.

3. The final stage is to calculate a total cost for each products, using both the details of the 'direct costs' the product incurs, plus a fair share of the 'indirect costs' (using the calculated OARs). A simple 50% mark-up is then added to calculate the selling price for each product.

Budgeted Factory Overheads

Factory Rent	£100,000
Heat & Light	£20,000
Canteen Costs	£10,000
Plant & Machine Depreciation	£30,000
Machine Maintenance	£20,000
Factory Cleaning	£10,000
Machining Dept. Supervisors	£40,000
Assembly Dept. Supervisor	£18,000
Finishing Dept. Supervisor	£15,000
Factory Manager	£40,000 (mainly deals with 'people' issues)
TOTAL FACTORY OVERHEADS	**£303,000**

Floor Space

Machining Department	2,500 metres^2
Assembly Department	3,500 metres^2
Finishing Department	4,000 metres^2
TOTAL FLOOR SPACE	**10,000 metres^2**

Number of Employees

Machining Department	10
Assembly Department	60
Finishing Department	30
TOTAL EMPLOYEES	**100**

Value of Machinery in each Department

Machining Department	£180,000
Assembly Department	£12,000
Finishing Department	£8,000
TOTAL MACHINERY	**£200,000**

6 Absorption Costing

Stage One

Either apportion or allocate each of the factory's overheads in order to calculate the total overhead which must be absorbed by each of the three production departments.

Overhead	Total	Sharing Basis?	Machining Dept.	Assembly Dept.	Finishing Dept.	Add to check
Factory Rent	£100,000	Apportion: Floor Area				
Heat & Light	£20,000	Apportion: Floor Area				
Canteen Costs	£10,000	Apportion: No. of employees				
Plant & Machinery Depreciation	£30,000	Apportion: Value of machinery				
Machinery Maintenance	£20,000	Apportion: Value of machinery				
Factory Cleaning	£10,000	Apportion: Floor Area				
Machine Dept. Supervisors	£40,000	Allocate to appropriate Dept.				
Assembly Dept. Supervisor	£18,000	Allocate to appropriate Dept.				
Finishing Dept. Supervisor	£15,000	Allocate to appropriate Dept.				
Factory Manager	£40,000	Apportion: No. of employees				
TOTAL FACTORY OVERHEADS	£303,000					

Stage Two

Now calculate an appropriate Overhead Absorption Rate (OAR) which will be used to determine how overhead should be absorbed by different products as they pass through the various production departments.

The budgeted Level of activity for each department in the coming year is as follows:

Budgeted Level of Activity for coming year

Machining Department	10,000 machine hours
Assembly Department	125,000 staff hours
Finishing Department	Output of 500,000 products

Transfer the total overhead for each department from the last table, and then calculate the three OARs. Remember to quote the appropriate units for each OAR!

	Machining Dept.	Assembly Department	Finishing Dept.
OAR Basis	Per Machine Hour	Per Labour Hour	Per Item
Total Budgeted Overheads			
Budgeted Activity			
Overhead Absorption Rate (OAR)			

6 Absorption Costing

Stage Three

Now using the additional data below and the calculated OARs, calculate the selling price for a garden fork and for an electric strimmer. The hourly rates for the three departments are as follows:-

- Machining Department   £10 per hour
- Assembly Department   £8 per hour
- Finishing Department   £6 per hour

	Garden Fork	Electric Strimmer
Machining Dept.		
Direct Labour		
Direct Materials		
Overheads Absorbed		
Assembly Dept.		
Direct Labour		
Direct Materials		
Overheads Absorbed		
Finishing Dept.		
Direct Labour		
Direct Materials		
Overheads Absorbed		
TOTAL COST		
50% Mark Up		
SELLING PRICE		

Garden Fork
Machining Department
Direct Labour	6 minutes (=0.1 hour)
Direct Materials	£1
Machine Time	12 minutes (=0.2 hours)

Assembly Department
Direct Labour	6 minutes (=0.1 hour)
Direct Materials	£0.75
Assembly Time	6 minutes (=0.1 hours)

Finishing Department
Direct Labour	6 minutes (= 0.1 hours)
Direct Materials	£0.50

Electric Strimmer
Machining Department
Direct Labour	6 minutes (=0.1 hour)
Direct Materials	£5
Machine Time	15 minutes (=0.25 hours)

Assembly Department
Direct Labour	30 minutes (=0.5 hour)
Direct Materials	£10.00
Assembly Time	30 minutes (=0.5 hours)

Finishing Department
Direct Labour	6 minutes (= 0.1 hours)
Direct Materials	£1.00

6 Absorption Costing

Question 6.12

Collegiate Ltd uses Activity Based Costing (ABC) to calculate the total cost of the products it manufactures. The company has identified four separate activities as shown in the table below. Calculate the cost driver rates for each area of activity (fully labelling the appropriate units for each cost driver rate).

Activity	Cost Driver	Annual Overhead	Level of Activity	Cost Driver Rate
Machining	Machine Hours	£18,000	6,000 hours	
Assembly	Labour Hours	£30,000	20,000 hours	
Quality Control	Inspections	£15,000	250 inspections	
Engineering Support	Machine Set Up	£12,500	25 Set Ups	

The direct costs for product X are as follows:

- Direct materials £30
- Direct Labour in Machining Department: 1 hour @ £12 per hour £12
  (Machine time in Machining Department = 1 hour)
- Direct Labour in Assembly Department: 3 hours @ £10 per hour £30
- Direct Expenses £5

Over the course of a full year 2,000 product X's are manufactured and this involves 3 full reconfigurations of the production line (i.e. Machine Set Ups) and 7 Quality Inspections

Using Activity Based Costing calculate the full cost of one single product X and the selling price (including VAT) if a 70% gross profit margin is required.

OVERHEAD ABSORPTION FOR PRODUCT X			
ACTIVITY	Cost Driver Rate	Level of Activity for Product X	Absorbed Overhead for Product X
Machining Overhead			
Assembly Overhead			
Quality Control Overhead			
Engineering Support Overhead			
Absorbed Overheads for 2,000 units of production			
Absorbed Overheads for 1 unit of production			

COST CARD – PRODUCT X	
Direct Materials	
Direct Labour - Machining	
Direct Labour – Assembly	
Direct Expenses	
Absorbed Overhead	
Total Cost (inc. Overheads)	
Selling Price (exc. VAT)	
Selling Price (inc. VAT)	

6 Absorption Costing

Question 6.13

Summarise the benefits & drawbacks of both absorption costing methods

Traditional Absorption Costing

Benefits

_____
_____
_____
_____

Drawbacks

_____
_____
_____
_____

Activity Based Costing

Benefits

_____
_____
_____
_____

Drawbacks

_____
_____
_____
_____

Chapter 7

Budgeting

INTRODUCTION

A **'Budget'** is simply a financial plan which outlines what a business hopes to achieve in the near future (typically the next 12 months).

In fact, it is simplistic to talk about 'the budget' as though it was a single document. In reality a business will produce multiple budgets (i.e. financial plans) which outline how they hope every aspect of their business will perform including sales, production, purchasing budgets etc. which cumulate in a 'Master Budget' which predicts the profitability and cash flow of the business in the coming months.

Virtually everyone working in business will encounter various aspects of the budgeting process from being asked to help set it, to subsequently being held accountable for his/her department's actual future performance compared to the budget.

OVERVIEW AND OBJECTIVES

By the end of this chapter you should be able to:

- understand what budgets are
- explain how budgets are set
- identify the benefits and drawbacks of budgeting

and answer questions relating to these areas.

7 Budgeting

7.1 Overview of budgets

What is a Budget?

Companies usually set themselves a set of strategic aims which reflect where they would like their business to be in (say) 3-5 years. Such strategy documents are periodically updated to reflect progress made so far and changing priorities, but tend to contain only high level aspirations with little detail of exactly how these are to be achieved.

Alongside the longer-term strategy, a company will also usually formulate a budget which details exactly what the business wishes to achieve over a shorter timescale (typically one year). The aim of the budget is to describe how the business means to achieve the *next stage* of the bigger journey towards the company's desired strategic aims.

DEFINITION

A Budget is a financial plan expressed in financial and/or other quantitative terms which extends forward for a period into the future

.... or put more simply, a business plan for the short-term.

TUTORIAL NOTE

The reference to *"and/or other quantitative terms"* simply means that not all budgets needs to be financial (£). Budgets can also contain information expressed in units, litres, kilogrammes etc.

To ensure consistency of message it is essential that the stated aims of the budget (over say the next 12 months) align themselves with the next stage of the longer-term stated strategy. If the budget and strategy seemed to be taking the business in two different directions then confusion (if not chaos) would result!

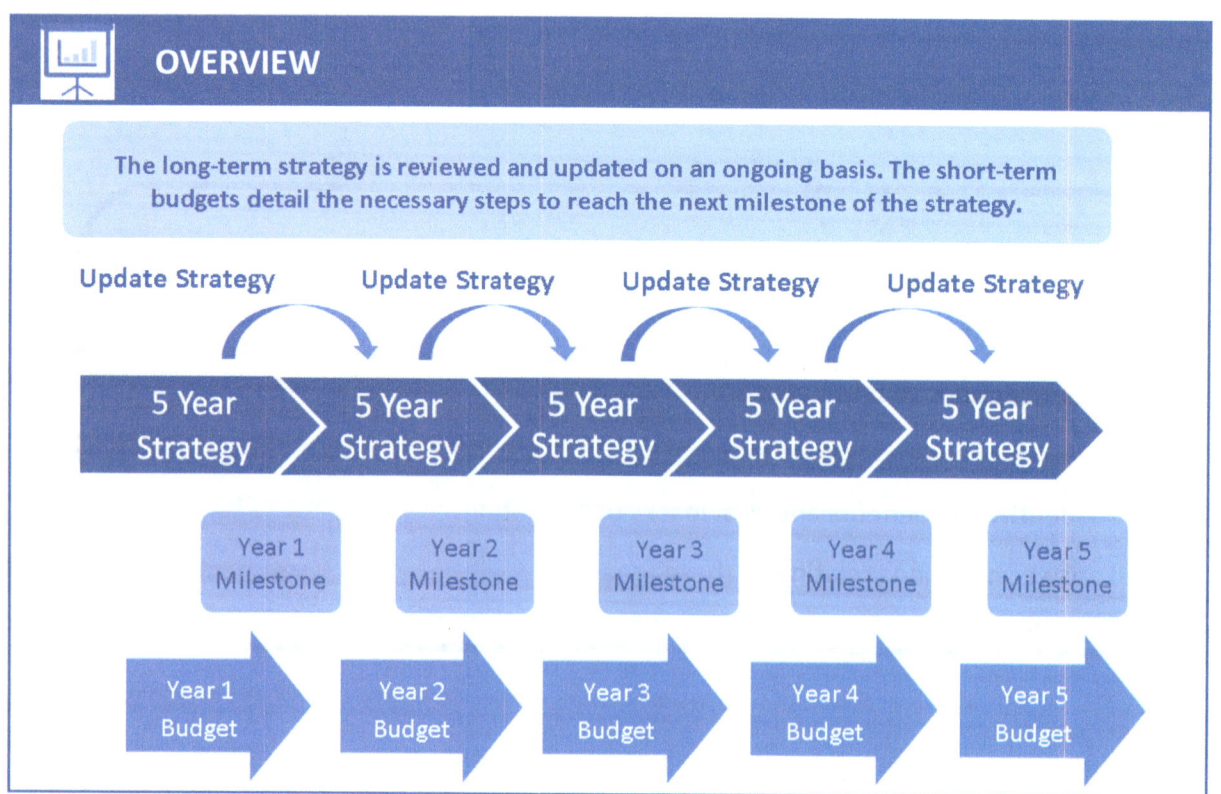

OVERVIEW

The long-term strategy is reviewed and updated on an ongoing basis. The short-term budgets detail the necessary steps to reach the next milestone of the strategy.

As we shall see, constructing budgets for companies can be time-consuming and their use is not without potential drawbacks in practice. However despite this, most businesses continue to use budgets as a key method of running their operations.

7.2 Use of budgets

Budgets are used for a range of purposes within a business, including:

Reinforcing the Business Strategy

As already mentioned, a good budget should reinforce the strategic aims of the business and deliver the company to the next milestone of the longer strategic journey. The budget spells out the necessary detail to ensure that the company's operation over the forthcoming months is in the right general direction for the business's desired aiming point on a longer timescale. Each year's budget can be viewed as an individual milestone to be reached as part of the longer journey towards the company's strategic aims.

Coordination within the Business

The budget encapsulates a business plan, and it is vital that all sections of the business not only know what that plan is, but what their individual roles and responsibilities are within that plan. For example, there is no point in the budget containing the proposed sale of 500 gizmos into a certain territory, if these products are not then available when required.

The full budget should contain sufficient detail to ensure that all sections of the business know what is required of each of them at each point throughout the year.

For example:

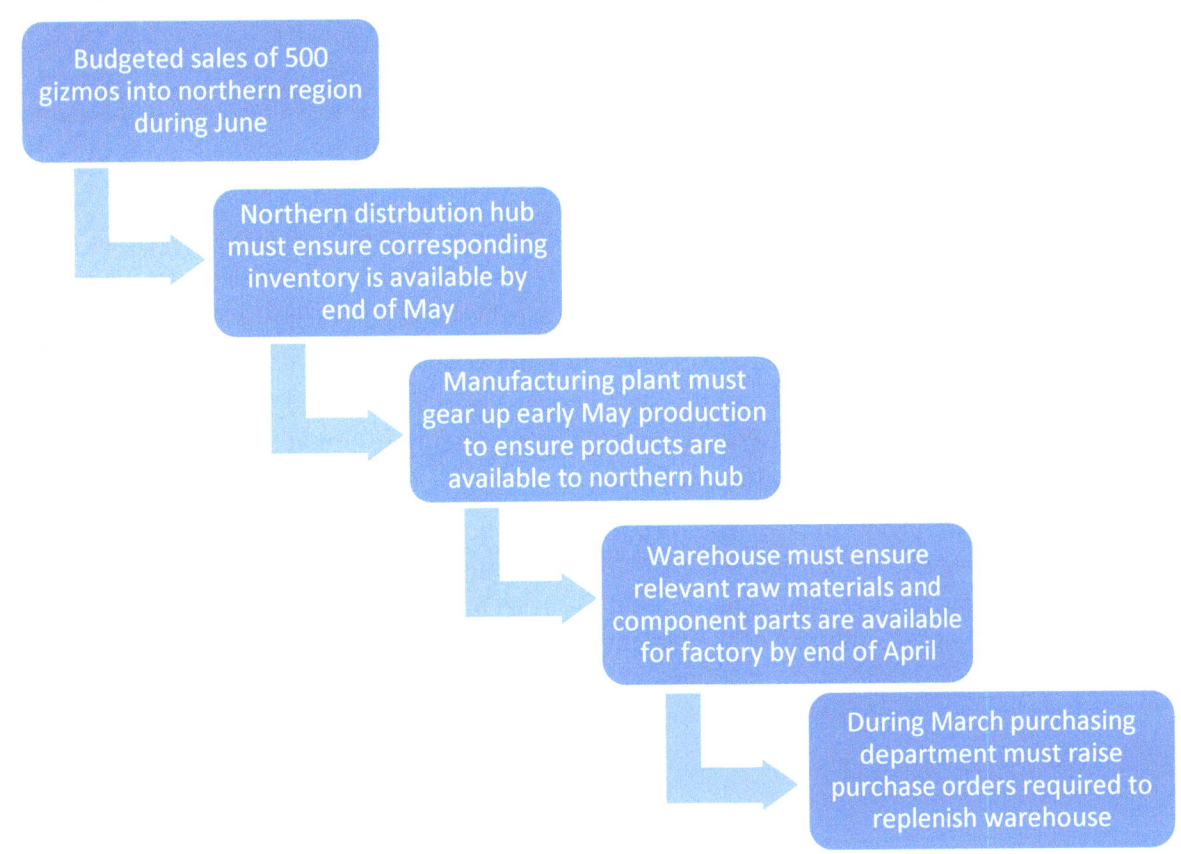

- Budgeted sales of 500 gizmos into northern region during June
- Northern distrbution hub must ensure corresponding inventory is available by end of May
- Manufacturing plant must gear up early May production to ensure products are available to northern hub
- Warehouse must ensure relevant raw materials and component parts are available for factory by end of April
- During March purchasing department must raise purchase orders required to replenish warehouse

As a System of Control

The budget provides a detailed plan of exactly what is required to be achieved by each individual department throughout each stage of the year. It can also then be subsequently used as a 'check-list' to ascertain who has and hasn't met their individual requirements.

Individual managers and departments can then be held to account for any shortcomings in their performance….. Or alternatively receive due recognition for having met their targets.

As a Means of Motivation

No-one likes to be left in the dark. Employees at all levels feel better about their role within the business if they can see 'the big picture' and understand their part within it. The fact that the budget facilitates communication therefore benefits both operational efficiency and staff motivation.

Performance against budget (at company level, departmental level and individual level) can then be used to drive a reward system for good performance, whether that be via:

- Performance related bonuses
- Recognition for future salary reviews
- Enhanced promotion prospects
- Or even just a simple 'thank-you' … which never goes amiss!

Conversely, failure to achieve budget targets can also trigger corrective action, including:

- Increased training and/or support if deemed necessary
- Increased resource being deployed to support what is now recognised as a tough budget
- Commencement of disciplinary process if appropriate

As a System of Authorisation

The budget will contain proposed levels of activity and expenditure and these can be allocated to individual managers and departments who then assume responsibility for either achieving or working within those levels. Thus a budget is often taken to be a formal pre-authorisation to:

- **Spend a certain sum of money** e.g. Head of Marketing holding a £50,000 advertising budget. This individual is then pre-authorised to spend up to £50,000 on advertising over the course of the year without seeking further clearance. If however he/she wishes to spend over this sum, additional permission would need to be sought.

- **Recruiting additional staff** e.g. the staff budget may have allowed for an expansion of the production workforce. The Production Manager is therefore pre-authorised to recruit these staff unless he/she hears to the contrary.

- **Purchase of Inventory** e.g. the raw materials budget may plan for a certain level of stockholding of a certain raw material. The Warehouse Manager should not then be criticised if it subsequently becomes apparent that this level of stock is excessive, as he/she was simply using the implied authority of the budget to follow the company's originally desired course of action.

The Language of Business

> **OVERVIEW**
>
> **Uses of the budget**
>
> **What's the budget used for?**
> - To support achievement of the strategic aims
> - To motivate staff to better performance
> - As a system of authorisation
> - To help co-ordinate different sections of the business
> - As a system of control

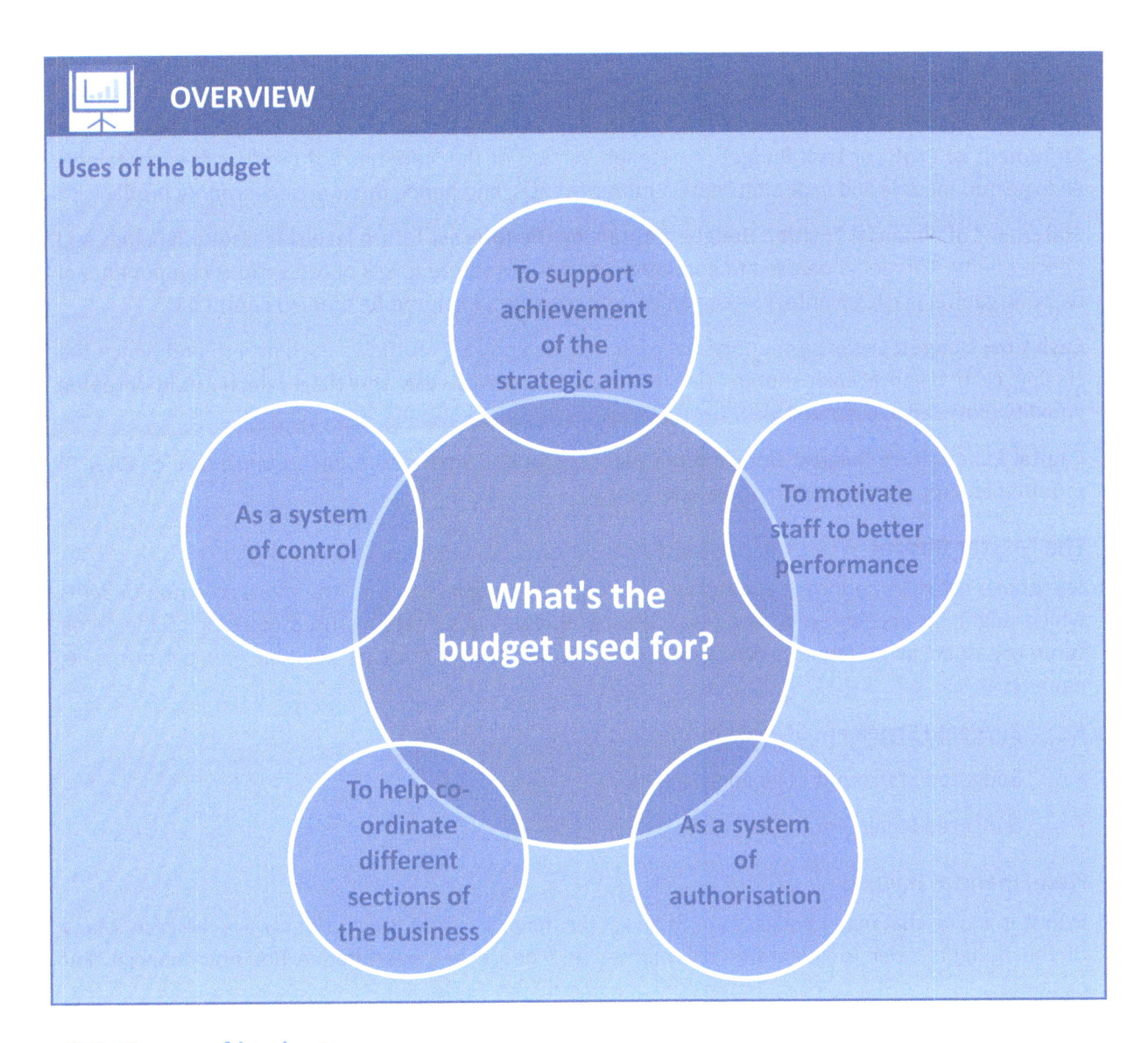

7.3 Types of budget

Referring to *the* budget makes it sound as if it were a single document. In fact (depending on the size and complexity of the company in question) the budget could consist of numerous interlinking documents which collectively describe the planned operation of the business over (say) the next year. Furthermore budgets are often 'calendarised' i.e. divided into months (typically) so that a month-by-month plan results.

A company's budget(s) could typically include any or all of the following:

Sales Budget: Detailing each month's forecast sales categorised by product type, region, sales channel, sales representative etc.

Production Budget: Detailing exactly what products need to be manufactured each month to support the budgeted level of sales.

Materials Usage Budget: Detailing each month's planned usage of raw materials and component parts to support the budgeted level of production.

Materials Purchase Budgets: Detailing how many component parts and what quantity of raw materials must be purchased each month to support the budgeted level of materials usage.

Staffing Budget: Detailing the required numbers of staff at different grades each month. Most typically used when these requirements vary with season or fluctuating demand.

Overheads Budget: Detailing the required level of expenditure necessary to support all the other budgeted activities.

Statement of Profit or Loss Budget: A detailed version of the statement of profit or loss containing all expected income and expenditure on a monthly basis, and hence the forecast monthly profit.

Statement of Financial Position Budget: Containing the forecast future levels of assets, liabilities and hence equity. This could be used to communicate desired future levels of the various components of working capital (cash, inventory, receivables, and payables, explored further in chapter 11).

Cash flow Budget: Detailing the forecast cash inflows and cash outflows each month and hence the closing cash balance each month. Can be used to predict cash shortfalls which could threaten liquidity (covered in chapter 10).

Capital Expenditure Budget: Detailing the planned capital expenditure each month (see chapter 9) required to support the growth of the company.

The Master Budget

The above list is by no means exhaustive but merely highlights some of the more common budgets which might be encountered. The term 'Master Budget' is sometimes used to refer to the three summary financial statements which describe the company's forecast position and performance, namely:

- Budgeted Statement of Profit or Loss
- Budgeted Statement of Financial Position
- Budgeted Statement of Cash flows

Non-Financial Budgets

Whilst it is true that many budgets are financial (i.e. have a £ sign), this is not always the case. Many of the budgets refer to quantities or volumes and hence are quantitative but not financial. For example:

- **Staffing Budget** – Number of staff hours required
- **Sales Volume Budget** – Number of units of a particular product sold
- **Production Budget** – Number of kilogrammes of a particular product manufactured
- **Purchasing Budget** – Number of litres of a particular raw material to be purchased

Different Requirements for Different Companies

Every company is unique and will therefore have varying requirements from a budgetary system. It is generally the case that the larger and more complex a business becomes, the greater its needs will be for a sophisticated budget system.

The Language of Business

> **EXAMPLE**
>
> - **New fledgling companies** employing only a handful of people will often manage in their early stages on a word of mouth basis. They can get away with this because everything about the business (e.g. number of customers, products and staff) is on a small scale. Moreover, the early culture is often a reactive one because everything is new and there is no historical data with which to forward plan.
>
> - **As the business grows** the managers will inevitably wish to plan ahead and this may well initially consist of setting sales budgets … which for a manufacturing company will then almost certainly also result in setting production budgets. The growing business is starting to gain experience of its exact requirements and this knowledge in turn facilitates proactive planning about its future requirements for staff, machinery, materials and overheads etc.
>
> - **The largest, most complex companies** are totally reliant on sophisticated planning methods which are generally either based on a budgetary system, or at least a system that emulates many of the features of a budgetary system. For example, a technology company planning its future investment in research and development and advanced manufacturing facilities, is reliant on the high level of coordination and control offered by a sophisticated budget system to ensure that the required resource is in the right place, at the right time. This 'resource' can consist of premises, staff, plant & machinery, inventory and cash!

7.4 Inter-dependence of budgets

The many and varied individual budgets do not exist in isolation, but are interdependent on each other, as the following comprehensive example will illustrate.

> **EXAMPLE**
>
> A toy manufacturer is planning a major expansion into the wider national market. Most of its toys are moulded from a plastic resin raw material in a highly automated manufacturing process. It is now late December and the company is finalising its budget for the following financial year (commencing 1st January).
>
> A popular toy is the scale model 'Doctor Who Tardis' (product code DWT) and next year's sales budget forecasts an ambitious increase in the sales of this toy to 20,000 units. There are currently 2,000 of these units in stock, but by the end of the following year the company wants to have increased the inventory level of DWTs to 5,000 units.
>
> **Sales Budget for DWTs = 20,000 units**
>
> Sales budget ▶ Production budget
>
> The sales budget has a knock-on effect on the production budget for DWTs.
>
> **How many DWTs does the company need to manufacture next year?**

7 Budgeting

The factory therefore needs to manufacture:

- 20,000 units to sell
- Plus 5,000 units to have in stock at the end of the year
- But it already has 2,000 units in stock

Production Budget for DWTs = 23,000 units (= 20,000 + 5,000 – 2,000)

Production budget → Materials usage budget

The production budget then has a knock-on effect on the materials usage budget for resin. Each DWT requires 0.3 kg of resin.

So the factory needs: 23,000 x 0.3Kg = 6,900 Kg of resin for production.

Material Usage Budget for resin = 6,900 Kg

Remembering that although it is planning on *selling* 20,000 units ….It is planning on *producing* 23,000 units!

Materials usage budget → Materials purchase budget

In turn, the materials usage budget has a knock-on effect on the materials purchase budget for resin. The company budgets on using 6,900 Kg of resin next year. There is currently 30,000 Kg of resin in stock, but by the end of the following year the company wants to have increased the inventory level of resin to 40,000 Kg.

How much resin will the company need to purchase next year?

The factory needs:

- 6,900 Kg of resin for production
- Plus 40,000 Kg of resin to have in stock at the end of the year
- But it already has 30,000 Kg of resin in stock

Material Purchase Budget for resin = 16,900 Kg (= 6,900 + 40,000 – 30,000)

The above illustrates how some of the budget setting process is linear in fashion with a cascading chain of events:

Sales budget → Production budget → Materials usage budget → Materials purchase budget

Additionally we must be aware of multiple knock-on effects from one element of the budget on *several* others, and that all of these effects (both linear and multiple) will always have corresponding effects on the Master Budget.

For example, our planned increase in sales of the 'Doctor Who Tardis' toy will not only affect the sales, production, materials usage & materials purchase budgets (as already seen) but also numerous *other* budgets as the following diagram illustrates.

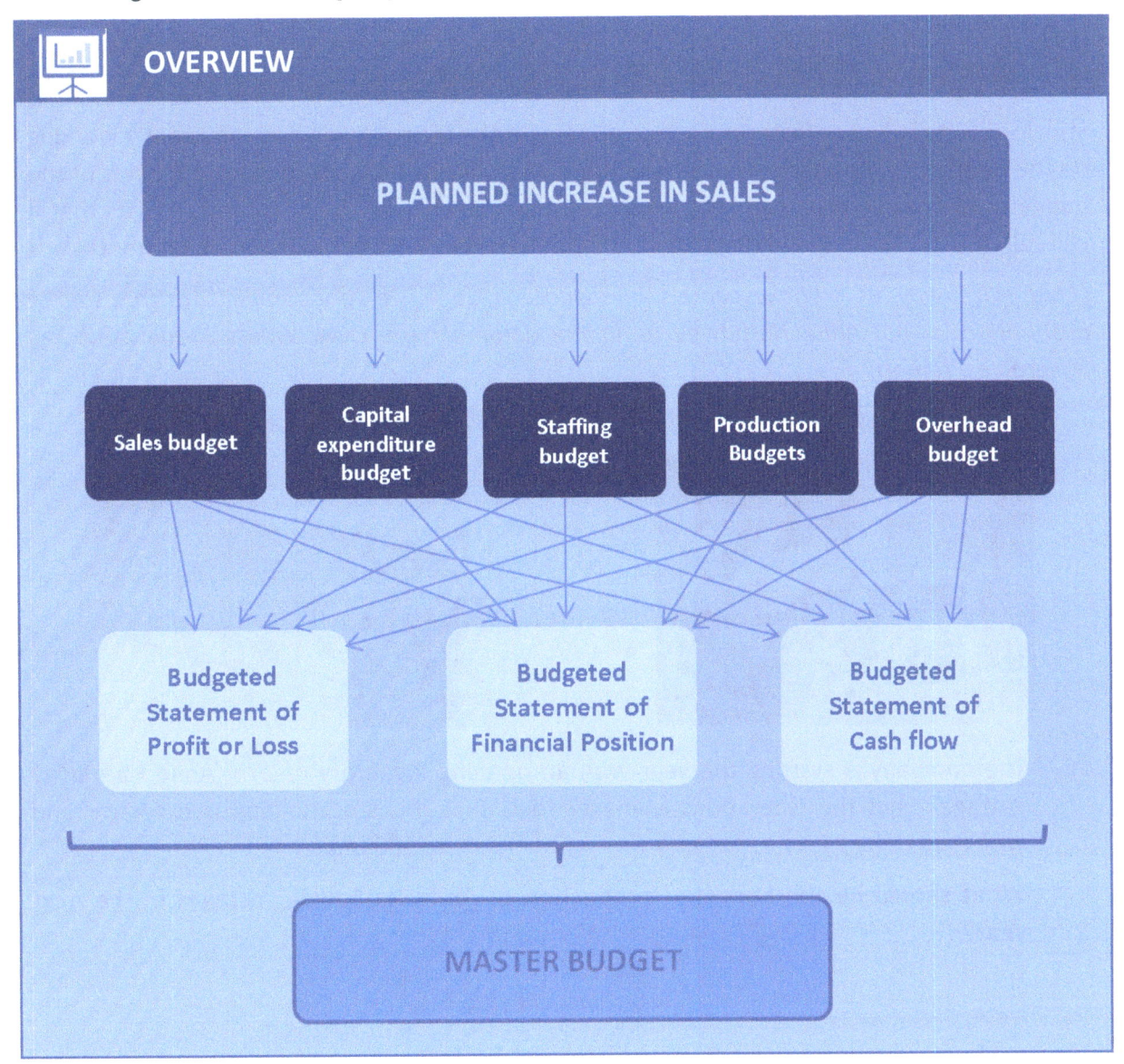

OVERVIEW

PLANNED INCREASE IN SALES

↓ ↓ ↓ ↓ ↓

- Sales budget
- Capital expenditure budget
- Staffing budget
- Production Budgets
- Overhead budget

↓

- Budgeted Statement of Profit or Loss
- Budgeted Statement of Financial Position
- Budgeted Statement of Cash flow

↓

MASTER BUDGET

So in addition to the effects on the budgets already mentioned (collectively summarised as the 'production budgets' in the above diagram), the simple planned increase in the sales of one toy will potentially impact on numerous other budgets, including:

- **Sales Budget -** Increased sales revenue
- **Capital Expenditure Budget -** New premises or manufacturing plant?
- **Staffing Budget -** Additional sales staff and/or production staff?
- **Production Budgets -** As already described
- **Overhead Budget -** Corresponding increase in all indirect costs

…. and every one of these will in turn have an effect on the Master Budget:

- Increased sales revenue and/or expenses → **Budgeted Statement of Profit or Loss**
- Closing Balances of Assets and/or Liabilities → **Budgeted Statement of Financial Position**
- Increased Cash inflows and/or Cash Outflows → **Budgeted Statement of Cashflows**

7 Budgeting

So around about now you are probably starting to realise that formulating a comprehensive budget is a fairly complex and time consuming affair!

TEST YOUR UNDERSTANDING 1

Stratford Gifts Ltd manufactures a range of gifts for the tourist trade and is currently working on the budget for the coming year. The Operations Manager is working on the aspects of the budget under his control, and sees from the sales budget that the company predicts that it will sell 2,000 resin moulded models of 'Anne Hathaway's Cottage' in the next 12 months.

(Anne Hathaway, as in Shakespeare's wife whose cottage is a very popular Stratford tourist destination...... not Anne Hathaway as in the actor of 'The Devil Wears Prada' and 'Les Miserables' fame!)

The actual cottage near Stratford

A model of the cottage

a) The company is starting the year with an opening inventory of 175 'Anne Hathaway cottages', but the Operations Manager feels that this stockholding is excessive and wishes to reduce it to a year-end closing inventory of 100 units.

What should be the budgeted production of Anne Hathaway cottages in the next year?

_____

b) Each moulded 'Anne Hathaway Cottage' requires 0.5Kg of special type X resin.

How much type X resin needs to be added to the material usage budget for this product for the coming year?

_____

c) The company has an opening inventory of 10Kg of type X resin. The Operations Manager would like to increase this stockholding to 30Kg by the year-end.

How much type X resin needs to be added to the materials purchasing budget?

_____

The Language of Business

7.5 How are budgets set?

Starting Point for the Budget Process

There are a variety of different ways in which a company can approach the task of creating next year's budget, but two common approaches are to start from either:

- **The sales budget,** which is then regarded as the principal budget *("How much can we sell")* with other budgets then being developed subsequently *("What resource will be required to support that level of sales")*….. or

- **The budgeted statement of profit or loss,** which is then regarded as the principal budget *("How much profit are we aiming to make")* and working backwards from there *("What level of sales & expenditure etc. will be required to make that profit?")*

Budgeting is often an iterative process that involves repeated adjustments and fine-tuning until the finished result appears both acceptable (to the shareholders and directors) and reasonable (in terms of being achievable).

Incremental versus Zero-Based Budgeting

The fundamental question is whether to start the budget process based on what was actually achieved in the previous year ('incremental budgeting') or whether to start completely afresh without reference to previous performance ('zero-based budgeting').

Incremental budgeting is more common in practice because of the obvious logic of using last year's performance (for sales, expenses, profit etc.) as a known achievable starting point and then considering what improvements could possibly be made. It is a relatively fast process because there is a known starting point, and it tends to produce more realistic budgets because they have originated from a known level of performance which has actually been achieved. The danger is that they have the potential to repeat last year's mistakes and poor performance.

EXAMPLE

Scenario

A company's performance for last year is summarised in the following abbreviated statement of profit or loss:

Sales Revenue	£500,000
Cost of Sales	(£200,000)
Gross Profit	£300,000
Overheads	(£230,000)
Net Profit	£70,000

If the business budgets to increase sales revenue by 2%, improve gross profit % by one percentage point, and decrease overheads by 3%, what amount of net profit will they budget to make?

Solution

This represents the incremental approach to budgeting where the previous year's performance is used as a starting point and then 'tweaked' based on what the company believes is achievable.

Sales

A 2% increase is calculated by multiplying by 1.02   £500,000 x 1.02 = **£510,000**

261

7 Budgeting

> **Gross Profit %**
>
> Note that the budget task was NOT to increase gross profit (£) by 1%, but rather to increase gross profit % by one percentage point!
>
> Last year's gross profit % = (£300,000 / £500,000) x 100% = 60%. A one percentage point increase is therefore an increase to 61% gross profit conversion of the budgeted sales revenue. So budgeted gross profit £ = £510,000 x 61% = **£311,100**   [61% = 0.61]
>
> **Overheads**
>
> A 3% decrease is the same as next year's overheads being 97% of the previous year's overheads i.e. £230,000 x 97% = **£223,100** [97% = 0.97]
>
> We can use these three figures to complete next year's budget, noting that 'cost of sales' and 'net profit' are merely balancing figures.
>
> | | | |
> |---|---|---|
> | Sales Revenue | £510,000 | |
> | Cost of Sales | (£198,900) | [balancing figure] |
> | Gross Profit | £311,100 | |
> | Overheads | (£223,100) | |
> | Net Profit | £88,000 | [balancing figure] |
>
> The company will therefore budget to make £88,000 net profit. This is a very healthy 26% increase achieved by a modest 2% increase to sales, an extra one percentage point on the gross profit %, and a 3% saving on overheads. Making all three of these things happen in practice is an altogether different matter but it gives the company a good target to aim for.

It is worth repeating that the cost of sales figure is not normally explicitly budgeted. Businesses instead focus on top-line sales and percentage gross profit performance. The cost of sales figure is then merely the balancing figure calculated afterwards.

Zero-Based Budgeting is used when a business wishes to have a completely fresh look at what it should be able to achieve, without limiting the process to what has previously actually been achieved. This approach is used for brand new activities where there simply isn't any performance history, but also where it is felt that previous performance is not indicative of what *could* be achieved. In these cases, a 'blank canvas' approach ensures that each budget figure is considered afresh and the business is invited to think about what *should* be achievable.

OVERVIEW

Benefits and drawbacks

	Benefits	Drawbacks
Incremental Budgeting	A faster process which tends to produce more realistic budgets.	Discourages innovative thinking and can result in last year's poor performance being repeated
Zero-Based Budgeting	Enforces a fresh look at every budget figure. Avoids last year's poor performance being rolled forward.	A more time-consuming process which can potentially result in unrealistic budgets

In practice a mixture of the two methods may be used e.g. starting with a broad-brush incremental approach based on last year's performance, followed by a close scrutiny of certain aspects of the budget to make sure they represent an appropriate target.

For instance, *all* of the company's sales figures might initially be increased by 3% from the previous year's figures, but then a closer look might be taken at the *online* sales figures (because the directors know that general online sales in the UK are increasing at 11% per annum).

Imposed versus Participative Budgets

The next question is 'who' should be involved in the budget setting process. The choice is basically one of whether to **impose** budgets onto the various departments and individuals who will ultimately be responsible for achieving them; or whether to invite them to actually **participate** in the budget setting process. Again there are pros and cons to both approaches.

In a perfect world it might be considered good practice to involve the people who will ultimately be responsible for achieving the budget, so that they feel as if they have some 'ownership' and are therefore more likely to strive to achieve it. After all, if someone participated in setting (say) a certain sales budget, it might then become a matter of personal pride to deliver what they originally said they could achieve.

Conversely if a sales budget is simply 'handed-down' to a salesperson they might resent it (particularly if it was a challenging target). Such resentment (although probably not openly displayed) might result in a lack-lustre effort to achieve *'someone else's target'*.

However, a particular problem which needs to be guarded against is that of 'budget slack'. This is when an individual is asked to participate in the setting of his/her own budget and uses this as an opportunity to set a 'soft' budget for him/herself i.e. either a low sales or profit budget (which can be easily achieved) or a high expenditure budget (which it is easy to stick within without having to particularly control costs). Imposed budgets avoid this potential problem altogether, but it needs to be borne in mind if a participative approach is adopted.

That said, there are times when the person ultimately responsible for achieving a budget is in fact the best placed person to decide what is actually achievable in the real world. An imposed budget set by someone 'remote' from the subsequent challenge, can end up being somewhat fanciful and hence not even taken seriously.

A significant factor in deciding between a participative and an imposed approach is the time available to conduct the budget process. Clearly, simply imposing budgets is far quicker than a time-consuming series of meetings where the budgets are negotiated.

OVERVIEW

Benefits and drawbacks

	Benefits	Drawbacks
Imposed Budgeting	A faster, simpler process which allows challenging targets to be set.	Imposed budgets can cause resentment and lead to a lack of 'buy-in'. Can result in unrealistic budgets.
Participative Budgeting	Promotes ownership and motivates individuals to strive to 'beat the budget. Can result in more realistic budgets.	A more complex time-consuming process which can result in softer budgets (e.g. budget slack).

Again, a common approach is often to adopt a 'hybrid' of the two approaches where the directors and senior managers have a clear idea of what they are hoping to achieve, but at least take the time to discuss the matter with those ultimately responsible for achieving the various targets. In this way unrealistic targets can be identified and re-visited, and the individuals concerned feel as though they have had a say in the process. For example, having stated that the company is (say) looking to save 1% on office costs, maybe the office manager can then suggest where best to make these savings … resulting in a win-win outcome.

7.6 Measuring performance against budget

We have already seen that a budget has several important uses including:

- Reinforcing the business's strategy
- Helping to coordinate the activities of the business
- Acting as a system of control
- As a means of motivating the team
- As a means of authorising expenditure and other activity

In addition the budget is used as one of the key benchmarks of company performance (typically on a monthly basis) and this process of performance appraisal automatically incorporates many of the above stated uses of budgets.

In order to appraise any type of performance (sales achievement, expenditure control, profit performance etc.) it is very useful to have some sort of benchmark against which to assess the actual level of performance. Merely producing a report that states a certain level of attainment is of little use unless there is also some form of comparative measure.

EXAMPLE

Scenario

A company achieved £100,000 profit last month. Was this a good performance?

Solution

Who knows? If the company in question is a major PLC then probably not, but then again maybe that PLC is trying to recover from a loss-making recent history in which case it might represent a good result. If it is small private company then maybe it is a good result, but we still can't really comment until we know what the *expected* results were.

In order to be able to assess any sort of performance figures, they need to be compared against some sort of expectation, which could be:

- **Year on Year:** The comparable figure from the same period in the previous year e.g. retail sales in the Sheffield branch are up 4% last month compared to the same month last year
- **Competitor Benchmark:** It would be excellent to be able to compare a business's performance against that of its competitors. Unfortunately, although all companies have to file their annual accounts at Companies House (at which point they are made publically available) these are highly summarised annual accounts which contain limited detail on which to base comparisons.

- **Against Budget:** For most companies this is the key performance measure. The budget represents the business's plan for the year and reviewing the company's actual performance against the budgeted performance reveals exactly where the plan is being achieved ... and where it isn't.

Variances against Budget

Most businesses will produce monthly reporting packs which (alongside numerous other reports) will contain a monthly statement of profit or loss (or 'P&L' as it is more likely to be referred to).

Not only will this state what the business's actual results were for the month in question, but also what the budget was, and how far apart the 'actual' was from the 'budget' in the form of a 'variance' figure.

Variances can either be:

- **Favourable Variances:** which are reported as positive numbers as they represent something which will result in a higher profit than the budgeted profit
- **Adverse Variances:** which are reported as negative numbers (often shown in brackets) as they represent something which will result in a lower profit than the budgeted profit

Care is needed interpreting results because a business wants sales and profit to be *higher* than the budget figure .... But wants expense figures to be *lower* than the budget figure!

OVERVIEW

This 'reversal' of treatment is best summarised in a table.

	(Negative Variance)	Positive Variance
Sales and Profit figures	'Actual' results lower than 'Budget' figures i.e. Lower profit as a result	'Actual' results higher than 'Budget' figures i.e. Higher profit as a result
Expense figures	'Actual' results higher than 'Budget' figures i.e. Lower profit as a result	'Actual' results lower than 'Budget' figures i.e. Higher profit as a result

Remembering that 'brackets are bad' often helps!

7 Budgeting

EXAMPLE

A typical monthly P&L (found in a business's management accounts) might look something like the following:

	Budget	Actual	Variance
Sales	**£10,000**	**£9,500**	**(£500)**
Cost of Sales	£3,000	£3,040	(£40)
Gross Profit (£)	**£7,000**	**£6,460**	**(£540)**
Gross Profit (%)	**70%**	**68%**	**(2%)**
Office Salaries	£3,000	£2,900	£100
Premises Costs	£1,000	£1,050	(£50)
Marketing	£500	£300	£200
Distribution	£500	£600	(£100)
Depreciation	£500	£500	£nil
Total Overheads	**£5,500**	**£5,350**	**£150**
Net Profit (£)	**£1,500**	**£1,110**	**(£390)**
Net Profit (%)	15%	12%	(3%)

The variance column immediately shows us what aspects of the business's performance have gone well and which haven't….

Favourable Variances:

- Office Salaries Budget underspent by £100
- Marketing Budget underspent by £200
- Overall Overheads Budget underspent by £150

Adverse Variances:

- Sales budget missed by £500
- Gross Profit budget missed by £540
- Conversion from sales to gross profit missed budget by 2%
- Distribution costs overspent by £100
- Net Profit £390 adverse to budget
- Conversion from sales to net profit missed by 3%

Although a detailed monthly performance review would entail examining every single line of the P&L (as every single line can affect the final profit figure to a greater or lesser extent), a 'quick' overview of a business's performance can be achieved by just considering five lines:

1) **Sales** – Are the business's 'top-line' sales higher or lower than expected?

2) **Gross Profit (£)** – Is there more or less gross profit (£) than expected? This of course can be due to two factors: the level of sales (higher or lower sales than budgeted), and/or the conversion from sales to gross profit (caused by higher or lower than budgeted cost prices and/or selling prices)

3) **Gross Profit (%)** – How many pence gross profit per £ of sales i.e. how efficient is the conversion from sales to gross profit? We need to look at this separately to establish if the conversion from sales (at whatever level they may be) to gross profit (£) is in line with expectations.

4) **Total Overheads** – How good is the business's cost control?

5) **Net Profit (£)** – Is the final 'bottom-line' better or worse than expected?

> **TUTORIAL NOTE**
>
> We don't tend to comment on the cost of sales figure because this performance is implied in the much more meaningful gross profit % result.

By reporting the 'actual' results against the 'budget' figures and by calculating either a favourable or adverse variance for each line of the P&L we can now see where any 'lost profit' has originated (or conversely how any surplus profit has arisen).

This is often the key method of assessing performance used internally within a company (i.e. in management accounting). In contrast the key measure of assessing performance used by external users (i.e. in financial accounting) is by 'year on year' comparison, as the highly confidential budget figures are simply not revealed to the outside world.

7 Budgeting

TEST YOUR UNDERSTANDING 2

Looking at the management accounts below, complete any blank fields and calculate the variances (indicating 'adverse' variances in brackets)

Identify the three most pressing specific issues for the music retailer "VMH Music" to take action to remedy.

"VMH MUSIC LTD": Year Ending 31st December 2015

	BUDGET	ACTUAL	VARIANCE
Sales Revenue	£1,800,000	£1,810,000	_____
Cost of sales	£810,000	£886,900	_____
Gross Profit	£990,000	_____	_____
GP%	55%	_____	_____
Less Expenditure			
Staff wages	£250,000	£330,000	_____
Staff Training	£25,000	£23,000	_____
Stock Losses	£30,000	£65,000	_____
Telephone	£20,000	£19,000	_____
Insurance	£50,000	£49,100	_____
Premises Costs	£400,000	£402,000	_____
Depreciation	£100,000	£150,000	_____
Total Expenditure	£875,000	£1,038,100	_____
Net Profit / (Loss)	£115,000	_____	_____

7.7 Benefits and drawbacks of budgets

Although producing budgets represent a significant cost both in terms of time and money, and despite budgets being open to the criticism that they can stifle innovation (by rigid adherence to 'the budget'), they continue to be the primary method of planning and performance appraisal for most companies.

The biggest 'budget-related' challenge for most organisations is to get the team to understand that whilst 'achieving budget' is important, that the budget itself is not 'written in stone'.

Circumstances change and that can mean that either:

- Something that was important when the budget was originally set is now less important
- Something that was possibly not even included in the original budget has now become a serious issue

Getting a large diverse team to both accept that budget achievement is very important, together with the truth that things change, is a difficult trick to pull off as some staff will seize on the opportunity to complain of mixed messages. No-one said that managing people was going to be easy!

OVERVIEW

Benefits of Budgeting	Drawbacks of Budgeting
A means of ensuring 'joined-up' thinking throughout an organisation	The significant time and cost necessary to develop and operate a budget
Reinforces and adds details to the company's strategic plan over the short-term	Unrealistic budgets (especially when not 'sold in') can demotivate staff
Supports planning and coordination of operations and activities	Participative budgeting can result in 'budget slack' being built into targets
Informs and motivates staff	Incremental budgeting can result in the previous year's poor performance being rolled forward and repeated
Provides a system of control and authorisation	Encourages a *use it or lose it* attitude to expenditure i.e. the budget *must* be spent, lest it is taken away next year
Facilitates performance appraisal and reward mechanisms	Stifles innovation by promoting rigid adherence to the budget

7 Budgeting

7.8 Static versus flexible budgets

As mentioned, one potential drawback of budgeting is that 'stuff happens' and what was appropriate when the budget was originally set, is now no longer relevant.

This potential problem can be addressed in two ways:

1) By using flexible budgets
2) By using Key Performance Indicators (KPIs)

Flexible Budgets

Up to this point we have discussed budgets as though they were formulated shortly before the start of a new financial year and then not altered under any circumstances i.e. that they are 'static budgets'. In fact this need not be the case. If circumstances alter then there is no reason why the budget should not be altered for the remainder of the year.

Of course, this can happen in either direction:

- If the reality of the market place is that trade has suffered a downturn, the entire budget can be revised downwards (lower sales, lower profit). After all, there is little point in demotivating your staff for every remaining month of the year by continually highlighting their failure to achieve what is now an impossible target.

- If however the market is now more buoyant than originally predicted then there is no reason why 'the bar' should not be raised to reflect better than expected trading conditions and urge the team onto the next level.

A good budget should be stretching...*but achievable!* Demanding the impossible simply demotivates employees. However, in contrast, giving them an 'easy life' is selling the shareholders short!

(Flexible) Key Performance Indicators (KPIs)

It can be useful to state key budget tasks in % terms so that they will *automatically* compensate for any changes (upwards or downwards) in the level of trade. A good example already encountered is gross profit % (aka GP%). A GP% simply states how many pence of gross profit has resulted from £1 in sales, and as such automatically 'flexes' with the actual level of sales.

EXAMPLE

Scenario

A budget requires a 55% gross profit conversion from sales of £10,000 i.e. £5,500 gross profit. In the event, the business achieves sales of £11,000 and gross profit of £5,600. Comment on the business's performance.

Solution

The business has exceeded its sales budget by £1,000 and that is to be applauded. However something appears to have gone awry on their conversion of these sales to gross profit (£).

They have exceeded the gross profit (£) budget by £100 which initially looks like good news until you consider that *if* they had achieved the budgeted 55% GP% they *should have* delivered £11,000 x 55% = £6,050 gross profit.

The Language of Business

> In the event they have only achieved 51% gross profit (£5,600 / £11,000 x 100%) which is 4% short of their targeted conversion rate. This is not particularly impressive and has thrown away virtually all of the benefit of the higher than expected sales figure.
>
> Ultimately the business should be striving for profit … not turnover *("Turnover is Vanity…Profit is Sanity")*. Have they been heavily discounting their selling prices to 'buy' sales … and sacrificing their profitability in the process?

The same principle can be applied to expenditure figures. In addition to quoting budgeted expenses in £ terms, they can also be quoted in % terms, as can be seen in the following example.

EXAMPLE

Scenario

A pub manager has a budget which states that in a certain week he should achieve £10,000 of drinks sales but is allowed to spend 10% of this on bar wages i.e. £1,000 in the week.

In the event the pub achieves drinks sales of £14,000 but spends £1,300 on bar wages. Is this a good performance or not?

Solution

Clearly the sales figure of £4,000 better than budget (positive variance) is an excellent performance. However, at first appearance there is a £300 adverse spend on bar wages … and normally adverse variances are bad news.

However it we look at the wage spend in % terms (which automatically adjust for higher or lower levels of trade) then we can see that the bar manager actually spent 9.3% of the sales figure on bar wages (£1,300 ÷ £14,000 x 100%) … as opposed to the target 10% figure. This represents a £100 underspend when compared to the 'flexed' budget (i.e. 10% of £14,000 = £1,400 'flexed' budget…as opposed the £1,300 actually spent).

The manager wisely increased the staff on duty so as to not miss any sales by over-long queues at the bar…but still managed to keep within the 10% guideline. The flexible budget has allowed common-sense to prevail.

7 Budgeting

> ⚠️ **KEY POINTS FROM CHAPTER 7**
>
> **Definition of a Budget**
> - A Budget is a financial plan expressed in financial and/or other quantitative terms which extends forward for a period into the future
>
>   *.... or put more simply, a business plan for the short-term*
>
> **Use of Budgets**
> - To reinforce the business strategy
> - To coordinate activities within the business
> - As a system of control
> - As a means of motivation
> - As a system of authorisation
>
> **Types of Budget**
> - Numerous budgets (i.e. financial plans) exist within a typical business including: sales, production, material usage, material purchase, staffing, overhead etc
> - These culminate in a **'Master Budget'** typically comprising of:
>   - Budgeted Statement of Profit or Loss
>   - Budgeted Statement of Cashflow
>   - Budgeted Statement of Financial Position
> - Individual budgets tend to be inter-dependent and changes to one budget will potentially affect one or more other budgets
>
> **Setting of Budgets**
> - **Incremental Budgeting** uses the previous year's performance as a starting point and then 'increments' it to produce the next year's desired targets. This is a fast process which produces realistic budgets, but which potentially discourages innovative thinking and can result in last year's poor performance being repeated.
> - **Zero-Based Budgeting** looks at the budgeting process afresh without reference to previous performance. This 'blank canvas' approach forces a fresh look at every budget figure and avoids last year's poor performance being rolled forward, but is a more time-consuming process which can potentially result in unrealistic budgets.
> - **Participative Budgeting** sets the various budgets by discussion and negotiation with the individuals who will ultimately be responsible for achieving each budget task. This promotes 'buy-in' and motivates individuals to strive to achieve the budget, but is a more time consuming process. Tends to produce realistic budgets, but runs the risk of 'budget slack'.
> - **Imposed Budgeting** is set by senior managers without prior negotiation. This is a faster process which allows challenging targets to be set, but can lead to unrealistic budgets and resentment.
>
> **Measurement of Performance against Budget**
>
> Businesses typically measure their actual performance against their budget on a monthly basis, and produce 'variances' to show the level of under-achievement (*adverse variances*) or over-achievement (*favourable variances*), always measured with reference to the ultimate effect on profitability.

Favourable Variances (increased profit) arise from either:

- Actual sales being *higher* than budgeted sales
- Actual expenditure being *lower* than budgeted expenditure

Adverse Variances (reduced profit) arise from either:

- Actual sales being *lower* than budgeted sales
- Actual expenditure being *higher* than budgeted expenditure

Overview of Statement of Profit or Loss Profit Performance

i. **Sales** – Are the business's 'top-line' sales higher or lower than expected?

ii. **Gross Profit (£)** – Is there more or less gross profit (£) than expected? This of course can be due to two factors: the level of sales (higher or lower sales than budgeted), and/or the conversion from sales to gross profit (caused by higher or lower than budgeted cost prices and/or selling prices)

iii. **Gross Profit (%)** – How many pence gross profit per £ of sales i.e. how efficient is the conversion from sales to gross profit? We need to look at this separately to establish if the conversion from sales (at whatever level they may be) to gross profit (£) is in line with expectations.

iv. **Total Overheads** – How good is the business's cost control?

v. **Net Profit (£)** – Is the final 'bottom-line' better or worse than expected?

Benefits & Drawbacks of Budgeting

- **Benefits** include the promotion of 'joined-up' thinking throughout a complex organisation and a common purpose which ultimately supports the business strategy. Acts as a motivator, system of authorisation and means of performance appraisal.

- **Drawbacks** include the time and cost required to develop and operate a budget system, and the potential for demotivation if budgets are unrealistic or badly 'sold-in'. Budgets can also promote dysfunctional behaviour such as unnecessary spending (fear of *'use it or lose it'*), and unethical or short-sighted behaviour to achieve the budget 'at any cost'.

Static versus Flexible Budgets

- **Static Budgets** are not subsequently modified in the light of actual trading conditions (whether better or worse than expected).

- **Dynamic Budgets** will be reviewed and modified to reflect actual trading conditions to allow targets to be amended where appropriate. The use of percentage based key performance indicators (KPIs) allow budgets to automatically flex to different levels of trade.

Chapter 7: Test Your Understanding Answers

TEST YOUR UNDERSTANDING 1

a) Budgeted production = Budgeted sales + budgeted closing inventory - opening inventory
Budgeted production = 2,000 + 100 – 175 = 1,925 units

b) Budgeted material usage = budgeted production x usage per unit
Budgeted material usage = 1,925 x 0.5 Kg = 962.5 Kg

c) Materials purchasing budget = budgeted material usage + budgeted closing materials inventory - opening materials inventory = 962.5Kg + 30Kg – 10Kg = 982.5 Kg

TEST YOUR UNDERSTANDING 2

"VMH MUSIC LTD" - Year Ending 31st December 2015

	BUDGET	ACTUAL	VARIANCE
Sales Revenue	£1,800,000	£1,810,000	£10,000
Cost of sales	£810,000	£886,900	(£76,900)
Gross Profit	£990,000	£923,100	(£66,900)
GP%	55%	51%	(4%)
Less Expenditure			
Staff wages	£250,000	£330,000	(£80,000)
Staff Training	£25,000	£23,000	£2,000
Stock Losses	£30,000	£65,000	(£35,000)
Telephone	£20,000	£19,000	£1,000
Insurance	£50,000	£49,100	£900
Premises Costs	£400,000	£402,000	(£2,000)
Depreciation	£100,000	£150,000	(£50,000)
Total Expenditure	£875,000	£1,038,100	(£163,100)
Net Profit / (Loss)	£115,000	(£115,000)	(£230,000)

i. Although the sales budget has been achieved, the conversion to gross profit is 4% less than expected resulting in the gross profit being £66,900 adverse to budget.

ii. The staff wage costs are £80,000 adverse to budget

iii. The stock losses are over twice the budgeted figure, resulting in an additional £35,000 loss to profit

The Language of Business

Chapter 7: End of Chapter Exercises

Section A Questions

Question 7.1
Which of the following are typical uses of a budget within a business?

- (A) Planning & Coordination
- B Controlling & Measuring Performance
- C Motivating and Rewarding
- D All of the above

Question 7.2
Which of the following statements relating to budgets is untrue?

- A Budgets typically outline shorter-term plans which support the longer-term strategy of the business
- (B) Budgets may contain non-financial information
- C The forthcoming year's budget will feature in the annual report filed at Companies House.
- D A budget may be changed if circumstances dictate

Question 7.3
Which of the following statements relating to incremental budgets is untrue?

- A They are typically based on last year's figures
- B They should result in more realistic targets
- (C) They are relatively simple to produce
- D They ensure that last year's mistakes are not repeated

Question 7.4
Which of the following statements relating to zero-based budgets is untrue?

- A They ignore previous performance and scrutinise each figure as though being undertaken for the first time
- B They always result in realistic targets
- C Previous poor performance is not automatically rolled forward from last year
- (D) They are relatively slow to produce

7 Budgeting

Question 7.5
Which of the following statements relating to a participative budget process is untrue?

- A   Participation promotes subsequent 'buy-in' to achieving the budget
- B   Can help to ensure that unrealistic budgets are not set
- C   They are relatively slower to produce compared to 'imposed' budgets
- D   They avoid any risk of 'budget slack'

Question 7.6
A manufacturing company uses its anticipated sales as its 'primary budget' but also needs to devise various other budgets for the coming year.

In what order would the company set the following budgets?

- i.   Material Usage Budget
- ii.   Production Budget
- iii.   Sales Budget
- iv.   Material Purchase Budget

Choose the option which shows the correct order:

- A   i, ii, iii, iv
- B   iii, ii, iv, i
- C   ii, i, iv, iii
- D   iii, ii, i, iv

Question 7.7
The materials usage budget predicts that 500 litres of a chemical will be required for production over the next year. There are 98 litres of this chemical in stock at the start of the year, but the business wishes to reduce that to a closing stock figure of 20 litres by the end of the year.

How many litres of this chemical should be included in the corresponding material purchase budget?

- A   382 litres
- B   422 litres
- C   578 litres
- D   618 litres

Question 7.8
The sales budget of a manufacturing company forecasts the sales of 10,000 of a certain product over the next year. It has 583 of the manufactured item in stock at the start of the year but wishes to increase this to 1,200 by the end of the year.

How many units of this product need to be included in the corresponding production budget?

- A   8,217 units
- B   9,383 units
- C   10,617 units
- D   11,783 units

The Language of Business

Question 7.9

In the past year a business spent £12,000 on heating & lighting its premises. It has now installed various energy saving measures and hopes to make 4% savings on the corresponding expenditure in the coming year.

What figure should be budgeted for heating & lighting expenses for the coming year?

A   £480
B   £11,520
C   £12,000
D   £12,480

Question 7.10

A company's budgeted Statement of Profit or Loss included the figure of £10,000 for equipment maintenance over the course of the next year. In the event it actually incurred £10,600 on equipment maintenance during the year, but the last £300 of maintenance expenses were actually paid shortly after the year-end.

What is the corresponding variance for equipment maintenance expenditure?

A   £300 Adverse
B   £300 Favourable
C   £600 Adverse
D   £600 Favourable

7 Budgeting

Section B Questions

Question 7.11

State three benefits of operating a budget within a business:

a) _____

b) _____

c) _____

Question 7.12

The budget for a large company can either be imposed on the managers within the company or devised with their participation.

What are the pros & cons of each approach?

Imposed Approach

_____
_____
_____
_____
_____

Participative Approach

_____
_____
_____
_____
_____

The Language of Business

Question 7.13 (Incremental Budgeting)

On the following template complete the 2018 budget for 'IncBudge Ltd' based on the following budget brief:

- B2B sales revenue to increase by 3%
- B2B GP % (*not* GP(£) !) to show a <u>1 percentage point</u> increase on the 2017 GP%
- B2C sales revenue to increase by 8%
- B2C GP% to achieve 80%
- Staff costs in the Operations Department to increase by 3%
- Staff costs in the Finance Department to increase by 8%
- Increase advertising spend by 10%
- Show savings of 7% on maintenance costs
- Show savings of 5% on all Travel & Accommodation costs
- The rent on the premises will increase by £100,000 in 2018. All other premises costs will remain static.
- 2018 depreciation has been estimated at £550,000

(GP% = figure ÷ 100 × %)

	2017 Actual	2018 Budget	Workings
B2B Sales Revenue	£5,000,000	5,150,000	
B2B Gross Profit	£3,000,000	3,141,500	
B2B GP%	60%	61%	
B2C Sales Revenue	£1,000,000	1,080,000	
B2C Gross Profit	£750,000	864,000	
B2C GP%	75%	80%	
TOTAL GROSS PROFIT	£3,750,000	4,005,500	
Staff Costs - Operations Dept.	£450,000	463,000	
Staff Costs - Finance Dept.	£100,000	108,000	
~~Research & Development Expenditure~~	~~£100,000~~		
Advertising Expenditure	£250,000	275,000	
Maintenance Costs	£120,000	111,600	
Travel & Accommodation Costs	£300,000	285,000	
Premises Costs	£1,200,000	1,300,000	
Depreciation Costs	£500,000	550,000	
TOTAL EXPENDITURE	£2,920,000	3,092,600	
NET PROFIT	£830,000	912	

7 Budgeting

Question 7.14

You are planning to launch a new retail business on the 1st January selling pet supplies. You have found a suitable high street premises available for rent and have applied for a business bank loan to finance the new operation. Your bank have said that they would like to say 'Yes' but first require a full business plan from you including a budgeted statement of profit or loss (properly prepared on the 'accruals' basis) for your first six months of trading. You have been advised to ignore any subsequent bank interest charges at this stage of budgeting.

Using the budget information below complete the separate template to estimate the monthly profit or loss you expect to make in your first six months of trading.

- January sales of £1,000 thereafter increasing by £1,000 each month.

- A steady gross profit of 70%

- Staff wage costs of £500 per month for January to March, then increasing to £1,000 from April onwards as the shop gets busier.

- Heat & light costs of £200 per month for January to April, but falling to £100 per month in May & June with the warmer weather.

- Telephone expenditure of £50 per month

- A business insurance premium of £900 per annum

- Advertising in the local newspaper in January and April at a cost of £500 each time

- Website hosting and maintenance via a local IT company at £50 per month

- The rent is £3,000 per calendar quarter.

- The local council has informed you that the annual business rates will be £2,400 payable in 10 instalments from January to October inclusive.

- You will have to spend £14,000 on fixtures and fittings, a computer and an EPOS till. These are expected to last for five years and have a residual value of £2,000 at the end of the five years.

The Language of Business

	January	February	March	April	May	June
Sales	1000	2000	3000	4000	5000	6000
Cost of Sales	300	600	900	1200	1500	1800
Gross Profit	700	1400	2100	2800	3500	4200
Staff Wages	500	500	500	1000	1000	1000
Heat & Light	200	200	200	200	100	100
Telephone	50	50	50	50	50	50
Insurance	150	150	150	150	150	150
Advertising	500	—	—	500	—	—
Website Hosting	50	50	50	50	50	50
Shop Rent	1000	1000	1000	1000	1000	1000
Business Rates	200	200	200	200	200	200
Depreciation	200	200	200	200	200	200
Total Expenditure	2850	2350	2350	2850	2350	2350
Net Profit	−2150	−950	−250	−50	1150	1850

7 Budgeting

Question 7.15

Budgets can either be devised by reference to last year's performance *('incremental budgeting')* or without reference to past performance *('zero-based budgeting')*.

What are the pros & cons of each approach?

Incremental Budgeting

___

Zero-Based Budgeting

___

Question 7.16

Despite the many benefits of operating a budget, they can also have some disadvantages and potential pitfalls. Briefly state some of these.

___

Chapter 8

Standard Costing and Variance Analysis

INTRODUCTION

Up to this point we have simply assumed a certain cost for each of the products a business sells. In reality this is seldom the case and this is especially true for manufacturing companies who might use more or less labour and/or materials than expected (and indeed pay a different rate for them).

Such businesses need a way of estimating what the **'standard cost'** (or budgeted cost) of each product should be so that they can set selling prices and properly value unsold inventory.

Furthermore, the manufacturer can then compare their actual costs to their expected 'standard costs' in order to produce variances, which tell them where they are performing well, and where they need to improve.

OVERVIEW AND OBJECTIVES

By the end of this chapter you should have developed an understanding of:

- Standard Costing and Cost-Plus Pricing
- The need for variance analysis and how variances are calculated and reconciled
- Flexed Budgets

and be able to answer questions relating to these areas.

This chapter does not contain any 'Test Your Understanding' questions. Instead you should work through the comprehensive example used throughout the chapter to demonstrate variance analysis.

8 Standard Costing and Variance Analysis

8.1 Standard Costs and Cost-Plus Pricing

A business manufacturing a fictional product called the 'Gizmo', believes that each Gizmo produced requires the following direct materials and direct labour:

- 10 kg of material which costs £5 per kg..... *plus*
- 4 hours of labour which is paid at a rate of £9 per hour.... *plus*
- £14 of variable overhead for every unit produced

These assumed costs are known as **'standard costs'** and are often used by businesses to calculate the overall expected cost of a product, which then allows an appropriate selling price to be calculated, as follows :

COST CARD	PRODUCT = 'Gizmo'		
	Quantity	Cost per Unit	Total
Direct Materials	10 kg	£5 per kg	£50
Direct Labour	4 hours	£9 per hour	£36
Variable Overhead		£14 per unit	£14
Standard Cost			£100

Manufacturing businesses typically produce *'cost cards'* for each product they manufacture similar to the one above (originally on actual cards, but nowadays far more likely to be computerised). Having established the cost of a product, the business can then add their required level of profit and hence calculate the required selling price.

This process is called **'Cost-Plus Pricing'** and simply means that selling prices are set by *first* calculating the cost and *then* adding the required profit (which may be quoted either as a required % margin or a required % mark-up - see Chapter 4).

Selling Price = Cost Price + Required Profit

TUTORIAL NOTE

Imagine that the business above wished to make a 60% mark-up on every Gizmo they sold. Their selling price would be calculated from the standard cost (as detailed on the cost card) as follows:

Selling Price	=	Cost Price + Required Profit
Selling Price	=	£100 + (60% x £100)
Selling Price	=	£100 + £60
Selling Price	=	**£160**

Remember mark-up is based on 'cost' ....so a 60% mark-up means that the profit element is equal to 60% of the cost.

> **EXAMPLE**
>
> A more complete cost card *(now including the standard selling price based on a 60% mark-up)* is shown below.
>
> | COST CARD | | PRODUCT = 'Gizmo' | |
> |---|---|---|---|
> | | Quantity | Cost per Unit | Total |
> | **Direct Materials** | 10 kg | £5 per kg | £50 |
> | **Direct Labour** | 4 hours | £9 per hour | £36 |
> | **Variable Overheads** | | £14 per unit | £14 |
> | **Standard Cost** | | | **£100** |
> | **Net Profit** | | 60% Mark-up | £60 |
> | **Standard Selling Price** | | | **£160** |

8.2 The need for variance analysis

In practice however, the actual costs which are incurred for materials and labour are rarely exactly the same as the standard costs originally anticipated. Furthermore the business may well sell the final product for a different selling price to the original 'standard selling price' and may achieve a greater or lesser volume of sales compared to that originally anticipated.

These differences can arise for a multitude of reasons, including:

- A greater or lesser quantity of materials being used compared to that originally anticipated *e.g. due to excessive wastage of raw materials*

- The purchase price of the material being higher or lower than expected *e.g. by gaining a bulk purchase discount from a supplier*

- A greater or lesser number of hours labour being used compared to that originally anticipated *e.g. less efficient, inexperienced workers taking longer than expected*

- The hourly rate paid for the labour being higher or lower than expected *e.g. using cheaper apprentice labour*

- The overheads (i.e. indirect costs) incurred being greater or less than expected *e.g. as a result of inaccurate budgeting*

- The final selling price for the item being different from the original standard selling price *e.g. offering discounts on the standard selling price to customers*

- The final sales volume being higher or lower than that originally budgeted *e.g. higher or lower than expected sales demand*

For all of these reasons, the final amount of profit a business actually makes from selling a certain product in a given period will probably be different to that originally budgeted. The important thing for the business is to fully understand *why* the final profitability has varied, so that it can better control its performance in the future by:

- **Identifying what things have gone well….** *so that it can try to repeat these*
- **Identifying what things have not gone so well….** *so that it can try to remedy these*

For this reason the use of standard costing and variance analysis is sometimes referred to as *'Accounting for Control'*.

8.3 Variance analysis in practice

We will now continue to use the 'Gizmo' example and see how *'standard costing'* can be used to set an initial profit budget for the manufacture and sale of this particular product within a particular period of time.

We shall then use *'variance analysis'* to carry out a financial appraisal of the actual profit performance and to establish what went well and what didn't. This process will involve producing three separate profit statements for the 'Gizmo', namely:

1. **Original Budget**… which will use a series of 'budget assumptions' (based on our 'standard costs') to forecast how much profit will result from the manufacture and sale of however many Gizmos we *budget* to make and sell in the period in question.

2. **Flexed Budget**… which will simply update the original budget to correspond to the *actual* sales volume of Gizmos achieved

3. **Actual Results**… which records the actual results achieved, and which we need to analyse to see exactly where our performance is better or worse than expected.

We will ultimately produce a series of 'variances' which will show how each separate aspect of the business's performance regarding this product has led to either an increase or decrease in the final net profit made.

Each variance will be described as either:

- **A Favourable Variance** – if it results in *more* profit being made

    (and will be shown as a *positive* number and/or labelled with an *'F'*)

- **An Adverse Variance** – if it results in *less* profit being made

    (and will be shown as a *negative* number and/or labelled with an *'A'*)

The Language of Business

> ## EXAMPLE
>
> A business manufactures and sells a product called the 'Gizmo' and uses the following budget assumptions to derive a profit budget for the following month.
>
> Each Gizmo:
>
> - requires 10Kg of raw material which costs £5 per Kg
> - requires 4 hours of labour which will cost £9 per hour
> - will incur a variable overhead expense of £14 per unit
>
> These are simply the [earlier] 'standard costs' for this product based on the business's expectations of how much the materials, labour and overhead will cost.
>
> The business would like to sell each item at a selling price of £160 each (in order to achieve a 60% profit mark-up) and hopes to manufacture and sell 200 units in the following month.
>
> At the end of the month in question the following *actual* results for this product were:
>
> - 2,700 Kg of material was used at a total cost of £12,690
> - 1,100 hours of labour were used at a total cost of £10,450
> - £3,450 of variable overhead expenses relating to this product were recorded
> - 250 Gizmos were actually manufactured & sold for a total sales revenue of £38,750
>
> We now need a way of understanding whether the actual results are good, bad or indifferent, compared to the business's original expectations! This is of course complicated by the fact that the business originally expected to make and sell only 200 units, but in the end made and sold 250 units. So we will need a way to adjust the figures to allow for a completely different level of activity.
>
> We now need to produce three profit statements to show:
>
> 1. The **original budget** (based on the original expectation of making and selling 200 units)
> 2. The **flexed budget** (which simply updates the original budget to the *actual* activity level of 250 units)
> 3. The **actual results** (for 250 units)

8.4 The original budget

Using the original budget estimates listed above we can produce a profit budget which shows the net profit which would be made if all of the original budget assumptions were subsequently proved to be 100% accurate in reality.

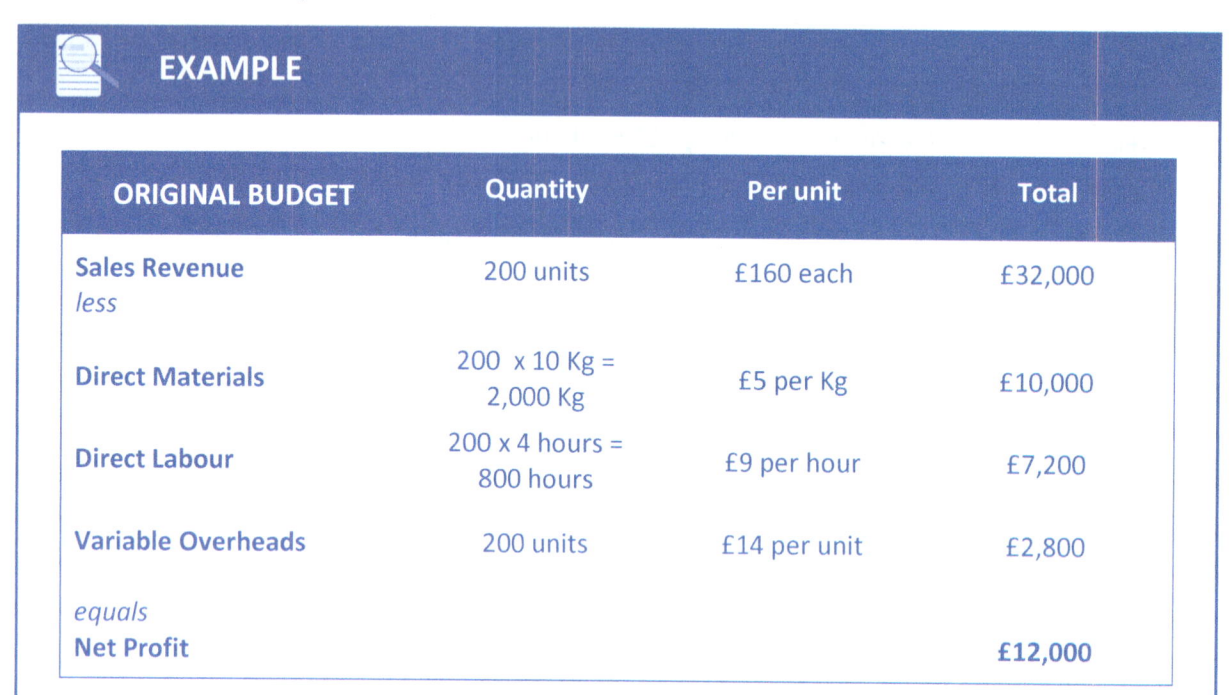

> **EXAMPLE**
>
> | ORIGINAL BUDGET | Quantity | Per unit | Total |
> |---|---|---|---|
> | **Sales Revenue** *less* | 200 units | £160 each | £32,000 |
> | **Direct Materials** | 200 x 10 Kg = 2,000 Kg | £5 per Kg | £10,000 |
> | **Direct Labour** | 200 x 4 hours = 800 hours | £9 per hour | £7,200 |
> | **Variable Overheads** | 200 units | £14 per unit | £2,800 |
> | *equals* **Net Profit** | | | £12,000 |

> **TUTORIAL NOTE**
>
> The above original budgeted net profit of £12,000 completely agrees with the original cost card which predicted a net profit of £60 per Gizmo (if the 'standard costs' and 'standard selling price' were accurate).
>
> The original budget (above) merely scales this up to a sales volume of **200 units** and therefore predicts 200 x £60 = **£12,000 net profit.**

8.5 The flexed budget

We will shortly want to compare the actual results achieved, to those predicted in the original budget (which were largely based on the standard costs etc. for the Gizmo). However it can be immediately seen that comparing the *actual* results (for *250* Gizmos) with the *original* budget (for *200* Gizmos) will be a largely meaningless exercise!

For instance there is little point in comparing:

- The budgeted material costs to make 200 Gizmos with the actual material costs to make 250 Gizmos, or …..

- The budgeted labour costs to make 200 Gizmos with the actual labour costs to make 250 Gizmos, or …..

- The budgeted overhead cost to make 200 Gizmos with the actual overhead costs to make 250 Gizmos.

The Language of Business

In each case we would fully expect the actual costs to be greater than the originally budgeted costs simply because we have manufactured 50 more Gizmos than originally planned!

The only way of making a sensible comparison is to update the original budget so that it accurately reflects the level of 'activity' which *actually* occurred. In this example the business actually made and sold 250 Gizmos, so we need to revise the original budget from being a budget for the manufacture and sale of 200 Gizmos…..to a new budget for the manufacture and sale of 250 Gizmos.

We call this process 'flexing the budget' and the end result is the 'flexed budget' in the example below.

EXAMPLE

FLEXED BUDGET	Quantity	Per unit	Total
Sales Revenue	250 units	£160 each	£40,000
less			
Direct Materials	250 x 10 Kg = 2,500 Kg	£5 per Kg	£12,500
Direct Labour	250 x 4 hours = 1,000 hours	£9 per hour	£9,000
Variable Overheads	250 units	£14 per unit	£3,500
equals			
Net Profit			£15,000

KEY POINT

It is very important to appreciate that the **only** 'variable' to change in the flexed budget is the change in sales volume (i.e. the level of activity) from 200 Gizmos to 250 Gizmos. All other original budget assumptions remain exactly the same, including:-

- Each Gizmo *still* requiring 10 Kg of materials
- The material *still* costing £5 per Kg
- Each Gizmo *still* requiring 4 hours of labour
- The labour *still* costing £9 per hour
- Each Gizmo *still* incurring £14 of variable overheads
- Each Gizmo *still* being sold for £160 each

The only thing to have changed is the level of activity i.e. an **actual** sales volume of **250** Gizmos compared to the **original budgeted** sales volume of **200** units.

ALL OTHER BUDGET ASSUMPTIONS REMAIN EXACTLY THE SAME!

> **TUTORIAL NOTE**
>
> The above flexed budget shows a net profit of £15,000 and again this completely agrees with the original cost card which predicted a net profit of £60 per Gizmo (if the 'standard costs' and 'standard selling price' prove accurate).
>
> The flexed budget (above) merely scales this up to the *actual* sales volume of **250** units and therefore predicts 250 x £60 = £15,000 net profit for the actual level.

8.6 Sales Profit Volume Variance

We earlier said that trying to compare aspects of the original budget (for 200 Gizmos) with the actual results (for 250 Gizmos) is a largely meaningless exercise.

However, there is in fact one single relevant comparison that we can and should make between the original budget (for 200 Gizmos) and the flexed budget (for 250 Gizmos) and that is to compare the two net profit figures. This comparison produces our first calculated variance known as the 'Sales Profit Volume Variance' and this is the ONLY variance which refers to the **original** profit budget.

All other variances compare the flexed budgeted figures (for 250 Gizmos) with the actual results (for 250 Gizmos) so that we are comparing the figures on a *'like for like'* basis.

Sales Profit Volume Variance = Flexed Budget Net Profit – Original Budget Net Profit

> **EXAMPLE**
>
> Returning to our example:
>
> **Flexed Budget Net Profit = £15,000**
>
> **Original Budget Net Profit = £12,000** so:
>
> Sales Profit Volume Variance = £15,000 - £12,000 = + **£3,000 F**
>
> This variance shows the difference in budgeted net profit **purely** as a result of the change in sales volume (hence the name). Nothing else has changed between these two budgets apart from the sales volume. In this example the flexed budget (for 250 Gizmos) forecasts £3,000 more net profit (hence *'Favourable'*) as a result of making and selling 50 additional Gizmos.

> **TUTORIAL NOTE**
>
> We can again reconcile this variance back to the original cost card which predicted a net profit of £60 per Gizmo. It therefore follows that an additional 50 Gizmos would make 50 x £60 = **£3,000** additional profit!

8.7 Actual results

Having briefly paused to look at the Sales Profit Volume Variance, we can now turn our attention to the third profit statement which reports the *actual* results. This time we have actually been given most of the figures and merely have to present them in an appropriate format for a profit statement.

EXAMPLE

ACTUAL RESULTS	Quantity	Total	Average per unit* (calculated below)
Sales Revenue	250 units	£38,750	Selling Price = £155 per unit
less			
Direct Materials	2,700 Kg	£12,690	Material Cost = £4.70 per Kg
Direct Labour	1,100 hours	£10,450	Labour Rate = £9.50 per hour
Variable Overheads	250 units	£3,450	Variable Overhead = £13.80 per unit
equals Net Profit		**£12,160**	Net Profit = £48.64 per unit

TUTORIAL NOTE

* Although not strictly necessary for variance analysis, it will later prove useful to have worked out an appropriate average for each given figure as follows:

Average Selling Price = £38,750 / 250 units = **£155 per unit**

Average Materials Cost = £12,690 / 2,700 Kg = **£4.70 per Kg**

Average Labour Rate = £10,450 / 1,100 hours = **£9.50 per hour**

Average Variable Overhead = £3,450 / 250 units = **£13.80 per unit**

Average Net Profit = £12,160 / 250 units = **£48.64 per unit**

We'll shortly use these averages to help us to *understand* the variances.

8.8 Main variances

Having 'flexed' the original budget to produce a budget which relates to the actual level of activity (i.e. manufacturing and selling 250 Gizmos) we can now compare the actual results against it and immediately ascertain the five main variances by simply comparing each flexed budget figure against the corresponding actual results figure.

To demonstrate this we will simply transfer the previously calculated figures from the flexed budget and the actual results into a new table and look at the difference between each corresponding pair of figures in turn.

8 Standard Costing and Variance Analysis

	FLEXED BUDGET (for 250 units)	ACTUAL RESULTS (for 250 units)	VARIANCE	VARIANCE NAME
Sales Revenue	£40,000	£38,750	- £1,250 A	Sales Price Variance
less				
Direct Materials	£12,500	£12,690	- £190 A	Direct Materials Total Variance
Direct Labour	£9,000	£10,450	- £1,450 A	Direct Labour Total Variance
Variable Overheads	£3,500	£3,450	+ £50 F	Overhead Variance
equals				
Net Profit	**£15,000**	**£12,160**	- £2,840 A	Net Profit Variance

TUTORIAL NOTE

Because we have flexed the budget we are now making meaningful comparisons of a **budget for 250 items** against the corresponding **actual results for 250 items** i.e. we are making a 'like for like' comparison.

This is a key point to understand! Every single variance *(apart from the Sales Profit Volume Variance discussed earlier)* is comparing the flexed budget* to the actual results. Because the flexed budget has been revised for the actual level of activity (250 Gizmos in this example) we are always making valid comparisons between figures which **both** relate to the **same** level of activity.

or figures derived from the flexed budget ….see sub-variances later

Getting the Variances the 'right way' around …..

As covered in Chapter 7 'Budgeting', we need to be careful with which figure is subtracted from which when working out whether a variance is a positive number (i.e. Favourable) or negative number (i.e. Adverse).

It is best to just use a logical approach, namely:

Sales Revenue and Net Profit

If the Actual results are larger than the Flexed Budget figures this represents greater profitability *(i.e. higher actual sales and/or profit than budgeted)*.

So calculate sales and profit variances as:

Actual – Flexed Budget … *to automatically produce a positive figure if favourable*

All Expense Items

If the Flexed Budget figures are larger than the Actual results this represents greater profitability *(i.e. lower actual levels of expense than budgeted)*.

So calculate expense variances as:

Flexed Budget – Actual … *to automatically produce a positive figure if favourable*

It is always worth sense checking the calculated sign (+ or -) of each variance to double check that:

- A **positive variance** does in fact represent something **Favourable**

    i.e. higher actual sales/profit or lower expenses, than the budget

- A **negative variance** does in fact represent something **Adverse**

    i.e. lower actual sales/profit or higher expenses, than the budget

Having sorted out which way around variances should go we can now look at each variance in turn.

8.9 Sales Price Variance

The formula for the Sales Price Variance is:

Sales Price Variance = Actual Sales Revenue - Flexed Budget Sales Revenue

Which is exactly what we did in the right-hand column of the last table *(see extract of original table below)* when the flexed budget sales revenue was simply deducted from the actual sales revenue.

	FLEXED BUDGET (for 250 units)	ACTUAL RESULTS (for 250 units)	VARIANCE	VARIANCE NAME
Sales Revenue	£40,000	£38,750	- £1,250 A	Sales Price Variance

KEY POINT

The Sales Price Variance tells us by how much the total net profit has changed **purely** as a result of **just** the change in the actual selling price (compared to the budgeted selling price).

EXAMPLE

Using the previous example:

Sales Price Variance	=	Actual Sales Revenue	-	Flexed Budget Sales Revenue
	=	£38,750	-	£40,000
	=	- £1,250 A		

i.e. the actual net profit is £1,250 less than it was budgeted to be **purely** because of a reduction in selling price.

What factors may potentially cause an adverse variance?

An adverse sales price variance means that the average actual selling price is less than the budgeted selling price. This arises whenever a business is forced to discount its selling prices. Lower selling prices will obviously result in lower profit.

8 Standard Costing and Variance Analysis

What factors may potentially cause a favourable variance?

A favourable sales price variance means that the average actual selling price is higher than the budgeted selling price. This would arise if a business increases its selling prices or charges an additional premium on its normal selling for some reason. Higher selling prices will clearly result in higher profit.

> **TUTORIAL NOTE**
>
> Understanding the Gizmo example result:
> - The standard selling price of the Gizmo was £160 per item
> - The actual average selling price was £155 per item (£38,750 / 250 units = £155)
> - 250 Gizmos were sold at £5 less each than budgeted   (£160 - £155)
> - Total lost profit = 250 x £5 = £1,250

8.10 Direct Materials Total Variance

The formula for the Direct Materials Total Variance is:

Direct Materials Total Variance = (SQ x SP) - (AQ x AP)

Where:

- **SQ** = **S**tandard **Q**uantity of material required *(to make the actual sales volume)*
- **SP** = **S**tandard **P**rice for material per unit (e.g. per Kg etc.)
- **AQ** = **A**ctual **Q**uantity of material used *(to make the actual sales volume)*
- **AP** = **A**ctual [average] **P**rice paid for material per unit (e.g. per Kg etc.)

Which is exactly what we did in the right-hand column of the last table *(see extract of original table below)* when the actual total direct material cost was simply deducted from the flexed budget total direct material cost.

Looking at the equation above it can be readily seen that:

- The first set of brackets **(SQ x SP)** is the cost of the materials **according to the flexed budget** which is £12,500 i.e. the standard quantity required *(for the actual sales volume!)* at the standard unit cost.
- The second set of brackets **(AQ x AP)** is simply the **actual cost** of the materials used *(for the actual sales volume)* which is £12,690. In fact this figure is often readily available as it is simply the actual cost of the materials and so it is often not even necessary to even work out the bracket (AQ x AP).

	FLEXED BUDGET (for 250 units)	ACTUAL RESULTS (for 250 units)	VARIANCE	VARIANCE NAME
Direct Materials	£12,500	£12,690	- £190 A	Direct Materials Total Variance

The Language of Business

> ⚠️ **KEY POINT**
>
> The Direct Materials Total Variance tells us by how much the total net profit has changed **purely** as a result of spending more or less on Direct Materials than the figure predicted in the flexed budget.

> 🔍 **EXAMPLE**
>
> Using the previous example:
>
> | **Direct Materials Total Variance** | = | (SQ x SP) | − (AQ x AP) |
> |---|---|---|---|
> | | = | (250 x 10kg x £5 per Kg) | − (£12,690) |
> | | = | (£12,500) | − (£12,690) |
> | | = | **− £190 A** | |
>
> i.e. the actual net profit is £190 less than it was budgeted to be **purely** because of a £190 overspend on direct materials.

What factors may potentially cause an adverse variance?

An adverse Direct Materials Total Variance could be caused by using a greater *quantity* of materials than budgeted (for the actual sales volume) and/or paying a higher unit *price* for the materials than budgeted.

What factors may potentially cause a favourable variance?

A Favourable Direct Materials Total Variance could be caused by using a smaller *quantity* of materials than budgeted (for the actual sales volume) and/or paying a lower unit *price* for the materials than budgeted.

> 🎓 **TUTORIAL NOTE**
>
> Understanding the Gizmo example result:
>
> According to the flexed budget, 2,500 Kg of direct materials (250 units x 10 Kg per unit) **should have been used** at a cost of £5 per Kg i.e. a total expenditure on direct materials of 2,500 Kg x £5 per Kg = £12,500.
>
> - However in reality £12,690 was **actually** spent on direct materials.
>
> - This represents an overspend of £190 compared to the [flexed] budget i.e. £190 less final profit because of overspending on direct materials.
>
> - At this stage we do *not* know how much of the overspend is as a result of using a greater **quantity** of material than budgeted, and how much of the overspend is as a result of paying a higher unit **price** for the material than budgeted. The variance just calculated simply gives the total effect of **both** of these factors.
>
> To understand how much of the total variance is due to each separate factor we will need to calculate a 'sub-variance' for each in turn (see later).

8.11 Direct Labour Total Variance

The formula for the Direct Labour Total Variance is:

Direct Labour Total Variance = (SH x SR) - (AH x AR)

Where:

- **SH** = **S**tandard number of **H**ours of labour required *(for the actual sales volume)*
- **SR** = **S**tandard **R**ate for labour (per hour)
- **AH** = **A**ctual number of **H**ours used *(for the actual sales volume)*
- **AR** = **A**ctual [average] **R**ate paid for labour (per hour)

Which again is simply what we did in the right-hand column of the last table *(see extract of original table below)* when the actual total direct labour cost was simply deducted from the flexed budget total direct labour cost. Looking at the equation above it can be readily seen that:

- The first set of brackets (SH x SR) is the direct labour cost **according to the flexed budget** i.e. the standard hours required *(for the actual sales volume)* at the standard hourly rate (=£9,000).

- The second set of brackets (AH x AR) is simply the **actual cost** of the direct labour used *(for the actual sales volume)* which was £10,450. In fact this figure is often given and so it is often not even necessary to even work out the bracket (AH x AR).

	FLEXED BUDGET (for 250 units)	ACTUAL RESULTS (for 250 units)	VARIANCE	VARIANCE NAME
Direct Labour	£9,000	£10,450	- £1,450 A	Direct Labour Total Variance

⚠ KEY POINT

The Direct Labour Total Variance tells us by how much the total net profit has changed **purely** as a result of spending more or less on direct labour than the figure predicted in the flexed budget.

EXAMPLE

Using the previous example:

Direct Labour Total Variance	=	(SH x SR)	–	(AH x AR)
	=	(250 x 4 hrs x £9 per hr)	–	(£10,450)
	=	(£9,000)	–	(£10,450)
	=	- £1,450 A		

i.e. the actual net profit is £1,450 less than it was budgeted to be **purely** because of a £1,450 overspend on Direct Labour.

What factors may potentially cause an adverse variance?

An adverse Direct Labour Total Variance could be caused by using more **hours** of labour than budgeted (for the actual sales volume) and/or paying a higher **hourly rate** for the labour than budgeted.

What factors may potentially cause a favourable variance?

A Favourable Direct Labour Total Variance could be caused by using less **hours** of labour than budgeted (for the actual sales volume) and/or paying a lower **hourly rate** for the labour than budgeted.

> **TUTORIAL NOTE**
>
> Understanding the Gizmo example result:
>
> - According to the flexed budget, 1,000 hours of direct labour (250 units x 4 hours per unit) **should have been used** at a cost of £9 per hour i.e. a total expenditure on direct labour of 1,000 x £9 per hour = £9,000.
>
> - However in reality £10,450 was **actually** spent on direct labour.
>
> - This represents an overspend of £1,450 compared to the [flexed] budget i.e. £1,450 less final profit because of overspending on direct labour.
>
> - At this stage we do *not* know how much of the overspend is as a result of using more **labour hours** than budgeted, and how much of the overspend is as a result of paying a higher **hourly rate** than budgeted. The variance just calculated simply gives the total effect of **both** of these factors.
>
> To understand how much of the total variance is due to each separate factor we will need to calculate a 'sub-variance' for each in turn (see later).

8.12 Overhead Variance

The formula for the Overhead Variance is:

Overhead Variance = Flexed Budgeted Overheads - Actual Overheads

Which again is simply what we did in the right-hand column of the last table *(see extract of original table below)* when the actual variable overhead was simply deducted from the variable overhead in the flexed budget.

	FLEXED BUDGET (for 250 units)	ACTUAL RESULTS (for 250 units)	VARIANCE	VARIANCE NAME
Variable Overheads	£3,500	£3,450	+ £50 F	Overhead Variance

> **KEY POINT**
>
> The Overhead Variance tells us by how much the total net profit has changed **purely** as a result of spending more or less on overheads than the figure predicted in the flexed budget.

8 Standard Costing and Variance Analysis

> ### EXAMPLE
>
> Using the previous example:
>
> | **Overhead Variance** | = | Flexed Budgeted Overheads | − | Actual Overheads |
> |---|---|---|---|---|
> | | = | £3,500 | − | £3,450 |
> | | = | **+ £50 F** | | |
>
> i.e. the actual net profit is £50 more than it was budgeted to be **purely** because of a £50 underspend on overheads.

What factors may potentially cause an adverse variance?

An adverse Overhead Variance could be caused by incurring **more** overhead expenditure than budgeted (for the flexed level of activity) and/or because the original budget assumptions had under-budgeted the likely level of overhead expenditure.

What factors may potentially cause a favourable variance?

A favourable Overhead Variance could be caused by incurring **less** overhead expenditure than budgeted (for the flexed level of activity) and/or because the original budget assumptions had over-budgeted the likely level of overhead expenditure.

> ### TUTORIAL NOTE
>
> Understanding the Gizmo example result:
>
> - According to the flexed budget, £3,500 of variable overhead (250 units x £14 per unit) **should have been** incurred.
> - However in reality £3,450 was **actually** incurred on variable overheads.
> - This represents an underspend of £50 compared to the flexed budget i.e. £50 more final profit because of underspending on variable overheads.

Fixed Overheads and Variable Overheads

In the Gizmo example we are considering overheads which happen to be variable overheads and therefore need to be 'flexed' when producing the flexed budget to allow for the different level of activity (250 units actual as opposed to 200 units originally budgeted).

In *other* examples the overheads might be fixed overheads which obviously do *not* need to be flexed; or there may even be both variable overheads and fixed overheads. If this is the case, handle them as two separate items of expense (flexing just the variable overheads) and produce two separate variances, namely:

Variable Overhead Variance	=	Flexed Budget Variable Overheads	−	Actual Variable Overheads

Fixed Overhead Variance	=	Flexed Budget* Fixed Overheads	−	Actual Fixed Overheads

* Obviously the Flexed Budget Fixed Overheads will be exactly the same as the Original Budget Fixed Overheads. You don't need to flex a fixed cost for different levels of activity…..because a fixed cost does not change with different levels of activity.

8.13 Net Profit Variance

The formula for the Net Profit Variance is:

Net Profit Variance = Actual Net Profit – Flexed Budget Net Profit

Again, this is simply what we did in the right-hand column of the last table *(see extract of original table below)* when the flexed budget net profit was simply deducted from the actual net profit.

	FLEXED BUDGET (for 250 units)	ACTUAL RESULTS (for 250 units)	VARIANCE	VARIANCE NAME
Net Profit	£15,000	£12,160	- £2,840 A	Net Profit Variance

> **KEY POINT**
>
> The Net Profit Variance tells us by how much the total net profit has changed (from the figure predicted in the flexed budget) as a result of **all** of the following factors:
>
> - Changes to the budgeted **Sales Price**
> - More or less expenditure on **Direct Materials** than budgeted
> - More or less expenditure on **Direct Labour** than budgeted
> - More or less **Overhead** expenditure than budgeted

> **EXAMPLE**
>
> Using the previous example:
>
> **Net Profit Variance** = Actual Net Profit – Flexed Budget Profit
> = £12,160 – £15,000
> = - £2,840 A

The fastest way to calculate the Net Profit Variance is to simply look at the difference between the flexed budget net profit and the actual net profit (as above), remembering that it is **F**avourable for the actual net profit to be *higher* than budgeted (and conversely **A**dverse if the actual net profit is *less* than budgeted).

8 Standard Costing and Variance Analysis

> **TUTORIAL NOTE**
>
> We can *also* find the Net Profit Variance by adding the four previously calculated variances together (remembering that Favourable variances are positive whilst Adverse variances are negative).
>
> - Sales Price Variance   - £1,250 A
> - Direct Materials Total Variance   - £190 A
> - Direct Labour Total Variance   - £1,450 A
> - Overhead Variance   + £50 F
>   TOTALLING …..   - £2,840 A
>
> i.e. The actual net profit is £2,840 less than it was budgeted to be because of the **cumulative** effect of:
>
> - Selling each Gizmo for less than budgeted
> - Overspending on direct materials
> - Overspending on Direct Labour
> - Less……the saving made on variable overheads

8.14 Sub-variances

Direct Materials

In the example above we identified a direct materials overspend of £190 compared to the expected expenditure on direct materials in the flexed budget and this is part of the reason for the shortfall on net profit. However, at this stage we are unsure exactly how this direct materials overspend has arisen. There are two possible reasons why the actual spend on direct materials exceeded the budget, namely:

1. As a result of using a greater **quantity** of material than budgeted
2. As a result of paying a higher **unit price** for the material than budgeted.

By calculating two direct material sub-variances we can separately quantify each of these two potential effects, and establish:

- How much of the £190 overspend resulted from the quantity of materials used
- How much of the £190 overspend resulted from the price paid for the materials.

Direct Labour

Similarly, in the example above we identified a direct labour overspend of £1,450 compared to the expected direct labour expenditure in the flexed budget and this is also part of the reason for the overall shortfall on net profit. Again, at this stage we are unsure exactly how this direct labour overspend has arisen. It could be:

1. As a result of using a greater **number of hours** of labour than budgeted
2. As a result of paying a higher **hourly rate** for the labour than budgeted.

By calculating two direct labour sub-variances we can separately quantify each of these two potential effects, and establish:

- How much of the £1,450 overspend resulted from the number of hours used
- How much of the £1,450 overspend resulted from the hourly rate paid.

> **TUTORIAL NOTE**
>
> Be clear in your own mind that one factor that *definitely did not* contribute to either the direct materials overspend or the direct labour overspend was the increase in production from 200 Gizmos in the original budget to the final 250 Gizmos. This increase in sales volume has *already* been accounted for when the budget was flexed and is therefore no longer relevant!

The four sub-variances we will calculate are:

- **Direct Materials Price Variance**

    → Effect on profit *solely* as a result of the unit price paid for materials

- **Direct Materials Quantity Variance** *(aka 'Direct Materials Usage Variance')*

    → Effect on profit *solely* as a result of the quantity of materials used

- **Direct Labour Rate Variance**

    → Effect on profit *solely* as a result of the hourly rate paid for labour

- **Direct Labour Efficiency Variance**

    → Effect on profit *solely* as a result of the number of hours labour used.

> **TUTORIAL NOTE**
>
> You will very quickly see parallels between the materials sub-variances and the labour sub-variances. They take the same mathematical form, albeit with slightly different terminology.
>
> For example:
>
> - Materials 'price', as opposed to labour 'rate'
> - Materials 'quantity' (or 'usage'), as opposed to labour 'efficiency'
> - AH or SH …..instead of AQ or SQ (i.e. 'Hours' replaces 'Quantity')
> - AR or SR …. instead of AP or SP (i.e. 'Rate' replaces 'Price')

8.15 Direct Materials Price Variance

The formula for the Direct Materials Price Variance is:

Direct Materials Price Variance = (AQ x SP) – (AQ x AP)

Where:

- **AQ** = **A**ctual **Q**uantity of material used *(to make the actual sales volume)*
- **SP** = **S**tandard **P**rice for material per unit (e.g. per Kg etc.)
- **AP** = **A**ctual [average] **P**rice paid for material per unit (e.g. per Kg etc.)

8 Standard Costing and Variance Analysis

The first set of brackets **(AQ x SP)** represents how much the actual quantity of materials used would have cost, if they had been purchased at the standard price.

The second set of brackets **(AQ x AP)** is simply the cost of the actual quantity of materials used, at the actual unit price paid. Again this figure is often readily available as it is simply the actual cost of the materials, and so it is often not even necessary to even work out the bracket (AQ x AP).

> ⚠️ **KEY POINT**
>
> The Direct Materials Price Variance tells us by how much the total net profit has changed **solely** as a result of paying a higher or lower unit price for materials compared to the standard unit price used in the budget.

> 🔍 **EXAMPLE**
>
> Using the previous example:
>
> | **Direct Materials Price Variance** | = | (AQ x SP) | – | (AQ x AP) |
> |---|---|---|---|---|
> | | = | (2,700kg x £5 per Kg) | – | (£12,690) |
> | | = | (£13,500) | – | (£12,690) |
> | | = | + £810 F | | |
>
> i.e. the actual net profit is £810 more than it was budgeted to be solely because of a £810 saving on the purchase price of the direct materials.

What factors may potentially cause an adverse variance?

An adverse Direct Materials Price Variance is caused by paying a higher unit **price** for the direct materials than budgeted.

e.g. Price increase from supplier, forced to use alternative more expensive supplier, seasonal price increase etc.

What factors may potentially cause a favourable variance?

A Favourable Direct Materials Price Variance is caused by paying a lower unit **price** for the materials than budgeted.

e.g. Bulk purchase discount, new cheaper supplier, use of lower grade/quality of material etc.

> 🎓 **TUTORIAL NOTE**
>
> Understanding the Gizmo example result:
>
> Looking at the formula……
>
> **Direct Materials Price Variance = (AQ x SP) - (AQ x AP)**
>
> It can be seen that both sets of brackets contain the term 'AQ' and so the formula could be 'factorised' into the simpler form:
>
> **Direct Materials Price Variance = (SP – AP) x AQ**

In words, this is stating that the Direct Material Price Variance can be simply found by working out the difference in unit price paid (compared to standard price) multiplied by the actual quantity used, thus:

- Standard materials price = £5.00 per Kg
- Actual materials price = £4.70 per Kg (= £12,690 / 2,700 Kg)
- Savings per Kg = £0.30
- Total Quantity Used = 2,700 Kg
- Actual Savings made = £810 F (= 2,700 Kg x £0.30 per Kg)

This is why it was helpful to work out all of the average prices etc. earlier. We could then see that we had purchased the materials for less than the budgeted price which would increase net profit.

8.16 Direct Materials Quantity Variance

The formula for the Direct Materials Quantity Variance is:

Direct Materials Quantity Variance = (SQ x SP) − (AQ x SP)

Where:

- **SQ** = **S**tandard **Q**uantity of material required *(to make the actual sales volume)*
- **SP** = **S**tandard **P**rice for material per unit (e.g. per Kg etc.)
- **AQ** = **A**ctual **Q**uantity of material used *(to make the actual sales volume)*

The first set of brackets **(SQ x SP)** represents how much the standard quantity of materials required would have cost, if they had been purchased at the standard price *(for the **actual** volume of units produced)*.

The second set of brackets **(AQ x SP)** represents how much the actual quantity of materials used would have cost if purchased at standard price.

> ⚠ **KEY POINT**
>
> The Direct Materials Quantity Variance tells us by how much the total net profit has changed **solely** as a result of using more or less materials compared to the standard amount which should have been used *(for the **actual** volume of units produced)*.

> 🔍 **EXAMPLE**
>
> Using the previous example:
>
> | **Direct Materials Quantity Variance** | = | (SQ x SP) | − | (AQ x SP) |
> |---|---|---|---|---|
> | | = | (250 x 10Kg x £5/Kg) | − | (2,700Kg x £5/Kg) |
> | | = | (£12,500) | − | (£13,500) |
> | | = | - £1,000 A | | |
>
> i.e. the actual net profit is actually £1,000 lower than it was budgeted to be purely because of using a great quantity of materials than expected.

8 Standard Costing and Variance Analysis

What factors may potentially cause an adverse variance?

An Adverse Direct Materials Quantity Variance is caused by using more materials than the standard quantity (*for the* **actual** *volume of units produced*)

e.g. Excess wastage due to unskilled workforce or lower quality material etc.

What factors may potentially cause a favourable variance?

A Favourable Direct Materials Price Variance is caused by using less materials than the standard quantity (*for the* **actual** *volume of units produced*)

e.g. Reduced wastage due to higher skilled workforce, or use of higher quality material etc.

> **TUTORIAL NOTE**
>
> Understanding the Gizmo example result:
>
> Looking at the formula......
>
> **Direct Materials Quantity Variance = (SQ x SP) - (AQ x SP)**
>
> It can be seen that both sets of brackets contain the term 'SP' and so the formula could be 'factorised' into the simpler form:
>
> **Direct Materials Quantity Variance = (SQ – AQ) x SP**
>
> In words, this is stating that the Direct Material Quantity Variance can be simply found by working out how much more or less materials were used (compared to standard quantity), valued at the standard price, thus:
>
> - Standard materials quantity = 2,500 Kg (250 x 10Kg each)
> - Actual materials quantity = 2,700 Kg
> - Additional material used = 200 Kg
> - Standard Material Price = £5 per Kg
> - Materials usage overspend = £1,000 A (200 Kg x £5 per Kg)

8.17 Reconciling the Direct Materials Sub-variances

If *(and only if)* the two sub-variances have been calculated correctly using the exact formulae given, then they will exactly add up to the Direct Total Materials Variance, thus:

Direct Materials Price Variance = + £810 F

Direct Materials Quantity Variance = - £1,000 A

Direct Materials Total Variance = - £190 A

... which reassures us that we have not made a mistake along the way!

> **TUTORIAL NOTE**
>
> Remember that Adverse variances are negative, whilst Favourable variances are positive.

> **TUTORIAL NOTE**
>
> If the exact formula is not used (for instance pricing out the 200Kg using actual price instead of standard price) you will get a variance which looks credible, but which will not reconcile as shown above.
>
> Don't trust to memory….always double the check the exact formula required.

8.18 Direct Labour Rate Variance

The formula for the Direct Labour Rate Variance is:

Direct Labour Rate Variance = (AH x SR) - (AH x AR)

Where:

- **AH** = **A**ctual **H**ours of labour used *(to make the actual sales volume)*
- **SR** = **S**tandard **R**ate (per hour) for labour
- **AR** = **A**ctual **R**ate (per hour) for labour

The first set of brackets **(AH x SR)** represents how much the actual hours of labour would have cost, if they had been paid at the standard rate.

The second set of brackets **(AH x AR)** is simply the cost of the actual labour hours used at the actual hourly rate i.e. the actual cost of the labour! Again this figure is often readily available and so it is often not even necessary to even work out the bracket (AH x AR).

> **KEY POINT**
>
> The Direct Labour Rate Variance tells us by how much the total net profit has changed **solely** as a result of paying a higher or lower hourly **rate** for labour compared to the standard hourly rate used in the budget.

> **EXAMPLE**
>
> Using the previous example:
>
> | Direct Labour Rate Variance | = | (AH x SR) | - | (AH x AR) |
> |---|---|---|---|---|
> | | = | (1,100 hrs x £9 ph) | - | (£10,450) |
> | | = | (£9,900) | - | (£10,450) |
> | | = | -£550 A | | |
>
> i.e. the actual net profit is actually £550 lower than it was budgeted to be solely because of the higher than budgeted hourly rate of pay.

What factors may potentially cause an adverse variance?

An Adverse Direct Labour Rate Variance is caused by paying a higher hourly rate for the direct labour than budgeted.

e.g. use of higher skilled labour or paying over-time rates

8 Standard Costing and Variance Analysis

What factors may potentially cause a favourable variance?

A Favourable Direct Labour Rate Variance is caused by paying a lower hourly rate for the labour than budgeted

e.g. use of apprentice workforce or lower skilled labour

> **TUTORIAL NOTE**
>
> Understanding the Gizmo example result:
>
> Looking at the formula……
>
> **Direct Labour Rate Variance = (AH x SR) - (AH x AR)**
>
> It can be seen that both sets of brackets contain the term 'AH' and so the formula could be 'factorised' into the simpler form:
>
> **Direct Labour Rate Variance = (SR – AR) x AH**
>
> In words, this is stating that the Direct Labour Rate Variance can be simply found by working out the difference in hourly rate paid (compared to standard hourly rate) multiplied by the actual number of hours used, thus:
>
> - Standard hourly rate = £9 ph
> - Actual hourly rate = £9.50 ph (= £10,450 / 1,100 hrs)
> - Overspend per hour = £0.50
> - Total Hours Used = 1,100 hrs
> - Actual Overspend = £550 A (= 1,100 hrs x £0.50 ph)
>
> Again, having already worked out the average prices & rates etc. earlier, we already knew that profit would be down because of a labour rate overspend.

8.19 Direct Labour Efficiency Variance

The formula for the Direct Labour Efficiency Variance is:

Direct Labour Efficiency Variance = (SH x SR) - (AH x SR)

Where:

- **SH** = **S**tandard **H**ours of labour required *(to make the actual sales volume)*
- **SR** = **S**tandard **R**ate for labour hours
- **AH** = **A**ctual **H**ours of labour

The first set of brackets **(SH x SR)** represents how much the standard quantity of hours required *(for the actual volume of units produced)* would have cost, if they had been paid at the standard hourly rate.

The second set of brackets **(AH x SR)** represents how much the actual number of labour hours used would have cost if paid at the standard hourly rate price.

The Language of Business

> ⚠️ **KEY POINT**
>
> The Direct Labour Efficiency Variance tells us by how much the total net profit has changed **solely** as a result of using more or less labour hours compared to the standard hours which should have been used (*for the* **actual** *volume of units produced*).

> **EXAMPLE**
>
> Using the previous example:
>
> **Direct Labour Efficiency Variance** = (SH x SR) - (AH x SR)
>
> = (250 x 4 hrs x £9 ph) - (1,100 hrs x £9 ph)
>
> = (£9,000) - (£9,900)
>
> = **-£900 A**
>
> i.e. the actual net profit is actually £900 lower than it was budgeted to be solely because of using a greater number of hours labour than expected.

What factors may potentially cause an adverse variance?

An Adverse Direct Labour Efficiency Variance is caused by using more hours of labour than the standard hours (*for the* **actual** *volume of units produced*)

e.g. lower skilled (slower) workforce, demotivated staff, poor materials requiring additional time etc.

What factors may potentially cause a favourable variance?

A Favourable Direct Labour Efficiency Variance is caused by using less labour hours than the standard hours (*for the* **actual** *volume of units produced*)

e.g. higher skilled (faster) workforce, motivated staff, efficiencies of scale for large production runs etc.

> **TUTORIAL NOTE**
>
> Understanding the Gizmo example result:
>
> Looking at the formula……
>
> **Direct Labour Efficiency Variance = (SH x SR) - (AH x SR)**
>
> It can be seen that both sets of brackets contain the term 'SR' and so the formula could be 'factorised' into the simpler form:
>
> **Direct Labour Efficiency Variance = (SH – AH) x SR**
>
> In words, this is stating that the Direct Labour Efficiency Variance can be simply found by working out how many more or less labour hours were used (compared to the standard number), valued at the standard rate, thus:
>
> - Standard labour hours = 1,000 hrs   (250 x 4 hrs)
> - Actual labour hours = 1,100 hrs
> - Additional hours used = 100 hrs
> - Standard labour rate = £9 ph
> - Labour Hours overspend = -£900 A   (100 hrs x £9 ph)

8.20 Reconciling the Direct Labour Sub-variances

Again, assuming the two sub-variances have been calculated correctly using the exact formulae given then they will exactly add up to the Total Direct Labour Variance, thus:

Direct Labour Rate Variance = - £550 A

Direct Labour Efficiency Variance = -£900 A

Direct Labour Total Variance = - £1,450 A

If these didn't reconcile, we would start double-checking our calculations!

> **TUTORIAL NOTE**
>
> In this case, both sub-variances are Adverse (i.e. negative).
>
> £900 of the total labour adverse variance was due to paying £0.50 per hour more than budgeted, whilst the remaining £550 was due to using 100 additional hours of labour compared to the standard amount which should have been required.

8.21 Summary of variances

Having now looked at every variance we need to *(Cost Accountants actually use many more variances than these... but we'll stop here!)*, lets recap on our progress so far using the diagram below.

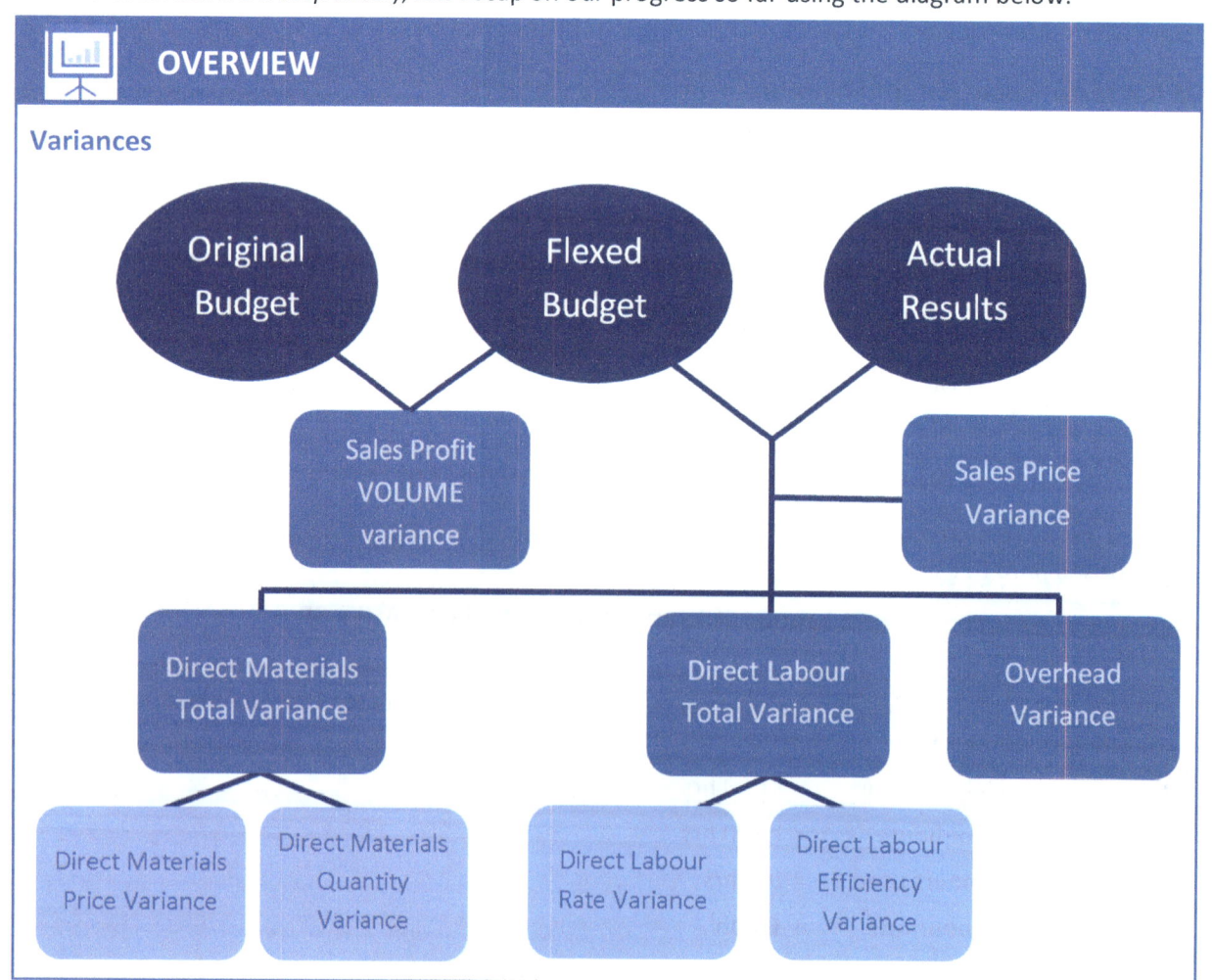

OVERVIEW

Variances

- Original Budget
- Flexed Budget
- Actual Results

- Sales Profit VOLUME variance
- Sales Price Variance

- Direct Materials Total Variance
  - Direct Materials Price Variance
  - Direct Materials Quantity Variance
- Direct Labour Total Variance
  - Direct Labour Rate Variance
  - Direct Labour Efficiency Variance
- Overhead Variance

- We 'flex' the original budget to the **flexed budget** by adjusting it to the actual level of activity. All of the original budget assumptions are retained, except for the level of activity (i.e. sales/production volume).
- The increase or decrease in net profit as a result of flexing the budget is called the **Sales Profit Volume Variance** and this is the only variance which refers to the original budget.
- The main variances are found by comparing the flexed budget figures to the actual figures (both of these relating to the actual level of activity). This produces:
    - **Sales Price Variance**
        - → *Change in profit due to change in unit selling price*
    - **Direct Materials Total Variance**
        - → *Change in profit due to change in unit price for materials and/or quantity of materials used*
    - **Direct Labour Total Variance**
        - → *Change in profit due to change in hourly labour rate paid and/or number of hours labour used*
    - **Overhead Variance**
        - → *Change in profit due to difference in level of overhead incurred*
- The **Direct Materials Total Variance** can then be further split down into:
    - **Direct Materials Price Variance**
        - → *Change in profit solely due to difference in unit price for materials*
    - **Direct Materials Quantity Variance**
        - → *Change in profit solely due to difference in quantity of materials used*
- The **Direct Labour Total Variance** can then be further split down into:
    - **Direct Labour Rate Variance**
        - → *Change in profit solely due to difference in hourly rate for labour*
    - **Direct Labour Efficiency Variance**
        - → *Change in profit solely due to difference in hours of labour used*

8.22 Profit reconciliation

> **TUTORIAL NOTE**
>
> In the previous Gizmo example we produced three separate profit figures, namely:
>
> - Original Budgeted Profit
> - Flexed Budgeted Profit
> - Actual Profit
>
> ….. and no fewer than eight separate variances & sub-variances.
>
> Wouldn't it be great if these all somehow married up together and made sense as some sort of big picture regarding the profitability of this product? Well it's your lucky day, as that is exactly what we will now do!

EXAMPLE

Profit Reconciliation	£	£
Original Budgeted Profit		**£12,000**
Sales Profit Volume Variance		+£3,000
Flexed Budget Profit		**£15,000**
Sales Price Variance		-£1,250
Direct Materials Price Variance	+£810	
Direct Materials Quantity Variance	-£1,000	
Direct Materials Total Variance		-£190
Direct Labour Rate Variance	-£550	
Direct Labour Efficiency Variance	-£900	
Direct Labour Total Variance		-£1,450
Overhead Variance		+£50
Actual Net Profit		**£12,160**

8.23 Accounting for control

At a glance we can now see what aspects of the production and sales of the Gizmo have gone well, and conversely what areas need to be focussed on to remedy current issues which are resulting in lost profit.

OVERVIEW

Good Performance to Repeat	Poor Performance to Remedy
Excellent sales volume 50 more units sold than budgeted, increasing profit by £3,000	**Weak average selling price** Average discount of £5 per unit, costing £1,250 in lost profit. Did the sales team over-discount to 'buy' the extra sales volume?
Good purchase price for materials A saving of £0.30 per Kg, increasing profit by £810… but see adverse quantity used!	**Excessive quantity of materials used** 200Kg more materials used than budgeted costing £1,000 in lost profit. Did the business buy cheap lower grade material? If so, it appears to be a false economy
Overheads Saving A saving of £0.20 per unit, resulting in £50 additional profit overall.	**Excessive hourly rate for labour** Average of £9.50 per hour paid compared to a budget of £9.00 per hour.
	Poor Labour Efficiency 100 excess labour hours used. Is this as a result of working with poor quality material?

Managers at all levels in a company should strive to maximise profit wherever and whenever they can. This example is a classic case of what initially looked like good news (additional £3,000 profit from selling 50 extra units) being progressively lost by a series of operational issues.

This sort of information needs to be included in the company's monthly management accounts to inform the subsequent discussions which should now be held. The company must urgently understand why virtually all of the extra potential profit generated has been lost …… and how to rapidly resolve these issues.

This combination of **'standard costing'** and subsequent **'variance analysis'** is often called **'Accounting for Control'** as it provides the company's managers with the sort of detail they need to understand how to better control their business and maximise profit.

8.24 Standard Costing in practice

The example used in this chapter has been kept deliberately simple to allow the basic principles to be understood. In practice a more complex product might:

- Be manufactured from several different types of material and several different component parts, and each of these would require a separate line on the cost card recording their respective quantities and cost per unit.

- Go through several different processes, each requiring a different grade of labour (e.g. machining, assembly, finishing etc.) and each of these would also need the amount of labour and labour rate per hour recording separately on the cost card.

- Include variable and/or fixed overhead costs which will need to be included in the standard cost *(obviously fixed overheads do not change when the original budget is flexed …. because they are fixed!)*

However, even though such products might appear more complex, the same basic principles that we have used above will still be employed to enable a business to accurately 'cost' products and hence set appropriate selling prices. Moreover the businesses will then review their actual performance against their planned performance using the techniques of variance analysis to allow poor practice to be identified and remedied, and outdated costing assumptions to be revised.

Standard Costing allows businesses to make properly informed decisions regarding their selling prices, which properly balance the need to achieve profitability with the need to remain competitive. The technique of variance analysis then allows the various standard costing assumptions made to be compared to the reality of the actual results, to see where (and to what extent) more or less profit has been made compared to that originally anticipated.

KEY POINTS FROM CHAPTER 8

Standard Costing

- Manufacturing businesses have to calculate the cost of the products they produce by considering the material, labour and overhead components of those products. These cost components do not remain static and so companies calculate 'standard costs' which can then be used to set selling prices, value inventory and on which to base subsequent performance appraisal.

Variance Analysis

- Variance analysis is used to show the profit effect of any of the standard costing assumptions varying in practice.
- Before any meaningful variances can be calculated the original budget must be flexed to the actual level of activity. This is a simple scaling up (or down) of all of the original budget assumptions for the various cost components to allow the flexed budget to reflect the actual level of activity.

Calculation of Variances & Sub-Variances

Sales Profit Volume Variance

- Sales Profit Volume Variance = Flexed Budget Net Profit – Original Budget Net Profit
- The effect on profit due to a change in the sales volume

Sales Price Variance

- Sales Price Variance = Actual Sales Revenue - Flexed Budget Sales Revenue
- The effect on profit due to a change in selling price

Direct Materials Total Variance

- Direct Materials Total Variance = (SQ x SP) - (AQ x AP)
- The effect on profit due to the combined effects of variations in quantity of material used and unit price paid

Direct Labour Total Variance

- Direct Labour Total Variance = (SH x SR) - (AH x AR)
- The effect on profit due to the combined effects of variations in labour hours used and hourly rate paid

Overhead Variance

- Overhead Variance = Flexed Budgeted Overheads - Actual Overheads
- The effect on profit of variations in the level of overheads incurred

Direct Materials Price Variance

- Direct Materials Price Variance = (AQ x SP) - (AQ x AP)
- The effect on profit of changes in the unit price of materials

8 Standard Costing and Variance Analysis

Direct Materials Quantity Variance

- Direct Materials Quantity Variance = (SQ x SP) - (AQ x SP)
- The effect on profit of changes in the quantity of materials used

Direct Labour Rate Variance

- Direct Labour Rate Variance = (AH x SR) - (AH x AR)
- The effect on profit of changes in the hourly rate for labour

Direct Labour Efficiency Variance

- Direct Labour Efficiency Variance = (SH x SR) - (AH x SR)
- The effect on profit of changes in the number of labour hours used

The Language of Business

Chapter 8: End of Chapter Exercises

Section A Questions

> **The following information relates to Questions 8.1 - 8.10.**
>
> A clothing factory manufactures woollen pullovers which it then sells to fashion retailers.
>
> In the month of May it expects to sell 5,000 pullovers for £12 each.   £60,000
>
> The standard costing information for the pullovers are as follows:
>
> - Direct Materials 0.5Kg wool per pullover at a standard cost of £1.80 per Kg   £4,500
> - Direct Labour 0.25 hours per pullover at a standard cost of £9 per hour   £11,250
> - Variable Overheads of £3 per pullover.   £15,000
>
> At the end of May it is ascertained that:
>
> - 6,000 pullovers were in fact produced and sold for total sales revenue of £69,000   variance of 9,000
> - 2,800 Kg of wool were used in production at a total cost of £5,180   300kg wool = £540
> - 1,800 hours of direct labour were used at a total cost £17,100 = 550 hours
> - £17,400 of variable overheads were incurred. = £24000

Question 8.1
What was the original budgeted profit in May?

- (A)   £29,250
- B   £35,100
- C   £38,250
- D   £44,250

Question 8.2
What was the flexed budgeted profit in May?

- A   £20,320
- B   £29,250
- C   £35,100
- D   £46,720

Question 8.3
What is the Sales Profit Volume Variance?

- A   £5,850 F
- B   £5,850 A
- C   £9,000 F
- D   £9,000 A

What exactly caused this variance?

315

8 Standard Costing and Variance Analysis

Question 8.4
What is the Sales Price Variance?

A £3,000 F
B £3,000 A
C £9,000 F
D £9,000 A

What exactly caused this variance?

_____

Question 8.5
What is the Direct Labour Rate Variance?

A £750 F
B £750 A
C £900 F
D £900 A

What exactly caused this variance?

_____

Question 8.6
What is the Direct Labour Efficiency Variance?

A £2,700 F
B £2,700 A
C £2,850 F
D £2,850 A

What exactly caused this variance?

_____

Question 8.7
What is the Direct Materials Price Variance?

A £140 F
B £140 A
C £150 F
D £150 A

What exactly caused this variance?

_____

Question 8.8

What is the Direct Materials Quantity Variance?

A   £360F

B   £360 A

C   £370 F

D   £370 A

What exactly caused this variance?

_____

Question 8.9

What is the Total Overhead Variance?

A   £600 F

B   £600 A

C   £2,400 F

D   £2,400 A

What caused this variance?

_____

Question 8.10

What is the Net Profit Variance?

A   £70 F

B   £70 A

C   £5,780 F

D   £5,780 A

What caused this variance?

_____

8 Standard Costing and Variance Analysis

Section B Questions

Question 8.11 – Standard Costs

Stratford Gifts Ltd manufacture a range of gifts for the tourist trade which are mainly sold in gift shops in and around their home town of Stratford. One of their products is a resin moulded model of the tourist attraction, Anne Hathaway's cottage

- Each cottage requires 0.5Kg of type X resin which has a standard cost of £3 per Kg. *£1.50 per item*
- Each cottage takes 6 minutes (=0.1 hours) of direct labour which is paid at a standard rate of £8 per hour

Calculate the standard marginal cost of an Anne Hathaway cottage.

Direct Materials   (Std. Qty. x Std. Cost)   £1.50

Direct Labour   (Std. Hrs. x Std. Rate)   0.1 × 8 = £0.80

Standard Cost (Marginal)   £2.30

The expression "Standard Cost" just means the expected budgeted cost!

Question 8.11 continued – Original Budget

In June, Stratford Gifts Ltd plan to make and sell 150 Anne Hathaway cottages at a standard selling price of £10.00 each. This is expected to incur fixed overheads of £100 in addition to the direct material & labour costs mentioned in question 1.

Complete the following budgeted profit statement for this product for June for the total anticipated sales volume.

Original Budget

	Working	£
Sales Revenue	150 × £10	£1500
Direct Materials	£1.50 × 150	£225
Direct Labour	0.8 × 150	£120
Fixed Overhead	100	£100
Net Profit		£1055

Standard Costing and Variance Analysis

Question 8.11 continued – Flexed Budget

In the event Stratford Gifts Ltd make and sell 170 Anne Hathaway cottages in June.

Complete the following budgeted profit statement for this product for June for the total actual sales volume by 'flexing' the original budget.

A flexed budget uses all of the original budget assumptions (unit costs, unit selling price, overheads etc.) but *just* changes the sales volume (or activity)

Flexed Budget

	Working	£
Sales Revenue	170 × £10	£1,700
Direct Materials	£1.50 × 170	£255
Direct Labour	0.8 × 170	£136
Fixed Overhead	100	£100
Net Profit	1700 − 491 =	£1209

What is the Sales Profit Volume Variance?

1209 − 1055 = 154

Complete:

The Sales Profit Volume Variance represents the change in __profit__ between the original budget and the __flexed__ budget purely due to the change in sales __volume__.

Sales Profit Volume Variance = Flexed Budget Net profit – Original Budget Net Profit
*It is the **only** variance to compare **original** budget to flexed budget.*

Question 8.11 continued – Actual Results

After the end of June the following information relating to the production and sales of the 170 Anne Hathaway Cottages during June is provided:

- The 170 cottages sold achieved total sales revenue of £1,632
- 100 Kg of type X resin was used at a cost of £330
- 15 hours of direct labour at a cost of £132
- The actual fixed overheads incurred totalled £95

Complete the following actual profit statement for this product for June for the total actual sales volume.

Actual Results

	£	(£ per unit / £ per Kg / £ per hour)
Sales Revenue	£1,632	£9.60 per unit (1632 ÷ 170)
Direct Materials	£330	£3.30
Direct Labour	£132	£8.80
Fixed Overhead	£95	
Net Profit	£1075	

Question 8.11 continued – Main Variances

Transfer your 'Flexed Budget' calculations and your 'Actual Result' calculations into the template below and hence work out the following variances (indicating whether Favourable or Adverse):

	Flexed Budget	Actual results	Variance
Sales Price Variance	1700	1632	68 A
Direct Materials Total Variance	255	330	75 A
Direct Labour Total Variance	136	132	4 F
Fixed Overhead Variance	100	95	5 F
Net Profit Variance	1209	1075	134 A

Complete the following statements:

- "The Sales Price Variance shows the effect on profitability caused by any variation in the ___price___ of the items sold".

- "The Direct Materials Total Variance shows the effect on profitability caused by any variation in the ___cost___ or ___quantity___ for Direct Materials".

- "The Direct Labour Total Variance shows the effect on profitability caused by any variation in the ___hours___ or ___rate___ for Direct Labour".

Note that we compare 'Actual' to 'Flexed'

Question 8.11 continued – Direct Materials Sub-Variances

Direct Materials Price Variance

Cost of actual quantity of materials used at std. price   300   £3 per kg × 100

Less Cost of actual quantity of materials used at actual price paid   330

Equals Direct Material Price Variance   −30 A

Complete:

"The Direct Materials Price Variance shows the effect on profitability caused by any variation in

_____ "

Direct Materials Quantity Variance *(aka 'material usage' variance)*

Cost of std. quantity of materials used at std. price   0.5 × 170 = 85 × 3 per kg = 255

Less Cost of actual quantity of materials used at std. price   300
100 × £3

Equals Direct Material Quantity Variance   −45 A

Complete:

"The Direct Materials Quantity Variance shows the effect on profitability caused by any variation in

_____ "

Check that sub-variances add back to Total Variance

Total Variance = Price Variance + Quantity Variance

_____

Note that we compare 'Actual' to 'Flexed'

Question 8.11 continued – Direct Labour Sub-Variances

Direct Labour Rate Variance

Cost of actual amount of labour used at std. rate   £120
15 × 0.8

Less Cost of actual amount of labour used at actual rate paid   £132

Equals Direct Labour Rate Variance   £12 A

Complete:

"The Direct Labour Rate Variance shows the effect on profitability caused by any variation in

_____"

Direct Labour Efficiency Variance *(aka 'labour usage' variance)*

Cost of Std. Amount of labour used at std. rate   £136

Less Cost of actual amount of labour used at std. rate   £120
15 × 0.8

Equals Direct Labour Efficiency Variance   £16 F

Complete:

"The Direct Labour Efficiency Variance shows the effect on profitability caused by any variation in

_____"

Check that sub-variances add back to Total Variance

Total Variance = Rate Variance + Efficiency Variance

_____

Note that we compare 'Actual' to 'Flexed'

The Language of Business

Question 8.11 continued – Reconciliation of:

i. Original Budgeted Profit…. to 1500
ii. Flexed Budgeted Profit …. to 1700
iii. Actual Results 1632

Original Budgeted Net Profit   (150 units)   £1055

+ / −   Sales Profit Volume Variance   154

= Flexed Budgeted Net Profit   (170 units)   £1209
                                                        −68
+ / −   Sales Price Variance   − 30

+ / −   Direct Material Price Variance   − 40

+ / −   Direct Materials Quantity Variance   −75

+ / −   **Direct Materials Total Variance**   −17

+ / −   Direct Labour Rate Variance   +16

+ / −   Direct Labour Efficiency Variance   4

+ / −   **Direct Labour Total Variance**   5

+ / −   Overhead Variance   1075

= Actual Net Profit   (170 units)

8 Standard Costing and Variance Analysis

Using the calculated variances describe and explain (i.e. reconcile) the major factors which have resulted in higher or lower profitability on this product and suggest possible reasons for why some of them might have occurred. You should include a numerical reconciliation of each variance.

Sale Profit Volume Variance

_____

_____

_____

_____

Sales Price Variance

_____

_____

_____

_____

Direct Materials Price Variance

_____

_____

_____

_____

Direct Materials Quantity Variance

_____

_____

_____

_____

Direct Labour Rate Variance

Direct Labour Efficiency Variance

Overhead Variance

Net Profit Variance

8 Standard Costing and Variance Analysis

Question 8.12

Norfolk Ltd manufactures a specialised metal component which is sold to manufacturers of heavy lifting machinery.

The standard cost card for one component is as follows:

Selling Price	£150.00 per unit	
Costs:		
Direct Materials	£35.00	7Kg of metal @ £5 per Kg
Direct Labour	£15.00	3 hours @ £5 per hour
Prime Cost	£50.00	

Using the separate template complete the Company's January Budget:

Selling price & prime costs as per cost card.

Budgeted Sales Volume	=	1,000 units
Fixed Overheads	=	£70,000

At the end of January the following actual results are reported:

Sales	1,100 units @ £145 each	£159,500
Costs:		
Direct Materials (8,250 Kg):		£37,125
Direct Labour (3,080 hours):		£16,940
Overheads		£73,250

Using the following template:

- Complete the flexed budget for January
- Complete the actual results for January
- Calculate all relevant variances
- Use the variances to reconcile : **Original Budgeted Profit** to **Flexed Budgeted Profit** ; and then **Flexed Budgeted Profit** to **Actual Results**

NORFOLK LTD

NORFOLK LTD	ORIGINAL BUDGET			FLEXED BUDGET			ACTUAL RESULTS	MAIN VARIANCES	
	Budget Assumptions	Workings	Total	Workings	Total				
Sales Revenue								*Sales Price Variance*	
Direct Materials								*Direct Materials Total Variance*	
Direct Labour								*Direct Labour Total Variance*	
Overheads								*Overhead Variance*	
Net Profit								*Net Profit Variance*	

Sales Profit Volume Variance = Flexed Budget Profit - Original Budgeted Profit = _____

SUB VARIANCES	DEFINITIONS	WORKINGS	SUB-VARIANCE
Direct Materials Price Variance	(AQ x SP) - (AQ x AP)		
Direct Materials Quantity Variance	(SQ x SP) - (AQ x SP)		
Direct Labour Rate Variance	(AH x SR) - (AH x AR)		
Direct Labour Efficiency Variance	(SH x SR) - (AH x SR)		

8 Standard Costing and Variance Analysis

	£	£
Original Budgeted Profit		
Sales Profit Volume Variance		
Flexed Budget Profit		
Sales Price Variance		
Direct Materials Price Variance		
Direct Materials Quantity Variance		
Direct Materials Total Variance		
Direct Labour Rate Variance		
Direct Labour Efficiency Variance		
Direct Labour Total Variance		
Overhead Variance		
Actual Net Profit		

Chapter 9
Capital Investment Appraisal

INTRODUCTION

We have already seen the two main ways that a company can raise long-term finance, namely via debt or equity. We also identified that the two main business requirements for such long-term finance are to fund both current assets (part of working capital) and non-current assets.

We will return to look at working capital in more detail in chapter 11, but for now let's turn our attention to exactly how a business decides which **non-current assets** to invest in.

Non-current assets are also known as **'fixed assets'** or **'capital assets'**, and the process of deciding whether or not to make a particular investment in a capital asset is known as **'Capital Investment Appraisal'**.

OVERVIEW AND OBJECTIVES

By the end of this chapter you should have developed an understanding of:

- Capital Investment Decisions
- Accounting Rate of Return (ARR)
- Payback
- Time Value of Money
- Net Present Value (NPV)
- Internal Rate of Return (IRR)

and be able to answer questions relating to these areas.

9 Capital Investment Appraisal

9.1 Capital-related jargon

Most specialisms have a generous scattering of jargon and unfortunately accounting and finance are no exception! If you can decipher the jargon you are often half-way there, so let's begin by clarifying some terms.

> **DEFINITIONS**
>
> **Capital**
>
> The word 'capital' is used in more than one context in accounting and finance. We have already used it to describe the investment made in a business e.g. 'share capital' (for a company) or the 'owner's capital' (for a sole trader or partnership).
>
> Additionally the term 'capital' is also used to differentiate between (generally) larger scale expenditure made for the longer term, known as 'capital expenditure' or just 'capex' and (generally) smaller scale expenditure made for the shorter term, which is known as 'revenue expenditure' (or 'operating expenditure').
>
> The reason for having different labels for these two types of expenditure is that they have two entirely different accounting treatments, thus:
>
> **Revenue Expenditure**
>
> *For example expenditure on rent, gas, electricity, wages, telephone, advertising, insurance etc.*
>
> Revenue expenditure is essentially treated as an immediate expense of the business and immediately charged to the statement of profit and loss when incurred (though 'accruals' and 'pre-payments' may be used to correct any short-term timing issues).
>
> **Capital Expenditure (Capex)**
>
> *For example expenditure on land & buildings, plant & machinery, computers, vehicles etc.*
>
> Capital expenditure is treated as a long-term investment which will be 'capitalised' and depreciated over its useful economic life. In contrast to revenue expenditure, capex will not immediately be charged to the statement of profit or loss in one go, but instead will be charged gradually in a series of depreciation charges over the entire life of the capital asset. The remaining value at any point in time (i.e. the remaining cost which has *yet to be* charged) is known as the Net Book Value (NBV) and is reported on the statement of financial position under the 'Non-Current Assets' section.
>
> **'Capital Assets'** are also known as **'Non-Current Assets'** or **'Fixed Assets'**.

9.2 Capital Investment decisions

There are many reasons why a business may consider investing in new capital assets and these are summarised in the table below.

The thing which is common to all of these decisions however is that they (generally) involve large sums of money and long timescales. It is therefore all the more important that the correct decision is made and for this reason we use a series of evaluation techniques to really scrutinise capital investment proposals.

If the wrong decision is made, the sums of money involved will be large, and the business may have to live with the consequences of that bad decision for a long time.

OVERVIEW

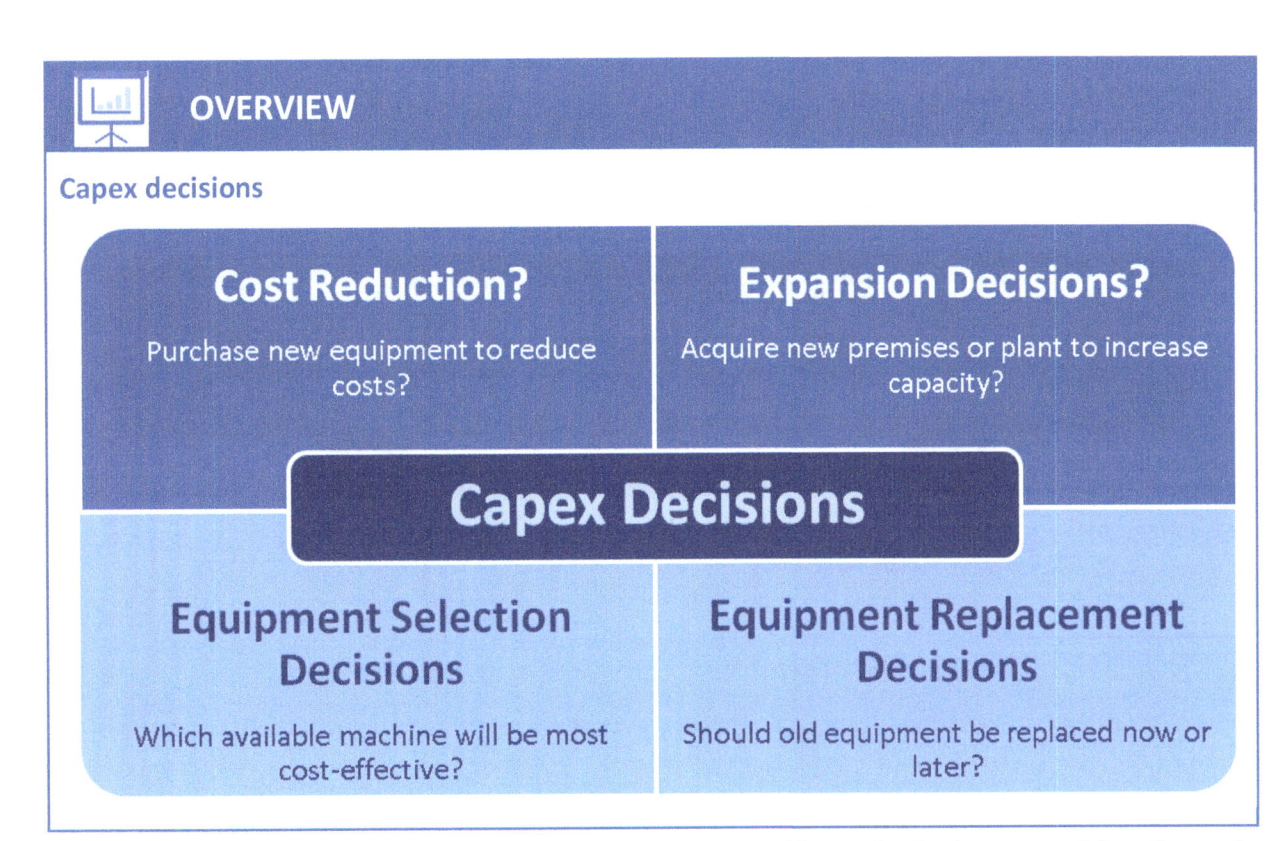

Capex decisions

- **Cost Reduction?** Purchase new equipment to reduce costs?
- **Expansion Decisions?** Acquire new premises or plant to increase capacity?
- **Capex Decisions**
- **Equipment Selection Decisions** — Which available machine will be most cost-effective?
- **Equipment Replacement Decisions** — Should old equipment be replaced now or later?

Moreover it is often the case that a business is either not able or simply does not wish to invest in every single capital investment project which is proposed within the company. A whole range of senior managers may be making competing bids for capital expenditure within their own departments.

For example:

- The Distribution Director may be bidding for new vehicles, whilst
- The IT Director is bidding for new computers, whilst
- The Production Director is bidding for new manufacturing equipment.

It is unlikely that every single bid for capital investment can be actioned ….*even if they all appear worthwhile on their own merits*. Companies are normally limited to how much capital investment they make each year for two main reasons.

Firstly, they may self-impose a limit on how much capital investment they wish to make and this will be largely based on how much cash they wish to preserve to pay dividends to the shareholders and to maintain a healthy cash flow. This type of self-imposed limiting is known as **Soft Capital Rationing**. Part of the budgeting process is to agree on the levels of capital expenditure for the year ahead (the 'Capex' budget).

Secondly, it may be the case that the company does not possess sufficient cash reserves itself and therefore needs to borrow the funds for any proposed capital investments. The external sources of finance such as the bank may well only be prepared to lend up to a certain amount and this type of limitation is known as **Hard Capital Rationing**.

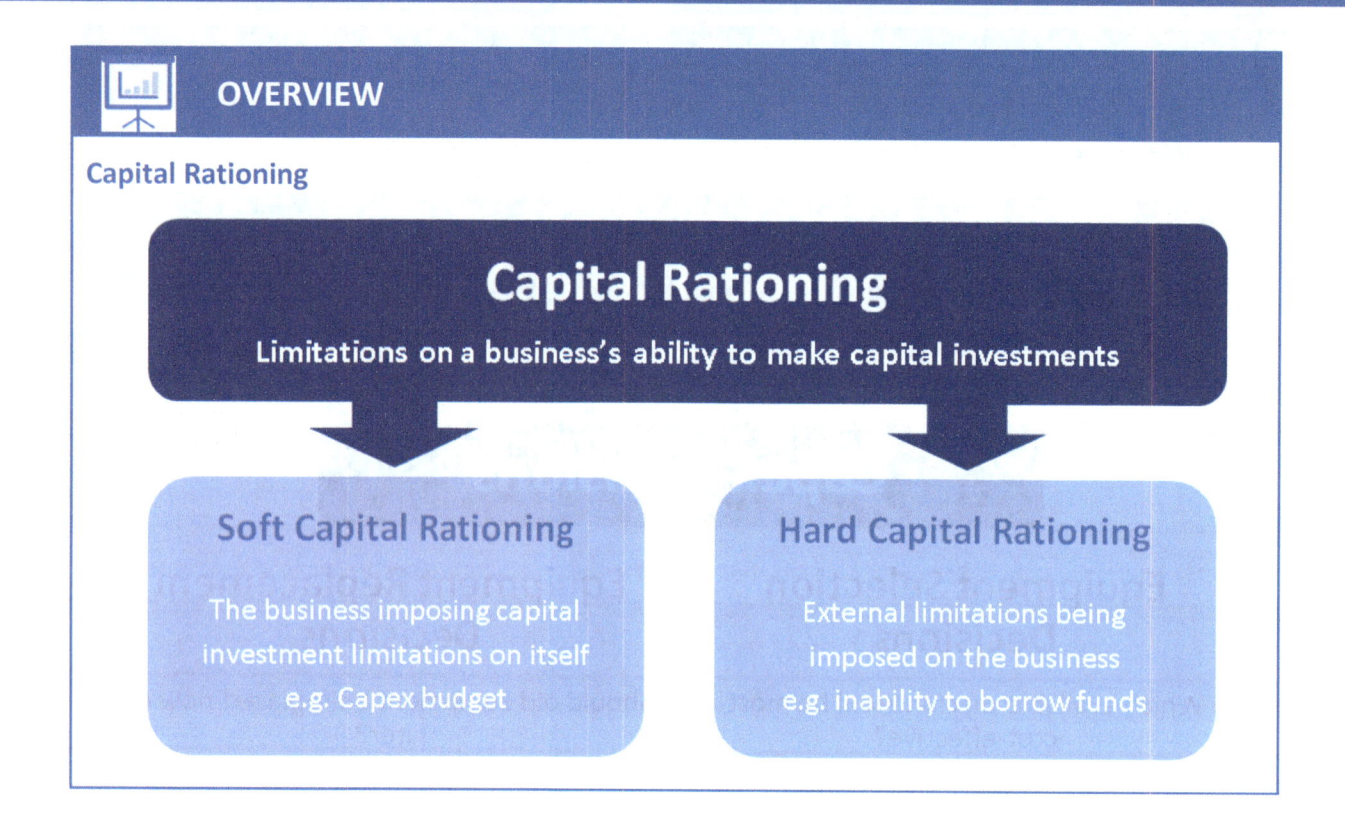

9 Capital Investment Appraisal

> **OVERVIEW**
>
> **Capital Rationing**
>
> **Capital Rationing**
> Limitations on a business's ability to make capital investments
>
> **Soft Capital Rationing**
> The business imposing capital investment limitations on itself
> e.g. Capex budget
>
> **Hard Capital Rationing**
> External limitations being imposed on the business
> e.g. inability to borrow funds

9.3 Capital Investment Appraisal methods

Ideally the outcome of any capital investment appraisal would be:

- To understand the likely returns from the project
- To decide whether the project is financially worthwhile or not
- To allow competing projects to be ranked in some way
- To provide an indication of any risk associated with the project

As we shall see, the fact that capital projects are long-term has a strong bearing on several of these factors and some sort of assessment is required which takes into account the timescales involved in different projects. It is always preferable to receive cash returns earlier rather than later, and this is known as the 'time value of money' (discussed later in the chapter).

Moreover, even if a project 'stacks up' financially it is still important to ensure that the proposed investment aligns with the business's strategic aims.

There are four main capital investment appraisal methods we shall consider. Two of these take into account the time value of money and two do not.

The Language of Business

OVERVIEW

Capital Investment Appraisal methods

- **Accounting Rate of Return (ARR)** — Ignores the time value of money
- **Payback** — Ignores the time value of money
- **Net Present Value (NPV)** — Takes the time value of money into account
- **Internal Rate of Return (IRR)** — Takes the time value of money into account

Capital Investment Appraisal methods

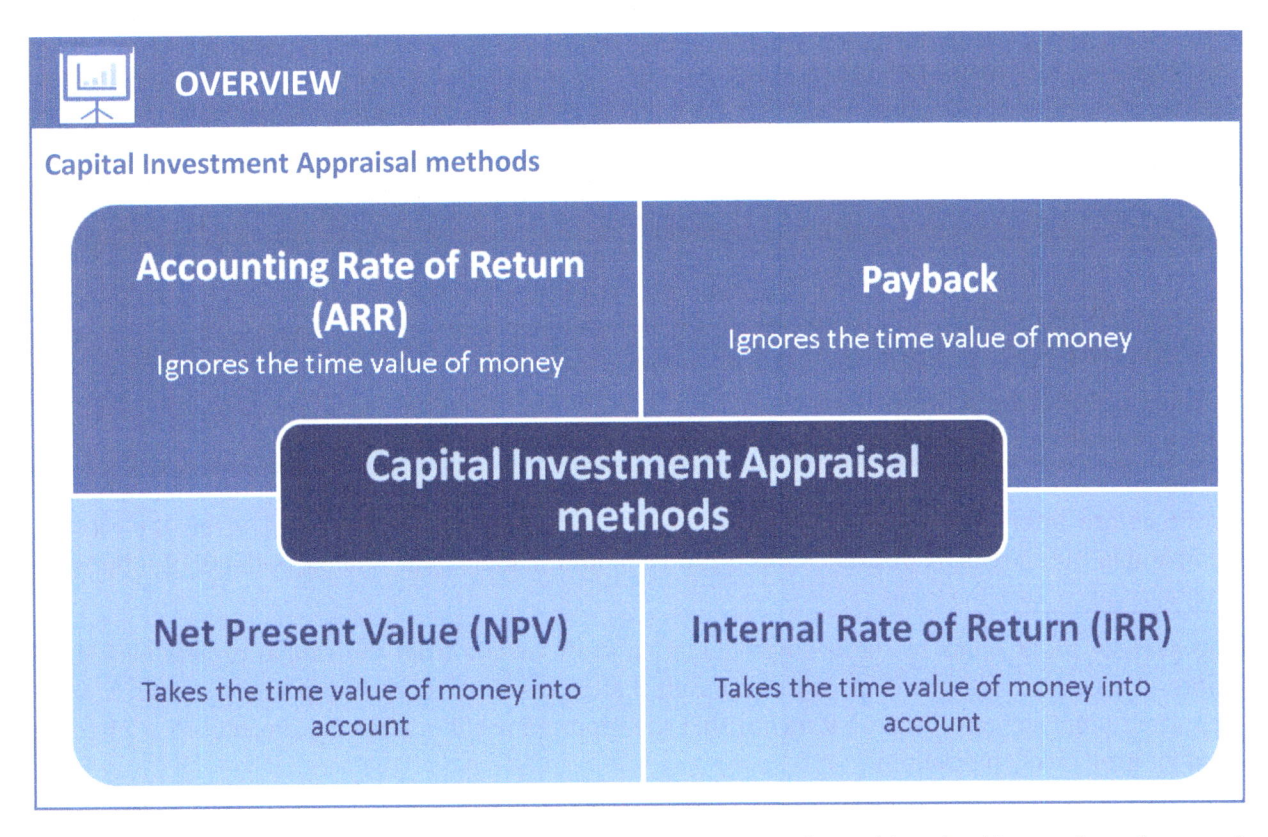

We shall now consider each one of these methods in turn and consider the 'time value of money' along the way.

9.4 Accounting Rate of Return (ARR)

A 'return' is simply what you **get out** compared to what you have **put in**.

EXAMPLES

- If a bank account pays 2% pa interest then putting £100 into the bank account (and leaving it there for a year) would allow a saver to get an additional £2 out at the end of the year, **a 2% return**.

- If an individual invests £5,000 in a portfolio of shares and receives £300 of dividends over the next 12 months then they have made **a 6% return** (£300 / £5,000 x 100%).

- If a buy-to-let landlord invests £150,000 in a residential property, lets it out and receives £12,000 of rent in the next year then they will have made **an 8% return** that year (£12,000 / £150,000 x 100%).

All of the above examples assume that the investments experience neither capital growth nor loss over the year (otherwise the calculations become a little more difficult).

The **Accounting Rate of Return** compares:

- What the business **'gets out'**...... Which in accounting terms is 'profit' calculated in accordance with accounting principles i.e. <u>after</u> depreciation has been deducted

...to...

- What the business **'puts in'** .... Which in accounting terms is measured by the Net Book Value (NBV) of the capital investment i.e. <u>after</u> the capital asset has been depreciated.

9 Capital Investment Appraisal

You might see alternative definitions of Accounting Rate of Return but the one we shall use is shown below.

DEFINITIONS

$$\text{Accounting Rate of Return (ARR)} = \frac{\text{Average Profit (£)}}{\text{Average Investment (£)}} \times 100\%$$

Average Profit

As we have already seen there are several different measures of profit, but the one used here is **Profit before Interest and Tax (PBIT) (aka Operating Profit)** as it is considered to be the most comparable measurement of profit before the (sometimes somewhat random) effects of interest and taxation confuse the issue.

The average profit refers to the average operating profit arising from the capital project over its entire life. Operating profit is of course measured after the deduction of depreciation. This is an important point to grasp because it means that the reported profit is **after** the project has in effect paid for itself (via depreciation).

Average Investment

In accounting terms the investment in the project (at any point in time) is the remaining Net Book Value (NBV) of the capital assets at that point in time. The capital investment is of course being depreciated each year and therefore the investment (i.e. NBV) is reducing each year. We need to calculate the *average* investment over the life of the project.

To find the average investment we could add each year's (reducing) NBV together and then divide by the number of different NBV values we have, or more simply (and only because we will always be using straight-line depreciation), we can simply add the initial NBV to the final NBV and divide by two.

EXAMPLE

Scenario

A proposed project involves purchasing machinery at a cost of £230,000. The machinery will have a 5 year life and a residual value of £50,000.

The project is expected to produce the following operating profits over its life:

Year 1	£20,000
Year 2	£25,000
Year 3	£30,000
Year 4	£20,000
Year 5	£15,000

What is the expected accounting rate of return?

The Language of Business

Solution

Accounting Rate of Return (ARR) = $\dfrac{\text{Average Profit (£)}}{\text{Average Investment (£)}}$ × 100%

The average profit = (£20,000 + £25,000 + £30,000 + £20,000 + £15,000) / 5 = £22,000

The average investment = (£230,000 + £50,000) / 2 = £140,000

ARR = £22,000 / £140,000 × 100% = 16%

TUTORIAL NOTE

A common mental block encountered by students is calculating the average investment because they are so used to *deducting* the residual value from the initial value (when calculating annual depreciation). In this case we are simply calculating the average of two figures (initial value & final value) so we simply add them and divide by two!

If you are still unconvinced, then calculate the Net Book Value (NBV) of the machinery each year and work out an average of *all* the values, thus:

Annual depreciation charge = (£230,000 - £50,000) ÷ 5 = £36,000 per annum i.e. the value of the machinery will reduce by £36,000 pa.

So the Net Book Values of the machinery over each year of its life will be as follows:

Year	Net Book Value (NBV)
Year 0	£230,000
Year 1	£194,000
Year 2	£158,000
Year 3	£122,000
Year 4	£86,000
Year 5	£50,000

Therefore to find the average investment (i.e. the average NBV) simply add up all six values above and divide by six, which will give exactly the same answer of an average investment of £140,000:

(£230,000 + £194,000 + £158,000 + £122,000 + £86,000 + £50,000) / 6 = £140,000

You will only need to do this once to convince yourself that simply adding the initial and final values together and dividing by two is not only valid but far quicker! However, remember that this short-cut only works for straight-line depreciation.

Assessing the calculated result for ARR

It is worth remembering that the various profit figures which were used in the ARR calculation showed the profit from the project after the deduction of depreciation i.e. after the project has paid back the initial investment.

9 Capital Investment Appraisal

The ARR is quoted as a percentage return and simply gives an indication of how well the capital investment is performing. A low percentage ARR indicates an investment that it producing only low returns which begs the question of whether the same money could produce a higher return if invested elsewhere. Conversely a high percentage indicates an investment that is producing good returns for the company and its shareholders.

Calculating a percentage return is a very useful way of making a *relative* comparison between alternative potential projects of different sizes and timescales, as it reduces the final assessment to a simple question of which project produces the biggest ARR i.e. the highest level of returns. If capital is rationed and a choice being made between competing projects then obviously a higher ARR will be preferable.

Because the ARR is calculated using the profit before interest and tax figure, it means that any financing costs involved with the project (e.g. interest on a bank loan) have *not* been taken into account. In fact the same project would give identical ARR figures regardless of whether it was funded from a company's own cash reserves or whether the company had to borrow money and pay interest on that borrowing.

It is therefore important to compare the calculated ARR to what is known as the company's 'cost of capital' (which we will return to later, but for now just regard it as the cost of borrowing or raising funds). Clearly there is no point in borrowing money at 8% interest, in order to invest it in a project that only makes 6% returns. This would simply lose money for the company and hence value for the shareholders.

Risk versus Return

The other factor which must always be considered alongside 'returns' is 'risk'. Put simply 'risk' is the **uncertainty** associated with any future events (such as a proposed capital investment). Just because someone has produced a shiny spreadsheet 'stating' that a certain level of profit will be made, does not mean that this will definitely be the case.

There are two sides to risk: *'upside risk'* where things go better than expected, and *'downside risk'* where thing go worse. However, it is usually the case that the person proposing the project has already built an over-exuberant level of optimism into their figures in the first place (known as 'optimism bias'), so it is normally just down-side risk which is encountered in practice! The basic principle of investment is that higher risk investments will usually require higher expected returns to compensate for the uncertainty.

The ultimate benchmark question for any investor (including companies considering capital investments) is what return they could expect on an alternative *risk-free* investment such as purchasing 'gilts' (=government loan stock). Why would a company invest in a risky project (virtually all capital projects carry some degree of risk) if they could get the same level of return from a risk-free alternative investment.

In practice most companies will state a 'target return' and if a project cannot be shown to achieve an ARR over this threshold then it won't even be considered. If a project is forecast to achieve an ARR over this target threshold figure then it will be considered…..alongside any other competing proposals.

Alternative definitions of ARR

Alternative definitions of Accounting Rate of Return exist, including ones which compare the average profits to the *initial* investment (as opposed to the *average* investment). The key message is to always check the exact definition of ARR being used and ensure that any comparisons (e.g. between alternative projects) are on a like for like basis i.e. both using the same definition of ARR.

The version of ARR adopted in this book has the advantage of taking the entire project into account as it compares average profits (over the whole life of the project) to average investment (over the whole life of the project).

ARR versus ROCE …..and ROI!

We encountered **Return on Capital Employed (ROCE)** in an earlier chapter and you may be (quite rightly) thinking that ARR sounds remarkably similar to ROCE, as both consider the percent returns enjoyed from capital investment.

This is absolutely true and the difference is really just down to alternative finance jargon.

- The term ARR is *normally* used to describe the profit returns from an individual project.
- The term ROCE is *normally* used to describe the profit returns from an entire company (or maybe an entire division of a company)

However you may encounter references to a *project* making a certain ROCE, and this is not in itself wrong. In fact, you may also encounter the phrase **'Return on Investment' (ROI)** which again means pretty much the same thing.

They say that Eskimos have 50 different words for snow, so we shouldn't be too surprised that accountancy has produced three different terms for profit returns!

OVERVIEW

Pros and Cons of ARR

Accounting Rate of Return

Pros (✓)	Cons (✗)
- Simple to calculate - Readily understandable - Provides relative assessment between different projects - Considers the whole life of a project	- Profits are more subjective than cash flows - Confusion caused by different definitions of ARR - Ignores time value of money

339

Capital Investment Appraisal

TEST YOUR UNDERSTANDING 1

Huyton Ltd is contemplating whether to invest in new production machinery. The machinery will have an initial cost of £50,000 and be expected to have a five year life and then have a residual value of £10,000.

It is estimated that the efficiencies resulting from the machinery will deliver the following additional profit in each year (after allowing for depreciation of the machine).

Year	Additional Profit
1	£12,000
2	£18,000
3	£30,000
4	£25,000
5	£5,000

What is the average additional net profit per annum?

_____

_____

_____

What is the average capital employed over the five year life of the project?

_____

_____

_____

What Accounting Rate of Return will the project deliver?

_____

_____

_____

If Huyton have a target ARR of 30% for new capital investment, should this project proceed?

_____

_____

_____

9.5 Payback period

Payback is the simplest of the four capital investment appraisal methods we will look at and although that simplicity is one of the advantages of the payback method it also means that it is of limited value.

> **DEFINITION**
>
> The **Payback Period** of a project is simply the length of time for cash inflows from the project to cover the initial cash outflow of the investment.
>
> In simple terms this gives an indication of how long a project will take to 'pay for itself' i.e. for the business to recoup the investment.

This of course assumes a 'standard' project which consists of an initial cash investment (cash outflow) followed by a series of cash inflows. Although this profile is typical, some projects require additional cash inflows later in the project and the payback method might not then give a meaningful result for such projects

EXAMPLE

Scenario

A project requires an initial cash outflow of £400,000 and then produces the following cash inflows:

Year 1	£120,000
Year 2	£180,000
Year 3	£240,000
Year 4	£200,000
Year 5	£180,000

What is the payback period of the project?

Solution

In these sort of cash flow problems we simplify matters by assuming that all of a particular year's cash flows happen on the last day of the year. We therefore signify the first day of the first year as 'Year 0'.

It's always worth adopting a methodical approach to avoid silly mistakes. Cash inflows are regarded as being positive numbers, whilst cash outflows are regarded as being negative numbers (signified by a minus sign or the use of brackets).

Year	Cash flow in Year	Cumulative Cash flow
0	(£400,000)	(£400,000)
1	£120,000	(£280,000)
2	£180,000	(£100,000)
3	£240,000	£140,000
4	£200,000	£340,000
5	£180,000	£520,000

9 Capital Investment Appraisal

The cumulative cash flow column above merely shows us the overall closing position at the end of each year e.g. at the end of the first year the net position is that the project has still had £280,000 more cash outflows than cash inflows i.e. -£400,000 + £120,000 = -£280,000

At the end of year 2 the cumulative position is still negative i.e. the project has still not paid for itself However by the end of year 3 the position has reversed and there is now a £140,000 cash surplus. So it can be seen that the project achieved payback at some point during year 3, i.e. after 2 years and a certain number of months

In order to ascertain how many months of year 3 were actually required for the project to achieve payback we note that:

- At the beginning of year 3 (which is the same as the end of year 2) the project was still £100,000 in deficit.

- During year 3 the project delivered £240,000 cash inflows

- So the question is what fraction of year 3 was required to turn a -£100,000 starting position into a nil level position. The answer is £100,000 / £240,000 = 0.417 of a year, which is better expressed in months £100,000 / £240,000 x 12 = 5 months

- **Payback period is therefore 2 years and 5 months.**

TUTORIAL NOTE

An alternative way of thinking about it is to say that during the 12 months of the third year, the project generated £240,000 cash inflows i.e. £20,000 cash inflow per month (= £240,000 ÷ 12).

It therefore took 5 months more to pay back the final £100,000 outstanding at the beginning of year 3 (= £100,000 ÷ £20,000 = 5).

Assessing the calculated result for Payback Period

In answer to the question *'What does the payback period tell us'* ... the answer is unfortunately *'very little'* apart from when the initial investment is recouped. However it continues to be a popular 'first screening' method of project appraisal.

Businesses are invariably attracted to projects which provide a rapid payback because this lessens the risks associated with a longer project *(time itself is always a risk factor .... no-one can predict what the future holds)*, and moreover a short payback period then allows the funds to be recycled into other projects.

However, if business and government always shied away from longer-term projects then no major infrastructure projects would ever be started, and no research and development ever undertaken ....so we must be cautious about saying that quick payback is a universally good thing!

Payback period is based on cash flows, which are a more objective measure of performance than profit (as measuring profit involves making accounting estimates, such as over what time period to depreciate capital assets). However the biggest weakness in the payback method of appraisal is that it does not measure the performance of the *whole* project. Any cash flows **after** the payback period are totally ignored which means that two very different projects may in fact produce identical payback periods, as the next example shows.

EXAMPLE

	Project A		Project B	
Year	Cash flow in Year	Cumulative Cash flow	Cash flow in Year	Cumulative Cash flow
0	(£250,000)	(£250,000)	(£250,000)	(£250,000)
1	£100,000	(£150,000)	£100,000	(£150,000)
2	£100,000	(£50,000)	£100,000	(£50,000)
3	£100,000	£50,000	£100,000	£50,000
4	£100,000	£150,000	£60,000	£110,000
5	£100,000	£250,000	£40,000	£150,000

Both project A and project B have identical cash flow profiles until year 3 and have exactly the same payback period of 2½ years. According to the payback period method of assessment therefore they both have equal merit.

However, in years 4 & 5 project A continues to perform strongly whilst project B slows down and ends up with £100,000 less cumulative cash flow than project A. This would not have been picked up purely by looking at payback period which is at best a rough measure of liquidity rather than a serious measure of performance.

OVERVIEW

Pros and Cons of Payback Period

Payback Period

Pros (✔)	Cons (✘)
▪ Simple to calculate	▪ Completely ignores cash flows after initial payback period
▪ Readily understandable	▪ Ignores time value of money
▪ Based on cash flow (so objective)	▪ No measure of project performance
▪ Favours projects which repay quickly	

9 Capital Investment Appraisal

TEST YOUR UNDERSTANDING 2

A company is assessing two projects which both require an initial capital outlay of £50,000.

The two projects are forecast to have the following cash flows:

Project A

Year	Cash flows	Cumulative Cash flow
0	(£50,000)	
1	£10,000	
2	£15,000	
3	£20,000	
4	£25,000	
5	£60,000	

What is the project's payback period (in years & months)?

_____

Project B

Year	Cash flows	Cumulative Cash flow
0	(£50,000)	
1	£40,000	
2	£30,000	
3	£20,000	
4	£25,000	
5	£60,000	

What is the project's payback period (in years & months)?

_____

What are the benefits of a short payback period?

_____

_____

_____

344

9.6 The Time Value of Money

Let's start with a question: *"Would you rather receive £1 today, or £1 in a year's time?"*

There are three reasons why it is preferable to receive money sooner rather than later:

1. **Inflation**

    Most economies tend to experience inflation, an increase in prices which results in a corresponding erosion of the buying power of the same sum of money. In short, £1 will be worth less (in terms of what it will purchase) in a year's time compared to now.

2. **Interest foregone**

    If there was no immediate use for the £1 it could be invested (maybe along with some friends!) and derive some form of return such that in a year's time it would be worth more.

3. **Risk**

    They say that nothing in life is certain ... except death and taxes! There is no certainty that a promise (or expectation) to receive £1 in a year's time will actually come about. Safer to have the £1 now before life's unexpected events get in the way!

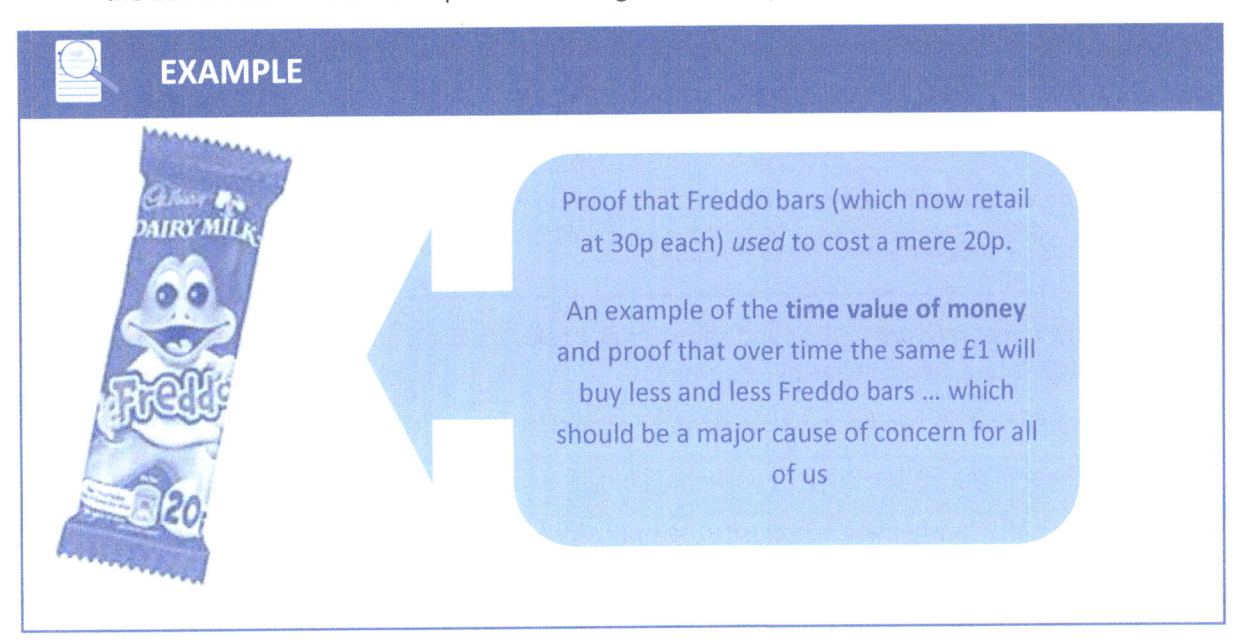

EXAMPLE

Proof that Freddo bars (which now retail at 30p each) *used* to cost a mere 20p.

An example of the **time value of money** and proof that over time the same £1 will buy less and less Freddo bars ... which should be a major cause of concern for all of us

Discounting

If we accept the principle that £1 received today, is worth more than £1 received in a year's time, then the next logical step is to try to quantify this i.e. *how much* **more is it worth?**

The answer to this apparently simple question is actually quite complex as it depends on all three of the reasons listed above as to why it is preferable to receive £1 now rather than £1 later.

To try to answer this question we would need to assess:

1. **Inflation**: By how much would the purchasing power of the £1 have decreased over the year we had to wait to receive it?

2. **Interest foregone**: How much return could have been achieved by investing the £1 received now over the 12 months we would otherwise have waited?

3. **Risk**: What level of risk is there that the £1 will not be paid in 12 months' time?

9 Capital Investment Appraisal

When combined together, these three factors will determine how much extra an investor would wish to receive in a year's time to financially compensate them for *not* receiving the money now. This required level of compensation is known as the investor's *'cost of capital'* and exactly how this is derived is a subject we will return to later.

However, to allow us to answer the immediate question of *'how much would £1 received now be worth in a year's time?'* we will simplify matters by assuming that the *only* relevant factor is the bank interest which could be gained if the £1 were invested now (the second reason on our list) i.e. so we shall ignore inflation (i.e. assume it is zero) and also ignore the risk of non-payment in a year's time.

To make the numbers simpler we will assume that the rate of bank interest which could be achieved is 10% per annum (which would be impressive to say the least when the Bank of England current base rate is 0.5%, but at least it makes the numbers easier to follow).

So £1 received now could be put into the bank where it would earn 10% interest so that in a year's time it would be worth:

$$£1.00 \text{ (Now)} \times 1.1 = £1.10 \text{ (1 year from now)}$$

> **TUTORIAL NOTE**
>
> **Why 1.1?**
>
> Because the '1' is the original £1 and the '0.1' is the 10% interest received.
>
> In 1 year's time we get both back our original £1 plus the 10% interest.
>
> Now grab *a pocket calculator and follow through………..*

We have gone 1 year *forward in time* and shown that £1.00 (received now) is worth £1.10 (in a year's time) when 10% interest could have been earned.

Now let's reverse that and go *back in time* remembering that:

- Going back in time is the 'time opposite' of going forwards in time
- Dividing is the 'mathematical opposite' of multiplication

If   £1.00 (now) x 1.1 = £1.10 (1 years' time)   i.e. Multiplying to go forwards

Then   £1.00 (1 years' time) / 1.1 = £0.909 (now)   i.e. Divide to go backwards in time

Try this out by entering 1.00 into a calculator and dividing it by 1.1. The answer will be 0.9090909090 etc. (about 91 pence approximately). Leave this figure in your calculator for a moment.

Now to prove to yourself that this figure of £0.909090909 etc. would be worth £1.00 exactly in a year's time (if invested in a bank account paying 10% interest) take the 0.9090909 etc. number in your calculator and multiply it by 1.1 as follows:

$$£0.909 \text{ etc. (now)} \times 1.1 = £1.00 \text{ (1 years' time)}$$

The Language of Business

> ### ⚠️ KEY POINT
>
> We have just proved that if we could earn 10% interest and we had £0.909 now we could invest it and it would be worth £1.00 in one years' time.
>
> i.e. The 'Present Value' of £1.00 received one year from now is £0.909 (with a 10% interest rate). We say that the 'discounted value' of £1.00 received a year from now is £0.909 with a 10% discount factor.

CALCULATIONS

Continue to follow through on a calculator ………

Question: How much would £1.00 (received now) be worth in 2 years' time if left in a bank earning 10% interest?

Answer: £1.00 x 1.10 x 1.10 = £1.21 ……… *or if you prefer £1.00 x (1.1)^2*

i.e. £1.00 x 1.1 = £1.10 after one year, and £1.10 x 1.1 = £1.21 after 2 years

Now going backwards in time ……

Question: How much is £1.00 received in 2 years' time worth today? (interest rate = 10%)

Answer: £1.00 ÷ 1.10 ÷ 1.10 = £0.826……… *or if you prefer £1.00 ÷ (1.1)^2*

i.e. The 'Present Value' of £1.00 received two years from now is £0.826 with a 10% interest rate. We say that the 'discounted value' of £1.00 received two years from now is £0.826 with a 10% discount factor.

- Again, to prove to yourself that these two figures are financially equivalent imagine you had £0.826 now and invested it in a bank paying 10% interest for two years.
- In two years' time you would have: £0.826 x 1.1 x 1.1 = £1.00   (you'll need all the decimal places to get exactly £1.00).
- So receiving £1.00 in two years' time is the same as receiving £0.826 now. They are equivalent amounts.

TUTORIAL NOTE

In practice we don't need to perform all these fiddly calculations (which would get increasingly onerous as we look further and further into the future) and instead we make use of 'discount tables' where all the 'number-crunching' has already been done for us.

A discount table follows. To find the present value of any figure simply select the appropriate discount rate column, and the row for the number of years into the future the sum will be received, and look-up the discount factor where they intersect.

9 Capital Investment Appraisal

OVERVIEW

Discount table

Years	1%	2%	3%	4%	5%	6%	7%	8%	9%	10%
1	0.990	0.980	0.971	0.962	0.952	0.943	0.935	0.926	0.917	0.909
2	0.980	0.961	0.943	0.925	0.907	0.890	0.873	0.857	0.842	0.826
3	0.971	0.942	0.915	0.889	0.864	0.840	0.816	0.794	0.772	0.751
4	0.961	0.924	0.888	0.855	0.823	0.792	0.763	0.735	0.708	0.683
5	0.951	0.906	0.863	0.822	0.784	0.747	0.713	0.681	0.650	0.621
6	0.942	0.888	0.837	0.790	0.746	0.705	0.666	0.630	0.596	0.564
7	0.933	0.871	0.813	0.760	0.711	0.665	0.623	0.583	0.547	0.513
8	0.923	0.853	0.789	0.731	0.677	0.627	0.582	0.540	0.502	0.467
9	0.914	0.837	0.766	0.703	0.645	0.592	0.544	0.500	0.460	0.424
10	0.905	0.820	0.744	0.676	0.614	0.558	0.508	0.463	0.422	0.386

EXAMPLE

The discount factor for a sum received in 2 years' time at a discount rate of 10% is 0.826 (as previously calculated manually).

Years	1%	2%	3%	4%	5%	6%	7%	8%	9%	10%
1	0.990	0.980	0.971	0.962	0.952	0.943	0.935	0.926	0.917	0.909
2	0.980	0.961	0.943	0.925	0.907	0.890	0.873	0.857	0.842	0.826
3	0.971	0.942	0.915	0.889	0.864	0.840	0.816	0.794	0.772	0.751
4	0.961	0.924	0.888	0.855	0.823	0.792	0.763	0.735	0.708	0.683
5	0.951	0.906	0.863	0.822	0.784	0.747	0.713	0.681	0.650	0.621

Now simply multiply whatever sum will be received in two years' time by 0.826 and the result will be its 'present value' i.e. the equivalent sum today.

Full sets of the discount tables will typically go up to 20% discount rates and 20 years into the future. The above is just an example extract of a full table.

9.7 The cost of capital

We have already mentioned that investors will demand a certain return before entering into a specific investment and that this required return will determined by:

1. **The rate of inflation in the economy ….** because there is little point in investing funds and receiving a return that is less than the rate of inflation, as effectively the investment would be losing money in real terms (i.e. with regard to its buying power).

2. **The interest (and alternative returns) foregone ….** because an investor always has choices in where to invest their money and any proposed investment has to look attractive compared to the alternatives.

3. **The level of risk associated with the potential investment….** because if an investment is perceived as being high risk then investors will demand a higher potential return to compensate for this additional risk. A base level of risk is often taken to be investing in government bonds ('gilts') which *should* be very low risk i.e. the government *should* repay you when the bond matures.

We are considering the cost of capital from the perspective of a company considering investing in a capital project, and realising that because some of the cash flows from the project will be received later rather than sooner, some adjustment needs to be made to their worth i.e. future cash flows need to be 'discounted' to their 'present value' as seen in the last section. The question is at what rate should these future cash flows be discounted i.e. what is the company's cost of capital?

The short answer to this is that a company's cost of capital will in turn depend on the expectations of the people financing the company. As we saw in chapter 3 the two main sources of long term finance are from either shareholders (equity finance), or lenders such as the bank (debt finance).

From the company's perspective they must ensure that any proposed capital projects deliver at least the levels of returns that they are having to pay out to their shareholders and lenders. Let's briefly look at each in turn:

Shareholders

will have a certain expectation of the level of dividends (i.e. return) they expect to receive compared to the value of the shares they hold. This will partly be based on the returns they could expect to receive from the stock market in general, and partly based on the level of risk associated with the specific company in question.

Lenders

such as banks and bondholders generally expect lower returns than shareholders because their investment risk is lower. Debt interest to lenders is paid in priority before dividends to shareholders. In the event of a company failing the lenders are paid before the shareholders. Furthermore bank lending is often 'secured' on the assets of the company giving the bank immediate recourse if the company fails to repay the loan.

Of course, depending on the level of gearing (see Chapter 3) some companies derive more or less of their total long-term funding from debt than others. The final average cost of capital for a company will be the '**Weighted Average Cost of Capital**' (WACC) based on the relative proportion of funding derived from debt and equity (and the costs of both respectively).

However, there is a body of opinion that the cost of capital that is used to discount future cash flows from a project should not be the WACC (weighted average cost of capital), but instead the cost of the actual direct source of capital that will fund the specific project in question!

9 Capital Investment Appraisal

> **TUTORIAL NOTE**
>
> There are many competing theories for how the cost of capital should be calculated and it remains a hotly debated area of corporate finance theory.
>
> However, you will be pleased to hear that for our purposes you will always be given a cost of capital which can be used to discount future cash flows to find their present value!

9.8 Net Present Value (NPV)

> **DEFINITION**
>
> **Net Present Value (NPV)** is an appraisal method that takes into account all the cash flows from a project and discounts all future cash flows to their equivalent present value (at whatever discount factor represents that particular company's cost of capital).
>
> This combination of:
>
> - including all cash inflows and all cash outflows over the entire life of the project, and
> - making an allowance for the timing of those cash flows
>
> makes the NPV method a powerful technique for capital investment appraisal.

> **EXAMPLE**
>
> **Scenario**
>
> A project requires the purchase of equipment costing £100,000. The project will then provide positive net cash inflows of £20,000 for a period of five years. The residual value of the equipment will be £10,000.
>
> The company has a 7% cost of capital.
>
> **What is the Net Present Value of the project?**
>
> **Based on the NPV alone, should the project proceed?**
>
> **Solution**
>
> A methodical approach should be adopted to ensure accurate results.
>
> - All cash flows are deemed to have occurred on the last day of each year, and the initial investment on day 1 is therefore indicated as having occurred on the last day of year 0
> - The un-discounted cash flows are entered, including the assumed sale of the equipment at the end of year 5 (which represents a cash inflow)
> - The discount factors are entered from the 7% column of the discount tables. The assumed sale of the equipment at the end of year 5 is put on a separate row for clarity but is also discounted at 7%

- Row by row, the non-discounted cash flow is multiplied by the discount factor to find the Present Value (PV) of each cash flow

- The initial ('day 1') cash outflow has a discount factor of 1.000 i.e. £1 today is worth £1

- The total figure for the non-discounted cash flows is not strictly required, but we include it now to show the effect of discounting

- The Present Values (PV) of the cash flows are totalled (remembering that cash outflows are negative whilst cash inflows are positive) to find the Net Present Value (NPV) for the project

Year	Cash flow	Discount Factor	PV of Cash flow
0	(£100,000)	1.000	(£100,000)
1	£20,000	0.935	£18,700
2	£20,000	0.873	£17,460
3	£20,000	0.816	£16,320
4	£20,000	0.763	£15,260
5	£20,000	0.713	£14,260
5	£10,000	0.713	£7,130
Total	£10,000		Net Present Value = (£10,870)

- **The project shows an NPV of (£10,870)** i.e. *having taken into account the time value of money* the project is returning £10,870 *less* than has been invested. The project is therefore clearly not worthwhile as it leads to reduced shareholder wealth.

- It is worth noting that if we had *not* discounted the cash flows then it would have appeared that the project delivered a £10,000 cash surplus and was therefore worthwhile. This flawed conclusion however assumes that inflation is zero, there is zero risk in the project and that the shareholders have zero expectations of a return i.e. a cost of capital of 0%!

- However when we include all of the above factors we realise that the business in fact has to 'pay' a **7% cost of capital** each year.

- By the time we have factored this in, it is obvious that the project is not viable. In today's value of money the project would be returning less to the company than the cost the company incurs to raise the original £100,000 in the first place.

Assessing the calculated result for Net Present Value (NPV)

As demonstrated above, the final NPV must be positive for the project to be worthwhile.

- **A positive NPV** means that at today's value of money the project is returning *more* money than it cost. It is therefore *worthwhile* as it *increases* shareholder value

- **A negative NPV** means that at today's value of money the project is returning *less* money than it cost. It is therefore *not worthwhile* as it will *decrease* shareholder value

The general rule is to proceed with projects with a positive NPV. If there are several competing projects, proceed with the project with the largest NPV. However one weakness of the NPV method is that it does not relate the final calculated NPV to the cash inflow required to achieve it... i.e. it does

9 Capital Investment Appraisal

not give a percentage return so that we can judge how hard the original investment has been made to work.

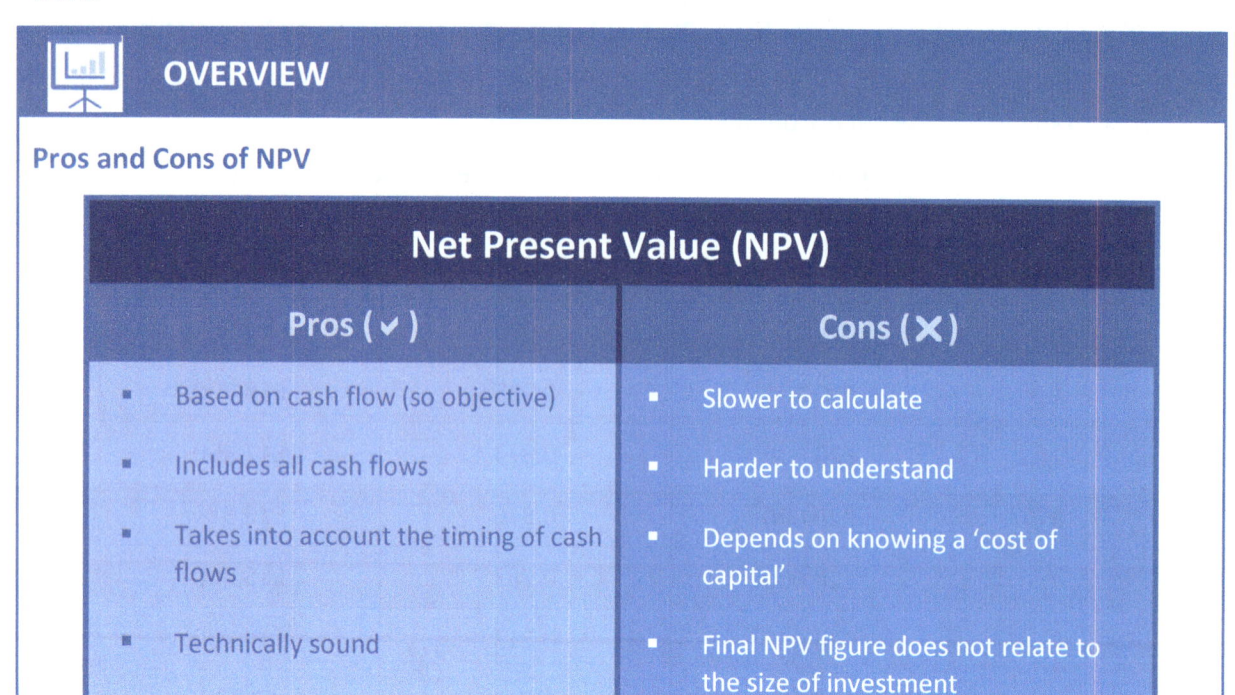

> **OVERVIEW**
>
> **Pros and Cons of NPV**
>
> | Net Present Value (NPV) | |
> |---|---|
> | **Pros (✓)** | **Cons (✗)** |
> | ▪ Based on cash flow (so objective) | ▪ Slower to calculate |
> | ▪ Includes all cash flows | ▪ Harder to understand |
> | ▪ Takes into account the timing of cash flows | ▪ Depends on knowing a 'cost of capital' |
> | ▪ Technically sound | ▪ Final NPV figure does not relate to the size of investment |

> **KEY POINT**
>
> Net Present Value is often considered to be the most robust of all the appraisal methods being based on objective cash flows, taking into account the whole project and the time value of money. Furthermore it is technically robust enough to handle irregular cash flow profiles (such as projects which require additional cash injections at a later date).
>
> However the big drawback with NPV is that it doesn't provide any indication of how the NPV performance compares to the size of the original investment i.e. although it reports an *absolute* return (i.e. in £), it does not report a *relative* return (i.e. in %).

9.9 Internal Rate of Return (IRR)

A 'conventional' project consists of an initial cash outflow (i.e. incurred now), followed by a series of subsequent cash inflows (i.e. received later). We need to recognise two factors relating to the discounting of future cash flows:

i. As we saw with the NPV technique ….the present value of these delayed cash inflows was lessened the longer we had to wait to receive the cash.

ii. In addition, the present value of the subsequent cash inflows is also lessened if a higher cost of capital is applied i.e. future cash flows are then more heavily discounted which results in smaller present values.

Both of these factors can be immediately seen by looking at a discount table (extract below).

The Language of Business

EXAMPLE

Years	1%	2%	3%	4%	5%	6%	7%	8%	9%	10%
1	0.990	0.980	0.971	0.962	0.952	0.943	0.935	0.926	0.917	0.909
2	0.980	0.961	0.943	0.925	0.907	0.890	0.873	0.857	0.842	0.826
3	0.971	0.942	0.915	0.889	0.864	0.840	0.816	0.794	0.772	0.751
4	0.961	0.924	0.888	0.855	0.823	0.792	0.763	0.735	0.708	0.683
5	0.951	0.906	0.863	0.822	0.784	0.747	0.713	0.681	0.650	0.621
6	0.942	0.888	0.837	0.790	0.746	0.705	0.666	0.630	0.596	0.564
7	0.933	0.871	0.813	0.760	0.711	0.665	0.623	0.583	0.547	0.513
8	0.923	0.853	0.789	0.731	0.677	0.627	0.582	0.540	0.502	0.467
9	0.914	0.837	0.766	0.703	0.645	0.592	0.544	0.500	0.460	0.424
10	0.905	0.820	0.744	0.676	0.614	0.558	0.508	0.463	0.422	0.386

If, for example, a cash inflow (being discounted at 5%) is received in 2 years' time it is discounted to 0.907 of its value. However if received in 3 years' time it is more heavily discounted to 0.864 of its value.

> *So the longer a business has to wait for future cash inflows the less they are worth (in today's terms)*

Similarly if (say) a cash flow being received in 4 years' time is subjected to a 9% cost of capital it will be discounted to 0.708 of its value, but if the cost of capital were increase to 10% it would be more heavily discounted, to 0.683 of its value.

> *So the higher a business's cost of capital the less future cash inflows are worth (in today's terms)*

Our final capital investment appraisal technique 'Internal Rate of Return', specifically looks at the effect that an increased cost of capital has on the overall viability of a project, as follows:

- A 'conventional' project consists an initial cash outflow (i.e. now), followed by a series of subsequent cash inflows (i.e. later).
- The higher a business's cost of capital, the more severe the discounting of future cash inflows will become (and so they will be worth less in today's value of money).
- Therefore, as the cost of capital increases the Net Present Value (NPV) will reduce.
- At a certain cost of capital the NPV will have reduced to £nil and at that cost of capital the project is no longer worthwhile i.e. at that cost of capital the present value of the future cash inflows no longer exceeds the cash outflows.
- The cost of capital at which the NPV=0 is known as the **'Internal Rate of Return'**.

9 Capital Investment Appraisal

Calculating the Internal Rate of Return

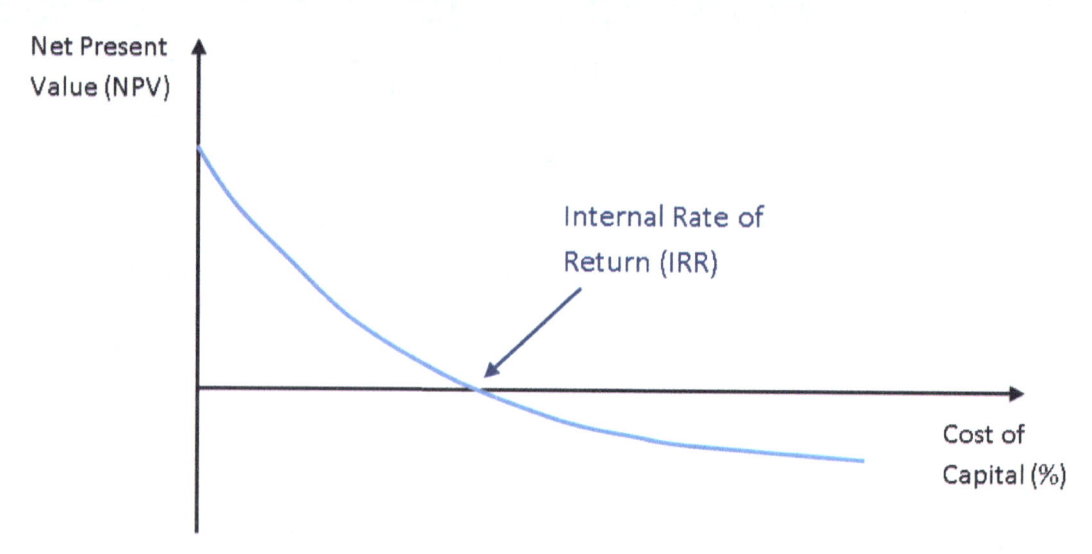

[Graph showing NPV decreasing curve against Cost of Capital (%), crossing the x-axis at the Internal Rate of Return (IRR)]

The above graph shows how the NPV of a project decreases as discounting (i.e. the cost of capital applied to future cash inflows) increases:

- **Lower costs of capital** (less than the IRR) result in **positive Net Present Values** i.e. the project is worthwhile and should proceed

- **Higher costs of capital** (more than the IRR) result in a **negative Net Present Values** i.e. the project is not worthwhile and should therefore be rejected

- At one certain cost of capital figure (the IRR) the Net Present Value is exactly £nil, and this represents the **'break-even' cost of capital**

In order to find this point where the NPV = £nil we use a mathematical technique called linear interpolation in which we calculate two NPVs:

- One using a *lower* cost of capital …. which should produce a *positive* NPV
- One using a *higher* cost of capital … which should produce a *negative* NPV

… and then use the formula below to estimate the cost of capital figure at which point the decreasing NPV line crosses the axis i.e. the IRR where NPV = £nil

$$IRR = A + \left（\frac{NPV(A)}{NPV(A) - NPV(B)}\right） \times (B-A)$$

Where:

- Discount Factor A produces NPV(A) and
- Discount Factor B produces NPV (B)

Remember NPV(B) is negative, and that a double negative means 'add'!

If you are mathematically minded you can quickly prove the above formula to yourself using the concept of 'similar triangles' (see below):

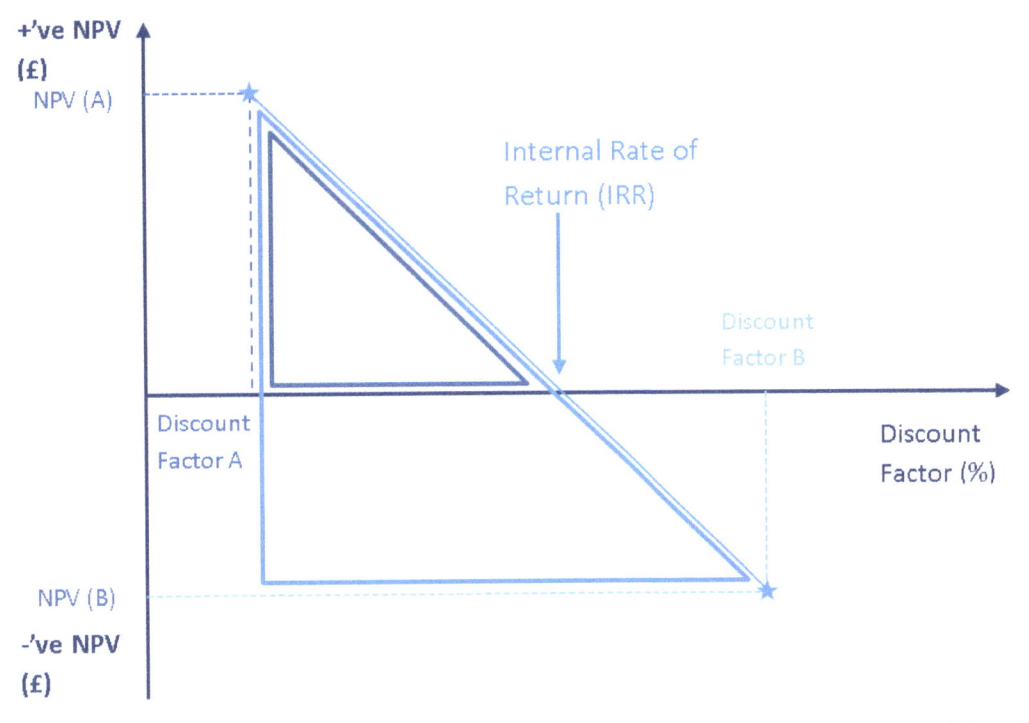

You can also use Microsoft Excel to calculate the IRR of a cash flow projection but this will give a slightly different (actually more accurate) answer to the formula above as Excel uses an iterative technique (i.e. multiple re-calculations to get ever closer to an accurate solution).

CALCULATIONS

Scenario

When discounted at 5% a project has an NPV of £30,000 but when discounted at 10% the same project has an NPV of (£12,000).

What is the IRR of the project?

Solution

$$IRR = A + \left(\frac{NPV(A)}{NPV(A) - NPV(B)} \right) \times (B-A)$$

A = Lower cost of capital = 5%

B = Higher cost of capital = 10%

NPV (A) = NPV at cost of capital A = £30,000

NPV (B) = NPV at cost of capital B = (£12,000)

(NPV(A) – NPV(B) = £30,000 + £12,000 = £42,000 ... because two negatives make a positive)

IRR = 5% + {£30,000 / (£30,000 + £12,000)} × (10% - 5%) = **8.6%**

The internal rate of return (i.e. the cost of capital at which the NPV = £nil) is 8.6%.

We can sense check this result as being reasonable because it falls between 5% (positive NPV) and 10% (negative NPV).

9 Capital Investment Appraisal

Interpretation of IRR

The IRR of a project is essentially a measure of risk ….namely the risk the project will not be worthwhile when the company's cost of capital is taken into account. We'll illustrate this using the IRR calculated above of 8.6%.

In all of these scenarios it is assumed that the cost of capital is based purely on the cost (or opportunity cost) of funding this specific project *(and not on the **Weighted Average Cost of Capital**)*.

EXAMPLES

Scenario 1

The company in question does not have spare cash reserves and so needs to borrow the funds for this project. The company does not have a particularly good credit rating and so the bank will only lend them money at a fixed rate of interest of 10%

- ➤ **Clearly the project should be rejected. An IRR of 8.6% shows that for any cost of capital higher than this (such as the 10% proposed by the bank) the Net Present Value will be negative. That is, the present value of the cash inflows (when discounted at 10%) will be less than the project cash outflows, meaning a cash loss in real terms.**

Scenario 2

The company in question does not have spare cash reserves and so needs to borrow the funds for the project. Their bank offers to lend the money at a variable rate of 7% over Bank of England base rate.

- ➤ **The Bank of England base rate is currently 0.5%, so the initial borrowing rate would be 7.5% (and this is therefore the initial cost of capital). At this rate the project would *just* be worthwhile as any cost of capital up to 8.6% will produce a positive NPV. The question is what is the risk of the Bank of England's base rate increasing to such a point that the project is no longer worthwhile (a base rate increase to anything over 1.6% would produce a cost of capital higher than the IRR).**

Scenario 3

The company in question has sufficient cash reserves to self-fund the project but those cash reserves are presently invested in an interest bearing bank account currently earning 2% pa (but this is a variable rate which might change). Therefore, if they are withdrawn and used for the project this will represent a 2% 'opportunity cost', which is the company's cost of capital (at least initially).

- ➤ **The cash for the initial investment into the project can be withdrawn from the bank account at which point it will stop earning interest, and as and when the project delivers cash inflows these can be repaid back into the interest bearing bank account (and start gaining interest again). These internal reinvestments of the cash inflows into the interest bearing bank account would have to earn 8.6% interest before the project ceased to be worthwhile i.e. if the variable rate of interest on the bank account rose to 8.6% or higher it would no longer be worthwhile investing the funds in the project, they may as well be left in the bank simply earning interest.**

- ➤ **The name "Internal Rate of Return" makes a little more sense when the idea of internally reinvesting the future cash inflows from the project is considered e.g. 'the project remains worthwhile whilst we can only internally re-invest at less than an 8.6% return". However, in truth *'Internal Rate of Return'* must surely win some sort of prize in the "Unhelpful Name" category of the accountancy & finance sector annual awards!**

OVERVIEW

Pros and Cons of IRR

Internal Rate of Return (IRR)

Pros (✓)	Cons (✗)
Based on cash flow (so objective)	Slower to calculate
Includes all cash flows	Harder to understand
Takes into account the timing of cash flows	Depends on knowing a 'cost of capital'
% result can be used to compare alternative projects	Can be technically flawed with irregular cash flows
IRR can be compared to business's cost of capital to identify risk	Does not distinguish between absolute size of projects

⚠ KEY POINT

Internal Rate of Return possesses many qualities considered desirable for a robust and objective appraisal of capital expenditure. It is based on cash-flow which is arguably more 'real world' than an appraisal of profit. It considers the whole life of the project and very importantly takes the time-value of money into account.

However what it *doesn't* do is to produce a final £ figure for how much net benefit a project is forecast to deliver. This is actually the inverse criticism of Net Present Value (which *does* provide a £ result, but *not* a % result) and so NPV and IRR are commonly used together in a complimentary fashion.

Although technically NPV is the more robust of the methods (as unconventional cash flows will still produce valid NPVs ... whereas they might produce meaningless multiple IRRs), many decision makers in business actually prefer to base a final choice of project on IRR because of the ease of simply ranking projects according to % return!

9 Capital Investment Appraisal

TEST YOUR UNDERSTANDING 3

A company is appraising a project which has the following cash flow forecast. The company can borrow funds at a variable rate of interest. The <u>current</u> rate of interest is 8%.

Complete the table below to ascertain whether the project would be worthwhile whilst the interest rate is 8%.

Year	Cash flow	Discount Factor @ 8%	Present Value
0	(£2,000)		
1	£500		
2	£500		
3	£600		
4	£600		
5	£440		
		Net Present Value =	

Is the project worthwhile whilst interest rates are 8%?

_____

Now evaluate whether the project would be worthwhile if the interest rate increased to 12%.

Year	Cash flow	Discount Factor @ 12%	Present Value
0	(£2,000)		
1	£500		
2	£500		
3	£600		
4	£600		
5	£440		
		Net Present Value =	

Is the project worthwhile whilst interest rates increase to 12%?

_____

Now estimate what rate of interest would result in the project delivering a Net Present Value of £nil......... and hence no longer being worthwhile

$$IRR = A + \left(\frac{NPV(A)}{NPV(A) - NPV(B)} \right) \times (B-A)$$

Do you consider the difference between the current interest rate and the 'break-even' interest rate to be a sufficient margin of safety to proceed with the project?

9 Capital Investment Appraisal

> ⚠️ **KEY POINTS FROM CHAPTER 9**
>
> **Capital Investment Decisions**
> - Capex decisions tend to involve significant sums of money being invested for long periods of time, hence the importance of appraisal methods to ensure the correct decision is taken.
> - Investment decisions often have to rank potential projects because of capital rationing:
>   - Soft Capital Rationing: self-imposed by the business itself
>   - Hard Capital Rationing: external limitations imposed by lenders.
>
> **Accounting Rate of Return (ARR)**
>
> $$ARR = \frac{\text{Average Profit (£)}}{\text{Average Investment (£)}} \times 100\%$$
>
> - Based on accounting principles, so average profit is measured after depreciation (i.e. after the potential project has paid for itself) and the average investment is the average Net Book Value (NBV) of the investment (i.e. after it has been depreciated each year). The standard profit figure to use is Operating Profit (i.e. Profit before Interest and Taxation).
> - ARR is simple to calculate and a readily understandable percentage measure, which can provide a relative assessment between different projects. It takes account of the entire life of the project but takes no account of the time value of money, and is based on profits which are more subjective than cash flows.
>
> **Payback Period**
> - The **Payback Period** of a project is simply the length of time for cash inflows from the project to cover the initial investment cash outflow.
> - It is a simple to calculate and simple to understand measure of how long a project will take to recoup the initial investment. It is based on cash flow (and so is objective) and favours projects which repay quickly. However it totally ignores cash flows after the initial payback period and the time value of money.
> - Payback gives no indication of project performance and is at best a rough measure of liquidity.
>
> **The Time Value of Money**
> There are three reasons why it is preferable to receive money earlier rather than later:
> i. Inflation - The buying power of money tends to lessen over time
> ii. Returns Forgone - Cash received now could be invested to produce a return
> iii. Risk - An expectation to receive money in the future is not certain
> - Discounting is the process of calculating an equivalent 'present value' of an anticipated future cash receipt. The further into the future cash receipts are expected the less their present value will be.
> - Every business must estimate its own 'cost of capital' which takes into account all three reasons why it is preferable to receive money sooner rather than later.
> - Discount tables are used to look-up a 'discount factor' which is then used to 'discount' every future anticipated cash flow back to today's 'present value'. The discount factor is based on both the delay in receiving the funds and the cost of capital.

The Language of Business

Net Present Value (NPV)

- NPV takes into account all the cash flows from a project and discounts all future cash flows to their equivalent present value (at whatever discount factor represents that particular company's cost of capital).
- **A positive NPV** means that at today's value of money the project is returning *more* money than it cost. It is therefore *worthwhile* as it *increases* shareholder value.
- **A negative NPV** means that at today's value of money the project is returning *less* money than it cost. It is therefore *not worthwhile* as it will *decrease* shareholder value.
- NPV is considered to be the most technically sound appraisal method. It is based on all of the project's cash flows, and takes into account the time value of money. However it is slower to calculate and harder to understand, and depends on knowing a 'cost of capital'. It provides an absolute £ result as opposed to a relative % measure.

Internal Rate of Return (IRR)

- As the cost of capital increases, future cash flows are more heavily discounted and become worth less at today's value of money (i.e. the NPV will be less). At a certain discount factor (i.e. cost of capital) the NPV will reduce to £nil.
- The cost of capital at which the NPV=0 is known as the 'Internal Rate of Return' (IRR).
- IRR is based on discounted cash flows and so is an objective measure, but unfortunately can be technically flawed with irregular cash flows. It is slow to calculate and harder to understand, and it requires the cost of capital to be known in order to assess the relative risk of the project.
- It provides a relative % measure as opposed to an absolute £ result and so is a valuable complimentary measure to NPV.

9 Capital Investment Appraisal

Chapter 9: Test Your Understanding Answers

TEST YOUR UNDERSTANDING 1

Average profit per annum = (£12,000 + £18,000 + £30,000 + £25,000 + £5,000) ÷ 5 = £18,000

Average capital employed = (£50,000 + £10,000) ÷ 2 = £30,000

ARR = Average profit per annum ÷ Average capital employed x 100%

= £18,000 ÷ £30,000 x 100% = 60%

Should this project proceed? **Yes, definitely!**

TEST YOUR UNDERSTANDING 2

Project A

Year	Cash flows	Cumulative Cash flow
0	(£50,000)	(£50,000)
1	£10,000	(£40,000)
2	£15,000	(£25,000)
3	£20,000	(£5,000)
4	£25,000	£20,000
5	£60,000	£80,000

Payback period = **3 years and 3 months** *(5,000 / 25,000 x 12 = 2.4 months)*

N.B. Always round up to a whole number of months

Project B

Year	Cash flows	Cumulative Cash flow
0	(£50,000)	(£50,000)
1	£40,000	(£10,000)
2	£30,000	£20,000
3	£20,000	£40,000
4	£25,000	£65,000
5	£60,000	£125,000

Payback period = **1 year and 4 months** *(£10,000 / £30,000 x 12 = 4 months)*

Benefits of a short payback period:

- Time equals risk, so a shorter payback always represents a lower risk

- The cash is recycled faster allowing lower borrowing and/or reinvestment in other projects.

TEST YOUR UNDERSTANDING 3

Year	Cash flow	Discount Factor @ 8%	Present Value
0	(£2,000)	1.000	(£2,000)
1	£500	0.926	£463
2	£500	0.857	£429
3	£600	0.794	£476
4	£600	0.735	£441
5	£440	0.681	£300
		Net Present Value =	£109

Is the project worthwhile whilst interest rates are 8%? **Yes, a positive return of £108 at today's value.**

Year	Cash flow	Discount Factor @ 12%	Present Value
0	(£2,000)	1.000	(£2,000)
1	£500	0.893	£447
2	£500	0.797	£399
3	£600	0.712	£427
4	£600	0.636	£382
5	£440	0.567	£249
		Net Present Value =	(£96)

Is the project worthwhile whilst interest rates increase to 12%? **No, it returns less that the original cost (at today's values).**

IRR = 8 + { £109 / (£109 - - £96) x (12-8) } = 10.1%

(N.B. Double negative = Addition, so £109 - - £96 = £205)

At an interest rate of ~10% the project delivers an NPV of £nil, hence the Internal rate of Return is 10%.

The variable interest rate would only need to increase by 2% for the project to no longer be worthwhile. An increase of *greater* than 2% would result in the project delivering less than its initial cost (at today's value of money), and hence would result in a reduction in shareholder value!

As such this project would appear to be too marginal in terms of its benefit and risk and it should be rejected.

9 Capital Investment Appraisal

Chapter 9: End of Chapter Exercises

Section A Questions

Question 9.1

Why is it important to fully appraise proposed capital investments before committing funds?

- A Capital expenditure typically involves large sums of money
- B Capital expenditure relates to long-term decisions
- C Businesses unable to undertake all desired capital projects will need a way of prioritising between them
- D All of the above

Question 9.2

Certain capital investment appraisal methods take into account the 'time value of money' which discounts the value of cash received in the future.

Which of the following statements explain this preference to receive cash sooner rather than later?

- A Inflation will erode the buying power of cash over time
- B Cash received now can be invested and make an immediate return
- C Time equates to risk. Receiving cash now eliminates the risk of not receiving it later.
- D All of the above

Question 9.3

Which of the following options represent the two appraisal methods which <u>both</u> take into account the 'time value of money'?

- i. Payback
- ii. Accounting Rate of Return
- iii. Net Present Value
- iv. Internal Rate of Return

Choose the correct combination of the options:

- A i & iv
- B ii & iii
- C iii & iv
- D ii & iv

Question 9.4

Which of the following is generally regarded as being the most technically accurate method of capital investment appraisal?

A   Payback

B   Accounting Rate of Return

C   Net Present Value

D   Internal Rate of Return

Question 9.5

A project costing £200,000 has the following expected cash flows:

Year	0	1	2	3	4	5
Annual Cash flow	(£200,000)	£100,000	£80,000	£60,000	£50,000	£45,000

What is the payback period of the project?

A   2 years 3 months

B   2 years 4 months

C   3 years 3 months

D   3 years 4 months

Question 9.6

A proposed project involves purchasing machinery at a cost of £620,000. The machinery will be depreciated on a straight-line basis over six years and have a residual value of £80,000.

The project is expected to deliver the following operating profits over its life:

Year	1	2	3	4	5	6
Annual Profit	£50,000	£55,000	£60,000	£60,000	£45,000	£40,000

What is the expected accounting rate of return?

A   8%

B   13%

C   15%

D   19%

9 Capital Investment Appraisal

Question 9.7

The details of a proposed project are as follows:

- Initial capital outlay = £300,000
- Subsequent annual cash inflows = £80,000 per annum
- Life of the project = 4 years
- Residual value of investment = £nil
- Cost of Capital = 6%

What is the Net Present Value of the project?

A £20,000

B (£20,000)

C £22,800

D (£22,800)

Is the project worth undertaking? _____

Question 9.8

The NPV on a proposed project has been evaluated at two different costs of capital as follows:

At a 10% cost of capital: NPV = £45,000. At a 20% cost of capital: NPV = (£15,000)

At what cost of capital will the Net Present Value be equal to zero?

A 13.3%

B 15.8%

C 17.5%

D 19.2%

Question 9.9

Which of the following statements best illustrates an example of 'soft capital rationing'?

A The company's bank refusing to lend above a certain amount of funds

B A lack of credible capital projects being proposed to use the available capital funds

C A 'soft' Finance Director who is easily convinced to sign-off on projects

D An internal self-imposed limit on a company's planned capital expenditure

Question 9.10

Which of the following statements best illustrates an example of 'hard capital rationing'?

A The company's bank refusing to lend above a certain amount of funds

B A lack of credible capital projects being proposed to use the available capital funds

C A 'hard' Finance Director who is resistant to signing-off on projects

D An internal self-imposed limit on a company's planned capital expenditure

Section B Questions

Question 9.11

You are acting as a management consultant to the company Kirkstall Ltd who are trying to decide which of two different proposed projects (Project Gemini & Project Taurus) to implement.

Both projects require an initial investment of £100,000 and are expected to last for 5 years but Kirkstall Ltd can only afford to progress one of the projects.

The projected cash flows & profits relating to both projects are as follows:

Project Gemini

Year	Cashflow	Profit
0	(£100,000)	
1	£45,000	£15,000
2	£40,000	£10,000
3	£35,000	£8,000
4	£10,000	£5,000
5	£10,000	£2,000

Project Taurus

Year	Cashflow	Profit
0	(£100,000)	
1	£10,000	£nil
2	£20,000	£5,000
3	£30,000	£8,000
4	£40,000	£12,000
5	£45,000	£20,000

The initial £100,000 investment will have no residual value at the end of the five year period. Kirkstall Ltd use a straight-line method of depreciation.

As their management consultant you are required to advise Kirkstall Ltd on the relative financial merits of each proposal using the following methods of capital investment appraisal:

a) Payback
b) Accounting Rate of Return
c) Net Present Value
d) Internal rate of Return

9 Capital Investment Appraisal

Complete all of the following tables to ascertain the relative merits of both potential projects. You should advise your client (Kirkstall Ltd) about the relative pros & cons of each method of capital investment appraisal. Kirkstall Ltd.'s cost of capital is 10% per annum.

(a) Payback Method

Project Gemini	Cash flow	Cumulative Cash flow
Year 0	(£100,000)	
Year 1	£45,000	
Year 2	£40,000	
Year 3	£35,000	
Year 4	£10,000	
Year 5	£10,000	

Project Gemini Payback Period: _____

Project Taurus	Cash flow	Cumulative Cash flow
Year 0	£100,000	
Year 1	£10,000	
Year 2	£20,000	
Year 3	£30,000	
Year 4	£40,000	
Year 5	£45,000	

Project Taurus Payback Period: _____

Using Payback which project looks more favourable?

_____

Benefits of Payback Method:

_____

_____

Drawbacks of Payback Method:

_____

_____

(b) Accounting Rate of Return (ARR) Method

$$ARR = \text{Average Profit} / \text{Average Investment} \times 100\%$$

Project Gemini Average Annual Profit: _____

Project Gemini Average Investment: _____

Project Gemini ARR: _____

Project Taurus Average Annual Profit: _____

Project Taurus Average Investment: _____

Project Taurus ARR: _____

Using ARR which project looks more favourable?
_____

Benefits of ARR Method:
_____
_____
_____

Drawbacks of ARR Method:
_____
_____
_____

9 Capital Investment Appraisal

(c) Net Present Value (NPV) Method

Kirkstall Ltd.'s cost of capital is 10%, so to estimate the benefit of *future* cash flows at *today's value* of money we must discount each future cash flow at a rate of 10% per annum [= *cost of capital 'A'*].

Project Gemini	Cash flow	10% discount factor	Discounted cash flow
0	(£100,000)		
1	£45,000		
2	£40,000		
3	£35,000		
4	£10,000		
5	£10,000		
		NPV (A) =	

Project Taurus	Cash flow	10% discount factor	Discounted cash flow
0	(£100,000)		
1	£10,000		
2	£20,000		
3	£30,000		
4	£40,000		
5	£45,000		
		NPV (A) =	

Using NPV which project looks more favourable?

_____

Benefits of NPV Method:

_____

_____

_____

Drawbacks of NPV Method:

_____

_____

_____

(d) Internal Rate of Return (IRR) Method

To estimate an Internal Rate of Return we now need to use a second higher discount factor which will produce a *negative* NPV. We will use 20%. **[= cost of capital 'B']**

Having ascertained both positive NPV(A) and negative NPV(B) we can use linear interpolation to estimate the cost of capital at which the NPV = 0. This NPV is the Internal Rate of Return (IRR).

$$IRR = A + \left[\frac{NPV(A)}{NPV(A) - NPV(B)} \right] \times (B-A)$$

Project Gemini	Cash flow	20% discount factor	Discounted cash flow
0	(£100,000)		
1	£45,000		
2	£40,000		
3	£35,000		
4	£10,000		
5	£10,000		
		NPV (B) =	

Project Gemini IRR: _____

Project Taurus	Cash flow	20% discount factor	Discounted cash flow
0	(£100,000)		
1	£10,000		
2	£20,000		
3	£30,000		
4	£40,000		
5	£45,000		
		NPV (A) =	

Project Taurus IRR: _____

Using IRR which project looks more favourable?

_____

Capital Investment Appraisal

Benefits of IRR Method:

_____

_____

_____

Drawbacks of IRR Method:

_____

_____

_____

Summarise your findings in the table below and based on an overall assessment of all four methods of capital investment appraisal recommend (with justifications) which project Kirkstall Ltd should implement.

	Project Gemini	Project Taurus
Payback		
ARR		
NPV		
IRR		

_____

_____

_____

_____

_____

_____

Question 9.12 (Payback)

A company is assessing a proposed project which requires an initial capital outlay of £50,000. The project will have a five year duration and will provide the following cash inflows.

Year	Cashflow	Cumulative Cashflow
0	(£50,000)	
1	£40,000	
2	£30,000	
3	£20,000	
4	£25,000	
5	£60,000	

Complete the 'Cumulative Cashflow' column and hence calculate the project's payback period (in years and months)

What does the calculated payback period represent?

What are the perceived benefits of the 'Payback Period' as a means of capital investment appraisal?

What are the disadvantages of 'Payback Period' as a means of capital investment appraisal?

9 Capital Investment Appraisal

Question 9.13 (NPV & IRR)

A company is appraising a five year project which will require an initial cash outlay of £2,000,000 on plant & machinery.

The project is then expected to deliver the following cash inflows:-

- Year 1   £500,000
- Year 2   £500,000
- Year 3   £600,000
- Year 4   £600,000
- Year 5   £400,000

At the end of the 5th year the plant & machinery will be sold for £40,000

The company can borrow funds at a variable rate of interest (with the initial rate of interest being 8%).

Complete the table below to calculate the Net Present Value of the project with an 8% cost of capital.

Year	Cashflow	Discount Factor	Present Value
		NET PRESENT VALUE =	

Hence state whether or not the project would be worthwhile whilst the interest rate is 8%

_____

Why is it considered preferable to receive cash sooner rather than later?

a) _____

b) _____

c) _____

The company fully appreciates that they would be borrowing the funds at a variable rate of interest. They have therefore also ascertained the Net Present Value of the project at a 12% cost of capital, and have calculated this to be (£97,000).

Is the project worthwhile at a 12% cost of capital?

_____

Calculate the Internal Rate of Return for the project (using the above Net Present Values for 8% and 12% costs of capital). Hence state at what cost of capital the project would cease to be worthwhile.

_____

_____

_____

_____

Do you consider the difference between the current interest rate and the 'break-even' interest rate to represent a sufficient margin of safety to proceed with the project?

_____

_____

9 Capital Investment Appraisal

Question 9.14 (using Discount Tables)

Using a 12% discount rate - What is the present value of £50 received in one year's time?

___

Using a 12% discount rate - What is the present value of £50 received in five years' time?

___

Using a 17% discount rate - What is the present value of £300 received in one year's time?

___

Using a 17% discount rate - What is the present value of £300 received in twenty years' time?

___

Question 9.15 (not using Discount Tables)

If you could invest cash and receive 6.5% interest:

What would £1 invested now be worth in one year's time?

___

What sum of money at today's value would be worth the same as receiving would £100 in one year's time? (Check your answer!)

___

What would £1 invested now be worth in two years' time?

___

What sum of money at today's value would be worth the same as receiving would £100 in two years' time? (Check your answer!)

___

Question 9.16

Discount Factor = 1 / (1 + r)^n

r = discount rate (expressed as a decimal); n = period (years)

What is the discount factor for money received in one year's time at a discount rate of 21%?

Using a 21% discount rate - What is the present value of £150 received in one year's time?

What is the discount factor for money received in two years' time at a discount rate of 21%?

Using a 21% discount rate - What is the present value of £150 received in two years' time?

Question 9.17

What does the expression *'Soft Capital Rationing'* mean?

What does the expression *'Hard Capital Rationing'* mean?

9 Capital Investment Appraisal

Chapter 10

Cash flow

INTRODUCTION

Many people assume that 'cash' and 'profit' mean broadly the same thing. This is definitely **not true**, and in this chapter we shall explore what the differences actually are and why it is vitally important to ensure that a business has sufficient cash.

In summary, we have two different ways of assessing business performance - 'profit' (as recorded on the Statement of Profit or Loss'), and cash flow (as recorded on the Statement of Cash flows).

OVERVIEW AND OBJECTIVES

By the end of this chapter you should have developed an understanding of:

- profit and cash flow
- measuring company performance
- timing differences of business transactions
- the Statement of Cash Flows

and be able to answer questions relating to these areas.

10 Cash flow

10.1 Profit versus cash flow

It is often wrongly believed that if a company reports a profit in the course of a financial year that means that they *must* have generated cash over that year ….and conversely if they made a loss that means that they *must* have ended the year with less cash than they started with.

In fact neither of these statements are *automatically* true, although they both often can be in practice. In this chapter we will explore the difference between profit and cash and why it is important to monitor both of these [different] measures of business performance.

To really appreciate the difference between cash flow and profit, we will consider a range of examples of business transactions and see what happens to profit and cash in each case, but let's start with simple separate explanations of what both profit and cashflow are.

> **DEFINITION**
>
> **What is Profit?**
>
> In general terms, profit is an accounting concept used to describe business performance and measured as the difference between the sales revenue earned in an accounting period less the corresponding expenses incurred:
>
> - It does not exist in reality. You *cannot* point to a 'pile' of profit.
> - It is merely the final figure on the bottom of the statement of profit or loss.
> - It is a measure of performance derived when the various transactions of a business are interpreted according to the rules of accountancy.
> - Its measurement involves a degree of subjectivity, as different people interpret financial reporting standards in different ways and make different accounting estimates.

More specifically, the profit of a business describes the performance of a business over a period of time and is derived in accordance with the **accruals concept**, which states:

- Income is recognised when *earned*
- Expenditure is recognised when *incurred*

We have already touched on the all-important accruals concept in Chapter 2 and will revisit it in detail in this chapter. Having a firm understanding of the difference between profit and cash is essential to your future business careers and separates out the 'financially fluent' from the 'financially illiterate'!

> **DEFINITION**
>
> **Accruals Concept: *"Income is recognised when earned"***
>
> - 'recognised' …… to acknowledge the existence of ….
> - 'earned' …… to obtain or be entitled to a reward …..
>
> So *'recognising income when earned'* simply means recording sales in the statement of profit or loss when the business becomes *entitled* to them ……..and *not* necessarily waiting until the cash is actually received.

Accruals Concept: *"Expenditure is recognised when incurred"*

- 'recognised' …… to acknowledge the existence of ….
- 'incurred' …… to become liable for …..

So *'recognising expenditure when incurred'* simply means recording expenses in the statement of profit or loss when the business becomes *liable* for them ……..and *not* necessarily waiting until the cash is actually paid.

DEFINITION

What is Cash flow?

In general terms, cash flow is the receipt or payment of cash:

- It is a reality. You *can* point to a 'pile' of cash.
- It is reported on the statement of cash flows.
- It is a measure of the liquidity of the business i.e. the extent to which a business can meet its liabilities as they fall due.
- Its measurement is completely objective, either cash is received or paid out (or it is not) … there is no need for an interpretation of whether or not it has occurred - a quick look at the bank statement will confirm whether a particular cash flow has occurred or not.

In more specific terms, cash consists of both 'cash in hand' (petty cash, floats in shop tills etc.), plus 'cash in bank' accounts. Some accounting standards extend the definition to include 'cash equivalents' which are certain financial investments which can be readily converted into cash (within 90 days).

Unlike profit, cash flow is not governed by a concept which dictates how it should be recorded and reported. The reason is simply that cash flow is almost entirely factual. It requires no special treatment. A simple examination of the company's bank statements will categorically reveal what sums of cash have been paid in, what sums of cash have been paid out and what the final closing balance of cash is at any point in time.

10.2 Measuring company performance

A company's performance can be measured by reference to either:

- Its **profit performance** … as recorded on the statement of profit or loss … or
- Its **cash flow performance** … as recorded on the statement of cash flow

As we shall see, the key difference between the two is the *timing* of when transactions are recorded:

- Profit records income when earned, and expenses when incurred

    This is known as the 'accrual accounting' or the 'accrual basis'

- Cash flow records cash inflow when it is actually received, and cash outflow when it is actually paid

    This is known as 'cash accounting' or the 'cash basis'

10 Cash flow

A **'cash business'** *(that is one always receiving immediate cash payment for sales, and always making immediate cash payment for expenses)* will have identical treatment on the statement of profit or loss, and the statement of cash flows for most of its transactions.

However most businesses sell their goods and services on a credit basis (where they allow their customers to pay for goods and services sold at a later date); and purchase their inventory and other items of expenditure on a credit basis (where their suppliers allow them to pay for goods and services purchased at a later date).

The statement of profit or loss and the statement of cash flow for such businesses will differ due to the various timing differences between:

- Selling goods and services to customers …… and being paid at a later date
- Purchasing goods and services from suppliers ….. and paying for them at a later date

Moreover both types of business (cash businesses and credit businesses) will 'capitalise' the purchase of non-current assets (aka capital assets), which will lead to differences in treatment between the statement of profit or loss, and the statement of cash flows.

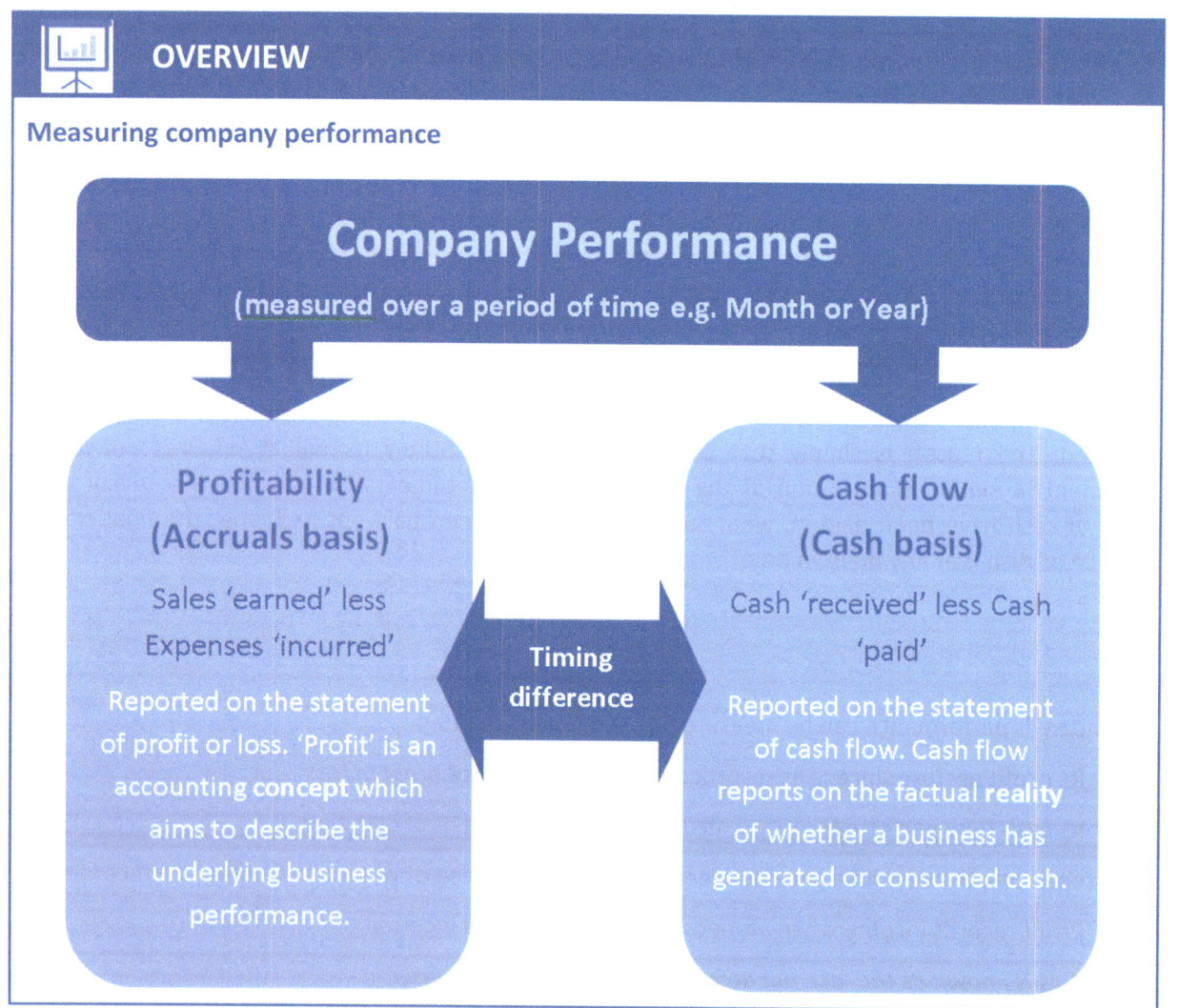

OVERVIEW

Measuring company performance

Company Performance
(measured over a period of time e.g. Month or Year)

Profitability (Accruals basis)

Sales 'earned' less Expenses 'incurred'

Reported on the statement of profit or loss. 'Profit' is an accounting **concept** which aims to describe the underlying business performance.

Timing difference

Cash flow (Cash basis)

Cash 'received' less Cash 'paid'

Reported on the statement of cash flow. Cash flow reports on the factual **reality** of whether a business has generated or consumed cash.

10.3 Timing differences of business transactions

Having given an overview of the differences between accruals accounting (to report profit) and cash accounting (to report cash flow), let's now look at a series of examples to see how these timing differences arise.

This is where the statement of financial position comes into its own by allowing a business to record amounts:

- which have yet to be received, or
- yet to be paid, or
- assets which have yet to be used.

All of these occur because of the timing differences which differentiate the 'accruals basis' from the 'cash basis'.

The financial statements which are of interest are:

- **The Statement of Profit or Loss** → Records the sales being earned, and the expenses being incurred, and the resulting profit (i.e. uses the accruals basis)
- **The Statement of Cash flows** → Records the corresponding cash being received or being paid, and the resulting net cash flow (i.e. uses the cash basis)
- **The Statement of Financial Position** → Handles the timing differences between:
  - Sales being incurred….. and the corresponding cash being received
  - Expenses being incurred….and the corresponding cash being paid

In each case we will identify how the transaction would appear on:

- The statement of cash flows ….. for reporting cash flow
- The statement of profit or loss …. for reporting profitability

In each case you should:

a) Identify where and why the timing differences are occurring which will lead to (temporary) differences between the statement of profit or loss, and the statement of cash flows.

b) Note that the statement of financial position is being used to account for the timing difference (by recording a corresponding asset or liability for the duration of the timing difference).

c) Verify that ultimately the cumulative amount that has been reported on the statement of profit or loss is exactly the same as the cumulative amount that has been reported on the statement of cashflows. …. albeit quite possibly with timing differences.

For brevity we shall refer to: the statement of profit or loss as 'P&L' (i.e. profit and loss account); and the statement of financial position as 'SOFP' in the following examples. We will assume that the business in question is producing monthly management accounts.

10 Cash flow

10.4 Cash sales

> **EXAMPLE**
>
> ABC Ltd supplies a customer with £1,000 worth of goods in January.
>
> The customer pays cash on delivery for the goods.
>
> | Statement of Profit or Loss | Statement of Cash Flows |
> |---|---|
> | The £1,000 **sales** are recorded in January's P&L. | The £1,000 **cash inflow** is recorded in January's Statement of Cash Flows. |
>
> - The £1,000 income is 'earned' in January when the customer is supplied with the goods, so the sale is recorded on January's P&L.
> - The customer pays cash on delivery (i.e. in January), and this is recorded as a cash inflow on January's statement of cash flows.
> - So in this instance there is *not* a timing difference between recording the sale and receiving the cash.

> **KEY POINT**
>
> This transaction **didn't have a timing difference** (between sales being earned and cash received) because it was a *cash transaction* i.e. the business received the cash immediately.
>
> The **same** £1,000 has been recorded on both the P&L and the statement of cash flows.

10.5 Credit sales

> **EXAMPLE**
>
> ABC Ltd supplies a customer with £1,000 worth of goods in January and grants the customer 60 days credit. The customer pays for the goods in March.
>
> **Statement of Profit or Loss**
>
> The £1,000 **sales** are recorded in January's P&L.
>
> **Statement of Cash Flows**
>
> The £1,000 **cash inflow** is recorded in March's Statement of Cash Flows.
>
> - The £1,000 income is 'earned' in January when the customer is supplied with the goods, so the sale is recorded on the P&L in January.
> - The customer has 60 day credit terms and so actually pays for the goods in March when the cash inflow is recorded on the statement of cash flows.
> - There **is** therefore a timing difference between recording the sale and receiving the cash.

> **KEY POINT**
>
> There is a **two month timing difference** between the sale being recorded on the P&L and the cash arriving two months later. During these two months the customer's debt is recorded on the SOFP as a 'Receivables' figure i.e. an asset. When the customer ultimately pays in March, the £1,000 receivables figure is then replaced with the corresponding £1,000 cash figure on the SOFP.
>
> The same £1,000 amount has **ultimately** been reported on both the P&L and the statement of cash flows (albeit at different times).

> **TEST YOUR UNDERSTANDING 1**
>
> A company supplies goods to a customer in January on 60 day credit terms. The customer pays late and the company does not receive the payment until May. In which month should the sale be recognised in the Statement of Profit or Loss and in which month should the payment be recorded in the Statement of Cash Flows?
>
> Statement of Profit or Loss _____
>
> Statement of Cash Flows _____

10 Cash flow

10.6 Cash purchases

> **EXAMPLE**
>
> ABC Ltd buys £100 of office stationery in January. They pay the supplier cash on delivery for the stationery.
>
> **Statement of Profit or Loss**
>
> The £100 **expense** is recorded in January's P&L.
>
> **Statement of Cash Flows**
>
> The £100 **cash outflow** is recorded in January's Statement of Cash Flows.
>
> - The £100 expense is 'incurred' in January when the supplier delivers the stationery to ABC Ltd and so the expense is recorded in January's P&L.
> - ABC Ltd pays cash on delivery (i.e. in January) and the cash outflow is therefore recorded on January's statement of cash flows.
> - In this instance there is **not** a timing difference between recording the expense and receiving the cash.

> **KEY POINT**
>
> This transaction didn't have a timing difference (between expense being incurred and cash paid) because it was a *cash transaction* i.e. the business paid the cash immediately.
>
> The **same** £100 amount has been reported on both the P&L and the statement of cash flows.

10.7 Credit purchases

> **EXAMPLE**
>
> ABC Ltd buys £100 of office stationery in January on 30 days credit terms. ABC actually pay the supplier for the stationery in February.
>
> **Statement of Profit or Loss**
>
> The £100 **expense** is recorded in January's P&L.
>
> **Statement of Cash Flows**
>
> The £100 **cash outflow** is recorded in February's Statement of Cash Flows.
>
> - The £100 expense is 'incurred' in January when the supplier delivers the stationery to ABC Ltd and so the expense is recorded on January's P&L.
> - ABC Ltd have 30 day credit terms and so actually pays for the stationery in February and it is recorded as a cash outflow in February.
> - Therefore there **is** a timing difference between recording the expense and paying the cash.

> **KEY POINT**
>
> There **is** a one month timing difference between the purchase being recorded on the P&L and the cash being paid one month later. During this month ABC's debt is recorded on the SOFP as a 'Payables' figure i.e. a liability. When ABC pays the supplier in February the £100 payables figure is then removed from the SOFP and the bank balance is correspondingly reduced by £100 on the SOFP.
>
> The same £100 amount has **ultimately** been reported on both the P&L and the statement of cash flows.

10 Cash flow

10.8 Pre-paid expenses

> **EXAMPLE**
>
> ABC Ltd pay their rent (£1,000 per month) quarterly in advance on 1st January.
>
> **Statement of Profit or Loss**
>
> The rent **expense** is recorded:
>
> January's P&L: £1,000
>
> February's P&L: £1,000
>
> March's P&L: £1,000
>
> **Statement of Cash Flows**
>
> The £3,000 **cash outflow** is recorded in January's Statement of Cash Flows.
>
> (nothing is recorded in February or March).

> **TUTORIAL NOTE**
>
> This is a slightly trickier example, so let's first consider exactly when the expense is 'incurred'. Each month that ABC Ltd occupy their premises they 'incur' rent:
>
> - £1,000 of rent is incurred in January… because they occupy the premises in January
> - £1,000 of rent is incurred in February… because they occupy the premises in February
> - £1,000 of rent is incurred in March… because they occupy the premises in March
>
> However they actually pay for all three months in advance in January i.e. they are pre-paying the rent. The pre-paid rent which they have paid for in advance (but not yet used) represents an asset i.e. they 'own' the right to occupy the premises for the next three months.
>
> - £1,000 of rent expense is 'incurred' each month so £1,000 rent expense is recorded on each of January's, February's and March's P&Ls.
> - The rent is paid in full in January….so January's statement of cash flows records a £3,000 cash outflow.
> - Therefore there **is** a timing difference between paying the cash and recording the rent expense for February and March (no timing difference for January's rent expense).

> **KEY POINT**
>
> At the end of January £1,000 rent has been charged to the P&L but £3,000 has been paid out of the bank, so there is a timing difference relating to the remaining £2,000. This £2,000 is recorded on January's SOFP as a **'pre-payment'** (in the 'current asset' section, because it is something paid for but not yet used).

In February another £1,000 of rent is charged to the P&L, so at the end of February the prepayment on the SOFP can be reduced by £1,000.

At the start of March there is only £1,000 rent prepayment left on the SOFP and this is then reduced to zero at the end of March as the final £1,000 is charged to March's P&L.

The same £3,000 amount has **ultimately** been reported on both the P&L and the statement of cash flows. The cash flow in one £3,000 outflow in January, and the P&L in 3 x £1,000 expenses in January, February and March.

10.9 Accrued expenses

EXAMPLE

ABC Ltd pay their telephone bill quarterly in arrears on 31st March. It is typically ~£100 per month, but this particular quarter the bill is £330.

Statement of Profit or Loss

The telephone **expense** is recorded:

January's P&L: £100 (accrued)

February's P&L: £100 (accrued)

March's P&L: £130 (balance)

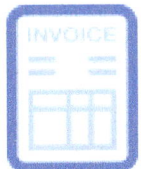

Statement of Cash Flows

The £330 **cash outflow** is recorded in March's Statement of Cash Flows.

(nothing is recorded in January or February).

TUTORIAL NOTE

Another slightly trickier example, again involving a quarterly bill, but this time the bill is received and paid 'in arrears' i.e. it is paid *after* the service has been used. Let's first consider exactly when the expense is 'incurred'. The answer is that every month that ABC Ltd use their telephone they 'incur' a corresponding expense.

The problem this time is that at the end of January (when the finance department are trying to finalise January's P&L) they don't actually know how much telephone expense they have in fact incurred during January .....because the actual bill will not arrive until the end of March. The expense they have incurred (but not yet paid for) represents a liability to ABC Ltd (something 'owed') and must be 'accrued' as follows.

It is better to include an estimate of the telephone costs (rather than just totally ignore them) and so they look back at previous bills and decide that ~£100 per month is typical.

- In January the P&L is charged with an accrued £100 telephone expense
- In February the P&L is charged with another accrued £100 telephone expense

10　Cash flow

- In March the £330 telephone bill is received. £200 worth of this has already been charged to the P&L in January & February, so just the remaining balance of £130 needs to be charged to March's P&L
- The £330 cash outflow is recorded on March's statement of cash flows
- There is therefore a timing difference during these three months between the P&L expense and the corresponding cash flow.

> **KEY POINT**
>
> **At the end of January** £100 telephone expense has been charged to the P&L but no cash has been paid, so there is a timing difference relating to this £100. This is resolved by recording the £100 liability on January's SOFP as an **'accrual'** (in the 'current liabilities' section). This records the fact that the business has incurred £100 of telephone costs but not yet paid for them (i.e. it 'owes' an estimated £100).
>
> *In February* the same happens again (another £100 expense without a corresponding cash outflow) so this is also recorded on February's SOFP as an additional £100 accrual. This now brings the total telephone accrual to £200 (£100 for January and £100 for February).
>
> **In March** the £330 telephone bill arrives and is paid. The £200 accrual on the SOFP is now removed (as the liability no longer exists), and the bank balance on the SOFP is reduced by £330.
>
> **Ultimately** £330 of telephone expense has been charged to the P&L, and a £330 cash outflow has been recorded.

> **TUTORIAL NOTE**
>
> It doesn't help matters that the word **'accrual'** is used to describe both:
>
> - The general rule of recognising 'income when earned' and 'expenses when incurred' i.e. the **accruals** basis …. and also….
> - A specific application of this general rule when we record an **'accrual'** to recognise one particular expense which has been incurred but not yet charged for!

10.10 Capital expenditure

The differences in timing encountered so far have been measured in months i.e. within a relatively short space of time any differences between the statement of profit or loss, and the statement of cash flows, would have resolved themselves.

However the timing differences caused by the different treatment of capital expenditure can remain for years…… but will *eventually* also be resolved.

You will recall that capital expenditure has a different accounting treatment to revenue expenditure:

Revenue Expenditure (e.g. wages, telephone, gas, rent etc.) is charged in full when the bill is received (albeit with some short-term allowances for pre-paid and accrued expenses as we have just seen, which will normally 'reverse out' within months).

Capital Expenditure (e.g. cars, computers, machinery etc.) is 'capitalised' … that is the value of the capital asset is held on the statement of financial position (in the Non-Current Asset section) and is then depreciated over the useful economic life of the capital asset … which is normally measured in years. This is because the cost of a capital asset which has (say) a three year life is deemed to be 'incurred' over all three years ….. after all, the capital asset is helping to generate profit for the business over these three years, and so it is only fair to 'match' the cost of the asset over the same time period during which it helps generate revenue. This results in a smoother, fairer profit figure being reported on a year by year basis.

EXAMPLE

ABC Ltd purchase a computer system for £4,000. They plan to use it for 3 years and then sell it for £1,000.

Statement of Profit or Loss

The depreciation **expense** is recorded:

Year 1 P&L: £1,000

Year 2 P&L: £1,000

Year 3 P&L: £1,000

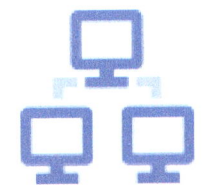

Statement of Cash Flows

Year 1 : £4,000 cash outflow

Year 2 : nothing!

Year 3 : £1,000 cash inflow

(net position = £3,000 cash inflow).

TUTORIAL NOTE

Let's start by working out the annual depreciation for the computer system.

$$\text{Depreciation} = \frac{\text{Initial Value} - \text{Residual Value}}{\text{Life in years}} = \frac{£4,000 - £1,000}{3} = £1,000 \text{ pa}$$

- In year 1 a cash outflow of £4,000 is recorded on the statement of cash flows
- In year 1 the P&L is charged with £1,000 of depreciation
- In year 2 the P&L is charged with £1,000 of depreciation
- In year 3 the P&L is charged with £1,000 of depreciation
- In year 3 there is a cash inflow of £1,000
- There are therefore timing differences in all three years between what is recorded on each year's P&L and what is recorded on the corresponding year's statement of cash flows.

In year 1 there is a £4,000 cash outflow but only £1,000 of depreciation expense charged to the P&L. Discrepancies then also occur in years 2 & 3. To understand how this is resolved we need to look at the accounting treatment for the 'life' of the computer system.

Profit & Loss Account

The expense of the computer system has been spread over its three year life by charging £1,000 of depreciation to the P&L each year.

10 Cash flow

P&L	Annual Depreciation Charge
Year One	£1,000
Year Two	£1,000
Year Three	£1,000

Statement of Financial Position

At each year-end the *remaining* value of the computer system (not yet charged to the P&L) is recorded on the SOFP (under non-current assets). This value is known as the Net Book Value (NBV) and represents the 'written down' value of the capital asset at the end of each year.

SOFP	Net Book Value of Computers
End of Year One	£3,000
End of Year Two	£2,000
End of Year Three*	£1,000

The SOFP has again been used to temporarily hold the difference between the values which has been recorded the P&L and the statement of cash flows to date. For example at the end of year one there has been a £4,000 cash outflow, but only £1,000 of this has been charged to the P&L. The remaining £3,000 of value remains as a capital asset recorded on the SOFP.

*This is immediately before the now redundant computer system is sold for £1,000 and the final value on the SOFP removed.

> ⚠️ **KEY POINT**
>
> Over a three year period £3,000 of depreciation expense been charged to the three separate year's P&Ls, and there has been a (net) £3,000 cash outflow on the statements of cash flow (-£4,000 + £1,000 = -£3000). Ultimately after three years they agree, but the SOFP has accounted for the timing differences during the three years.

TEST YOUR UNDERSTANDING 2

On the 1st January 2018 a business invests £100,000 in new manufacturing machinery. The machinery is anticipated to have a four year life after which it will have a residual value of £24,000 (and will be sold for this amount in January 2022). The business has a 31st December financial year-end and produces annual financial statements.

Complete the following extracts from the business's financial statements to show for each year how:

- The expense of the machinery will be charged to the statement of profit or loss
- The remaining Net Book Value (NBV) of the machinery will be recorded in the Statement of Financial Position
- Any corresponding cash flows are recorded in the Statement of Cash Flows

Statement of Profit or Loss	Depreciation Charge
Year Ending 31st Dec 2018	
Year Ending 31st Dec 2019	
Year Ending 31st Dec 2020	
Year Ending 31st Dec 2021	

Statement of Financial Position	Net Book value
As at 31st Dec 2018	
As at 31st Dec 2019	
As at 31st Dec 2020	
As at 31st Dec 2021	

Statement of Cash Flows	Cash Flows
Year Ending 31st Dec 2018	
Year Ending 31st Dec 2019	
Year Ending 31st Dec 2020	
Year Ending 31st Dec 2021	
Year Ending 31st Dec 2022	

10 Cash flow

10.11 Cost of Sales

Finally let's look at the purchase of inventory (i.e. goods for resale). ABC Ltd purchase and pay for £5,000 of inventory in February so we can immediately see that a cash outflow of £5,000 will have occurred during February.

The £5,000 cash payment is recorded in February and therefore appears as a cash outflow on February's statement of cash flows.

EXAMPLE

During February, ABC Ltd purchase and pay for £5,000 worth of inventory.

Statement of Profit or Loss

?

Statement of Cash Flows

The £5,000 **cash outflow is** recorded in February's Statement of Cash Flows.

The question is whether this is also an expense which should appear in February's statement of profit or loss, and that boils down to the question of has an expense occurred i.e. has any wealth left the company as a result of buying £5,000 of inventory?

TUTORIAL NOTE

The short answer is **'No'** ….

All that has happened is that ABC Ltd have exchanged one asset (£5,000 cash) for an alternative asset (£5,000 inventory). True, cash has left the business … but not wealth.

In fact the expense is not incurred until the inventory is actually sold. At that point wealth has left the business (because the value of the sold inventory is no longer there), but this is hopefully more than compensated for by the corresponding sales receipts for this inventory (which should obviously be greater if the business is to actually make some gross profit!).

Of course, any inventory which is sold will be a mixture of unsold inventory from previous months (which forms the 'opening inventory' for the month) plus some of the newly purchased inventory. To calculate the value of the inventory sold we use the formula:

Cost of Sales = Opening Inventory + Purchases − Closing Inventory

… where 'Purchases' is the £5,000 inventory purchased in the month in question.

Assuming that at the start of February there was £1,000 of opening inventory and at the end of February there was £2,000 of closing inventory, then:

Cost of Sales (February) = £1,000 + £5,000 - £2,000 = £4,000

The £4,000 cost of sales expense is recorded in February's statement of profit or loss

Note that again the entries on the statement of cash flow and statement of profit or loss are different but (in this case over the entire life of the company) would ultimately reconcile.

The key point to understand is that the **'cost of purchases'** is not an expense ….but *the* **'cost of sales'** is!

TEST YOUR UNDERSTANDING 3

At the beginning of June a business has £75,000 worth of inventory. During June it makes further purchases of inventory totalling £18,000. At the end of June it is left with £71,000 worth of inventory. What cost of sales figure should appear on June's statement of profit or loss? What inventory figure should appear on the statement of financial position as at 30th June?

Statement of Profit or Loss - Cost of Sales

_____

Statement of Financial Position - Inventory

_____

TEST YOUR UNDERSTANDING 4

During the month of November a business records sales revenue of £200,000 and gross profit of £130,000. If the business had £20,000 of inventory on the 1st November and £24,000 of inventory on 30th November, then what were its total purchases of new inventory during November?

_____

_____

_____

_____

10 Cash flow

10.12 Profit versus cash flow differences on a larger scale

Firstly, let us recap:

Net Profit = Income Earned – Expenses Incurred (Accruals Basis)

Net Cash flow = Cash Received - Cash Paid (Cash Basis)

The differences between the two arise because of the timings of cash flows e.g.

- Credit Sales
- Credit Purchases
- Year End Accruals & Prepayments etc.
- Capital Expenditure (often the biggest single factor)

We have already seen several examples of individual transactions which result in differing 'profit' and 'cash flow' treatments. The following table summarises some of the reasons why the statement of profit or loss, and the statement of cash flows might vary on a *large-scale basis* e.g. for an entire financial year. Many of the effects listed are simply the same issues we have already examined…..but on a 'macro-scale'.

Examine the following table:

- Firstly, note that the two sets of reasons why cash flow might either be higher or lower than profit are in fact exact opposites.

- Secondly, make sure you can explain in your own words why each of these effects occurs. This will pay dividends *(finance pun fully intended!)* when we look at the 'indirect method' for cash flow statements shortly.

OVERVIEW

Possible Causes for Cash flow to be higher than Profit	Underlying Reason
Capital Expenditure: Lower capital investment than in previous years	Modest cash being spent on capex in year just finished, but residual high depreciation charges from previously higher levels of capex
Receivables: Lower at end of year than at start of year	At end of year customers owe less cash to the business … because they have 'overpaid' cash during the year to clear their outstanding bills
Payables: Higher at end of year than at start of year	At end of year more cash is owed to suppliers … because the business has held back on payments and therefore 'preserved' cash in the business
Inventory: Lower at end of year than at start of year	The business has 'run down' the amount of inventory it holds over the year, and turned the surplus inventory into cash

Possible Causes for Cash flow to be lower than Profit	Underlying Reason
Capital Expenditure: Higher capital investment than in previous years	Significantly higher cash being spent on capex in year just finished, with correspondingly lower depreciation charges from previously lower levels of capex
Receivables: Higher at end of year than at start of year	At end of year customers owe more cash to the business … because they have 'underpaid' cash during the year allowing their outstanding bills to increase
Payables: Lower at end of year than at start of year	At end of year less cash is owed to suppliers … because the business has over-paid during the year and therefore used up cash
Inventory: Higher at end of year than at start of year	The business has increased the amount of inventory it holds over the year, and effectively turned cash into inventory

10.13 Statement of Cash Flows

The Statement of Cash flows reports the actual cash inflows and cash outflows for a business over a period in time, and hence the increase or decrease in cash (and cash equivalents) in the business.

It is the final statement we need to consider of the four key statements in financial accounting:-

1. Statement of Profit or Loss
2. Statement of Financial Position
3. Statement of Changes in Equity
4. Statement of Cash Flows

Cash is regarded as the life-blood of business because the **immediate** reason for companies failing is *not* lack of profit …… *it is lack of cash!*

Remember that profit is simply an accounting concept which we use to 'smooth out' the somewhat random timings of cash flows and instead provide a 'cleaned up' version of a business's underlying performance.

To understand just how useful the concept of 'profit' is in assessing a business's performance, imagine if it didn't exist and business instead only had cash flow on which to gauge how well it was doing. The Finance Director's boardroom (cash flow based review) on recent performance would then go something like:

"Well we seem to have ended the month with more cash than we started, but I'm not sure it's really as good as it looks. We actually have very low levels of inventory at the moment and need to spend cash to increase these. The amount we owe to our suppliers at the moment is

10 Cash flow

very high, and we also need make some urgent payments to them. Moreover the manufacturing machinery we bought ten years ago needs replacing and that will take a lot of cash.

I think I need to make some adjustments for all these factors and then come back and tell you how much 'spare' cash we might have really generated once we have dealt with all these issues. Only then will we see how well we have really done".

The 'adjustments' which the Finance Director is considering making to get a 'true picture' of performance are all the things which are *already included* within a profit figure, because :

- Profit is based on how much expense has been *incurred* in (say) a month… not on what payments have actually made to suppliers
- Profit is measured after deducting the *cost of sales* (i.e. inventory actually sold)….. not on whether the levels of inventory in the warehouse have increased or decreased in the month
- Profit is calculated using *depreciation* so that the cost of capital investment is spread out over the entire period that benefits from this investment

So profit is an incredibly useful way of understanding how well a business is performing, free from the vagaries of random cash flow events ……. **but profit remains nothing more than a concept!**

- You cannot bank profit
- You cannot pay the staff wages with profit
- You cannot pay suppliers, or premises rent, or bank loan repayments with profit

…… for all of these a business needs **cash**, and whilst it has cash, it can remain liquid (i.e. able to pay debts as they become due) and hence continue to trade.

- **A loss-making company can still generate cash …..**

……. and hence survive (at least in the short term)

- **However even a profitable company which runs out of cash …..**

…….. will fail !

For these reasons it is vital for companies to consider **both** their:

- **Profit** – so the underlying business performance can be understood
- **Cash flow** – so that the immediate liquidity (and therefore survival) of the business can be understood

The ideal combination is *'high quality'* profit (meaning that the profit arises from sustainable core operations and not one-off accounting anomalies such as property revaluations), together with strong cash flow i.e. the strong profit performance is leading to a corresponding strong cash flow performance.

The directors of a business will therefore use both historic cash flow statements (which report on past cash flows) and forward-looking cash flow budgets (which forecast future cash flow) to ensure that the business will remain liquid. Because these are used internally they form part of the unregulated management accounting information used by a business to operate. They can therefore take whatever form the Directors find most useful.

However, the external users of financial information (such as shareholders, suppliers and lenders) will also wish to see the company's cash flow performance and so the financial accounts filed at Companies House will also contain a statement of cash flows, but this time prepared in accordance with financial reporting standards. Financial accounting never contains future forecasts and the annual accounts will *not* therefore contain a cash flow *budget*, merely a historical report of the cash flow over the financial year just ended.

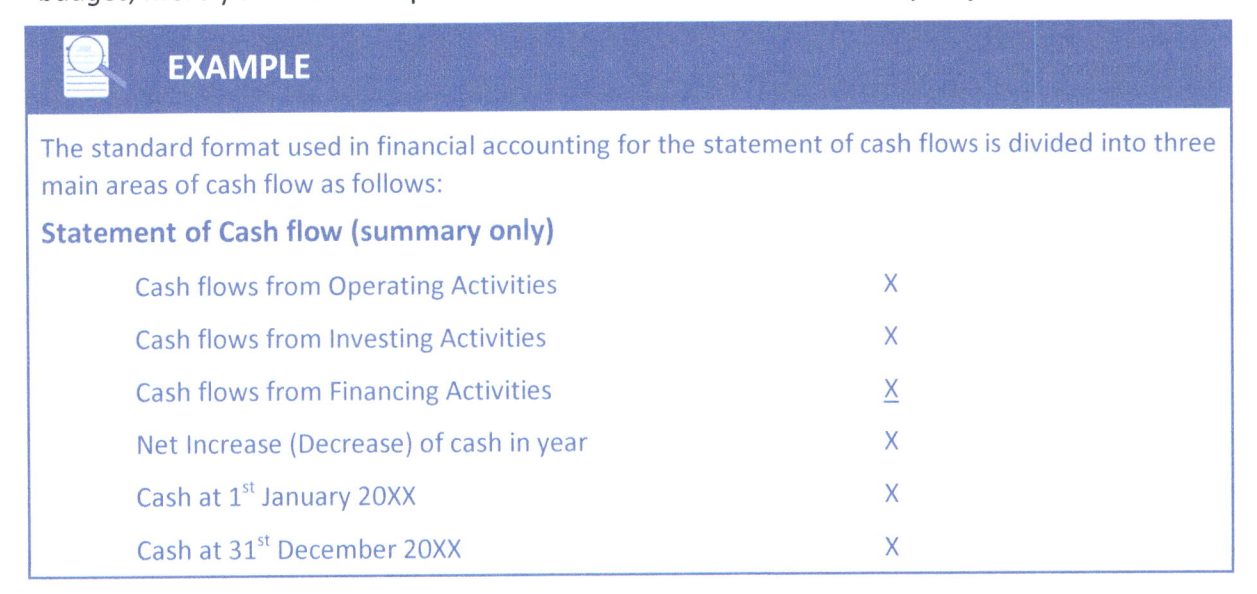

EXAMPLE

The standard format used in financial accounting for the statement of cash flows is divided into three main areas of cash flow as follows:

Statement of Cash flow (summary only)

Cash flows from Operating Activities	X
Cash flows from Investing Activities	X
Cash flows from Financing Activities	X
Net Increase (Decrease) of cash in year	X
Cash at 1st January 20XX	X
Cash at 31st December 20XX	X

The three main sections show:

Operating Activities

How much cash has been generated (or alternatively used up) in the normal day to day trading of the business. This is the section which will often reveal whether the business is viable on an ongoing basis. To survive **in the long-term** a business needs its core operations to be able to generate cash

The precise way in which we identify every single operating cash flow throughout the year (which might be millions of transactions!) is discussed later.

Investing Activities

In this section any cash outflows used for new capital expenditure are recorded. This would typically be for the purchase of land & buildings or plant & machinery, but could also include (say) the purchase of shares if the business was buying another company. Conversely, any investments sold would be recorded as a cash inflow in this section.

Financing Activities

We know that the two main sources of long-term finance are debt and equity, and any cash flows relating to these are recorded here. This could include cash inflows from new bank loans received or new shares issued. Or alternatively, cash outflows for bank loan repayments or dividends paid to shareholders.

The total net cash flow from all three of these activities is summed and then used to reconcile the difference between the cash* held by the company at the start of the year and the cash held at the end of the year. Of course, a company can actually choose any financial year-end date it chooses ….it does not have to be 31st December!

including 'cash equivalents' - certain investments which can be turned into cash within 90 days

10 Cash flow

Cash flow from Operating Activities

This is normally the most complex section which aims to summarise all of the cash flows from the multitude of transactions which have occurred over the year. The financial reporting standards allow for two alternative ways of presenting this information, as follows:

Direct Method

The direct method simply reports the various cash inflows and outflows according to their source or destination:

	Cash receipts from customers
less	Cash payments to suppliers
less	Cash payments to employees
equals	Cash flow from Operating Activities

... which seems quite straightforward but unfortunately in practice is not! Accounting systems are primarily designed to record transactions in accordance with the accruals basis, so that they may then readily report profit performance (which is based on the accruals concept).

Therefore, to try and summarise potentially millions of operational transactions over a year into the format of the Direct Method would require a complete revisit of every operational transaction during the year, or of the fundamental way in which the accounting system operates.

Indirect Method

The Indirect Method provides a short-cut to the problem of finding the operational cash flow by instead actually starting with the profit figure. This initially sounds counter-intuitive, as the preceding chapter has been emphasising why profit and cash flow are different! However the indirect method then proceeds to effectively 'undo' all of the aspects of accruals accounting that produced the profit figure, and in the process gets back to the original cash flows.

	Profit (Loss) for period
+	Depreciation Charge
+/-	Change in Inventory
+/-	Change in Receivables
+/-	Change in Payables
=	**Cash flow from Operating Activities**

We have already covered most of the above, but as a quick recap:

- Depreciation is deducted in calculating profit, but is not actually cash flow and so must be added back to the profit figure to get back to cash flow

- The cost of sales figure used to calculate profit does not take in to account whether or not the levels of inventory are altering. However, if they are this definitely affects cash flow and hence must be adjusted for (so an increase in inventory absorbs cash and vice versa)

- The sales figure used to calculate profit does not take into account whether or not the customer has actually paid for the sale or not. However, customers who do not pay effectively withhold cash from the business (so an increase in receivables absorbs cash and vice versa)

- The expenses charged against profit do not take into account whether or not the supplier has actually been paid. However, not paying suppliers has the effect of preserving cash within the business (so an increase in payables generates cash and vice versa)

TEST YOUR UNDERSTANDING 5

At the beginning of a financial year a business had payables (i.e. amounts owing to its suppliers) of £67,000, and at the end of the year it had payables of £78,000. What will be the corresponding effect on cash flow purely as a result of the change in the payables figure?

___

___

___

This 'reverse-evolution' of converting profit back into cash flow is actually far easier to achieve in practice than the previous direct method, and therefore far more widely used. The accounting system provides the starting profit figure and a simple examination of this years' and last years' financial statements provides the necessary adjustments.

A full Statement of Cash flows (using the indirect method) is shown on the following page and this would be studied closely by anyone with a serious interest in the company, whether they be:

- A potential investor wanting reassurance that the company is cash positive and therefore viable and able to pay a good level of dividends before purchasing shares in the company

- A potential supplier who wants to check that the company is able to pay its debts as they fall due, before offering the company credit terms

- A potential lender who wants to check that the company generates enough cash to allow it to pay interest and loan repayments, before advancing loan finance to the company.

10 Cash flow

> **EXAMPLE**
>
> ### Statement of Cash Flow for Year ending 31st December 2017
>
> | | £'000 |
> |---|---:|
> | **Cash flow from operating activities** | |
> | Operating Profit | 2,546 |
> | plus Depreciation | 10 |
> | less increase in inventory | -200 |
> | less increase in receivables | -700 |
> | plus increase in payables | 335 |
> | Cash generated from Operations | **1,991** |
> | less interest paid | -20 |
> | less taxation paid | -540 |
> | **Net cash inflow from operations** | **1,431** |
> | | |
> | **Cash flow from investing activities** | |
> | Purchase of non-current assets | -100 |
> | Disposal of non-current assets | 0 |
> | **Net cash flow from investing activities** | **-100** |
> | | |
> | **Cash flow from financing activities** | |
> | New Share Capital issued | 50 |
> | Loan repayments | -35 |
> | Dividends paid | -520 |
> | **Net Cash flow from financing activities** | **-505** |
> | | |
> | **Net Increase in cash** | **826** |
> | Cash as at 1st January 2017 | 290 |
> | Cash as at 31st December 2017 | 1,116 |

We saw in Chapter 3 that businesses should think more about profit than turnover…. and have now seen that a business must not only look at profit, but also at cash flow.

The fundamental aim of any business is to maximise profitability and to ensure its survival. Making profit will not by itself ensure business survival …. For that you also need cash flow!

Remember: "Turnover is vanity, profit is sanity, but cash is king!"

The Language of Business

⚠ KEY POINTS FROM CHAPTER 10

Profit
- Is an accounting concept used to describe business performance
- Does not exist in reality but is merely the final figure on the bottom of the P&L
- It is a measure of performance derived when the various transactions of a business are interpreted according to the rules of accountancy
- Its measurement involves a degree of subjectivity, with varying interpretations of financial reporting standards and accounting estimates

Cash
- Is a reality. Cash is tangible.
- Is reported on the statement of cash flows.
- It is a measure of the liquidity of the business i.e. the extent to which a business can meet its liabilities as they fall due.
- Its measurement is completely objective. Either cash is received or it's not.

A company's performance can be measured by reference to either:

Profit Performance
- Recorded on the statement of profit or loss
- Profit records income when earned and expenses when incurred
- Known as 'accrual accounting' or the 'accrual basis'

Cash flow Performance
- Recorded on the statement of cash flow
- Cash flow records cash inflow when it is actually received, and cash outflow when it is actually paid
- Known as 'cash accounting' or the 'cash basis'

The divergence between 'profit performance' and 'cash flow performance' is due to timing differences, which over a long enough time period will ultimately resolve themselves.

The Statement of Profit or Loss
- Records the sales being earned, and the expenses being incurred, and the resulting profit (i.e. uses the accruals basis)

The Statement of Cash flows
- Records the corresponding cash being received or being paid, and the resulting net cash flow (i.e. uses the cash basis)

The Statement of Financial Position
- Handles the timing differences between:
  - Sales being earned….. and the corresponding cash being received
  - Expenses being incurred….and the corresponding cash being paid

Cash flow Performance
- Is regarded as being as important (if not more so) than the profitability of a company
- *'Profit is a concept… cash is a reality'.*

10 Cash flow

Chapter 10: Test Your Understanding Answers

TEST YOUR UNDERSTANDING 1

The transaction is recorded on the **Statement of Profit or Loss in January** (when the sale was 'earned') and recorded on the **Statement of Cash Flows in May** (when the cash was actually received).

TEST YOUR UNDERSTANDING 2

Statement of Profit or Loss	Depreciation Charge
Year Ending 31st Dec 2018	£19,000
Year Ending 31st Dec 2019	£19,000
Year Ending 31st Dec 2020	£19,000
Year Ending 31st Dec 2021	£19,000

Statement of Financial Position	Net Book value
As at 31st Dec 2018	£81,000
As at 31st Dec 2019	£62,000
As at 31st Dec 2020	£43,000
As at 31st Dec 2021	£24,000

Statement of Cash Flows	Cash Flows
Year Ending 31st Dec 2018	(£100,000)
Year Ending 31st Dec 2019	-
Year Ending 31st Dec 2020	-
Year Ending 31st Dec 2021	-
Year Ending 31st Dec 2022	£24,000

TEST YOUR UNDERSTANDING 3

Statement of Profit or Loss: Cost of Sales = Opening inventory + Purchases – Closing Inventory = £75,000 + £18,000 - £71,000 = **£22,000**

Statement of Financial Position: Inventory = **£71,000**

TEST YOUR UNDERSTANDING 4

Cost of Sales = Sales Revenue – Gross Profit = £200,000 - £130,000 = **£70,000**

Cost of Sales = Opening Inventory + Purchases – Closing Inventory

So, Purchases = Cost of Sales + Closing Inventory – Opening Inventory = £70,000 + £24,000 - £20,000 = **£74,000**

TEST YOUR UNDERSTANDING 5

There is a **£11,000 cash inflow** (£78,000 - £67,000) as a result of the change in Payables i.e. the suppliers have been underpaid by £11,000 in the year compared to what has been purchased from them. This underpayment is equivalent to a cash inflow (when comparing the effect on the P&L and the effect on the Statement of Cash Flows).

10 Cash flow

Chapter 10: End of Chapter Exercises

Section A Questions

Question 10.1
Which of the following statements best summarises when transactions are recognised on the Statement of Profit or Loss?

A   Sales are recognised when cash is received. Expenses are recognised when the cash is paid.
B   Sales are recognised when cash is received. Expenses are recognised when incurred.
C   Sales are recognises when earned. Expenses are recognised when the cash is paid
D   Sales are recognised when earned. Expenses are recognised when incurred.

Question 10.2
Which of the following statements best summarises when transactions are recognised on the Statement of Cash flows?

A   Cash flows from sales are recognised when the cash is actually received. Cash flows relating to expenses are recognised when the cash is actually paid.
B   Cash flows from sales are recognised when cash is actually received. Cash flows relating to expenses are recognised when the expense was originally incurred.
C   Cash flows from sales are recognised when the original sale was earned. Cash flows relating to expenses are recognised when the cash is actually paid.
D   Cash flows from sales are recognised when the original sale was earned. Cash flows from expenses are recognised when the expense was originally incurred.

Question 10.3
A business purchases £120,000 of new manufacturing machinery in Year 1. It expects to use it for 5 years, and then sell it for £20,000 at the end of Year 5.

What figure relating to this machinery will appear on the Statement of Cash flows in Year 3?

A   £nil
B   £20,000 cash outflow
C   £24,000 cash outflow
D   £20,000 cash inflow

Question 10.4

Which of the following do **not** represent a cash flow:

i. The sale of goods on 60 day credit terms
ii. The partial repayment of a bank loan
iii. The monthly depreciation charge on Plant & Machinery
iv. Receiving payment from a credit customer

Choose the correct combination of statements:

A   i & ii
(B)   ii & iii
C   i & iv
D   i & iii

Question 10.5

In its first month of trading a new business purchased £500 of inventory from a supplier on 30 day credit terms, and then in the same month sold all of this inventory to a customer for £800 on 60 day credit terms.

What were the corresponding profit and cash flows in this first month?

	Profit	Cash flow
A	£nil	£nil
(B)	£300	£nil
C	£nil	£300
D	£300	£300

Question 10.6

Which of the following statements is false?

A   A loss making company may end the year with more cash than it started the year
B   Profit is a concept whereas cash is a reality
(C)   A company will immediately go bankrupt if it makes a loss
D   A profitable company may end the year with less cash than it started the year

Question 10.7

If a company ends the year with £10,000 more inventory than it had at the start of the year then it will have...

A   ..... Correspondingly reduced its cash by £10,000 as a result"
B   ..... Neither had its cash increased nor decreased as a result"
(C)   ..... Correspondingly increased its cash by £10,000 as a result"

10 Cash flow

Question 10.8

A company made an operating profit for the year of £500,000 (after accounting for depreciation of £20,000). Over the course of the year:

- It paid out £150,000 in dividends
- It repaid a £50,000 bank loan
- It invested £75,000 in capital expenditure
- Its inventory increased by £10,000
- Its receivables decreased by £5,000
- Its payables increased by £15,000

What was the corresponding increase in the company's cash over the course of the year?

A   £215,000
B   £235,000
C   £255,000
D   £405,000

Question 10.9

Which of the following would result in a cash outflow for a company?

i.   Payment of a Dividend to Shareholders
ii. New shares being issued
iii. Payment of a Corporation Tax liability
iv. Receipt of a new bank loan

Choose the most appropriate combination of statements from the options given:

A   i & iii
B   ii & iv
C   iii & iv
D   i & iv

Question 10.10

The following is an incomplete (summarised version) of a company's year-end Statement of Cash flows.

Cash flow from Operating Activities	£295,000
Cash flow from Investing Activities	(£310,000)
Cash flow from Financing Activities	(£123,000)
Net Increase in cash in year	???
Cash at 1st January 2018	£197,000
Cash at 31st December 2018	???

What is the company's cash as at 31st December 2018?

A £59,000
B £335,000
C £679,000
D £925,000

10 Cash flow

Section B Questions

Question 10.11

For each of the following financial transactions explain how:

- profit will be affected (as recorded on the monthly statement of profit or loss)
- cash flow will be affected (as recorded as the monthly statement of cash flows)

...when entered into the monthly management accounts of a business with a 31st Dec. year-end.

Sales made to a customer in January on 60 day credit terms

In which month(s) are the sales 'recognised' (*i.e. recorded*) on the statement of profit or loss?

January

In which month(s) is the corresponding cash inflow recorded on the statement of cash flows?

March

£18,000 annual rent for the business premises paid in advance on 1st January annually

In which month(s) is the rent 'recognised' on the statement of profit or loss?

All months – 1,500 per month

In which month(s) is the corresponding cash outflow recorded?

_____

£38,000 cash purchase in January of manufacturing plant intended to be used for 3 years and then sold for £2,000

How will this be recorded on the statement of profit or loss?

£1,000 per month

How will this be recorded on the statement of cash flows?

£38,000 out in Jan

The cash payment In December of a £500 expense which relates to the next financial year

How is this recorded on December's statement of profit or loss?

£0

How is this recorded on the statement of cash flows?

£500 outgoing

Which other financial statement would record this payment?

Statement of Financial Position – Asset (prepayment = CA)

£2,000 of equipment repairs carried out in December. The corresponding invoice was not received until January and was then paid in March

How and when is this recorded on the statement of profit or loss?

January

How and when is this recorded on the statement of cash flows?

March

Which other financial statement might record this transaction in December?

Statement of Financial Position – Liability – Accrual

During April £28,000 of inventory is purchased on 30 day credit terms. The opening inventory on 1st April was £8,000. The closing inventory on 30th April was £11,000

What 'cost of sales' figure appears on April's statement of profit or loss?

£17,000

When is the cash outflow corresponding to April's purchases recorded on the statement of cash flows?

April

Which financial statement is the £11,000 April closing inventory recorded on?

Cash flow

10 Cash flow

Question 10.12

You are planning to launch a new business on the 1st January selling spare parts for the automotive industry to car repairers in the north of the UK. You will not carry any inventory of these spare parts but will simply purchase the parts that your customers need from your various suppliers and deliver them to your customers the same day (making a 30% gross profit margin).

On 1st January you deposit £20,000 of your own savings into your business bank account. Your bank has offered you a £50,000 overdraft facility on this bank account, on condition that you provide a satisfactory 6 month cash flow budget for your new business.

Using the following information, complete the template to provide the bank with the required **cash flow budget.**

- Budgeted sales are:

    - January   £10,000
    - February   £16,000
    - March   £20,000
    - April   £24,000
    - May   £28,000
    - June   £30,000

- Your customers are all 'trade customers' who will insist on standard 30 days credit terms. You know from experience that this will result in 50% of the sales being paid on time the following month (i.e. 30 days), but the other 50% being paid late 2 months (i.e. 60 days) after being supplied.

- You set your prices to achieve a standard 30% gross profit margin.

- Your suppliers have all offered you 30 day credit terms, with the promise of an additional 5% year-end 'retro' discount if all of your purchases are paid within the agreed 30 days. You are keen to secure the additional 5% retro-discount at the end of your first year's trading and so will pay all purchase invoices within 30 days.

- On 1st January you make a £14,000 cash purchase of a delivery van. This is expected to have a residual value of £2,000 in four years' time and will be depreciated on a straight-line basis

- Van running costs (mainly diesel) are expected to be £500 per month payable in cash

- You rent a premise at a cost of £500 per month payable quarterly in advance commencing on 1st January.

- You estimate that gas & electricity costs will be £200 per month payable quarterly in arrears at the end of each calendar quarter.

- You will pay your delivery driver a salary of £24,000 per annum payable monthly in the same month as he works.

- The local council has informed you that the annual business rates will be £2,400 payable in 10 monthly instalments from February to November inclusive.

- You agree a series of six adverts in a monthly trade magazine to appear from the January to June editions at a cost of £200 per month. You are required to pay for them all in advance in January.

The Language of Business

Enter no figures other than cash flows!

	January	February	March	April	May	June
30 day Sales Receipts	—	£5,000	£8,000	£10,000	£12,000	£14,000
60 day Sales Receipts	—	—	£5,000	£8,000	£10,000	£12,000
Total Cash Inflows	—	£5,000	£13,000	£18,000	£22,000	£26,000
Stock Purchases	—	£7,000	£11,200	£14,000	£16,800	£19,600
Van Purchase	£14,000	—	—	—	—	—
Van running costs	£500	£500	£500	£500	£500	£500
Rent	£1,500	—	—	£1,500	—	—
Gas & Electricity	—	—	£600	—	—	£600
Wages	£2,000	£2,000	£2,000	£2,000	£2,000	£2,000
Business Rates	—	£240	£240	£240	£240	£240
Advertising	£1,200	—	—	—	—	—
Total Cash Outflow	£19,200	£2,740				
NET CASH FLOW	-£19,200	£				
Opening Bank Balance	£20,000	£800				
Closing Bank Balance	£800	£				£-200

↳ narrative question — explain overdraft

413

10 Cash flow

Question 10.13

The following financial information relates to Sparkright Ltd for its financial year ending 31st December 2018.

	£'000
Operating Profit	3,000
Depreciation	400
Inventory as at 1st January 2018	500
Inventory as at 31st December 2018	600
Receivables as at 1st January 2018	200
Receivables as at 31st December 2018	180
Payables as at 1st January 2018	400
Payables as at 31st December 2018	350
Bank interest paid during year	20
Taxation paid during year	600
Purchase of new delivery vehicles during year	120
Sale of old plant & machinery during year	5
Proceeds from issue of new shares in Sparkright Ltd during year	12
Bank loan repayments during year	280
Dividends paid to shareholders during year	950
Bank balance on 1st January 2018	250

By completing the following (financial accounting format) statement of cash flows for year-ending 31st December 2018, determine what Sparkright Ltd's net cash flow was during 2018 and what its closing bank balance would be on 31st December 2018?

Sparkright Ltd Statement of Cash flows
Year ending 31st December 2018

	£'000
Cash flow from operating activities	
Operating Profit	£3,000
plus Depreciation	+ 400
+/- change in inventory	- 100
+/- change in receivables	+ 20
+/- change in payables	- 50
Cash generated from Operations	3,270
less interest paid	- 20
less taxation paid	- 600
Net cash inflow from operations	2,650
Cash flow from investing activities	
Purchase of non-current assets	-120
Disposal of non-current assets	+ 5
Net cash flow from investing activities	-115
Cash flow from financing activities	
New Share Capital issued	+12
Loan repayments	-280
Dividends paid	-950
Net Cash flow from financing activities	-1,218
Net Increase /(decrease) in cash	1,317
Cash as at 1st January 2018	250
Cash as at 31st December 2018	£1,567

10 Cash flow

Chapter 11

Working capital management

INTRODUCTION

We have already seen that a business needs to finance its investment in working capital and also in non-current assets such as buildings and plant and machinery, and we have explored the ways in which we evaluate proposed investment in non-current assets.

We will now turn our attention to the working capital requirements of a business. What is working capital, how much is required, and how can it be most efficiently managed?

OVERVIEW AND OBJECTIVES

By the end of this chapter you should have developed an understanding of:
- Working Capital and Liquidity
- Managing Receivables
- Managing Payables
- Managing Inventory
- Operating Cycle
- Managing Cash

and be able to answer questions relating to these areas.

Working capital management

Working capital

The working capital of a business can be considered to be the level of funding required to enable a business to operate on a day-to-day basis and give it sufficient liquidity to enable it to pay its debts as they become due.

In order to be able to trade, a business requires sufficient funding to allow it to have:-

- **Cash** – so that it can pay debts as they fall due
- **Inventory** – so that it has something to sell
- **Receivables** – so that it can offer its customers credit terms

A business which could not fund the above would find it difficult (if not impossible) to trade.

However, on the other side of the coin it is quite possible that a business will itself be granted credit terms from its suppliers i.e. **Payables** which are themselves a form of funding which helps offset the funding requirement for cash, inventory and receivables.

> ### DEFINITION
>
> The formal definition of working capital is:
>
> **Working Capital = Current Assets – Current Liabilities**
>
> Where **Current Assets** are what the business 'owns' and which will be 'used up' in the next 12 months, such as:
>
> - Inventory   (unsold goods)
> - Receivables   (amounts owed by credit customers waiting to be received)
> - Cash   (cash in hand, and cash in bank)
> - Pre-payments   (Payments made in advance for an expense which has not yet been incurred)
>
> And where **Current Liabilities** are what the business 'owes' and which must be paid in the next 12 months, such as:
>
> - Payables *(amounts owed to credit suppliers waiting to be paid)*
> - Taxation *(VAT, Corporation tax etc. owed to HMRC)*
> - Accruals *(Expenses which have been incurred but not yet charged)*

The figures for total current assets and total current liabilities can be read straight from the statement of financial position, and hence a figure for the working capital of a business can be quickly calculated.

Although the formal definition of working capital includes all current assets less all current liabilities, we will focus on those over which a business can exert some control: cash, inventory, receivables and payables *(accruals and pre-payments are basically book-keeping adjustments, whilst the payment of tax to HMRC is not normally negotiable!)*

The working capital within a business can be regarded as a 'money-go-round' as visualised in the diagram below.

Starting from Payables:

- Inventory is purchased from suppliers on credit terms:

    Payables → Inventory

- Sometime later the inventory is sold to customers on credit terms:

    Inventory → Receivables
- Sometime later the customers pay off their outstanding bills:

    Receivables → Cash
- The cash is then used to pay the original suppliers [+ others] and the suppliers will then be happy to supply more inventory on credit.

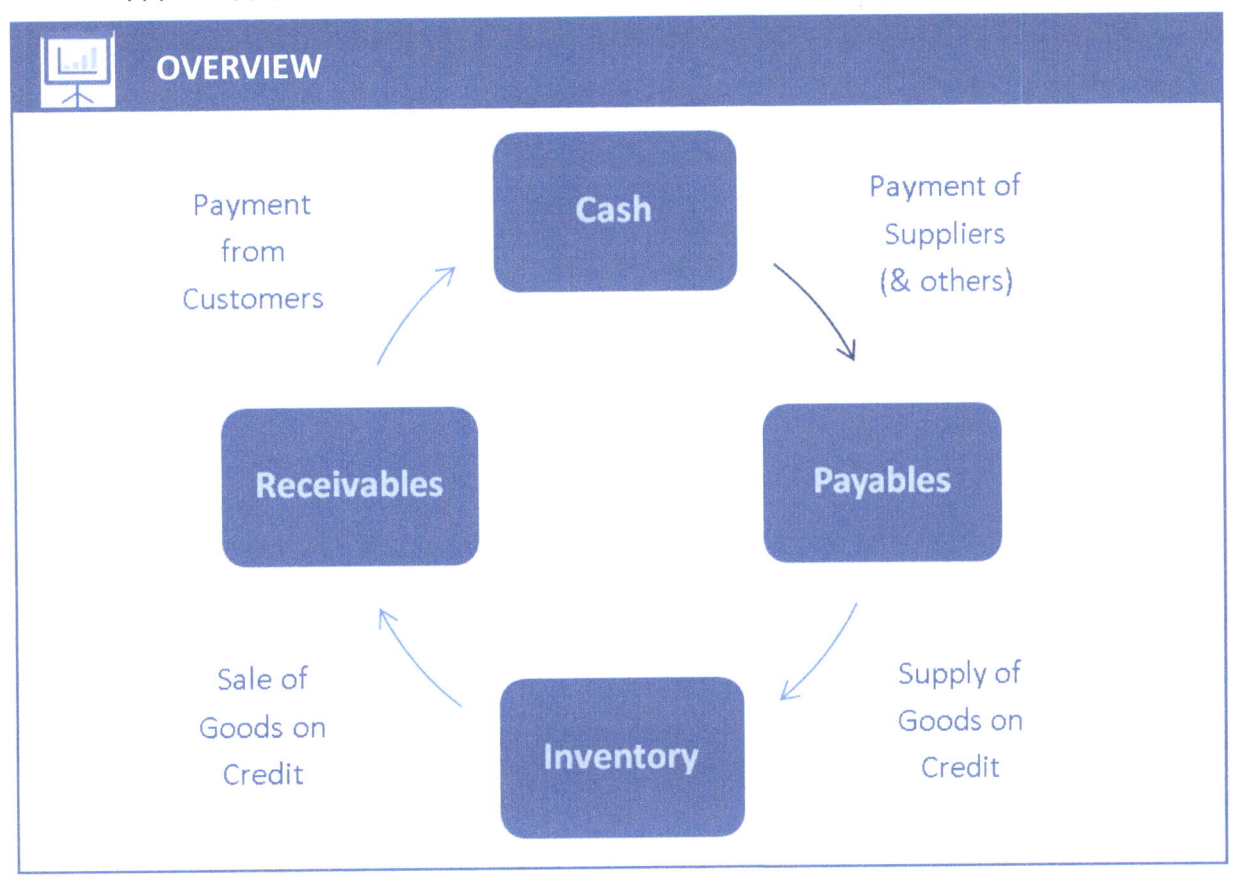

OVERVIEW

Cycle: **Cash** → (Payment of Suppliers (& others)) → **Payables** → (Supply of Goods on Credit) → **Inventory** → (Sale of Goods on Credit) → **Receivables** → (Payment from Customers) → **Cash**

The challenge for a company is:

a) To ensure that it has enough long-term funding available to allow it to hold sufficient cash, inventory and receivables …. less any funding contribution provided from payables

b) To ensure that at any point in time there is sufficient liquidity (i.e. cash) to enable it to pay debts as they fall due

The rest of this chapter will be devoted to seeing where this funding might come from and how to minimise the level of working capital required, whilst maximising liquidity.

11.2 Funding working capital

We have previously seen that virtually all businesses require long-term finance to allow them to:

a) Invest in the non-current assets (capital assets) required by their business

   e.g. land & buildings, computers, manufacturing machinery etc.

b) Invest in their current assets (part of working capital) also required by the business

   e.g. receivables, inventory & cash

… and that this long-term finance can be provided by either:

11 Working capital management

a) **Equity Finance**

   Shareholder funds comprising share capital + retained profit

b) **Debt Finance**

   Bank loans and/or corporate bonds

> ### ⚠️ KEY POINT
>
> **Remember... financing comes at a cost.**
>
> **Debt finance incurs interest payments, whilst shareholders expect returns.**
>
> In addition to **long-term finance**, funding requirements can also come from **short-term finance** ... which because it is short-term is categorised as a *current* liability e.g. using supplier credit terms (payables) or a bank overdraft. These are both ways of partially funding the business ... *but both may need to be paid off in the near future.*

We have now highlighted two **destinations for the financing** in a business, namely:

- Non-Current Assets (NCA) *e.g. land & buildings and plant & machinery*
- Current Assets (CA) *e.g. receivables, inventory & cash*

And three possible **sources of finance**, namely:

- Equity (EQ) *e.g. Shareholder funds*
- Non-Current Liabilities (NCL) *e.g. Bank loans, corporate bonds*
- Current Liabilities (CL) *e.g. Payables, overdraft*

> ### 🎓 TUTORIAL NOTE
>
> If you are a 'left-brained' student (*Google it!*) you might like to consider that:
>
> The accounting equation [Assets – Liabilities = Equity] can be expanded by splitting both assets and liabilities into their 'current' and 'non-current' components, and then re-arranged into:
>
> **NCA + CA = EQ + NCL + CL** ..... which shows that:
>
> **Non-Current Assets (NCA) + Current Assets (CA)** [on left]
>
> **are funded by Equity (EQ) + Long term Finance (NCL) + Short Term Finance (CL)** [on right]

Another complication is that as businesses grow they tend to need more funding for both:

- **Non-Current Assets** (bigger premises, more plant & machinery etc.)
- **Current Assets** (more credit customers, more inventory, higher cash reserves etc.)

..... and so will need to increase both the level of long-term and short-term funding within the business.

The *final* complication (promise!) is that the level of funding a business requires for its current assets does not remain constant over the trading year, but varies according to the seasonality of the market sector it operates in.

For example, a toy manufacturer (who sells into the retail sector) might need to significantly increase both inventory and receivables in the run up to Christmas, but will then receive large customer payments in January and February.

Put all of these factors together and the funding picture resembles the graph below, which shows that a business:

- Requires funding for non-current assets (land & buildings, plant & machinery etc.)
- Requires funding for current assets (receivables, inventory, cash etc.)
- Grows over time and requires more funding for both of the above
- Usually has a bedrock of funding from long-term sources (equity + long-term debt)
- Can top up the long-term funding with short-term funding (payables, overdraft etc.)

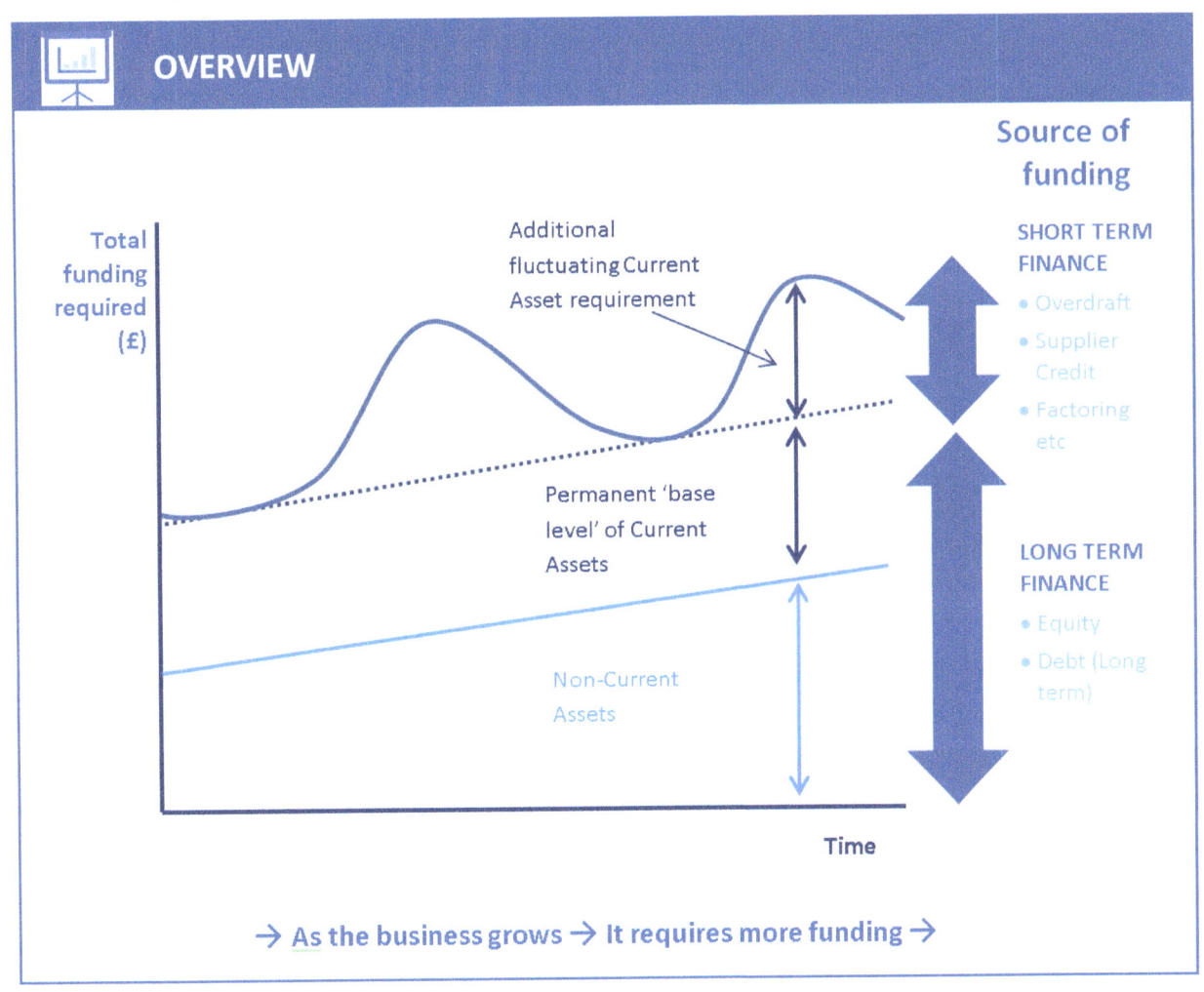

OVERVIEW

Graph showing Total funding required (£) over Time, with Non-Current Assets at the base, Permanent 'base level' of Current Assets above, and Additional fluctuating Current Asset requirement on top.

Source of funding

SHORT TERM FINANCE
- Overdraft
- Supplier Credit
- Factoring etc

LONG TERM FINANCE
- Equity
- Debt (Long term)

→ As the business grows → It requires more funding →

There are two broad ways in which a company can approach the problem of ensuring the required level of funding:

1. **A Conservative Funding Policy**

    Which favours the use of more long-term finance (more shares issued, higher long-term debt) to ensure that the company always has ample liquidity.

    This makes the company lower risk but it comes at a price. The providers of semi-permanent long-term finance (shareholders and banks etc.) will both require a return (dividend or interest) regardless of whether or not their finance is needed at any point in time.

    Safer, but more expensive.

11 Working capital management

2. **An Aggressive Funding Policy:**

   Which minimises the amount of semi-permanent long-term finance and instead relies on increased short-term finance sources such as delaying payments to suppliers, using bank overdrafts and even selling receivables (for a fee) to 3rd parties to generate cash when needed (so called 'debt factoring').

   This is undoubtedly a riskier method of operation (as it is not always clear where the cash to pay debts is coming from!) but can lead to higher profits, because long-term debt interest etc. is reduced (a company only pays overdraft interest for the days its bank account is actually overdrawn).

   Riskier, but cheaper.

Having given a recap and overview of all the sources and destinations for the financing of companies, we will now focus on the **working capital aspects** of this bigger problem, namely:

a) How can effective management of working capital actually reduce the amount of funding required for current assets i.e. how can a business survive with less cash, less inventory and less receivables, and therefore a lower funding requirement?

   Lower funding requirements → less cost → more profit

b) How can effective management of working capital actually increase the amount of short-term funding which is available from supplier credit (payables) and the use of overdrafts?

c) How can a business ensure its liquidity i.e. have sufficient cash available when needed?

… and we will focus on the four aspects over which a business can exert control:

- Inventory
- Receivables
- Cash
- Payables.

11.3 Measuring liquidity

> **DEFINITION**
>
> **Current Ratio (aka Working Capital ratio)**
> The current ratio is an indication of the business's liquidity i.e. ability to pay its debts as they fall due.
>
> $$\text{Current Ratio} = \frac{\text{Current Assets}}{\text{Current Liabilities}}$$
>
> - For a company to be able to pay its debts as they fall due it would seem preferable for its current assets to be greater than its current liabilities (i.e. Current Ratio > 1).
> - If this were the case then even if all the current liabilities became due for payment on the same day (unlikely!) they could all be paid, so long as all the current assets could also be converted to cash on the same day (even more unlikely!)
> - In practice, current liabilities become due for payment throughout the year, and the various current assets are converted to cash throughout the year, and so the aim is to always have sufficient cash at any point in time to pay the next bill.

The current ratio is used to provide a general overview of how liquid a company appears to be. The ratio is interpreted thus:

Current Ratio <1 → Current liabilities are greater than current assets.

This *might* indicate a liquidity problem.

Current Ratio 1-2 → Current assets are greater than current liabilities.

The company *should* have sufficient liquidity.

Current Ratio >2 → The company should have ample liquidity.

Possibly holding too many current assets (at a cost)

Any such general guidelines should be treated with the utmost caution as every industry sector (and indeed every business within every sector) is unique. For example, supermarkets generally have a very low current ratio. This does not mean they are suffering liquidity problems, but is instead a result of the market they operate in (fast turnover of stock, cash sales and credit purchases) meaning they can easily manage to operate on a very low current asset base.

The current ratio is most useful when used as a comparative measure for example:

- Comparing the current ratio year-on-year trend for the same company
- Comparing the current ratio to the industry norm for that sector.

However, one significant weakness of the current ratio is that it treats all types of current asset as though they had equal liquidity which is clearly not the case. In particular, inventory is the *'least liquid'* current asset because it is two steps away from being cash …. Inventory has to first be sold to a customer (normally on credit) and then that customer has to actually pay.

Businesses which hold high levels of inventory might appear to have high current ratios as a result and this might be hiding underlying liquidity problems caused by a combination of high payables with low cash/receivables.

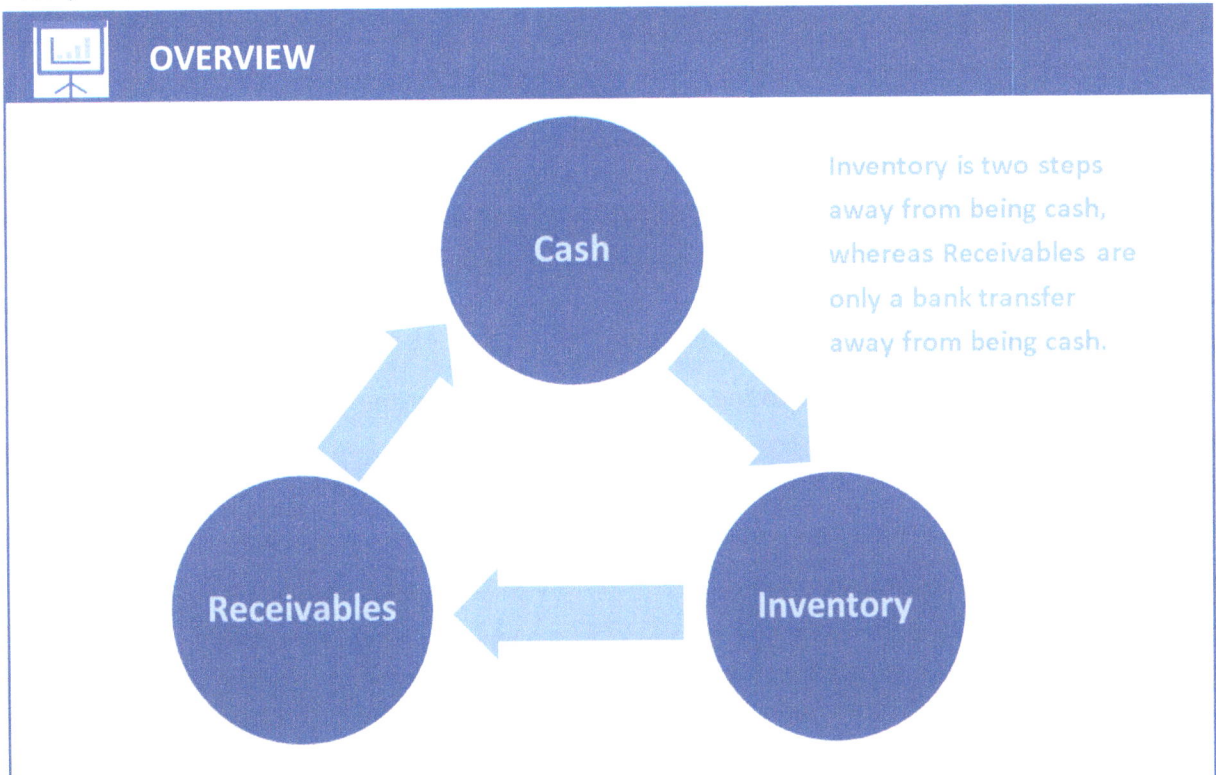

OVERVIEW

Inventory is two steps away from being cash, whereas Receivables are only a bank transfer away from being cash.

Cash → Inventory → Receivables → Cash

...king capital management

...se reasons it is also advisable to calculate the Quick Ratio which ignores inventory.

> **DEFINITION**
>
> **Quick Ratio (aka Acid Test ratio)**
>
> $$\text{Quick Ratio} = \frac{\text{Current Assets - Inventory}}{\text{Current Liabilities}}$$

The quick ratio of a certain business will clearly always be less than its current ratio (since it excludes inventory). However, the exclusion of inventory *(the least 'liquid' current asset)* means that the quick ratio will be a more robust measure of liquidity than the current ratio. Again the quick ratio is best used as a comparative measure.

> **TEST YOUR UNDERSTANDING 1**
>
> A company's statement of financial position shows it to have current liabilities of £550,000 and current assets of £625,000. However a closer examination of the current assets reveals that £330,000 of the total figure of £625,000 current assets is made up of inventory.
>
> Calculate the current ratio and quick ratio for the company and comment on its apparent liquidity.
>
> Current Ratio _____
>
> Quick Ratio _____
>
> Liquidity? _____
>
> _____
>
> _____

11.4 Managing working capital

The rest of the chapter is devoted to the efficient management of the key components of working capital, namely:

- Receivables
- Payables
- Inventory
- Cash

In each case the overall aims are to reduce the level of funding required for working capital (to allow the company to reduce its financing costs) and to reduce the time it takes to convert inventory into receivables, and receivables into cash.

These aims will often involve a profit versus liquidity balancing act and it is up to individual businesses to prioritise which one is more important at any point in time.

11.5 Receivables

> **DEFINITION**
>
> **Receivables (aka Debtors)** are the sums owed to the company by customers who have purchased goods or services on credit terms.
>
> They are typically managed by a sub-team from within the finance function known as the Sales Ledger Department, or Credit Control Department, or Accounts Receivable (AR) Department.

The responsibilities of these teams include:

- Screening potential new credit customers to ensure that they are credit worthy. This might involve seeking trade references from other businesses who have previously offered the same customer credit terms. It will also probably involve using a credit rating agency such as Experian who can provide an assessment of the level of risk involved with selling to this customer on a credit basis, plus a suggested initial credit limit for them.

- On an ongoing basis: sending sales invoices and periodic statements of account to the customers, and processing the corresponding payments received. As the relationship with the customer grows and more trust is built, the credit limit may be reviewed upwards if there are no causes for concern.

- A key function which this department fulfils is to encourage prompt payment from the credit customers. This is a balancing act between maintaining good ongoing relations with the customers, whilst not allowing the customer to take advantage and consistently pay late.

- The ultimate dilemma is when payment is simply not forthcoming and the credit control department then have a key role in maintaining lines of communication with the defaulting customer and gaining an understanding of exactly what the problem is and therefore how best to tackle it. Every company is different, but a suggested sequence could involve:

    - Sending a copy statement or polite email reminder of overdue balance and requesting payment
    - Telephone call to ascertain nature of problem and encourage payment
    - Withhold further supplies if no satisfactory response (i.e. 'put on stop')
    - Possible involvement of debt collection agency
    - Possible legal action

.... which can be summarised as *'PNS'* .... Polite ... Nasty .... Solicitor!

> **DEFINITION**
>
> **Receivables Days (aka Debtor Days)**
>
> A key measure used by the Sales Ledger Department is to calculate the average number of days the company's customers are taking to pay:
>
> $$\text{Receivables Days} = \frac{\text{Trade Receivables}}{\text{(Credit) Sales}} \times 365$$
>
> *Strictly speaking we should use just credit sales to calculate receivables days. However it is not always possible to establish what a company's credit sales, as opposed to its cash sales, actually are and we will then have no choice but to use the total sales figure.*

11 Working capital management

> **TUTORIAL NOTE**
>
> Receivables represents the value of the sales made to customers and these are obviously at the selling price. The above formula is comparing this with a sales figure which is also clearly measured 'at selling price' i.e. a like-for-like comparison.

> **EXAMPLE**
>
> **Scenario**
>
> At the end the financial year a company reports £45,000 of Receivables on its Statement of Financial Position.
>
> In the year just ended it reported sales revenue of £580,000 (comprised wholly of credit sales).
>
> At the year-end how many days of sales remained unpaid?
>
> **Solution**
>
> Receivables Days = $\dfrac{\text{Trade Receivables}}{\text{Credit Sales}} \times 365 = \dfrac{£45,000}{£580,000} \times 365 =$ **28 days**
>
> The £45,000 of outstanding customer payments represents 28 days' worth of sales.

As with all 'Key Performance Indicators' (KPIs) it is always useful to compare the result to some form of benchmark, such as:

- The standard credit terms for the company. If these are standard 30 day terms then the Sales Ledger Department appear to be doing a good job.

- Receivables Days result from previous year. Is the credit control function more or less efficient at collecting debt than last year?

- Receivables Days of major competitors in the same sector (possible selling to the same customers). How well is the credit control function doing compared to the credit control departments of the competitors? Remember the competitors' annual accounts will be publically available at Companies House to enable this sort of benchmarking.

Receivables Balancing Act: Liquidity versus Profitability

As with many aspects of business there can be a potential difference of priorities between different sections of the business, and indeed different priorities from one month to another as circumstances change.

For example, the sales department is obviously keen to sell as much as they can to their customer base. If a particular customer has exceeded their credit limit (the maximum they are allowed to owe at any point in time) then the business's computer systems would normally automatically put that customer 'on stop' i.e. not allow any more sales orders to be processed until the customer makes a payment and reduces the outstanding balance. At this point the customer would typically ask for an increase to the credit limit and this may even be supported by the business's own sales department, who are keen to secure as many sales as possible.

It is then a judgement call (led by the credit control team, but in discussion with others) as to whether or not the company should hold firm and demand a payment to bring the customer back within the credit limit ... or simply increase the limit!

There is no right or wrong answer to such quandaries, but it is important that everyone appreciates the big picture so that a fully informed discussion can take place. The credit control team need to appreciate the importance of seizing the opportunity to drive sales and hence profit, whilst the sales team have to appreciate the importance of safeguarding cash flow and reducing bad debt risks.

Similar dilemmas arise when deciding on credit terms i.e. how many days credit to allow (30, 60, 90 days etc.). Some companies offer incentives for customers to pay early by offering early settlement discounts (e.g. 2.5% discount if payment is made within 15 days). Again this presents a choice, this time between improving cash flow at the cost of profitability.

Some of the conflicting choices faced when dealing with receivables are summarised in the table below.

OVERVIEW

Receivables Balancing Act	Liquidity versus Profitability
Providing long credit terms *Drives sales .... but worsens cash flow*	Customers are attracted by long payment terms ... after all, they might have cash flow problems of their own. So this might help to grow sales and profit. However until they ultimately pay, all you have is 'paper profit' which is a poor substitute for cash.
Providing high credit limits *Drives sales ... but ties up cash and increases risk of bad debt*	Providing high credit limits will certainly attract customers, but this can increase the risk of non-payment as well as potentially slowing down customer payments.
Offering early payment discounts *Improves cash flow .... but reduces profitability*	Offering a modest discount for early payment certainly encourages early payment (at least from customers who have the cash), but at a cost. The discount is reducing the company's bottom line profit.
Overly assertive credit control function *Improves cash flow ..... but risks goodwill and future trade*	Continual hounding of customers for payment might result in some earlier payments, but in the long-term might also sour the future trading relationship.

11 Working capital management

11.6 Payables

> **DEFINITION**
>
> **Payables (aka creditors)** are the sums owed by the company to its suppliers from whom they have purchased goods or services on credit terms. They are typically managed by a sub-team from within the finance function known as the Purchase Ledger Department, or Accounts Payable (AP) Department.

The responsibilities of these teams include:

- On an ongoing basis: processing purchase invoices received from suppliers and ensuring that they agree with the volume of material/services actually received and that the prices are as agreed.

- Arranging payment for purchase invoices at the appropriate time and with regard to the current cash flow position of the business. In businesses with cash flow issues this can involve juggling & diplomacy.

- Payment meetings (typically between Purchase Ledger Department and Finance Director) to decide exactly which overdue invoices to pay. If cash flow is currently strained then this will involve trying to:
    - Keep all key suppliers at least 'satisfied' (even if not happy) to maintain ongoing supply
    - Maintaining contact with suppliers as failure to communicate sends out a bad message
    - Negotiating payment plans with suppliers (to avoid situations 'going legal')

Developing good supplier relationships can secure the supply chain even when cash is short! Remember, the Payables of a company are one of its short-term sources of finance and 'stretching' supplier payments can help a business get through a difficult period. However stretching too far or too often, can risk being 'put on stop' and potentially halting production due to loss of supply, or at least gaining a bad reputation which will prove a hindrance with future supplier price negotiations.

> **TUTORIAL NOTE**
>
> In many ways, the Purchase Ledger department (looking after Payables) is the mirror image of the Sales Ledger Department (looking after Receivables):
>
> - The **business's** Sales Ledger Department is trying to *speed up receipt of payments* from customers by negotiating with the **customer's** Purchase Ledger Department …. whilst
>
> - The **business's** Purchase Ledger Department is often trying to *slow down payments* to suppliers by negotiating with the **supplier's** Sales Ledger Department.

> **DEFINITION**
>
> **Payables Days (aka Creditor Days)**
>
> A key measure used by the Purchase Ledger Department is to calculate the average number of days the company is taking to pay its suppliers:
>
> $$\text{Payables Days} = \frac{\text{Trade Payables}}{\text{Cost of Sales}} \times 365$$

The Language of Business

> **TUTORIAL NOTES**
>
> You may see quoted an alternative formula for Payables Days which uses 'purchases' in place of 'cost of sales'.
>
> The two formulae usually produce very similar results (unless the opening and closing inventory figures have varied significantly) but the 'purchases' figure is not so readily available from a company's accounts as the 'cost of sales' figure.
>
> Payables represents the *cost* of the stock purchased and the above formula is comparing it with Cost of Sales which is also measured 'at cost' i.e. a like-for-like comparison.

> **EXAMPLE**
>
> **Scenario**
>
> At the end the financial year a company reports £60,000 of Payables on its Statement of Financial Position.
>
> In the year just ended it reported Cost of Sales of £1,200,000 (comprised wholly of credit sales).
>
> At the year-end how many days of payables remained unpaid?
>
> **Solution**
>
> Payables Days = $\dfrac{\text{Trade Payables}}{\text{Cost of Sales}}$ x 365 = $\dfrac{£60,000}{£1,200,000}$ x 365 = **18 days**
>
> The £60,000 of outstanding supplier payments represents 18 days' worth of payables.

Again we should always compare the result to some form of benchmark. For example:

- The standard purchasing credit terms from suppliers. If these are the standard 30 day terms then the Purchase Ledger department appears to be paying too quickly!

- Payables Days result from previous year. Is the business paying faster or slower than a year ago?

- Payables Days of major competitors in the same sector (possibly buying from the same suppliers). Is the business paying suppliers faster or slower than its competitors? Again, this sort of benchmarking is possible because the competitors' annual accounts will be publically available at Companies House.

Payables Balancing Act: Liquidity versus Profitability

The Purchase Ledger Department also face a series of choices between profitability and liquidity, which are often the opposite choices to those faced by the Sales Ledger Department.

- The Purchase Ledger Department are to some extent 'in the driving seat' when it comes to deciding when to pay, whilst the corresponding suppliers are in the driving seat when it comes to decide whether or not to maintain ongoing supplies, whereas…

- The situation is exactly reversed for the Sales Ledger Department who can decide whether or not to continue supplying a particular customer depending on whether or not that customer has paid on time or not.

11 Working capital management

The truth is that the Sales Ledger Department have a key role to play in working capital management by ensuring that the customers keep paying i.e. keep turning receivables into cash. The Purchase Ledger Department have an equally vital role to play by managing whatever cash is available to keep all of the business's suppliers satisfied and thereby ensuring that the supply chain is maintained.

OVERVIEW

Payables Balancing Act	Liquidity versus Profitability
Slow down payments to suppliers *Preserves cash … but risks reputation*	Slowing down payments to suppliers to get through a 'lean period' is not uncommon in business, but doing it too often might damage the business's reputation, credit rating and future supply.
Taking advantage of early payment discounts *Improves profitability … but uses valuable cash prematurely*	If the company has spare (!) cash then it may as well take advantage of early payment discounts and increase profitability. However if cash is short then the discounts can wait. Securing cash flow is more important.
Developing reputation as a prompt payer *Builds good reputation … but worsens cash flow*	If cash flow was not an issue then it might be wise to always pay within the agreed terms and develop a reputation as a good payer. This might lead to more favourable supplier treatment in future (e.g. next price negotiation).

11.7 Inventory

DEFINITION

Inventory (aka stock) is the goods or materials held by a company for resale. These can be 'finished goods' held by a wholesaler or retailer, or raw materials and components which will be used by manufacturers in their production process. Inventory also includes part manufactured goods, known as 'work in progress' or WIP, and finished manufactured items awaiting sale.

Inventory can therefore comprise of:

- Raw Materials and Components
- Work in Progress (WIP)
- Finished Goods

The Language of Business

Valuation of Inventory

The total value of a company's inventory (for all of the above) is ascertained at the end of each financial period and recorded on the Statement of Financial Position (SOFP) under the 'Current Assets' section.

Financial reporting standards require all inventory to be valued at:

"...the lower of cost and net realisable value...'

The key point being that inventory is recorded on the SOFP at its original cost and not at its expected selling price (which would be pre-empting profit for goods not yet sold!)

The exception is if the inventory is now considered to be worth less than when purchased, in which case it is 'written down' to whatever the final (lower) selling price is expected to be realised (less any additional estimated costs to make the sale).

The 'cost' should include all costs of purchase, costs of conversion (including fixed and variable manufacturing overheads) and other costs incurred in bringing the inventories to their present location and condition.

TEST YOUR UNDERSTANDING 2

A computer retailer purchases a number of laptop computers for £180 each with the intention of selling them for £210 each.

At what value should any of the unsold laptops be recorded for inventory purposes?

_____
_____

TEST YOUR UNDERSTANDING 3

Some months later the computer retailer still has a number of the original laptops remaining unsold but feels he will not now be able to sell them at the original selling price because everyone appears to be buying a new, more powerful model that has recently been launched. However, by installing increased memory into each laptop at a cost of £20 he believes they can be sold for the discounted sum of £190.

At what value should any of the unsold laptops now be recorded for inventory purposes?

_____
_____
_____

11 Working capital management

FIFO & AVCO

A problem arises when a business repeatedly purchases the same item and at some point in time the purchase cost of the item increases. For example imagine that component X is being purchased on a monthly basis. The new components are added into the storage bin (along with the previously purchased components) and then (a mixture of old and new) component X's are withdrawn from the storage bin whenever they are needed for production.

At the end of the financial period it is impossible to determine how many of the remaining component X's in the storage bin are old and how many are new, so how can their value be determined for inventory purposes?

There are two allowed methods of valuing this inventory:

1) **First In First Out (FIFO)** where it is assumed that the oldest components were sold first
2) **Weighted Average Cost (AVCO)** where a weighted average cost is used

EXAMPLE

Scenario

On the 1st January there were zero component X's in stock.

What is the total inventory valuation at the end of February on a FIFO basis?

	Purchased	Used in Production
January	200 units costing £1.00 each	80
February	50 units costing £1.20 each	90

Solution

No. of component X remaining in stock = 250 purchased − 170 used = 80

The component X's are being used on a First In First Out basis so the 170 used in production ALL came from the first batch of 200 bought for £1.00 each.

The 80 component X's remaining in stock are therefore deemed to comprise of:

- 30 @ £1.00 each = £30.00 (remaining January batch)
- 50 @ £1.20 each = £60.00 (as yet untouched February batch)
  £90.00

TUTORIAL NOTE

FIFO is the standard method in practice.

The alternative AVCO method simply recalculates a new weighted average cost, each time items are added or subtracted (i.e. total value divided by total number = weighted average cost).

The older method of 'Last In First Out' (LIFO) is no longer allowed by financial reporting standards.

The Language of Business

Management of Inventory

The ordering of inventory is typically managed by a team known as the Purchasing Department, or Procurement Department.

Their responsibilities typically include:

- Managing the tendering process for new supply contracts and ensuring that the business has a secure supply chain (to prevent potential loss of supply), of goods and services of the required quality, at the keenest prices and best trading terms possible.

- On an ongoing basis: issuing purchase orders for all required supplies and ensuring that the subsequently received purchase invoices agree with the volume of material/services actually received and that the prices are as agreed.

- Managing the level of inventory held to ensure that the lack of any single item does not halt production or result in lost sales. This is no small task…

> **EXAMPLES**
>
> - Supermarkets can stock 40,000 different product lines
> - A typical family car contains 30,000 parts
> - Estimates for the number of different components parts required to manufacture a large airliner vary from hundreds of thousands … to millions!

In practice, any company of a reasonable size will run a computerised inventory system which keeps track of all items purchased and sold (or withdrawn for manufacture) and their inventory valuation (on FIFO or AVCO basis depending on how the system has been configured).

The best solution is for an 'integrated' system which 'talks' to the other systems within the business (sales, purchasing, production, accounting etc.). The most sophisticated inventory systems are known as 'Warehouse Management Systems' (WMS) which actually 'map out' every single storage location in the business and are able to provide a real-time calculation of exactly what components are where, and what their FIFO/AVCO value is. Quite handy if you are running a car manufacturing plant and trying to track 30,000 different items of stock!

Measurement of Inventory Management

From a working capital perspective, a business is keen to understand how much valuable cash they have tied up in unsold inventory and whether this represents an appropriate level of inventory. The most common business metric is Inventory Days, which calculates the average number of days stock is held for (or alternatively how many days it would take to sell the closing inventory).

$$\text{Inventory Days} = \frac{\text{Inventory}}{\text{Cost of Sales}} \times 365$$

> **TUTORIAL NOTE**
>
> Inventory is measured 'at cost' and the above formula is comparing it with Cost of Sales which are also measured 'at cost' i.e. comparing on a like-for-like basis.

11 Working capital management

> **EXAMPLE**
>
> **Scenario**
>
> At the end of the financial year a company has £550,000 of Inventory on its statement of financial position. In the year just ended it reported cost of sales of £1,200,000.
>
> At the year-end how many days' worth of Inventory is the company holding?
>
> **Solution**
>
> Inventory Days = $\dfrac{\text{Inventory}}{\text{Cost of Sales}}$ x 365 = $\dfrac{£550,000}{£1,200,000}$ x 365 = 167 days
>
> **The £550,000 of inventory represents sufficient stock for 167 days' worth of sales.**

> **EXAMPLE**
>
> **Scenario**
>
> How much less working capital would be required if the company above reduced its stock holding to 60 days of inventory?
>
> **Solution**
>
> Rearranging: Inventory Days = $\dfrac{\text{Inventory}}{\text{Cost of Sales}}$ x 365
>
> Into: Inventory = $\dfrac{\text{Inventory Days x Cost of Sales}}{365}$ = $\dfrac{60 \times £1,200,000}{365}$ = £197,260
>
> The company would require £550,000 - £197,260 = £352,740 less working capital if it could operate with 60 days of inventory instead of 167 days' worth. This would represent a significant saving in the funding costs of working capital and hence potentially higher profitability.

As usual we should ideally compare the Inventory Days result to some form of benchmark:

- Inventory Days result from previous year. Is the business increasing or decreasing its stock holding (when compared to the level of trade)?

- Inventory Days of major competitors in same sector. Are the business's competitors managing to survive on a lower level of inventory? If so what can be done to achieve the desired stock reductions? As before, this sort of benchmarking will involve scrutinising the competitors' annual accounts available online at Companies House.

Inventory Levels

The efficient management of inventory involves a great deal of skill in ensuring that the entire production process of a manufacturing plant does not come to a standstill for the lack of an individual component part or raw material. Similarly, in the wholesale and retail sectors losing sales through lack of stock is considered a cardinal sin!

However, every company has to balance the desire to hold huge quantities of inventory (just in case!) against the additional costs (and hence lost profit) which would be incurred.

These additional costs include:

- Increased requirement for working capital ….. at a cost!
- Larger warehouses with more warehouse staff required.
- Greater chance of redundant stock due to changed specifications, fashions or even sell by dates!

There are several different ways of managing inventory levels, including:

- **Ordering according to anticipated demand** i.e. based on what the budget believes will be required for the period ahead (possibly modified by recent trends … plus a safety level of 'buffer stock').

- **Re-ordering back up to pre-determined 'par' levels of stock**. This involves knowing how much inventory of each item is currently being held, and then ordering the difference between this actual level, and the pre-determined par level. Unfortunately this requires a physical stock-take (i.e. someone counting items in individual warehouse storage bins etc.) … unless a computerised inventory control system is used which knows (at least in theory) how much stock is currently available, and can therefore calculate a requirements list to take each item back up to the 'par' value held in the system.

- **Replenishment ordering based on actual sales/usage.** Simply ordering replacement stock for that sold/used since the previous order. For example, each night a supermarket places a replenishment order to the hub depot for the items sold through the store's EPOS (Electronic Point of Sale) till system the day before. The stock is 'picked' in the hub depot overnight and arrives with the supermarket branch early the next morning.

- **Just In Time (JIT) Ordering** is a philosophy being increasingly considered in manufacturing, which aims to eliminate inventory altogether so that raw materials and components arrive 'just in time' to go onto the beginning of the production line when needed. The consequences of getting this wrong are horrendous, and for that reason many companies are still talking about it rather than implementing it. It has its origins in Japan and requires a completely robust supply chain including suppliers who are prepared to deliver small quantities of inventory on a daily basis to avoid the business having to hold any inventory at all.

EXAMPLE

Scenario

A manufacturing company orders inventory based on anticipated demand. The materials usage budget forecasts that 100 Kg of grade 316 stainless steel will be required in April to produce components for the marine industry. The last two months have seen the corresponding sales budgets exceeded by 5%. The opening stock of grade 316 stainless steel will be 30Kg on the 1st April, and a buffer stock of 50Kg is usually aimed for.

How much grade 316 stainless steel should be ordered for April?

Solution

Ordering Quantity = (Forecast Requirement + 5%) + buffer level − stock on hand

= (100 Kg x 1.05) + 50 Kg − 30Kg

= **125 Kg**

11 Working capital management

> **OVERVIEW**
>
> | **Inventory Balancing Act** | **Liquidity versus Profitability** |
> |---|---|
> | **Maintain High Levels of Inventory**

Safer … but more cash tied up in inventory | Ordering in bulk reduces ordering costs and reduces the risk of 'stock-outs' … but incurs high holding costs, and results in more cash being tied up in inventory.

With perishable goods higher stock levels can result in more stock write-offs, whilst with fashion goods higher stock levels can lead to increased stock write-downs (via clearance houses etc.). |
> | **Maintain Low Levels of Inventory e.g. JIT**

More risk of 'stock-outs' but less cash tied up in inventory | Making smaller but more frequent orders in an attempt to reduce inventory levels will increase ordering and handling costs, but lower holding costs and reduce the amount of cash tied up in inventory. |

11.8 Operating cycle

We have now examined three of the components of working capital and in each case have looked at a measure to describe how long that part of the working capital operating cycle ties up funds for:

Inventory Days: Which measures how long on average funds are tied up in Inventory before it is sold.

Receivables Days: Which measures how long on average funds are tied up in Receivables before the customers settle their accounts.

Payables Days: Which measures how long on average the business benefits by withholding the Payables required to settle supplier accounts.

If all three of these factors are taken into account then an estimate can be made of the length of time taken for money to complete the working capital cycle on the following page.

The Language of Business

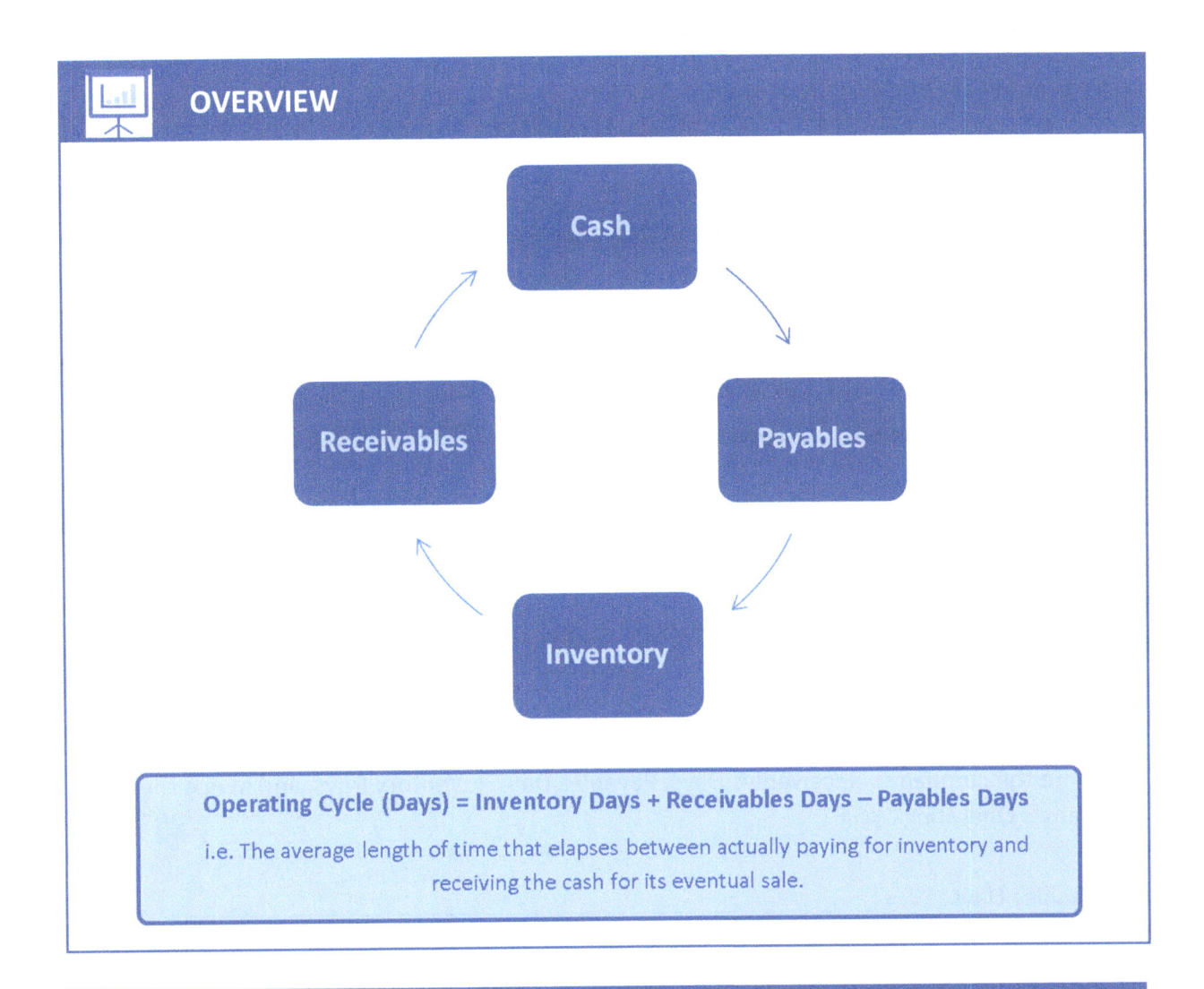

OVERVIEW

```
         Cash
       ↗      ↘
Receivables   Payables
       ↖      ↙
        Inventory
```

Operating Cycle (Days) = Inventory Days + Receivables Days − Payables Days

i.e. The average length of time that elapses between actually paying for inventory and receiving the cash for its eventual sale.

EXAMPLE

Scenario

A company has the following working capital KPIs (Key Performance Indicators):

- Inventory Days   = 140 days
- Receivables Days = 65 days
- Payables Days   = 45 days

How long is cash 'tied up' on average in this company between paying the supplier for inventory and subsequently receiving payment for it from the customer?

Solution

Operating Cycle = Inventory Days + Receivables Days − Payables Days

= 140 days + 65 days − 45 days

= **160 days**

This represents a considerable time for the business to be 'out of pocket' and having to fund the transaction. Anything that could be done to reduce this time (and move funds around the operating cycle faster) would reduce the amount of working capital required by the company and hence improve financial performance.

11 Working capital management

As we have already seen such ideas could include:

- Reducing inventory levels to promote faster turnover of stock
- Encouraging faster payments from customers
- Stretching (within limits) the time taken to pay suppliers

As with any other calculated business metric it is useful to measure trends over time within the business in question (i.e. is the operating cycle getting faster or slower over time), and to compare it to competitors in the same trade sector.

> **TEST YOUR UNDERSTANDING 4**
>
> A company's year-end financial statements include the following figures:
>
> - Credit Sales   £700,000
> - Cost of Sales   £245,000
> - Receivables   £76,500
> - Payables   £30,200
> - Inventory   £45,600
>
> Calculate the company's Receivables Days, Payables Days, Inventory Days, and hence the company's Operating Cycle.
>
> Receivables Days _____
>
> Payables Days _____
>
> Inventory Days _____
>
> Operating Cycle _____

11.9 Cash management

The final component part of working capital is cash itself, and this is undoubtedly the most sought after current asset. It is the only way of paying staff, rent and suppliers to say nothing of dividends or loan interest. With sufficient cash a company can continue to trade through difficult periods, whilst the market picks up or they re-align their product offering.

The final question then is how much cash should a business aim to hold. The instinctive response might be to say 'as much as possible' in the belief that you can't have too much of a good thing. However we have to remind ourselves where the cash came from. Like the other current asset components of working capital (receivables and inventory) it is all funded from a combination of long-term wond short-term funding, most of which comes at a cost or at least an expectation of a return.

If the level of working capital is too high (for instance because the company is holding too much cash) then the costs of finance are arguably also too high, particularly from:

- Long-term bank loans or corporate bonds which incur interest costs

- Shareholder funds which are accompanied by the expectation of dividends

If the overall level of working capital can be restricted to the required optimal levels (including cash levels) then less long-term borrowing is required, thereby reducing financing costs, and less share capital is required meaning that the profits of the company can be shared among fewer shareholders, thereby potentially increasing dividends *per share.*

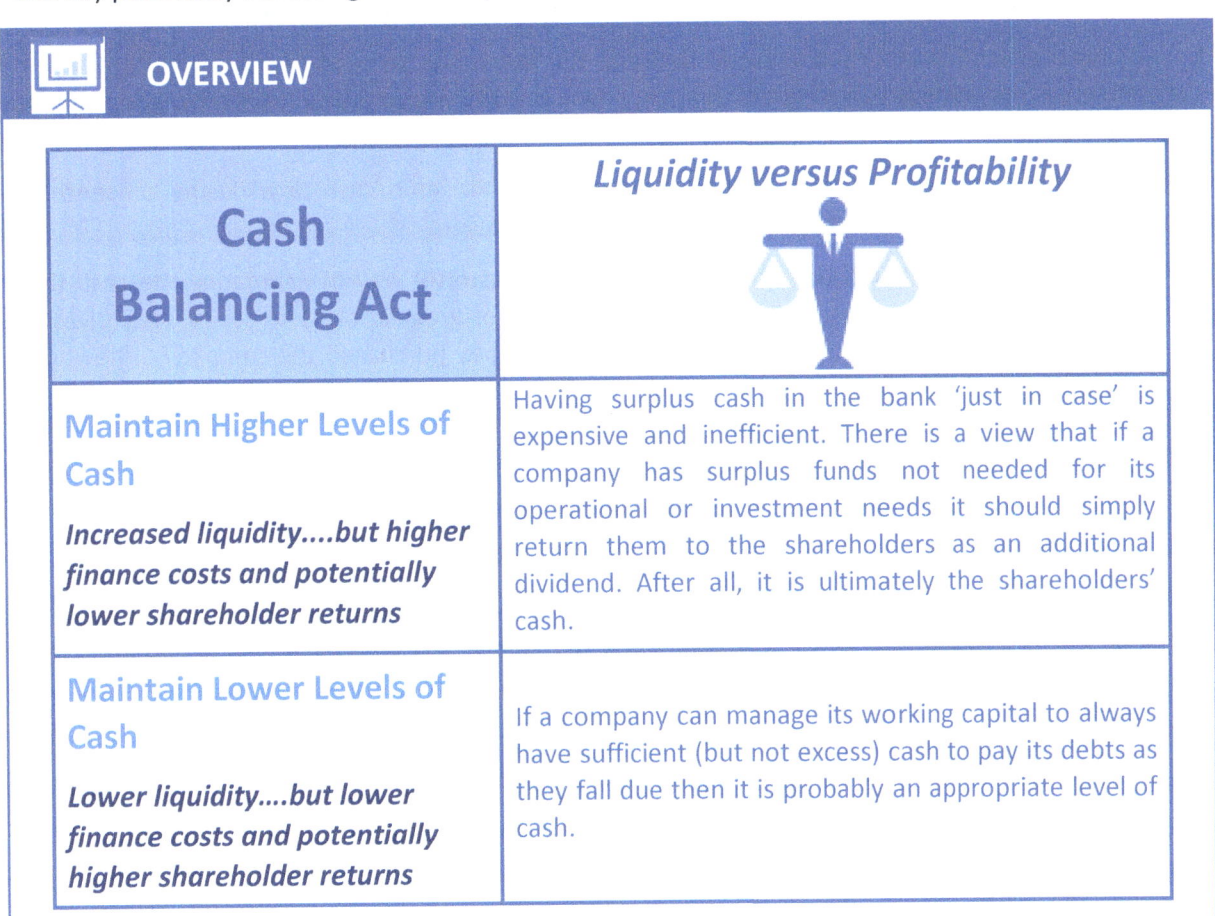

OVERVIEW

Cash Balancing Act	Liquidity versus Profitability
Maintain Higher Levels of Cash *Increased liquidity….but higher finance costs and potentially lower shareholder returns*	Having surplus cash in the bank 'just in case' is expensive and inefficient. There is a view that if a company has surplus funds not needed for its operational or investment needs it should simply return them to the shareholders as an additional dividend. After all, it is ultimately the shareholders' cash.
Maintain Lower Levels of Cash *Lower liquidity….but lower finance costs and potentially higher shareholder returns*	If a company can manage its working capital to always have sufficient (but not excess) cash to pay its debts as they fall due then it is probably an appropriate level of cash.

11.10 EBIDTA

DEFINITION

EBITDA is a performance measure frequently used at senior levels of company management because it is a figure which can be quickly derived from the statement of profit or loss (which tends to be the most frequently produced and used financial statement) but which gives a good approximation of the cash being generated from the operations of the business.

EBITDA = Earnings Before Interest Taxation Depreciation & Amortisation

Although looking slightly formidable, it is actually an easier term to understand than might at first appear. Let's decipher it ....

- 'Earnings' is simply another word for 'Profit'
- 'Earnings before Interest and Tax' (EBIT) is exactly the same as 'Profit before Interest & Tax' (PBIT) … which we also know as Operating Profit and which is a readily available profit figure on

the statement of profit or loss, and regarded as the best indicator of company profit performance

- Depreciation is the (accruals basis) method of spreading the cost of capital expenditure over the life of the non-current assets….rather than recording it all at once when the assets are first purchased. Depreciation is NOT a cash flow but rather a book-keeping adjustment

- Amortisation is exactly the same as depreciation but is the term used when the non-current assets in question are 'intangible' (i.e. no physical form) e.g. copyright, patents, goodwill etc. Again, amortisation is NOT a cash flow.

- Invariably the biggest single difference between 'profit' and 'cash flow' is the presence of depreciation (and amortisation) charges.

- So EBITDA gives a very quick (though not entirely accurate) way of estimating the cash flow generated from operating activities, which would be of great interest to senior executives …. and also prospective purchasers of a company i.e. if they purchased the company … how long would it take to recoup the cost?

The Language of Business

> ⚠️ **KEY POINTS FROM CHAPTER 11**

Working Capital

- The level of funding required to enable a business to operate on a day-to-day basis and give it sufficient liquidity to enable it to pay its debts as they become due
- **Working Capital = Current Assets – Current Liabilities**
- Working capital should be reduced to the lowest level possible (to reduce financing costs) whilst ensuring that the business has sufficient liquidity to allow it to pay debts as they fall due.

Current Ratio (aka Working Capital ratio)

- The current ratio is an indication of the business's liquidity i.e. ability to pay its debts as they fall due.
- $\text{Current Ratio} = \dfrac{\text{Current Assets}}{\text{Current Liabilities}}$

Quick Ratio (aka Acid Test ratio)

- The quick ratio is a more robust measure of liquidity which excludes inventory as it is the *'least liquid'* current asset.
- $\text{Quick Ratio} = \dfrac{\text{Current Assets - Inventory}}{\text{Current Liabilities}}$

Receivables Days (aka Debtor Days)

- A key measure used by the Sales Ledger Department is to calculate the average number of days the company's customers are taking to pay.
- $\text{Receivables Days} = \dfrac{\text{Trade Receivables}}{\text{[Credit] Sales}} \times 365$
- Offering customers higher credit limits and longer credit terms might drive sales and hence profitability, but at the cost of worsening liquidity and possibly increasing bad debt.

Payables Days (aka Creditor Days)

- A key measure used by the Purchase Ledger Department is to calculate the average number of days the company is taking to pay its suppliers.
- $\text{Payables Days} = \dfrac{\text{Trade Payables}}{\text{Cost of Sales}} \times 365$
- Paying suppliers promptly will promote good supplier relations and possibly help with future price negotiations, but will worsen liquidity in the short term. Supplier credit is a valuable (and usually free) source of short-term finance.

Inventory Days

- Calculates the average number of days stock is held for (or alternatively how many days it would take to sell the closing inventory).
- $\text{Inventory Days} = \dfrac{\text{Inventory}}{\text{Cost of Sales}} \times 365$
- High levels of inventory reduce the risk of interrupted production or lost sales due to 'stock-outs', but are costly in terms reduced liquidity and increased holding costs.

11 Working capital management

Operating Cycle (aka Working Capital Cycle)

- **Operating Cycle (Days) = Inventory Days + Receivables Days – Payables Days**
- The average length of time that elapses between actually paying for inventory and receiving the cash for its eventual sale.
- Reducing the operating cycle, correspondingly reduces the required level of funding for working capital.

Chapter 11: Test Your Understanding Answers

TEST YOUR UNDERSTANDING 1

Current Ratio = Current Assets / Current Liabilities = £625,000 / £550,000 = **1.14**

Quick Ratio = (Current Assets – Inventory) / Current Liabilities = £295,000 / £550,000 = **0.54**

The current ratio shows that current assets are larger than current liabilities which is usually a healthy indicator of liquidity. However the quick ratio reveals that once inventory (with poor liquidity) is disregarded that the liquidity position appears far less healthy with current liabilities outweighing (liquid) current assets by nearly twice over.

TEST YOUR UNDERSTANDING 2

If the retailer valued the unsold laptops at £210 in the inventory valuation this would have the effect of generating £30 of profit which does not yet exist. The laptops are therefore valued at **£180 each** (which is the **lower** of cost and net realisable value).

TEST YOUR UNDERSTANDING 3

The net realisable value is now £190 - £20 = £170.

The unsold laptops still in inventory are therefore valued at **£170 each** (being the **lower** of cost and net realisable value).

TEST YOUR UNDERSTANDING 4

Receivables Days = Trade Receivables / [Credit] Sales   x 365 = £76,500 / £700,000 x 365 =   **40 days**

Payables Days = Trade Payables / Cost of Sales   x 365 = £30,200 / £245,000   x 365 = **45 days**

Inventory Days = Inventory / Cost of Sales   x 365 = £45,600 / £245,000   x 365 = **68 days**

Operating Cycle = Inventory Days + Receivables Days – Payables days = 68 + 40 – 45 = **63 days**

In other words, the company has to wait 63 days between paying their supplier, and then ultimately receiving payment from their customer (for the sale of a particular batch of inventory).

11 Working capital management

Chapter 11: End of Chapter Exercises

Section A Questions

The following information relates to Questions 11.1 – 11.10:

Pinters Ltd: Statement of Financial Position as at 31st December 2018

Non-Current Assets		
Land & Buildings	£700,000	
Plant & Machinery	£600,000	
		£1,300,000
Current Assets		
Inventory	£70,000	
Trade Receivables	£60,000	
Cash	£10,000	
		£140,000
TOTAL ASSETS		**£1,440,000**
Equity		
Share Capital	£10,000	
Retained Profit	£1,160,000	
		£1,170,000
Non-Current Liabilities		
25 Year Mortgage	£200,000	
		£200,000
Current Liabilities		
Trade Payables	£45,000	
Tax Liability	£25,000	
		£70,000
TOTAL EQUITY & LIABILITIES		**£1,440,000**

Pinters Ltd: Statement of Profit or Loss. Year Ending 31ˢᵗ December 2018

Sales Revenue	£750,000
Cost of sales	(£150,000)
Gross Profit	£600,000
Selling & Distribution	(£180,000)
Administration	(£175,000)
Operating Profit (PBIT)	£245,000
Finance Costs	(£12,000)
Profit before Tax (PBT)	£233,000
Taxation	(£23,000)
Profit after Tax (PAT)	£210,000

Question 11.1
What is the level of Pinders' working capital?

A   £70,000

B   £1,030,000

C   £1,170,000

D   £1,370,000

Question 11.2
What is the Pinders' current ratio?

A   0.7

B   1.0

C   2.0

D   5.3

Question 11.3
What is the Pinders' quick ratio?

A   0.7

B   1.0

C   2.0

D   5.3

11 Working capital management

Question 11.4

The 'quick ratio' is regarded as a preferable measure of liquidity compared to the 'current ratio' because ....

A   The quick ratio excludes any current asset other than cash

B   The quick ratio is faster to calculate than the current ratio.

C   The current ratio takes non-current assets into account

D   The quick ratio gives a more robust indication of liquidity

Question 11.5

Find the average length of time Pinders' customers take to pay them by calculating their 'Trade Receivables Days'

A   29 days

B   68 days

C   146 days

D   341 days

Question 11.6

Find the average length of time Pinders' take to pay their suppliers by calculating their 'Trade Payables Days'

A   22 days

B   34 days

C   110 days

D   170 days

Question 11.7

Find the average length of time Pinders' hold inventory for by calculating their 'Inventory Turnover Days'

A   34 days

B   68 days

C   170 days

D   341 days

Question 11.8

Find the average length of time between Pinders' paying their suppliers for inventory purchased, and finally receiving payment from their customers for the subsequent sale of that inventory by calculating their Operating Cycle Days:

A   31 days

B   65 days

C   89 days

D   251 days

Question 11.9

A company may aim to improve its cash flow by which of the following techniques?

- i. Rapid chasing of late paying customers
- ii. Increasing the credit limits & credit terms offered to customers
- iii. Offering an early settlement discount to credit customers
- iv. Early payment of purchase invoices

Which of the following describes the two correct techniques?

A   i & ii

B   ii & iii

C   ii & iv

D   i & iii

Question 11.10

Why is it important for a business to optimise the level of its investment in working capital?

A   Too lower a level of working capital can result in insufficient liquidity

B   Too higher level of working capital might require excessive debt financing which incurs interest costs and hence reduces profitability

C   Too higher level of working capital might require excessive equity financing to produce the same level of profit and hence reduces individual shareholder returns

D   All of the above

11 Working capital management

Section B Questions

Data for Question 11.11 to Question 11.13

Financial Accounting information relating to Public Limited Companies is open to public scrutiny. The table below contains some **extracts** from the Annual Reports of three major PLCs which all feature in the FTSE 100 index of the London Stock Exchange.

	Rolls Royce PLC	Taylor Wimpey PLC	J Sainsbury PLC
	Engineering	House Building	Food Retailer
STATEMENT OF PROFIT OR LOSS	£m	£m	£m
Sales Revenue	13,736	2,686	23,775
Cost of Sales	10,533	2,046	22,567
Gross Profit (£)	3,203	640	1,208
Gross Profit (%)	23%	24%	5%
STATEMENT OF FINANCIAL POSITION	£m	£m	£m
Inventory	2,768	3,490	997
Trade Receivables	1,531	45	101
Cash	2,862	213	1,285
CURRENT ASSETS	11,188	3,813	4,421
Trade Payables	1,361	506	2,089
CURRENT LIABILITIES	7,685	958	6,923
STATEMENT OF CASH FLOWS	£m	£m	£m
From Operating Activities	1,301	193	911
From Investing Activities	(1,966)	(10)	(900)
From Financing Activities	(468)	(76)	(314)
Increase (decrease) in cash	(1,133)	107	(303)
Cash at start of year	3,995	106	1,588
Cash at end of year	2,862	213	1,285

Question 11.1 - Rolls Royce PLC

Working Capital

What is the formal definition of 'Working Capital'?   WC = CA - CL

level of funding required to enable operations

In everyday simple terms what does 'Working Capital' represent?

Cash, inventory and receivables

What is Rolls Royce's level of working capital (£m)?

£3,503   (11,188 - 7,685)

Liquidity

What is Rolls Royce's Current Ratio?   CA ÷ CL

1.46

What is Rolls Royce's Quick (acid test) Ratio?   CA - INVENT ÷ CL

1.09

Why is the 'Quick Ratio' often believed to be a more robust measure of liquidity than the 'Current Ratio'?

- because current ratio doesn't use inventory

What might these two ratios tell us about the liquidity of Rolls Royce?

(above 1) higher the ratio the more capable the company is to repay debts

Inventory Turnover (Days)   inventory days = inventory ÷ cost of sales × 365

What is the average length of time (in days) for which inventories are held? In the case of Rolls Royce this could include: raw materials, work in progress and finished goods.

96

11 Working capital management

Trade Receivables (Days) Receiv ÷ sales × 365

What is the average length of time (in days) it takes customers to pay?

41

Trade Payables (Days) payables ÷ cos × 365

What is the average length of time (in days) it takes to pay suppliers?

47

Operating Cycle

Using the above three figures what is the average length of time (in days) between paying for goods and receiving the cash from the sale of those goods?

61

What do the component parts of the Operating Cycle reveal about how Rolls Royce funds their Working Capital requirement?

It takes 61 days to come back to the business

per

Statement of Cash flows

Despite generating £1.3 billion cash from operating activities, Rolls Royce ended the year with a £1.1 billion decrease in cash. What areas of activity caused this? Give some examples of possible specifics which might have occurred?

The Language of Business

Question 11.2 – Taylor Wimpey PLC

Taylor Wimpey PLC

Working Capital

What is Taylor Wimpey's level of working capital (£m)?

£2,855

Liquidity

What is Taylor Wimpey's Current Ratio?

3.98

What is Taylor Wimpey's Quick Ratio?

0.33

Why are these two ratios so markedly different?

Assets + inventory are very similar. Liabilities are quite low.

What might these two ratios tell us about the liquidity of Taylor Wimpey?

Less able to pay debt.

Inventory Turnover (Days)

In the case of Taylor Wimpey what might the constituent parts of inventory be?

Raw materials + equipment - houses

What is the average length of time (in days) for which inventories are held?

622

Trade Receivables (Days)

What is the average length of time (in days) it takes Taylor Wimpey's customers to pay?

6

11 Working capital management

Trade Payables (Days)
What is the average length of time (in days) Taylor Wimpey takes to pay its suppliers?

91   (90.2)

Operating Cycle
Using the above three figures what is the average length of time (in days) between paying for the component parts of inventory and receiving the cash from the sale of the finished houses?

239.3

The nature of Taylor Wimpey's Operating Cycle reveals a particular problem which affects this industry sector. What is this problem and what is the knock-on effect it has on the required level of Working Capital?

Slow sales vs how long inventories are held

Statement of Cash flows
Briefly summarise Taylor Wimpey's cash flow performance for the year

What are the most obvious two <u>possible</u> explanations for the £76m cash outflow from Financing Activities?

The Language of Business

Question 11.13 - J Sainsbury PLC

Working Capital

What is Sainsbury's level of working capital (£m)? *(We will comment on it later!)*

−2,502

Liquidity

What is Sainsbury's Current Ratio?

0.63

What is Sainsbury's Quick Ratio?

0.49

Suggest a fundamental difference between the operation of a retailer such as Sainsbury's and other industries such as Rolls Royce that could account for these ratios being so different.

Sainsbury's sell stock before they receive/pay for it.

Inventory Turnover (Days)

What is the average length of time (in days) which Sainsbury's holds inventory for?

17

Trade Receivables (Days)

What is the average length of time (in days) it takes Sainsbury's customers to pay?

1.55 or 2

Why is this figure so low?

because the customer pays there and then

Trade Payables (Days)

What is the average length of time (in days) Sainsbury's takes to pay its suppliers?

33.7 or 34

Working capital management

Operating Cycle

Using the above three figures what is the average length of time (in days) between Sainsbury's paying for its inventory and receiving the cash from the sale of it?

17.6

Explain this figure.

Due to the nature of the business, selling stock before they recieve it = low operating cycle

What is the extremely beneficial consequence of this and how does it relate to the calculated figure for Working Capital?

No long term holding stock therefore no money is wasted.

Statement of Cash flows

Briefly summarise Sainsbury's cash flow performance for the year

In this year Sainsbury's actually made a net loss of £166m. Explain (with possible examples) how this can be the case when there was a positive cash inflow from operating activities of £911m.?

Question 11.14

Receivables Balancing Act

The policies a company adopts with respect to pursuing its customers for payment of unpaid sales invoices can affect both its Liquidity and its Profitability.... often in opposite directions.

Provide some examples which illustrate this.

Actions which will *increase* **Liquidity** (but possibly *decrease* Profitability)	Actions which will *increase* **Profitability** (but possibly *decrease* Liquidity)

11 Working capital management

Question 11.15

Payables Balancing Act

The policies a company adopts with respect to paying its supplies for goods and services received can affect both its Liquidity and its Profitability.... often in opposite directions.

Provide some examples which illustrate this.

Actions which will *increase* **Liquidity** (but possibly *decrease* Profitability)	Actions which will *increase* **Profitability** (but possibly *decrease* Liquidity)

Question 11.16

Inventory Balancing Act

The policies a company adopts with respect to the levels of inventory it holds can affect both its Liquidity and its Profitability.... often in opposite directions.

Provide some examples which illustrate this.

Actions which will *increase* **Liquidity** (but possibly *decrease* Profitability)	Actions which will *increase* **Profitability** (but possibly *decrease* Liquidity)

11 Working capital management

Chapter 12

Performance Appraisal

INTRODUCTION

Over the past eleven chapters we have explored many ways of analysing and appraising business performance. In this final chapter we are now going to bring all of these methods together.

We will recap and summarise the various **performance ratios** we have encountered, and see how these together with **Key Performance Indicators** (KPIs) may be used within a **'responsibility accounting'** framework.

Finally we will look at **non-financial performance appraisal** and the balanced scorecard.

OVERVIEW AND OBJECTIVES

By the end of this chapter you should have developed an understanding of:

- Ratio Analysis
- Market Capitalisation
- Vertical & Horizontal Analysis
- Responsibility Accounting
- Key Performance Indicators
- Balanced Scorecard

and be able to answer questions relating to these areas.

12 Performance appraisal

12.1 Ratio analysis

Ratio analysis is often used to evaluate financial statements as it provides certain advantages compared to simply looking at the original numbers, including:

1. **Identifying relationships between separate numbers on a financial statement**

    For example on a statement of profit or loss the gross profit (£) figure can be restated as gross profit (%) i.e. as a percentage of the sales revenue.

    $$\text{Gross Profit \%} = \frac{\text{Gross Profit (£)}}{\text{Sales Revenue (£)}} \times 100\%$$

    This instantly shows how efficient a business is at converting sales into gross profit.

2. **Allowing information to be rebased into a more meaningful measure**

    For example, looking at the level of inventory (quoted in £) on the statement of financial position might not really help to understand how much inventory the company is currently holding. However, rebasing it to quote how many days it will take to sell that amount of inventory immediately makes the figure more meaningful.

    $$\text{Inventory Days} = \frac{\text{Inventory}}{\text{Cost of Sales}} \times 365$$

    A company can then see if the level of inventory held will take (say) 7 days or 7 months to sell through.

3. **Allowing a relative comparison between different years or different companies**

    To allow performances of different magnitudes to be compared e.g. The Return on Capital Employed (ROCE) achieved by two companies of different size.

    $$\text{ROCE} = \frac{\text{Operating Profit (£)}}{\text{Total Capital Employed (£)}} \times 100\%$$

    Despite the different size of the two companies the use of a ratio allows relative comparisons to be made.

4. **Allowing risk to be identified**

    Simply expressing the amount of long-term debt a company has does not immediately indicate how heavily a company has borrowed.

    $$\text{Gearing \%} = \frac{\text{Debt Finance (£)}}{\text{Total Capital Employed (£)}} \times 100\%$$

    Whereas quoting (say) 70% gearing immediately shows that the company has very high levels of debt.

12.2 The ratio family

We have already encountered many ratios and still have a final few to introduce in this chapter. It is therefore useful to give an overview of the whole ratio family (and recap of those already covered), before introducing yet more!

These are split into four categories, as follows:

Profitability & Return

- Used to describe the business's profitability

Liquidity
- Used to describe the business's liquidity

Efficiency
- Used to describe how efficiently the business is managing its working capital

Investment & Finance
- Used to describe the business from the perspective of a potential investor or lender.

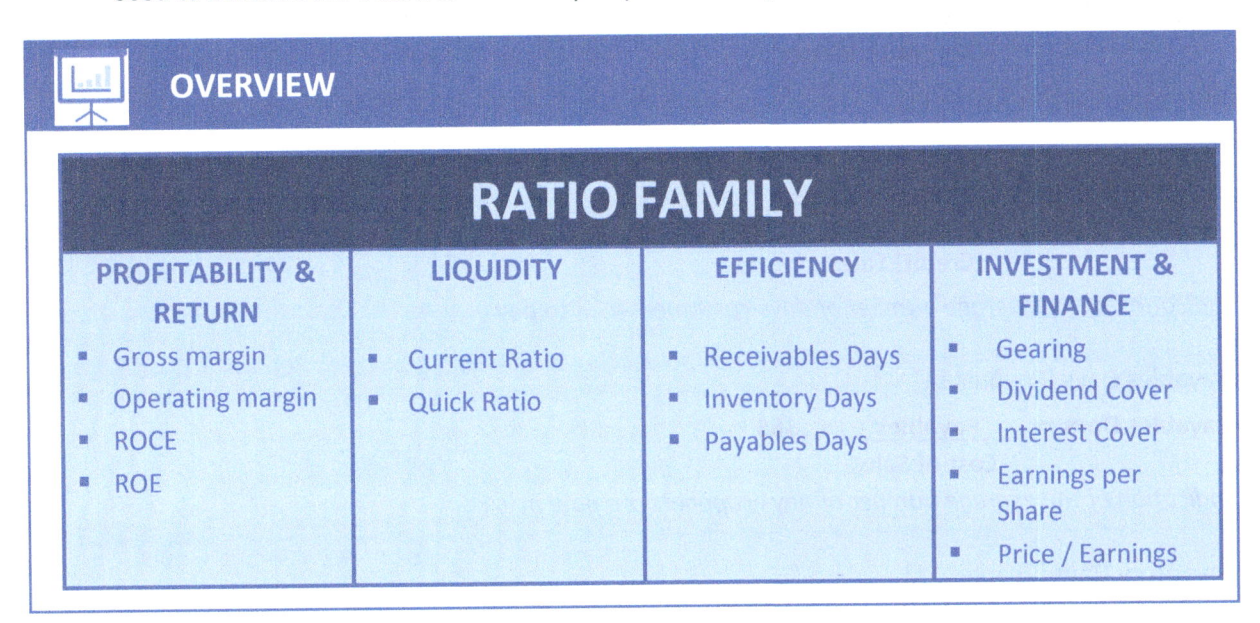

OVERVIEW

RATIO FAMILY

PROFITABILITY & RETURN	LIQUIDITY	EFFICIENCY	INVESTMENT & FINANCE
- Gross margin - Operating margin - ROCE - ROE	- Current Ratio - Quick Ratio	- Receivables Days - Inventory Days - Payables Days	- Gearing - Dividend Cover - Interest Cover - Earnings per Share - Price / Earnings

We have already met many of the above ratios (including all of the first three groups) scattered throughout the preceding chapters, but we'll briefly remind ourselves of them before then moving onto the new Investment & Finance ratios.

Gross Profit Margin (GP %) [Chapter 2]

Gross Profit Margin % = $\dfrac{\text{Gross Profit}}{\text{Sales Revenue}}$ x 100%

Measures the efficiency with which sales revenue is converted into gross profit.

Operating Profit Margin [Chapter 2]

Operating Profit Margin % = $\dfrac{\text{Operating Profit}}{\text{Sales Revenue}}$ x 100%

Measures the efficiency with which sales revenue is converted into operating profit (so overheads are now also taken into account)

Return on Capital Employed (ROCE) [Chapter 3]

Return on Capital Employed = $\dfrac{\text{Operating Profit}}{\text{Total Capital Employed}}$ x 100%

Measures the profit returns (PBIT) from the <u>total</u> *long term capital employed (Debt + Equity)*

Return on Equity (ROE) [Chapter 3]

Return on Equity = $\dfrac{\text{Profit after Tax}}{\text{Equity}}$ x 100%

Measures the profit returns (PAT) enjoyed by the Shareholders from **their** *capital employed (i.e. just Equity)*

12 Performance appraisal

Current Ratio [Chapter 11]

$$\text{Current Ratio} = \frac{\text{Current Assets}}{\text{Current Liabilities}}$$

Broad indication of the ability of a business to pay its liabilities as they fall due

Quick Ratio [Chapter 11]

$$\text{Quick Ratio} = \frac{\text{Current Assets - Inventory}}{\text{Current Liabilities}}$$

More robust indication of the ability of a business to pay its liabilities as they fall due

Receivables Days [Chapter 11]

$$\text{Receivables Days} = \frac{\text{Receivables}}{\text{[Credit] Sales}} \times 365$$

Indication of the average number of days customers take to pay

Payables Days [Chapter 11]

$$\text{Payables Days} = \frac{\text{Payables}}{\text{Cost of Sales}} \times 365$$

Indication of the average number of days suppliers are paid in

Inventory Days [Chapter 11]

$$\text{Inventory Days} = \frac{\text{Inventory}}{\text{Cost of Sales}} \times 365$$

Indication of the average number of days' worth of sales held in stock

Gearing [Chapter 3]

$$\text{Gearing \%} = \frac{\text{Debt}}{\text{Total Capital Employed}} \times 100\%$$

How much of a company's long-term finance (i.e. Debt + Equity) comes from borrowing

12.3 Investment and financial ratios

Existing and potential new investors and lenders will wish to evaluate a company's financial health to make invest-divest decisions (i.e. should they buy, or should they sell).

The following ratios are the most commonly ones used:

- **Gearing** — Already covered, and recapped above
- **Interest Cover** — How affordable interest payments are to the company
- **Dividend Cover** — How affordable dividend payments are to the company
- **Earnings per Share** — How much profit does each share make?
- **Price / Earnings** — How expensive are shares compared to the profit they make?

We'll now look at each of the new ratios in more detail, taking in the market valuation of companies along the way.

12.4 Interest Cover

Any prospective lender will wish to see how much debt the company already has, and to assess how affordable its current level of debt is, before considering further lending.

The gearing % would almost certainly be calculated to understand how heavily laden with debt the company already is. An additional test would then be to calculate how many 'times over' the company could afford to pay the interest on this debt, by calculating the interest cover.

Interest Cover = Operating Profit / Interest Costs

The interest cover simply shows how many times over the interest costs could be paid out of Operating Profit i.e. how 'affordable' the interest costs are. To fully appreciate this formula we need to revisit the standard format for the statement of profit or loss below.

Statement of Profit or Loss

	£
Sales Revenue	X
Cost of Sales	(X)
Gross Profit	X
Selling & Distribution Costs	(X)
Administration Costs	(X)
Operating Profit (PBIT)	X
Finance Costs	(X)
Profit before Tax	X
Taxation	(X)
Profit after Tax	X

From this we can see that finance costs (e.g. loan interest) are paid out of the operating profit figure (aka Profit before Interest and Tax - PBIT).

The interest cover figure therefore reports how many times larger the operating profit figure is, than the loan interest i.e. how many times over the loan interest could have been paid from that level of operating profit. This gives a good indication of how affordable the loan interest is.

EXAMPLE

Scenario

A company has an operating profit of £40,000 per annum. It has £20,000 of long-term borrowing on which it pays a 10% fixed interest rate.

What is the interest cover and does this suggest that the current level of borrowing is affordable?

Solution

The annual loan interest is £20,000 x 10% = £2,000. The interest cover is therefore:

Interest Cover = Operating Profit / Interest Costs = £40,000 / £2,000 = 20

The current loan interest could be paid 20 times over out of the current level of profitability, and therefore appears quite affordable.

12 Performance appraisal

> **TUTORIAL NOTE**
>
> By default loan interest is quoted 'per annum' (unless otherwise stated).

> **TUTORIAL NOTE**
>
> You may be wondering why we have just focussed on the affordability of the *loan interest* and not considered any *capital repayments*. The answer is that commercial loans are often paid back in full at the *end* of the loan term, with no intermediate capital repayments.
>
> The crucial factor during the term of the loan therefore, is whether the company can afford the interest payments! At the end of the term the company might even take out *new* borrowing to repay the *old* borrowing and the whole cycle starts over again!

12.5 Dividend Cover

A potential investor will always be interested in the level of dividends a company has recently paid, after all this will represent the investor's level of immediate return. However, the company directors are free to increase or decrease the dividends declared each year at will. The only say the shareholders have is to vote to confirm that the year's proposed final dividend is *not* too high (they cannot however vote to increase it!).

The directors can even propose total dividends which are in excess of the final profit for the year, so long as there is sufficient retained profit from previous years out of which to pay the dividends. They may do this in an attempt to 'prop up' the current share price by the lure of high dividends…. even if these high dividends are not sustainable in future years.

Investors will therefore be interested to see how sustainable the current level of dividends actually is and this can be ascertained by calculating the dividend cover, as follows:

$$\text{Dividend Cover} = \frac{\text{Profit after Tax}}{\text{Dividends}}$$

The dividend cover shows the number of times over the dividend could be paid out of Profit after Tax, and therefore how 'affordable' the dividends are.

> **TUTORIAL NOTE**
>
> Dividend Cover uses 'profit after tax' because it is this very final profit figure (after all direct & indirect costs, finance costs and taxation have been paid) that 'belongs' to the shareholders. Look at the standard format for the statement of profit or loss above, and you will see that profit after tax really is the ultimate 'bottom line' profit.

The Language of Business

EXAMPLE

Scenario

A company makes £375,000 profit after tax. It has 200,000 shares in issue and proposes a dividend of 75p per share.

What is the dividend cover and does it appear affordable?

Solution

The total dividend paid out will be 200,000 x £0.75 = £150,000. The dividend cover is therefore:

Dividend Cover = $\dfrac{\text{Profit after Tax}}{\text{Dividends}}$ = $\dfrac{£375,000}{£150,000}$ = 2.5

The proposed dividend could be paid 2.5 times over out of the current level of profit after tax, and therefore appears quite sustainable. The directors seem to be proposing paying 40% of the final profit to the shareholders and retaining 60% for onward investment in the company.

TUTORIAL NOTE

When we are operating at 'share' level the convention is to quote dividends etc. in pence e.g. a dividend of 75p per share in the example above.

TEST YOUR UNDERSTANDING 1

Elgar Ltd have 12,000 issued shares and have just announced a dividend of 500p per share.

Using the P&L below calculate Elgar Ltd's Interest Cover and Dividend Cover.

Elgar Ltd: Statement of Profit or Loss Year Ending 30th June 2018

Sales Revenue	£2,000,000
Cost of Sales	(£950,000)
Gross Profit	£1,050,000
Selling & Distribution Costs	(£350,000)
Administration Costs	(£400,000)
Operating Profit (PBIT)	£300,000
Finance Costs (bank interest)	(£25,000)
Profit before Tax	£275,000
Taxation	(£52,000)
Profit after Tax	**£223,000**

Interest Cover _____

Dividend Cover _____

12 Performance appraisal

12.6 Earnings Per Share (EPS)

'**Earnings**' is simply another name for '**profit**' and whenever we are looking at profit relating to shares or shareholders we use profit after tax.

The earnings per share (EPS) is simply the amount of profit after tax that has been made by each individual share over the previous year.

$$\text{Earnings per Share} = \frac{\text{Profit after Tax}}{\text{No. of Shares in Issue}}$$

> **EXAMPLE**
>
> Continuing on from the previous example... what is this company's EPS?
>
> **Solution**
>
> The Company made £375,000 profit after tax, and had 200,000 shares in issue.
>
> $$\text{Earnings per Share} = \frac{\text{Profit after Tax}}{\text{No. of Shares in Issue}} = \frac{£375,000}{200,000} = 187.5\text{p per share}$$
>
> Again the answer is quoted in pence because we are operating at 'share' level. Each share made 187.5p profit and out of that a dividend of 75p was paid.

12.7 Market share price

How much is a £1 share worth? The answer is simply however much an investor is willing to pay for it... which will typically be in excess of £1.

The '£1' label simply refers to the 'nominal value' of the share which was probably the value that equivalent shares were issued at, to the original subscribers who first bought them. However as time goes on shares tend to increase in value as the company grows. So an original £1 may well be worth considerably more as time goes on.

Furthermore if a **mature** company issues new additional shares (but wishes them to have the same voting and dividend rights as the original shares) they will still issue £1 shares …. But at a price premium. So later subscribers might pay (say) £3 to buy a £1 share (£1 nominal share capital + £2 share premium).

> **TUTORIAL NOTE**
>
> A '**subscriber**' is an investor who buys a brand new share **direct from the company** i.e. **not** an investor who buys a second-hand share from an existing shareholder.

> **TUTORIAL NOTE**
>
> Companies generally pay out a proportion of their profit after tax to shareholders in the form of dividends, and retain the rest for onward investment and growth. This means that the equity in the company is naturally growing (**Equity = Share Capital + Retained Profit**), and as the equity grows the market price of the shares should also increase.

Quite aside from the company itself offering brand new shares to 'subscribers', most companies (particularly 'listed' PLCs) have an active trade in their existing second-hand shares via stock markets. It must be remembered that the sale and purchase of a second-hand share is a transaction between two investors (normally via a stock exchange) and does not directly involve the company itself. Nonetheless the directors will still have a keen interest in the market share price as they are acting on behalf of shareholders who obviously wish the share price to increase.

Market Capitalisation

The share price of existing shares quoted on a stock market will vary on a daily basis but at any point in time the share price on that day can be used to derive a 'market value' for the company known as the 'market capitalisation':

Market Capitalisation = Current Market Price of Shares x Number of Shares in Issue

EXAMPLE

A company has 500,000 issued shares and the current market share price is 550p each.

What is the market capitalisation?

Solution

The market capitalisation gives the market's (i.e. the investor community's) valuation of the company at that point in time = 500,000 x £5.50 = **£2.75 million.**

What affects Market Price?

Investors tend to be influenced by both their assessment of the individual company and also their assessment of the wider environment, when evaluating how much they are willing to pay for shares in a particular company.

Assessing the individual company is of course sensible and logical. An investor will wish to have an understanding of the company's current trading performance and its future prospects (profit levels, growth, risk etc.). Additionally investors know that the share price of a company which is the target of a takeover bid, will inevitably rise and this will also be factored into their assessment of how much they are willing to pay for the shares.

What seems *less* logical is the 'herd instinct' which investors tend to exhibit when they base their judgement on what *other* investors are doing, rather than on the information available on a particular company. Some of this investor confidence (or lack thereof) is based on general economic indicators which has some merit to it, but it is often also based on a primitive herd instinct:

- *"If everyone else is buying then I will also buy"* (a **'bull market'** where share prices tend to increase)… but…

- *"If everyone else is selling then I will also sell"* (a **'bear market'** where share prices tend to fall).

12 Performance appraisal

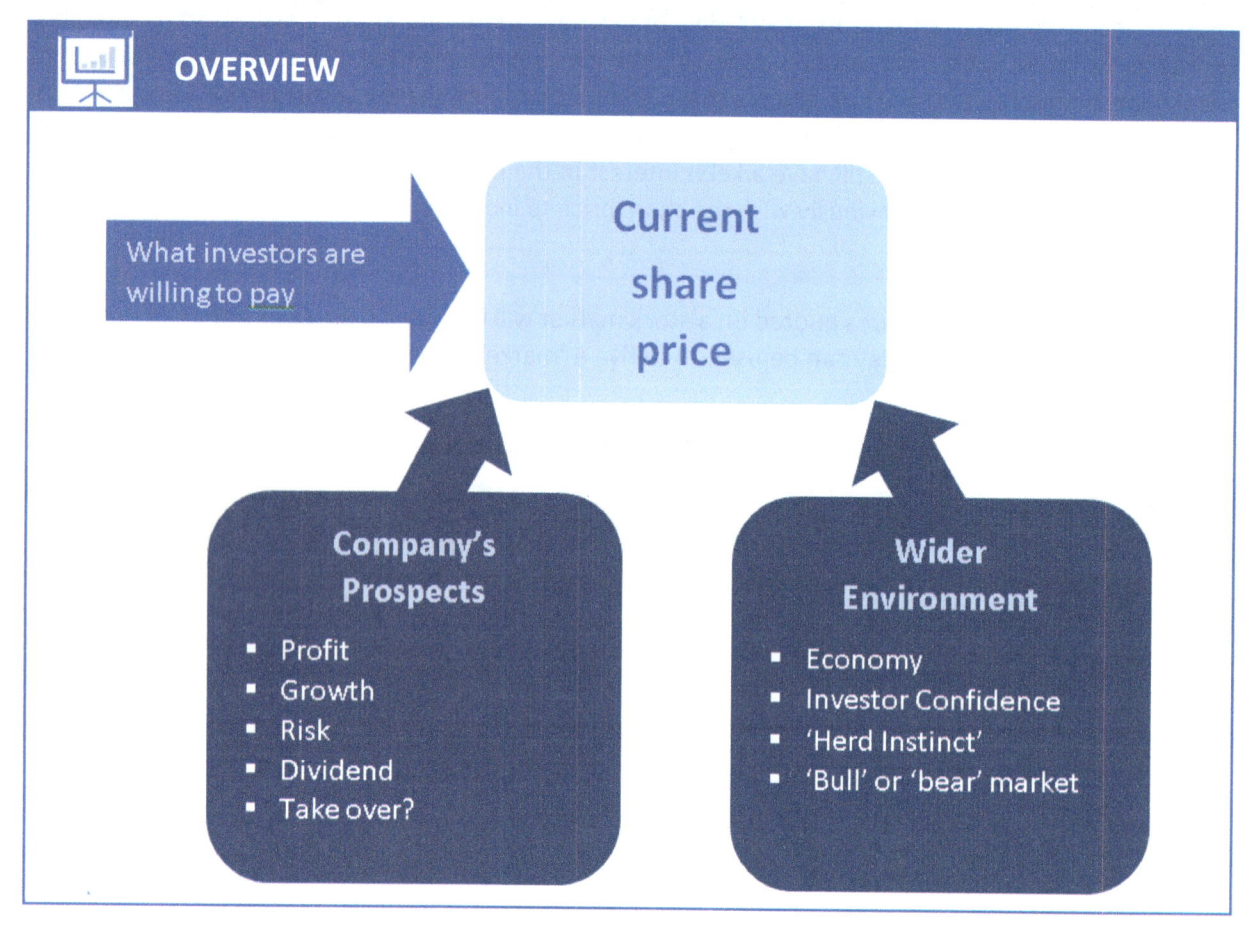

> **OVERVIEW**
>
> What investors are willing to pay → **Current share price**
>
> **Company's Prospects**
> - Profit
> - Growth
> - Risk
> - Dividend
> - Take over?
>
> **Wider Environment**
> - Economy
> - Investor Confidence
> - 'Herd Instinct'
> - 'Bull' or 'bear' market

Equity Valuation versus Market Capitalisation

We have now encountered two different ways of valuing a company:-

- **Equity Valuation:** The 'balance sheet' value of a company based on an accountancy valuation of its assets less it liabilities. The valuation is simply the 'book value' of the company according to the accounting rules laid down in financial reporting standards.

- **Market Capitalisation:** What the market thinks the company is currently worth, evidenced by how much the shares of the company are currently being traded for.

The market capitalisation is generally higher than the equity valuation because investors are less interested in the 'book values' of the company's net assets, and more interested in the company's perceived future prospects (and likely future dividends and growth in the share price).

Moreover, intangible assets (such as trademarks, brand names etc.) are often not included on the company's balance sheet because their exact value cannot be reliably measured. However potential investors *do* attach a value to them and are willing to pay a higher share price as a result.

Unsurprisingly the market capitalisation of a company (based on not always entirely rational investors) is somewhat more volatile than the equity valuation of a company (based on 'prudent' accounting principles).

The Language of Business

> **TEST YOUR UNDERSTANDING 2**
>
> Handel Ltd's Balance Sheet shows total assets of £2.5m and total liabilities of £1.6m. It has 100,000 issued shares and these have a current market value of £12.60 each.
>
> Calculate Handel Ltd's equity valuation and market capitalisation.
>
> Equity Valuation _____
>
> Market Capitalisation _____

12.8 Price/Earnings Ratio

The final ratio we are going to consider is the Price/Earnings Ratio (P/E Ratio) which gives an indication of investors' confidence in a particular company.

Price / Earnings Ratio = $\dfrac{\text{Current Share Price}}{\text{Earnings per Share}}$

The P/E ratio indicates how much an investor is willing to pay to get £1 worth of profit earning ability.

> **EXAMPLE**
>
> The shares of a company are currently trading at 650p whilst the company's Earnings per Share are 130p.
>
> What is the P/E ratio?
>
> **Solution**
>
> The P/E ratio is calculated as follows:
>
> P/E ratio = $\dfrac{\text{Current Share Price}}{\text{Earnings per Share}}$ = $\dfrac{650}{130}$ = 5
>
> This means that investors are currently willing to pay five times as much to purchase a single share than the amount of profit that that share made in the previous year … or put another way are willing to pay £5 for every £1 of profit the share produces each year.

P/E ratios are widely used in financial circles because they reveal how much investors are currently willing to pay to *'buy into'* the profit-making potential of a particular company, as follows:

High P/E ratio: Investors are willing to pay a lot to buy into the profit-making potential of the company. This either reveals:

- Well-founded investor confidence in the future prospects of that company… or
- Simply that the company's shares are currently over-priced!

Low P/E ratio: Investors are not willing to pay a lot to buy into the profit-making potential of the company. This either reveals:

- Perceptive investors lacking confidence in the future prospects of that company…… or
- Simply reveals that the company's shares are currently under-priced!

12 Performance appraisal

> **TUTORIAL NOTE**
>
> The smart investor will seek out companies with low P/E ratios, but which have better prospects than their P/E ratio would suggest. These companies are currently under-priced (in comparison to their profit potential) but if they continue to perform the market will eventually realise their value and their share price will then rise.

> **TEST YOUR UNDERSTANDING 3**
>
> Bach Ltd have 50,000 issued shares, which have a current market value of £18 each. The company's recent results show a Profit after Tax of £150,000.
>
> What is Bach Ltd's Earnings per Share and Price Earnings Ratio based on this information?
>
> Earnings per Share _____
>
> Price Earnings Ratio _____

12.9 Analysis of financial information

To allow a meaningful analysis of financial results they must be compared against:

- Budget → *How well is the business performing compared to its plan?*
- Previous Year → *Is the performance improving or worsening over time?*
- Benchmark → *How is the business performing compared to its competitors?*

Two techniques which are commonly used to better understand financial data, are vertical analysis and horizontal analysis.

Vertical Analysis

This simply involves the calculation of ratios within data *from the same time period*. In fact we have already seen examples of this technique when calculating the gross profit % and operating profit % for a business, but it can be extended to any other item of data.

EXAMPLE

Year Ending 31/12/17	£'000	%
Sales Revenue	**500**	100%
Less cost of sales	170	34%
Gross Profit	**330**	**66%**
Wages Costs	135	27%
Premises Costs	70	14%
Distribution Costs	40	8%
Marketing Costs	15	3%
Operating Profit	**70**	**14%**

In the example above we have calculated the size of the various expense and profit figures as a percentage of the sale revenue. So it can now be seen that (for example):

- The business is converting its sales into gross profit at the rate of 66%
- 27% of the sales revenue is being spent on wages
- 3% of the sales revenue is being spent on marketing
- The business is converting sales into operating profit at the rate of 14% etc.

Now this type of analysis might by itself throw up some interesting observations, for example:

- "At 27% of our sales, wages are by far our biggest expense. Can we not make some savings here?"
- "A 3% marketing spend seems pretty modest. If we increased this could we grow our sales revenue?"

So vertical analysis can be useful to highlight the relative size of numbers within a given period of time.

TUTORIAL NOTE

The Cost of Sales % is included for completeness (businesses normally focus on the more meaningful Gross Profit %).

However you may find it useful to note that if all the various cost percentages are added up (including costs of sales) they total 86%....**of the sales revenue**. *(Ignore the GP% for this exercise as it is merely providing an additional interim measure of profit, which if included would be 'double-counting')*. The remaining 14% **of the sales revenue** is of course the final bottom-line operating profit.

Horizontal Analysis

This involves the comparison of data from across *successive time periods*. At its simplest this merely comprises of showing last year's comparable figures (see below) and this is routinely done in financial

12 Performance appraisal

accounts to allow an instant assessment of whether each element of performance has improved or worsened.

EXAMPLE

Continuing from the previous example, the table below now compares the previous set of results, to the comparable results from the year before:

	2016 (£'000)	2017 (£'000)
Sales Revenue	530	500
Less cost of sales	185	170
Gross Profit	345	330
Wages Costs	130	135
Premises Costs	70	70
Distribution Costs	42	40
Marketing Costs	26	15
Operating Profit	77	70

TUTORIAL NOTE

Using the table, it can be immediately seen that:

- Sales Revenue has worsened
- Gross Profit has worsened
- Wage costs have increased
- Premises costs are unchanged
- Distribution costs have decreased
- Marketing costs have decreased
- Operating profit has worsened

On the face of it, many aspects of the 2017 performance seem disappointing with both sales and profit worsening. However, merely presenting two years' worth of figures alongside each other is not really scratching the surface of what has happened here. So, in the next table, we will calculate year-on-year variances for each line of the P&L (expressed in both £ and % terms).

EXAMPLE

	2016 (£'000)	2017 (£'000)	Variance (£)	Variance (%)
Sales Revenue	**530**	**500**	**(30)**	**(6%)**
Less cost of sales	185	170	15	8%
Gross Profit	**345**	**330**	**(15)**	**(4%)**
Wages Costs	130	135	(5)	(4%)
Premises Costs	70	70	-	-
Distribution Costs	42	40	2	5%
Marketing Costs	26	15	11	42%
Operating Profit	**77**	**70**	**(7)**	**(9%)**

TUTORIAL NOTE

We can now see how each element of performance has changed over the two year period (a 'year-on-year' comparison). This information now allows the business to more properly appraise their performance:

Sales Revenue has shown a 6% decrease and dropped by £30,000

Clearly a 6% shrinking of 'top-line' sales is worrying. The question is 'why?' The business needs to quickly review their selling prices, promotion, product range, customer feedback, competitor activity etc. to understand what has caused this.

Gross Profit (£) has shown a 4% decrease and fallen by £15,000

On the face of it a falling Gross Profit (£) is bad news but we still don't fully understand the full causes behind this. Is it all because of falling sales, or is it partly due to a lack of efficiently in converting sales revenue into gross profit?

Wage Costs have shown a 4% rise and increased by £5,000

With the top-line sales falling by 6%, the business might have hoped for the partial consolation of a corresponding saving on wages, due to lower levels of activity. However the wage costs have gone in the opposite direction!

Premises Costs have remained unchanged

The premises costs will largely consist of fixed costs and they therefore remain unchanged with lowered levels of activity.

Distribution Costs are 5% lower which represents a £2,000 drop

The distribution costs seem in line with where they should be. They will largely be variable costs and so a 5% fall in distribution is to be expected with a 6% fall in sales activity.

12 Performance appraisal

> **Marketing Costs** *show a £11,000 saving – a 42% year on year fall*
>
> Normally a year-on-year cost saving would be welcomed, but this 42% reduction in marketing needs to be closely examined to see to what extent it is responsible for the 6% drop in sales. If the two are linked *(and that remains to be proved)* then the £11,000 saving on marketing is a false economy if it has led to a £30,000 fall in sales (which then produces £19,800 less gross profit i.e. £30,000 less sales x 66% GP in 2017).
>
> **Operating Profit** *is £7,000 down on previous year i.e. 9% lower*
>
> The £7,000 fall in the business's 'bottom-line' profit is the cumulative effect of all of the above. The business cannot *directly* address a falling operating profit figure. It instead needs to separately address each of the above operational aspects which have led to this.

Combining Horizontal and Vertical Analysis

Of course there is no reason why the two techniques looked at (vertical analysis and horizontal analysis) should not be combined and used simultaneously.

EXAMPLE

Continuing with the previous example and combining the results:

	2016		2017	
	£'000	%	£'000	%
Sales Revenue	530	100%	500	100%
Less cost of sales	185	35%	170	34%
Gross Profit	345	65%	330	66%
Wages Costs	130	24%	135	27%
Premises Costs	70	13%	70	14%
Distribution Costs	42	8%	40	8%
Marketing Costs	26	5%	15	3%
Operating Profit	77	15%	70	14%

This now helps to answer one of the earlier queries, namely why had the gross profit (£) fallen so much. We can now see that it was NOT due to an inability to convert sales revenue into gross profit (as the GP% has improved from 65% to 66%), so it looks like it was simply due to a fall in sales revenue.

TUTORIAL NOTE

In fact looking at both gross profit % and operating profit % is regarded as being so useful that in management accounting these tend to be permanent features of 'vertical analysis' which are always added onto statements of profit or loss.

The Language of Business

For example the top of a P&L might look like this:

Sales Revenue	£500,000
Cost of Sales	(£170,000)
Gross Profit (£)	**£330,000**
Gross Profit (%)	*66%*

We can also see that the wage bill has not only increased in £ terms, but also in % terms and this underlines the need for immediate action on this largest single area of expense in the business.

Finally the fall in marketing spend is now even more apparent. When the business cut it back from 5% to 3% (whether this was done knowingly or not) it appears to have potentially had the corresponding effect of a 6% fall in sales. Perhaps the directors should consider their marketing strategy and decide whether (say) 5% of sales revenue should be ring-fenced for sales support via marketing to prevent this happening again.

TEST YOUR UNDERSTANDING 4

Complete the following table to allow basic vertical & horizontal analysis on the Mozart Ltd's sales and gross profit performance.

Mozart Ltd	2016	2017	Year on Year Variance (£)	Year on Year Variance (%)
Sales	£950,000	£970,000		
Cost of Sales	£285,000	£310,000		
Gross Profit (£)	£665,000	£660,000		
Gross Profit (%)				

12.10 Responsibility accounting

The bigger any organisation becomes the harder it is to ensure effective communication, coordination and control. For example Tesco PLC employ approaching ½ million staff, so it's quite hard for the CEO to keep track of them all individually!

Large companies therefore tend to use a system of 'responsibility accounting' to delegate responsibility downwards throughout the organisation. However, the corresponding *authority* needs to also be delegated hand-in-hand with *responsibility*. You cannot ask someone to take responsibility for an aspect of the business unless they also have the authority required to see the task through.

Of course different operating units of the business (at different levels) will require different forms of authority in order to assume different types of responsibility. The following general categories are used to describe the nature of the responsibility being delegated:

Revenue Centres: Operating units whose responsibility is to ensure that certain levels of sales revenue are delivered. However they are not in control of their own costs, and therefore if they wanted to (say) increase the size of the sales team they would need to get prior authorisation for this.

12 Performance appraisal

> *e.g.   A telesales office, whose role is to follow up sales leads and turn them into sales orders, and will be largely judged on whether they have achieved their sales budget or not.*

Cost Centres: Operating units whose responsibility is to ensure that certain levels of expenditure are kept within stated limits. They do not however have any responsibly for generating sales revenue.

> *e.g.   A Human Resources Department where part of its performance appraisal will be whether they have operated within their budgeted level of expenditure or not.*

Profit Centres: Operating units who are responsible for both generating sales revenue and at the same time controlling expenditure. They are therefore responsible for delivering a certain level of profit. However if capital investment was required this must be evaluated and authorised at a higher level.

> *e.g.   An individual restaurant in a fast food chain, which will be expected to deliver a certain level of operating profit each month.*

Investment Centres: Operating units that are not only responsible for delivering a certain profit performance (and all that entails), but who are also responsible for making their own capital investment decisions (within the capital spending budget allocated to them).

> *e.g.   A regional operating division of a company which is not only judged on its level of profitability, but also on the returns it makes on its investment decisions (e.g. achieving target ROCE or ARR)*

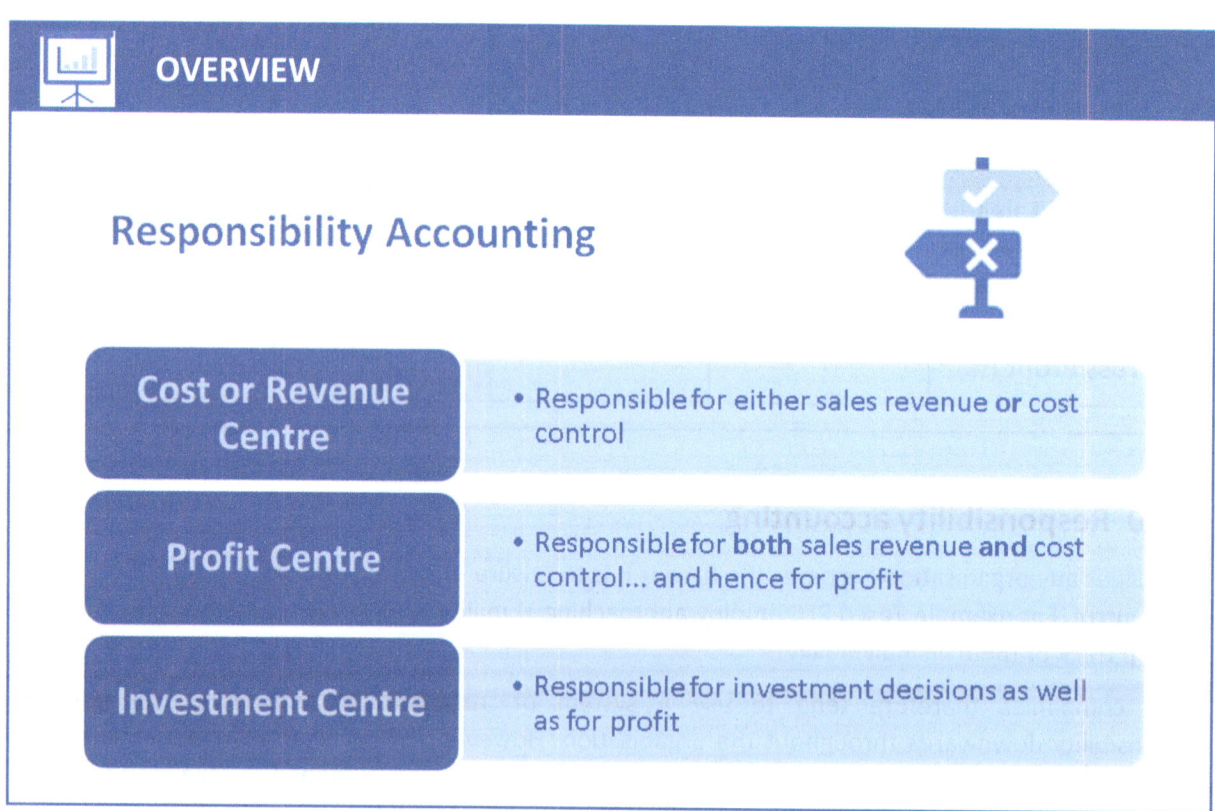

OVERVIEW

Responsibility Accounting

Cost or Revenue Centre	• Responsible for either sales revenue **or** cost control
Profit Centre	• Responsible for **both** sales revenue **and** cost control... and hence for profit
Investment Centre	• Responsible for investment decisions as well as for profit

The Language of Business

> ## EXAMPLE
>
> A national double-glazing company is split into four regionally based operating divisions (North East, North West, South East and South West). Each region is empowered to 'bid' for capital funds from the corporate finance department to expand the number of local sales offices and teams of installers as it sees fit. The company runs national TV market campaigns and has a national call centre which receive sales enquiries and tries to convert them into firm sales orders to be shipped out to the relevant region. The company runs a factory which produces all of the double glazed windows and doors and ships them out to the relevant region.
>
> The business was started 25 years ago by a sole trader but has now become a multi-million pound business employing 20,000 staff. The founder originally knew his handful of staff by name as they all worked in the same office, but now (as Managing Director) he hasn't even met the majority of the company's employees.
>
> How can he hope to control such a large business?
>
> Solution
>
> He can do so by organising it into separate operating units, each empowered with a certain level of authority and each being held responsible for achieving certain targets, as follows:
>
> | | Operating Unit | Responsible for: | Not responsible for: | Methods of Appraisal |
> |---|---|---|---|---|
> | Factory | Cost Centre | Maintaining cost control of all factory staff and overheads. | Sales revenue. Profit. Investment Decisions. | Expenditure maintained within budget. |
> | National Call Centre | Revenue Centre | Generating sales revenue by converting enquiries into orders. | Cost control. Profit. Investment Decisions. | Achieving budgeted levels of sales. |
> | Individual Sales Offices | Profit Centre | Maximising branch sales revenue and controlling branch expenditure. | Capital Investment Decisions. | Achieving budgeted level of branch profit. |
> | Regional Operating Division | Investment Centre | Expanding its network of sales offices to maximise returns. | Setting the level of its overall Capex budget. | Achieving budgeted level of divisional profit and budgeted ROCE. |

12 Performance appraisal

> ### TEST YOUR UNDERSTANDING 5
>
> Large companies are often split into smaller divisions and/or departments each holding specific financial responsibilities. If each department or division achieves its specified targets then the company as a whole will achieve the overall corporate target.
>
> **'Responsibility Accounting'** categorises departments and divisions into:
>
> - Cost Centres
> - Revenue Centres
> - Profit Centres
> - Investment Centres
>
> Which of the above categorisations best describes each of the following?
>
> a) **The Northern Operating Region** of a high street retailer. All acquisition and refurbishment decisions relating to the high street outlets it operates are made by head office, but the northern region is responsible for achieving both sales and expenditure targets in the day to day operation of the company's northern branches.
>
> _____
>
> b) **The Distribution Centre** of an online retailer which receives 'picking lists' from the separate Sales Department detailing the products on customer orders which are to be 'picked, packed & despatched' to the customers.
>
> _____
>
> c) **The European Operating Division** of a multi-national petro-chemical company. The division operates on a largely autonomous basis and is appraised on the Return on capital Employed (ROCE) it achieves on the investment funds it received from the corporate headquarters.
>
> _____
>
> d) **The Sales Team** based in the call centre of an Insurance Company. Responsible for handling telephone enquiries from prospective customers and encouraging them to sign up for a new insurance policy.
>
> _____

12.11 Key Performance Indicators

A common way of expressing both targets and measuring results is to use **Key Performance Indicators (KPIs).** These are designed to identify the most critical aspects of an organisation's performance and encapsulate a corresponding target in the simplest and most meaningful way possible.

The underlying principle is that in business *'less is more'*. There is no point in giving someone twenty different 'top priorities'. Not only will the individual definitely fail to succeed in achieving all twenty, but more frustratingly he/she will inevitably focus on just the handful which appeal to him/her or appear easier to 'tick off'.

It is far preferable to narrow the focus down to the really critical priorities and just give these to the individual in question. Not only will this mean that he/she is now actually working on what really are the [very] top priorities, but the increased focus given to each will improve the chances of success on (what is now) a much smaller list.

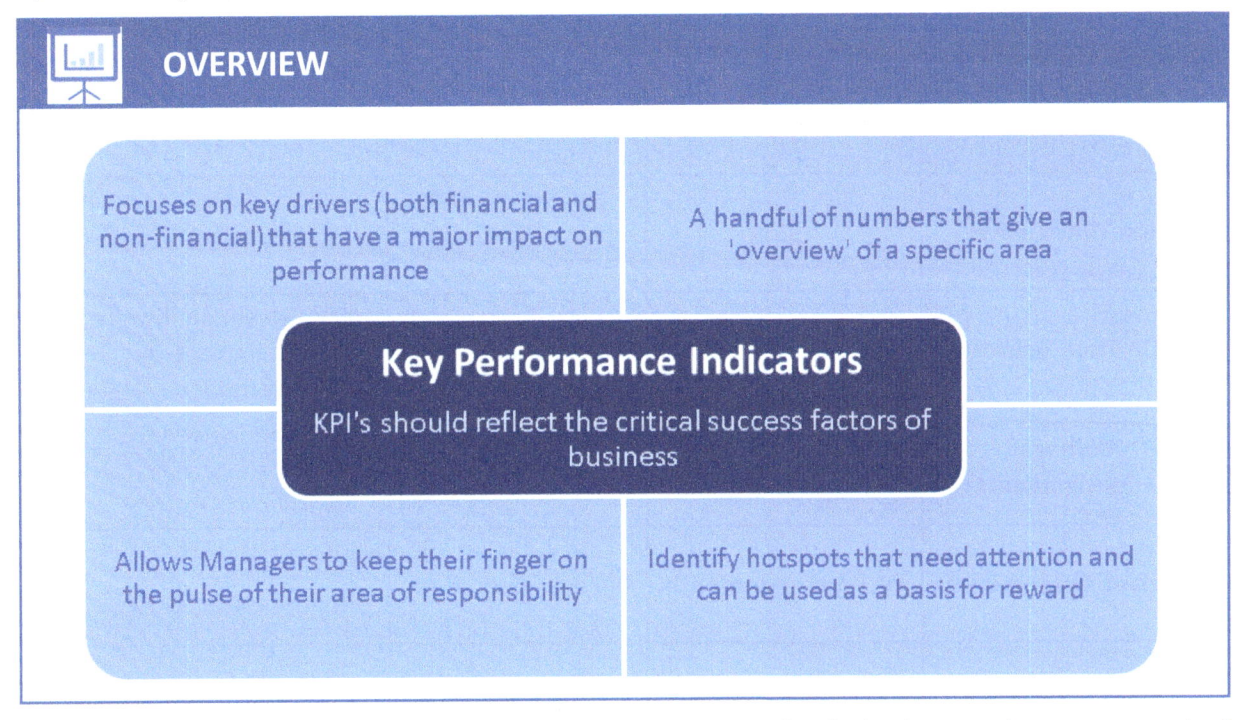

OVERVIEW

Focuses on key drivers (both financial and non-financial) that have a major impact on performance

A handful of numbers that give an 'overview' of a specific area

Key Performance Indicators

KPI's should reflect the critical success factors of business

Allows Managers to keep their finger on the pulse of their area of responsibility

Identify hotspots that need attention and can be used as a basis for reward

All that is now needed is to establish the critical success factors for the business and to express each of these in the form of an easy to understand measure. The measure need not necessarily be financial, but it does need to be quantitative to allow the KPI be stated and subsequently measured in a completely objective fashion.

EXAMPLE

The Operations Director of a transport company needs to identify the top factors which will ultimately determine the success or otherwise of the business. The chosen KPIs will then be used to challenge each separate distribution depot to meet the operational standards required, and to appraise the performance of each depot manager.

Solution

There is of course no right or wrong answer to such a question, but from the perspective of an operations director the following might appear on a short list of potential KPIs:

- **Distribution Costs:**   Cost per mile < £0.55
- **First Time Delivery:**   >95% success at first time delivery
- **On Time Delivery**   >98% deliveries on time
- **Damaged Consignments:** Less than 1% of consignments damaged
- **Driver Availability:**   Average driver absenteeism < 0.5 days per annum
- **Vehicle Availability:**   Average vehicle off road <1 day per month

A subsequent monthly management information report could then compare a depot's performance against these KPIs, and this would ensure that the Operations Director and the depot managers would be working towards a common set of priorities. This is shown on the next page.

12 Performance appraisal

PDQ Logistics Ltd : South Yorkshire Depot June 2018 : Performance against KPIs			
KPI	**Target Performance**	**Actual Performance**	**Comments**
Distribution Costs	<£0.55 per mile	£0.53	Good performance
First Time Delivery	>95%	97%	Excellent
On Time Delivery	>98%	96%	Needs attention if we're not to damage our reputation.
Damaged Consignments	<1%	1.3%	Is there a need to retrain certain warehouse staff?!?
Driver Absenteeism	<0.5 days per month	0.9 days per month	Please discuss regular offenders with HR Dept.
Vehicle Off Road	<1 day per month	0.7 days	Well done

12.12 Balanced Scorecard

"What is the fundamental aim of a business?"

The standard answer to this question is normally along the lines of maximising profitability for the benefits of the shareholders. And since profitability is reported using the statement of profit or loss, it should be no surprise that the humble P&L is one of the primary tools used to measure a business's level of success. But is this enough?

The answer is clearly "No". Successful businesses need to pay far more attention to all aspects of their operation than simply studying a single financial report on a monthly basis, but what else should they be looking at?

Two American business academics (Kaplan and Norton) researched this question in the 1990's, and asked leading U.S. companies exactly what information *they* used to gauge the success and prospects for their own business. Clearly they received a variety of different answers but certain common themes were present in those answers.

Kaplan & Norton distilled these down into four fundamental viewing perspectives that encompassed the different categories of information that these top U.S. businesses were using to appraise themselves, namely:

Financial Perspective

e.g. cash flow, sales growth, operating income, return on equity etc.

To answer the question *"How do we look to shareholders?"*

Of the four perspectives this is the closest to the traditional way of appraising company performance by means of financial information.

Customer Perspective

e.g. market share achieved, customer satisfaction, delivery lead-times etc.

To answer the question *"What is important to our customers and stakeholders?"*

This perspective confirms the ultimate dependence that any business has on its customers.

Internal Business Processes

e.g. staff satisfaction, manufacturing & operating efficiency, etc.

To answer the question *"What must we excel at?"*

These are all about the company striving to improve the key factors specific to that business.

Learning and Growth

e.g. research & development, fostering innovation etc.

To answer the question *"How can we continue to improve, create value and innovate?"*

This perspective is about looking forward to ensure the future of the business.

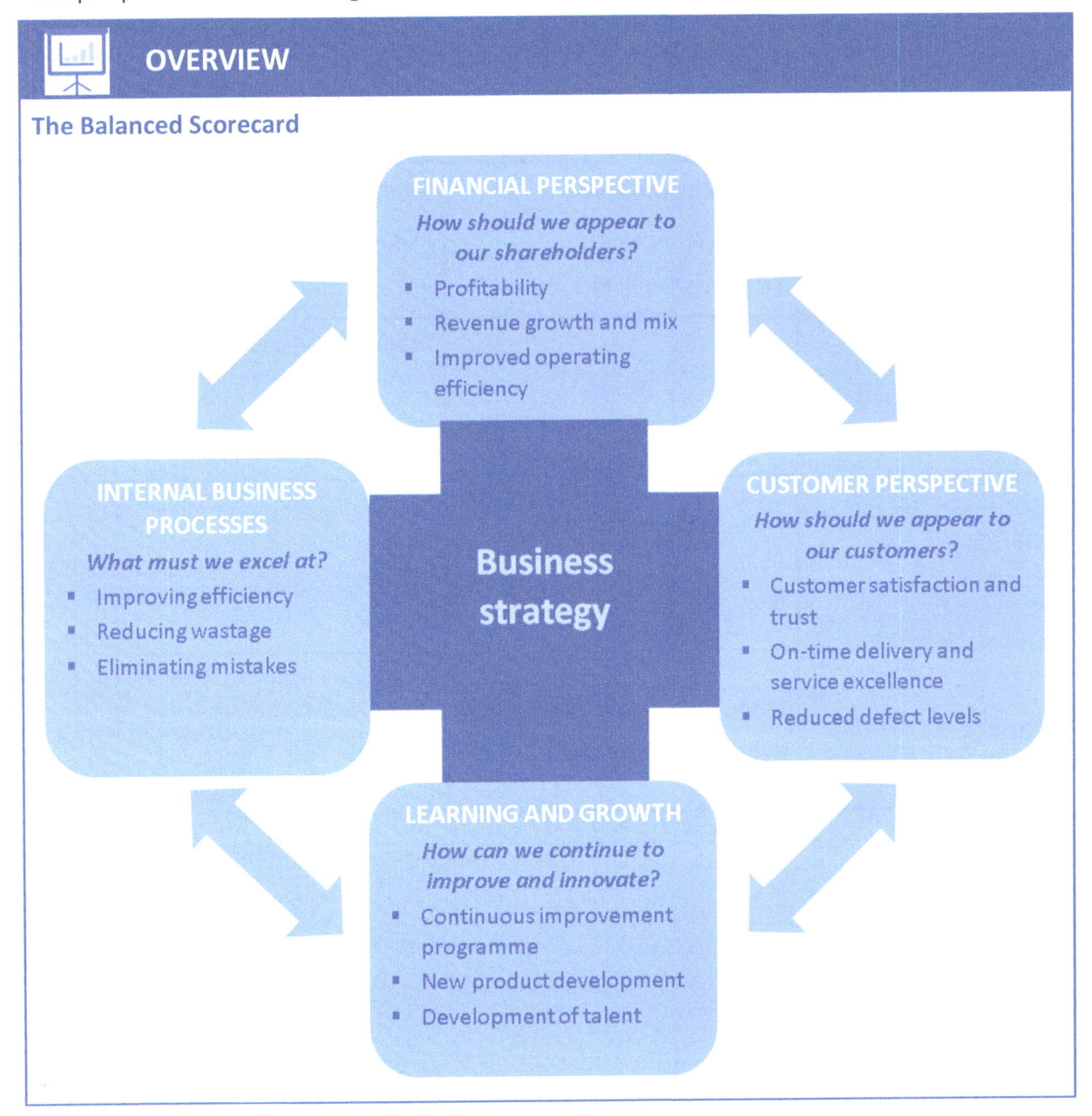

OVERVIEW

The Balanced Scorecard

FINANCIAL PERSPECTIVE
How should we appear to our shareholders?
- Profitability
- Revenue growth and mix
- Improved operating efficiency

INTERNAL BUSINESS PROCESSES
What must we excel at?
- Improving efficiency
- Reducing wastage
- Eliminating mistakes

Business strategy

CUSTOMER PERSPECTIVE
How should we appear to our customers?
- Customer satisfaction and trust
- On-time delivery and service excellence
- Reduced defect levels

LEARNING AND GROWTH
How can we continue to improve and innovate?
- Continuous improvement programme
- New product development
- Development of talent

12 Performance appraisal

The exact wording of the four different perspectives have evolved over the years, and organisations who adopt this model invariably adapt it to their own needs. The key use of the Balanced Scorecard is to encourage businesses to think beyond the traditional financial statements and see the bigger picture of their company's performance and prospects. This does not mean that financial measures are not important. They clearly are, and will undoubtedly feature in the various perspectives of the balanced scorecard, but they are not the whole story.

The Balanced Scorecard model is a template to encourage a company to consider what factors are vital to ensure the future of its business, what objectives should be set to support these key factors, and how the level of success will be measured?

> **EXAMPLE**
>
> A technology company is considering introducing a Balanced Scorecard to provide some focus to the key areas it needs to work on. Suggest suitable objectives and KPIs for the four perspectives of the Balanced Scorecard.
>
> **Solution**
>
> | PERSPECTIVE | OBJECTIVE | MEASURE |
> |---|---|---|
> | Financial | Increased profitability | Profit after Tax +5% |
> | | Reduce borrowing | Reduce gearing to < 30% |
> | | Enhance shareholder return | Increase dividend to 30p |
> | Customer | Improve customer ranking | Achieve top 5 position in industry ranking tables |
> | | Improve customer satisfaction | Achieve 90% approval in independent surveys |
> | Internal business processes | Reduce design lead times | Average 'concept to product' lead time reduced < 6 months |
> | | Reduce staff turnover in design dept. | Decrease design staff turnover to <30% pa |
> | Learning & growth | Encourage innovative thinking | All design staff to attend Las Vegas Tech. conference |
> | | Refresh product range | >50% of sales to come from products launched in last 2 years |

The Language of Business

> ⚠ **KEY POINTS FROM CHAPTER 12**

Ratio Analysis

Ratio analysis provides certain advantages compared to simply looking at the original numbers, including:

- Identifying relationships between separate numbers on a financial statement
- Allowing information to be rebased into a more meaningful measure
- Allowing a relative comparison between different years or companies
- Allowing risk to be identified

The Ratio Family

Four main categories of ratio, as follows:

- **Profitability & Return:** Used to describe the business's profitability
- **Liquidity:** Used to describe the business's liquidity
- **Efficiency:** How efficiently the business is managing its working capital
- **Investment & Finance:** Describing the business from the perspective of a potential investor or lender

Market Capitalisation

Market Capitalisation = Current Market Price of Shares x Number of Shares in Issue

Market Share Price affected by both:

- **The company's prospects:** profit, growth, risk, dividend history, takeover bid?
- **The wider environment:** the economy, investor confidence, herd instinct (bull or bear?)

Performance Appraisal

- **Vertical Analysis**: Calculation of ratios within data *from the same time period*.
- **Horizontal Analysis:** Comparison of performance across time periods

Responsibility Accounting

- **Cost Centres** — Responsible for controlling expenditure
- **Revenue Centres** — Responsible for generating sales revenue
- **Profit Centres** — Responsible for achieving required profit
- **Investment Centres** — Responsible for achieving required profit returns on investment

Key Performance Indicators

- Focuses on key drivers that have a major impact on performance
- A handful of numbers that give an 'overview' of a specific area
- Allows Managers to keep their finger on the pulse of their area
- Identify hotspots that need attention and can be used as a basis for reward

Balanced Scorecard

- **Financial Perspective:** *"How do we look to shareholders?"*
- **Customer Perspective:** *"What is important to our customers?"*
- **Internal Business Processes:** *"What must we excel at?"*
- **Learning and growth:** *"How can we continue to improve, create value and innovate?"*

Chapter 12: Test Your Understanding Answers

TEST YOUR UNDERSTANDING 1

Interest Cover = Operating Profit / Interest Costs = £300,000 / £25,000 = **12**

Total Dividend = 12,000 x £5.00 = £60,000

Dividend Cover = Profit after Tax / Dividend = £223,000 / £60,000 = **3.7**

TEST YOUR UNDERSTANDING 2

Equity Valuation = Total Assets – Total Liabilities = £2,500,000 - £1,600,000 = **£900,000**

Market Capitalisation = No. of issued shares x current market price of each share = 100,000 x £12.60 = **£1,260,000**

TEST YOUR UNDERSTANDING 3

Earnings per Share = Profit after Tax / No. of shares in issue = £150,000 / 50,000 = **£3.00** (i.e. 300p) per share

Price Earnings (P/E) Ratio = Market Price per Share / Earnings per Share = £18 / £3 = **6**

TEST YOUR UNDERSTANDING 4

Mozart Ltd	2016	2017	Year on Year Variance (£)	Year on Year Variance (%)
Sales	£950,000	£970,000	£20,000	2.1%
Cost of Sales	£285,000	£310,000		
Gross Profit (£)	£665,000	£660,000	(£5,000)	(0.75%)
Gross Profit (%)	70.0%	68.0%		(2.0%)

> **TEST YOUR UNDERSTANDING 5**
>
> a) **The Northern Operating Region -** Responsible for sales & expenditure i.e. **a Profit Centre**
>
> b) **The Distribution Centre -** Just responsible for expenditure i.e. **a Cost Centre**
>
> c) **The European Operating -** Makes its own investment decisions and is responsible for then delivering the required level of profit returns i.e. **an Investment Centre**
>
> d) **The Sales Team -** Just responsible for generating sales i.e. **a Revenue Centre**

Chapter 12: End of Chapter Exercises

Section A Questions

The following information relates to Questions 12.1 – 12.6.

Coopers Ltd: Statement of Financial Position as at 31st December 2018

Non-Current Assets		
Land & Buildings	£900,000	
Plant & Machinery	£300,000	
		£1,200,000
Current Assets		
Inventory	£90,000	
Trade Receivables	£50,000	
Cash	£20,000	
		£160,000
TOTAL ASSETS		**£1,360,000**
Equity		
Share Capital	£100,000	
Retained Profit	£960,000	
		£1,060,000
Non-Current Liabilities		
7% Corporate Bond (repayable 2030)	£200,000	
		£200,000
Current Liabilities		
Trade Payables	£65,000	
Tax Liability	£35,000	
		£100,000
TOTAL EQUITY & LIABILITIES		**£1,360,000**

The Language of Business

Coopers Ltd: Statement of Profit or Loss. Year Ending 31ˢᵗ December 2018

Sales Revenue	£450,000
Cost of sales	(£140,000)
Gross Profit	£310,000
Selling & Distribution	(£80,000)
Administration	(£75,000)
Operating Profit (PBIT)	£155,000
Finance Costs	(£14,000)
Profit before Tax (PBT)	£141,000
Taxation	(£25,000)
Profit after Tax (PAT)	£116,000

Coopers Ltd have 100,000 (£1 nominal) shares in issue and these had a market value of 1,200p on 31ˢᵗ December 2018 They issued a final dividend of 50p per share.

Question 12.1
What is Cooper Ltd's equity valuation and market capitalisation?

	Equity Valuation	Market Capitalisation
A	£200,000	£200,000
B	£860,000	£1,100,000
C	£1,060,000	£1,200,000
D	£1,260,000	£2,400,000

Question 12.2
What is Cooper Ltd's interest cover?

- A 8
- B 10
- C 11
- D 22

Question 12.3
What is Cooper Ltd's Dividend Cover?

- A 1.2
- B 2.3
- C 2.8
- D 3.1

12 Performance appraisal

Question 12.4

What is Cooper Ltd's Earnings per Share?

A   58p

B   116p

C   141p

D   155p

Question 12.5

What is Cooper Ltd's Price Earnings ratio?

A   7

B   8

C   9

D   10

Question 12.6

What is Cooper Ltd's Return on Capital Employed?

A   9%

B   11%

C   12%

D   15%

The following information relates to Questions 12.7 – 12.10:

Neptune Ltd is a national logistics company which operates throughout the UK from numerous depots and operates a large fleet of lorries. They are organised into four largely autonomous operating divisions, each based on a geographical region of the UK.

Question 12.7

Each operating division of Neptune Ltd is regarded as an 'Investment Centre'.

In the context of 'Responsibility Accounting' which of the following would be the most appropriate performance measure for each of these individual divisions?

A   Sales Revenue

B   Expenditure control

C   Gross Profit %

D   Return on Capital Employed

Question 12.8

A key determinant of profitability for Neptune Ltd is keeping their costs under control.

With this in mind which of the following possible Key Performance Indicators (KPIs) would be suitable to measure the success of their individual depot managers?

- A The delivery cost per mile of each depot
- B Market share price of Neptune Ltd shares
- C Neptune Ltd market share of the logistics sector
- D Results of a national customer service survey

Question 12.9

On Neptune Ltd's Balanced Scorecard which of the following would be the most appropriate objective for the 'Financial Perspective'?

- A £1m funding into research & development of next generation logistics software
- B All staff to undergo annual appraisal to identify individual training needs.
- C Ensure 98% achievement on independent customer satisfaction survey
- D Increase Operating Profit by 5% year on year

Question 12.10

On Neptune Ltd's Balanced Scorecard which of the following would be the most appropriate objective for the 'Customer Perspective'?

- A £1m funding into research & development of next generation logistics software
- B All staff to undergo annual appraisal to identify individual training needs.
- C Ensure 98% achievement on independent customer satisfaction survey
- D Increase Operating Profit by 5% year on year

12 Performance appraisal

Section B Questions

Question 12.11

In the past The Directors of BG Ltd have relied solely on a financial budget to set their plans and to measure their performance.

However they are now considering introducing a Balanced Scorecard in order to give a more rounded approach to their management of the company.

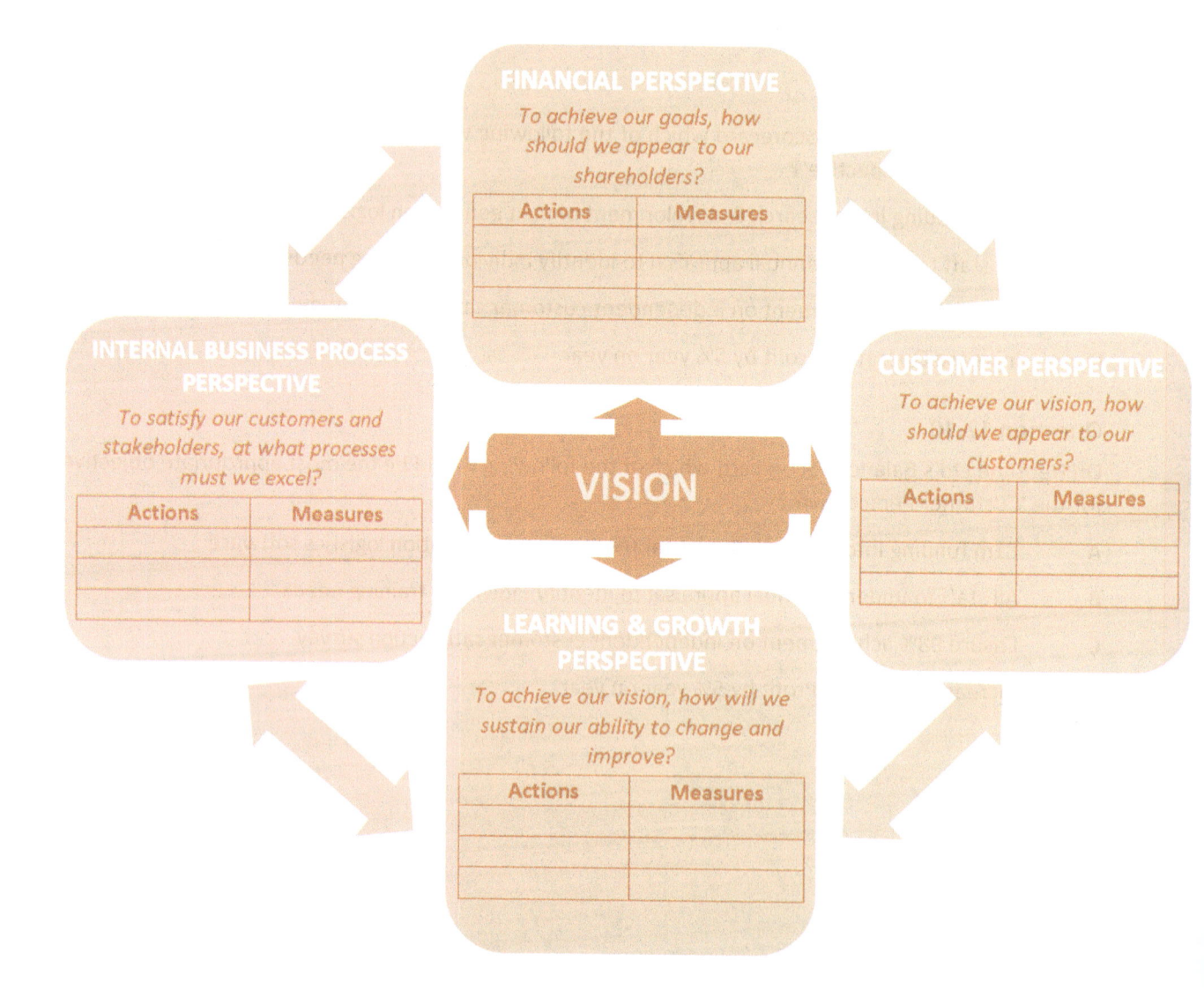

FINANCIAL PERSPECTIVE
To achieve our goals, how should we appear to our shareholders?

Actions	Measures

INTERNAL BUSINESS PROCESS PERSPECTIVE
To satisfy our customers and stakeholders, at what processes must we excel?

Actions	Measures

CUSTOMER PERSPECTIVE
To achieve our vision, how should we appear to our customers?

Actions	Measures

LEARNING & GROWTH PERSPECTIVE
To achieve our vision, how will we sustain our ability to change and improve?

Actions	Measures

VISION

For each perspective of the Balanced Scorecard suggest two or three actions which would support the strategic goals of a manufacturer of precision steel components such as BG Ltd.

Each action should be accompanied by a quantitative measure to allow progress to be verified. The measures can be financial or non-financial, and can include figures, percentages, ratios, or any other Key Performance Indicator (KPI).

The Language of Business

Financial Perspective *"To achieve our goals how should we appear to our Shareholders?"*

Actions	Measures

Customer Perspective *"To achieve our goals how should we appear to our Customers?"*

Actions	Measures

Learning & Growth Perspective *"How will we sustain our ability to change and improve?"*

Actions	Measures

Business Process Perspective *"What business processes must we excel at?"*

Actions	Measures

Question 12.12

The following financial statements are from the annual accounts of BG Ltd a manufacturer of precision steel components for the automotive trade.

BG Ltd - Statement of Financial Position as at 31st December 2018

ASSETS
Non-Current Assets

Premises	£900,000	
Plant & Machinery	£963,092	
		£1,863,092

Current Assets

Inventory	£128,677	
Receivables	£265,900	
Cash	£100,000	
		£494,577
		£2,357,669

EQUITY & LIABILITIES
Equity

Share capital	£500,000	
Retained Profit	£1,457,249	
		£1,957,249

Non-Current Liabilities

Bank Loan (repayable 2025)	£93,300	
		£93,300

Current Liabilities

Trade Payables	£170,470	
Tax Payable	£136,650	
		£307,120
		£2,357,669

The Language of Business

BG Ltd - Statement of profit or loss - Year Ending 31st December 2018

Sales Revenue	**£2,762,444**
Cost of Sales	£1,715,478
Gross Profit	**£1,046,966**
Selling & Distribution Costs	£458,290
Administration Expenses	£136,662
Operating Profit	**£452,014**
Finance Costs	£53,938
Profit before Tax	**£398,076**
Taxation	£136,650
Profit after Tax	**£261,426**

From this Profit after Tax figure BG Ltd paid out **£100,000 of dividends** to the shareholders who in total hold **40,000 shares**.

The current **share price is 9000p** per share

Required:

Calculate the following financial ratios for BG Ltd.

Then, in plain English, give a simple meaning for each one

Profitability

Gross Profit (%) _____

Meaning _____

Operating Profit % _____

Meaning _____

Returns

ROCE _____

Meaning _____

ROE _____

Meaning _____

12 Performance appraisal

Liquidity

Current Ratio _____

Meaning _____

Quick Ratio _____

Meaning _____

Working Capital

Working Capital (£) _____

Meaning _____

Inventory Days _____

Meaning _____

Receivables Days _____

Meaning _____

Payables Days _____

Meaning _____

Operating Cycle _____

Meaning _____

Lending Ratios

Gearing _____

Meaning _____

The Language of Business

Interest Cover _____

Meaning _____

Investor Ratios

Dividend per share _____

Meaning _____

Dividend Cover _____

Meaning _____

Earnings per share _____

Meaning _____

P/E Ratio _____

Meaning _____

Company Valuation

Market Capitalisation _____

Meaning _____

Equity Valuation _____

Meaning _____

Performance appraisal

Question 12.13

The management accounts of a company contain the following statements of profit or loss for 2017 and 2018.

Compared to 2017 by what £ figure, and by what % have the following increased by in 2018:

	£ Increase	% Increase
Sales Revenue (£)	_____	_____
Gross Profit (£)	_____	_____
Operating Profit (£)	_____	_____

	2017 £	2017 %	2018 £	2018 %
Sales Revenue	£850,000	100%	£1,000,000	100%
Cost of Sales	£370,000		£450,000	
Gross Profit	£480,000		£550,000	
Salaries	£230,000		£275,000	
Travel & Accommodation	£8,000		£11,000	
Customer Entertaining	£5,000		£7,000	
Marketing	£25,000		£30,000	
Legal & Professional	£15,000		£19,000	
Heat & Light	£6,000		£8,000	
Insurance	£5,000		£5,100	
Telephone & Broadband	£12,000		£15,000	
Rent	£100,000		£100,000	
Operating Profit	£74,000		£79,900	

Using the template carry out 'vertical analysis' on the statements of profit or loss of both years.

Using the relevant year's sales revenue as a base (i.e. sales revenue = 100%), comment on the performance that the vertical analysis has revealed for:

- Gross profit performance
- General expense control
- Operating profit performance

_____

_____

_____

_____

_____

_____

If the 2018 statement of profit or loss had the same gross profit % as the 2017 statement of profit or loss, how much gross profit (£) would the business have made in 2018?

_____

_____

_____

_____

_____

If the 2017 statement of profit or loss had the same operating profit % as the 2017 statement of profit or loss, how much operating profit (£) would the business have made in 2018?

_____

_____

_____

_____

_____

12 Performance appraisal